Making the San Fernando Valley

Making the
San Fernando Valley

RURAL LANDSCAPES, URBAN DEVELOPMENT, AND WHITE PRIVILEGE

LAURA R. BARRACLOUGH

THE UNIVERSITY OF GEORGIA PRESS
Athens & London

© 2011 by the University of Georgia Press
Athens, Georgia 30602
www.ugapress.org
All rights reserved
Designed by Walton Harris
Set in 10/13 Minion Pro

Printed digitally in the United States of America

Library of Congress Cataloging-in-Publication Data

Barraclough, Laura R.
Making the San Fernando Valley : rural landscapes, urban development,
and White privilege / Laura R. Barraclough.
  p.   cm. — (Geographies of justice and social transformation ; 3)
Includes bibliographical references and index.
ISBN-13: 978-0-8203-3562-9 (hardcover : alk. paper)
ISBN-10: 0-8203-3562-2 (hardcover : alk. paper)
ISBN-13: 978-0-8203-3680-0 (pbk.   )
ISBN-10: 0-8203-3680-7 (pbk.   )
1. San Fernando Valley (Calif.) — Race relations. 2. Whites —
California — San Fernando Valley — History. 3. San Fernando Valley
(Calif.) — Rural conditions. 4. Landscapes — Social aspects —
California — San Fernando Valley — History. 5. San Fernando Valley
(Calif.) — Geography. 6. San Fernando Valley (Calif.) — Social condi-
tions. 7. Urbanization — California — San Fernando Valley — History.
8. Social change — California — San Fernando Valley — History.
9. Cultural pluralism — California — San Fernando Valley — History.
I. Title.
F868.L8B35 2011
979.4′94 — dc22   2010015808

British Library Cataloging-in-Publication Data available

CONTENTS

ILLUSTRATIONS

FIGURES

TABLES

ACKNOWLEDGMENTS

Completing this book offers a welcomed opportunity to reflect back on my intellectual trajectory and the many, many people who have shaped my growth, both personal and academic.

The questions that I raise in this book have been with me for a long time — certainly since my time as an undergraduate at the University of California, San Diego's Thurgood Marshall College, whose staff and the faculty teaching the Dimensions of Culture sequence launched me into a lifetime of exploration into the study of culture, inequality, identity, and social systems. How fortuitous that I chose, on the casual suggestion of a friend, to enroll in George Lipsitz's "Ethnic Diversity and the City" class. The core ideas that Professor Lipsitz introduced to me then and in subsequent courses are everywhere in this book and in my teaching; he also offered a critically important model to me, especially at that juncture in my life, of the way that a white person can work authentically for racial justice. To this day, he continues to inspire. I am deeply thankful to all of the ethnic studies faculty at UCSD, especially Yen Le Espiritu, Ross Frank, Jorge Mariscal, and Leland Saito (now at the University of Southern California), as well as David Gutiérrez in history and then–graduate assistants Ruby Tapia and Albert Lowe. You have all provided me with an intellectual and political foundation that guides my life's work. Thank you. My academic work in ethnic studies was integrated at every step with my involvement at UCSD's Cross-Cultural Center, where I was extremely fortunate to learn from and work with Edwina Welch, Juan Astorga, and Nancy Magpusao, each of whom helped me to reflect honestly upon the person that I was becoming and pushed me forward in important ways. Edwina, Juan, and Nancy: thank you for the work that you continue to do for students and for justice in higher education.

I count my experience in the American Studies and Ethnicity graduate program at the University of Southern California as among the most formative moments in my intellectual and personal life. I am deeply thankful to the many faculty and students there, too many now to name, who have worked so hard to build a different model of graduate education and of academia. I am especially grateful for the support and friendship of colleagues who entered ASE as part of the very first cohort with me: Michan Connor, Hillary Jenks, Reina Prado, Jenny Stoever-Ackerman, Cam Vu, and Karen Yonemoto. Gerardo

Licón, Lorena Muñoz, Ana Rosas, and Sharon Sekhon welcomed me enthusi-astically during my first few days at USC and have since become great friends and respected colleagues. I have deep appreciation for my fellow participants in the 2003 Irvine Foundation Summer Dissertation Workshop at USC — I'm very glad to have shared the experience with you. Special thanks and hugs to my *querida amiga* Perla Guerrero for long walks around the neighborhood, trips to Mexico, and chats about anything and everything. To my friend James Thing, thank you for constantly reminding me to think in more complex terms. James, along with Ilda Jiménez y West, Lalo Licón, Hillary Jenks, Jerry Gonzales, and Cynthia Willis, provided support and friendship as part of two writing groups in which I worked through an early draft of this project. And some of my very favorite memories revolve around Sunday-morning writing sessions with my dear friends Hillary Jenks and Marci McMahon. Although we are now scattered around the country, I hope we'll find a way to do that again someday!

I am profoundly appreciative of the opportunity to work with Laura Pulido, my dissertation advisor, mentor, collaborator, and friend. Laura, from our first meeting, I felt an instant connection — intellectual, political, personal — that has only grown in the years since. Thank you for all that you have done to make me a better writer, scholar, teacher, and activist. I look forward to many more years of friendship and collaboration. Similarly, I can't begin to thank George Sánchez, who was the main driving force behind the establishment of ASE, and who devoted so much of his time and energy to building a new kind of academic community and socializing all of us to be responsible, imaginative, productive scholars. George, thank you for your commitment to me and to the visions you hold dear. We have all benefited from your wisdom. Special thanks also to Bill Deverell, who served on my dissertation committee almost immediately after arriving at USC and helped me to think strategically and honestly about my future. Many other USC faculty supported me and this project in various ways from the beginning, especially Carolyn Cartier, Ruthie Gilmore, Roberto Lint Sagarena, Leland Saito, and Jennifer Wolch — thanks to each of you for your guidance. ASE staff Sonia Rodríguez, Sandra Hopwood, and Kitty Lai fostered a wonderful atmosphere in which to be a student.

In so many ways, I was truly blessed to find a somewhat unconventional first academic job in the Liberal Studies program at Antioch University Los Angeles. Antioch's distinctive pedagogical approach has forever shaped the way I think about and carry out my role as an educator. Thank you to my valued colleagues Al Erdynast, Rosa Garza Mourino, MeHee Hyun, Andrea Richards, Donald Strauss, and David Tripp for your inspirational work to make a transforma-tive education accessible to so many people. I am especially appreciative of the support and friendship of Kirsten Grimstad, chair of the BA program at Antioch, whose encouragement and support of faculty enabled me to thrive, and to Neal King for his leadership. All of Antioch's students are extraordinary people, but I am especially grateful to Amanda Garcés, Tyler Daly, Robin Garcia, Rob Wilton, and Jackie Legg for our long talks about justice and the role we might play in achieving it. I value the opportunity to have worked with you and learned from you.

I find myself now at Kalamazoo College and part of a wonderful intellectual community. Kiran Cunningham, Espelencia Baptiste, and Maksim Kokushkin, my colleagues in the Department of Anthropology and Sociology, are like kindred spirits. I am excited about the department we are building together; thanks for making my transition to K College smooth and gratifying. Eileen Wilson Oyelaran and Mickey McDonald provide outstanding leadership to the college and make it an idyllic place in which to work.

Many people have provided critical feedback on this project over the years. I am especially thankful to Don Mitchell and Frieda Knobloch, who read the manuscript in its entirety and offered generous comments and suggestions, as well as Colleen O'Neill, Luis Álvarez, Paul Spickard, Jennifer Price, Kristen Maher, and David Roediger. I am also grateful to have had the extraordinary opportunity to participate in the 2007 Summer Institute for the Geographies of Justice in Athens, Georgia. Special thanks to the coordinating committee and to all the participants with whom I spent that glorious week talking radical theory and politics. Derek Krissoff at the University of Georgia Press has shown his support and excitement for this project since well before I knew what it would really be about. I thank him for his long-standing commitment and diligent work on its behalf, as well as Nik Heynen, Andy Herod, and Melissa Wright, the editors of this important new series, of which I am very excited to be a part.

Of course, the nitty-gritty work of visiting archives and conducting interviews would not have been possible without funding or staff support. I am fortunate to have received fellowships from the College of Letters, Arts, and Sciences and the Urban Initiative at USC, the Haynes Foundation, and the Mellon Foundation to work on this project at the dissertation stage. Thanks to the staffs of the Huntington Library, California State University Northridge's Special Collections, USC Special Collections, and L.A. City Records and Archives; and to Lloyd Hitt and Marlene Hitt at Bolton Hall. A month-long residency at the Autry National Center in July 2007, made possible by a fellowship awarded by the Los Angeles Corral of Westerners, was like an overdue vacation, a retreat that really enabled me to finish the research for this project. Many thanks to Marva Felchlin, Kim Walters, and Manola Madrid at the Autry and the Southwest Museum of the

American Indian for their help locating materials and for conversations about the San Fernando Valley. Special thanks to the many people in the northeast Valley who shared their opinions and life experiences with me. I am quite certain that we will not always agree on the analysis; nonetheless, I thank you for your honesty and hope that you will find your stories portrayed fairly.

My family and friends have supported me and my interests in this project for many years. To my parents, Mike Barraclough and Bette Barraclough; my sister, Robin Campbell; my brother-in-law, Rick Campbell; and my nephew, Loudoun, and my niece, Avalon — your love and encouragement have meant the world to me, and I feel humbled trying to thank you here. My dear life-long friends Brigid Morales, John Grande, Carrie Dubin Aguilar, Steve Aguilar, Ella Serrano, Jennifer Cogan, Bethany Lockhart, Fernando Estrada-López, and Carlos Estrada-López all helped me remember that life is much bigger than this book. And finally, all my love and gratitude to my partner, Emerson Marroquín, who watched this project unfold with all its twists and turns and who consistently found the words to help me move forward when I got stuck. Emerson, this book owes much to your brilliant analysis, ethical and political commitments, and humor. Thank you.

Making the San Fernando Valley

INTRODUCTION

In 1965, Lifetime Savings and Loan, a bank serving Los Angeles's suburban San Fernando Valley, mailed an advertisement for the vast new Porter Ranch subdivision to potential home buyers. Carved out of the former property of real-estate tycoon George Porter, Porter Ranch would be the largest residential subdivision in the San Fernando Valley's history to date, housing more than forty-three thousand people in nearly twelve thousand units; sixteen schools and twenty churches were also included in the plans. Total development costs were estimated at over $350 million, and construction would take more than ten years to complete. When finished, Porter Ranch covered six and a half square miles in the neighborhood of Granada Hills.[1] Despite the project's massive, master-planned quality, however, Lifetime reassured potential home buyers that Porter Ranch would be less "cookie-cutter" and more authentic than most postwar subdivisions because of its unique and deliberate blend of rural and suburban landscapes. The brochure promised that "with the many recreational areas being planned, [the subdivision would] provide its residents with ideal conditions for prestige family living in a rural atmosphere." Miles of land had been set aside for "rustic bridle trails" — as well as two golf courses and several shopping centers. The sales pitch also claimed that the subdivision would represent and extend the area's rural western heritage amid the San Fernando Valley's dramatic postwar transformation from agricultural empire to residential and industrial suburb. It noted, "While Porter Ranch has a promising future as an outstanding residential community, it also has an interesting past, steeped in the rich heritage of California history." As evidence, the advertisement narrated the historic layers of conquest in the San Fernando Valley, from the sale of the former Spanish mission at San Fernando to Eugelio de Celis in 1848, at the tail end of the U.S. war with Mexico; to the split of the property between wheat farmers and real-estate tycoons Isaac Lankershim, I. N. Van Nuys, George Porter, Ben Porter, and Charles Maclay — Anglo men whose names now appear in street signs, strip malls, and gated communities throughout the Valley. It also celebrated the San Fernando Valley's preeminent role as the center of western film and television production through a full-page advertisement for Lifetime Savings and Loan endorsed by western film actor Andy "Jingles" Devine, who was then a San Fernando Valley resident and honorary mayor of the Valley community of Van Nuys. The ad featured a sketch of Devine with reference to one of the actor's most famous on-screen lines: "When Andy Devine comes into Lifetime . . . that'll be the day!"[2] Lifetime used Devine's endorsement to promote its new save-by-mail function and, in turn, the Porter Ranch master-planned community. In all these ways, the brochure intoned that new suburban homeowners could carry out California and the American West's rich legacy of dons, ranchers, and frontiersmen — both real and celluloid — when they purchased a new tract home at Porter Ranch. As white home buyers purchasing property in the last years of state-sanctioned residential segregation, they would also be the newest generation carrying out a long legacy of Anglo-American conquest.

The Porter Ranch subdivision is only one of countless real-estate and land-use projects in the San Fernando Valley that has deliberately drawn upon ideas about rural land and western heritage as a strategy of urban development. In this book, I conceptualize this process as "rural urbanism," or the production of rural landscapes by the urban state, capital, and other urban interests, and I argue that it is vital to understanding the relationships between American imperialism, racial formation (especially the socio-spatial construction of whiteness), and the urban geographies of Los Angeles and cities of the U.S. West. The process of rural urbanism occurs through the dialectics of myth making about rural land and western heritage and the formulation of urban policy. The concept builds on Raymond Williams's and William Cronon's insights, made in two separate contexts, that the development of city and countryside go hand in hand, both in terms of their material, physical development and their cultural and symbolic meanings.[3] My primary concern in this book is to investigate how the ideologies of rural land embedded in mythologies of the frontier West, the Spanish mission system, and agriculture have influenced the urban-planning practices of cities in the U.S. West during the twentieth and twenty-first centuries, and how the physical places created by urban policies and practices in turn affirm romantic ideologies about rural land. Following postcolonial theorists, I conceive of such myths and ideologies as American variants on the global, five-hundred-year-old "transition narratives" that explain and justify imperial conquest and white supremacy. Applying a critical humanist lens to urban policy, I suggest that efforts to shape and influence policy are crucial sites for the formation and negotiation of identity; more specifically, processes of rural urbanism have been, and continue to be, fundamentally generative of American identity and what it means to be both white and middle class in Los Angeles.

In this book, I analyze the practice of rural urbanism as a racial project in the San Fernando Valley from 1900 to 2005. The San Fernando Valley is a particularly appropriate place to investigate the workings of rural urbanism. Though often dismissed as a prototypical postwar suburban landscape of residential subdivisions and strip malls, the San Fernando Valley actually has a far more complex past in which rurality, suburbia, and urbanity have coexisted, often tensely. As Kevin Roderick reminisces in his popular and personal history of the Valley, his childhood during the 1950s and 1960s was defined by the "quirky swirl of country and suburb." He and his friends "patronized the San Fernando Valley Fair every summer and cheered at local parades like the Northridge Stampede, led by cowboy rider [and movie star and local resident] Montie Montana, the honorary sheriff of the Valley." Roderick observes that depictions of other suburbs, like Lakewood in Los Angeles or Levittown in New York, as "featureless blobs of sameness that rose from nothing" were foreign to him, because the San Fernando Valley so obviously had a past—a rural western one.[4] That history was—and still is—visible in the Valley's physical landscapes. Roderick notes that nowadays, "newcomers are often startled to discover signs of a rural past. Pockets of dirt streets and horse trails remain, along with faded farmhouses, backyard chicken coops, gurgling creeks, and overgrown orchards, if you know where to look."[5] These pockets of rurality, in turn, are nestled among the Valley's more recognizable strip malls and tract homes. In this book, I suggest that the Valley's distinctive mélange of rural, suburban, and urban landscapes attests to competing visions of the kind of place the San Fernando Valley has been and will become—visions that are intimately linked to the ways in which racial, class, and national identities are being negotiated in Los Angeles and the metropolitan U.S. West.

I grew up in one of the Valley's pockets of rurality: the horse-keeping community of Shadow Hills, in the northeast San Fernando Valley. When I was eight years old, my parents moved my sister and me from Northridge, where we lived in a typical post–World War II–era suburban tract home with a pool, to a home with a barn and pipe corrals in the backyard on a half-acre lot in Shadow Hills. There, my mother, who had ridden horses as a teenager in the industrial, working-class white suburbs of Hawthorne and Torrance, reignited her love of horses and introduced her two young daughters to a rural horse-keeping lifestyle that had all but disappeared elsewhere in the city, including the neighborhoods where she grew up. My sister and I were bussed to magnet schools in more typically suburban Valley neighborhoods, but in the afternoons, we threw bridles on our horses and rode bareback through the hills of our neighborhood and into the adjacent Hansen Dam recreational area. Our schoolmates no doubt considered us lucky and perhaps a bit spoiled; they were right, but for reasons that I did not understand at the time, since I did not yet possess the language of white structural and cultural privilege and certainly did not grasp the ways

FIGURE 1 The San Fernando Valley, part of the city of Los Angeles, California. Map by Jacky Woolsey.

in which whiteness and social class privilege had been inscribed within the Valley's rural landscapes, relative to central Los Angeles, throughout the twentieth and twenty-first centuries. Back then, I simply felt lucky that I could have such an experience — that I could navigate the differences, and the tensions, of rural and suburban life and landscape as a formative part of my childhood and adolescence.

Although people in my neighborhood frequently spoke about the community's "natural" quality in comparison to the dense hubbub of Los Angeles, the newsletters mailed to my family from the local homeowners association, highlighting their work before the city council and the city planning commission, and the amount of time, energy, and money that my family alone spent on maintaining our horses and property suggested a different reality — that the rural landscape in the San Fernando Valley was a great deal of work. Untangling these histories and performances of physical and symbolic labor in the twentieth and twenty-first centuries has produced this book: a historical geography of the "rural" San Fernando Valley in relationship to the political, economic, and cultural evolution of Los Angeles. As an adult and a scholar, I returned to the northeast San Fernando Valley, armed with the tools and methods of ethnic studies, radical geography, and ethnography, and pursuing questions designed to make sense of my own experience, as well as that of my family and neighbors: How could these rural places still exist in a global city like Los Angeles? Why had they not evolved into suburban tract-home subdivisions like so many other places in the San Fernando Valley? What did they mean to the people who lived in them? And why was the rural northeast Valley, where I lived, primarily white and middle class, while the schools I had attended and the neighborhoods where my friends lived were majority Latino and Asian American and far more economically diverse?

To answer these questions, I combined archival and ethnographic methods. I immersed myself in the city's major archival institutions, where I analyzed planning documents, promotional materials, films, local history texts, and newspapers. I also conducted four years of ethnographic research in the legally designated rural communities of Shadow Hills and, to a lesser extent, Lakeview Terrace, La Tuna Canyon, and Sunland-Tujunga. From 2001 to 2005, I attended monthly or bimonthly meetings of a local homeowners association, the neighborhood council, and recreational equestrian organizations; as well as meetings associated with election campaigns, redistricting, and equestrian-oriented land-use policy. I observed special events, such as the annual Day of the Horse celebration, and meetings sponsored by the local city council district office, the planning commission, and other city and state agencies. I also conducted sixteen in-depth, semistructured interviews with rural residents, including active neighborhood leaders as well as those who are relatively uninvolved in neighborhood politics. Throughout all these experiences, the rural landscape itself remained foremost in my mind, both because it has been such a powerful source of identity for rural dwellers, and because, as I learned, it has been so closely connected to the negotiation of whiteness.

The history of the San Fernando Valley reveals the crucial but underappreciated role that notions of "rurality" have played in the urban development of Los Angeles and the city's changing racial formation. Lest we imagine that the urbanization of Los Angeles has followed a smooth and continuous arc, the history I narrate in these pages suggests instead that urban development has occurred only in convulsive fits and starts. Throughout the twentieth and twenty-first centuries, ideas about rural land have acted as a mirror held up to reflect, slow, and channel the city's growth and transformations. Yet the city's partial and contested construction as a "rural" place is not often captured in either popular culture's representations of the city or in the growing, interdisciplinary body of scholarship on Los Angeles. So much of Los Angeles's popular image, especially the city that is broadcast to the world via the local news and feature films, is high density, gang ridden, and poor; alternatively, Los Angeles is portrayed as the playground of rich and famous Hollywood celebrities. Existing scholarship on Los Angeles, too, has focused almost exclusively on the city's racially and economically exclusive Westside, with its much-celebrated beach communities and celebrity lifestyles; its industrial, multiethnic, and working-class Eastside; and its Southside, with histories of entrenched segregation, deindustrialization and reindustrialization, civic neglect, and occasional rebellion. But within the San Fernando Valley there are four legally recognized horse-keeping districts, a regional park devoted to the history and mythology of the frontier West, numerous country-western-themed bars and musical venues, and tack and feed stores where engineers, financial investors, and janitors can buy cowboy boots and silver belt buckles as well as hay for their horses. These landscapes are unfamiliar to many, perhaps most, of the city's residents, even those who have lived in Los Angeles all their lives; certainly they are invisible to those who view and study Los Angeles from afar. For those who use and inhabit these places on a regular basis, however, rurality is a powerful source of identity — a crucial way in which they make sense of who they are, and who they are not — in the globally interconnected and deeply unequal city that is Los Angeles.

Moreover, Los Angeles, via the San Fernando Valley, symbolizes the scope of change under way in cities of the U.S. West and the shifting ways in which Anglo-American conquest of the region has been and continues to be negotiated through the dynamics of urban policy making and everyday life. According to historian Carl Abbott, during the "imperial century" of American expansion (which he bounds from 1840 to 1940), cities in the U.S. West were created in two distinct waves of urban development. The first wave, lasting from roughly 1840 to 1880, consisted of the laying of urban foundations in newly conquered regions; in the second wave, from 1890 to 1940, these initial steps were consolidated and complex social institutions were established, transforming boomtowns into full-fledged cities that were not all that different from their East Coast counterparts. Abbott's perspective, which I share, is that cities in the U.S. West have never been merely "frontier outposts." Instead, from the earliest moments of American expansion and conquest, cities *led* development of the West, facilitating Anglo settlement of a newly conquered region that was, at best, tenuously and jealously held.[6]

In this respect, cities played several crucial, interlocking roles. On the one hand, cities connected rural places to the world economy, particularly through the extraction, manufacture, and distribution of resources. As John Reps has argued, the most important "settlers" of the West were not the rugged cowboys or Pony Express riders of popular culture but rather the real-estate developers, town-site builders, railroad companies, and corporations investing in resource extraction who ensured American economic control of the region. Cities also coordinated the legal infrastructures that attempted to impose order on newly acquired territories across the American West. Boosters and land speculators in the West's expanding cities frequently hired surveyors, planners, and town-site companies that were connected to projects of American empire. Much of their work involved regulating property disputes between indigenous, Mexican, and Anglo-American people with conflicting claims on land as they designed, then implemented, their urban design visions.[7] Reps argues that these individuals "brought to the West all of the techniques of urban land development that had been thoroughly tested on older frontiers of settlement," both in the United States and in European imperial possessions around the globe.[8] Finally, western cities functioned as cultural epicenters that produced and distributed a distinct regional culture. Cities drew together concentrations of artists, novelists, universities, archives, and museums dedicated to making sense of the frontier experience. Many of the resulting cultural representations produced by western artists constructed the idea of a unique Anglo-American relationship with rural land in the West. In each of these ways, urban interests produced rural places, both as material landscapes and as cultural representations, and in doing so played an important role in consolidating Anglo-American supremacy in the U.S. West.[9]

World War II transformed western cities, especially Los Angeles and other Sunbelt metropolitan regions. Thanks to their excellent year-round weather, substantial open space, and the extensive promotional efforts that urban elites engaged in to attract federal investment, western cities received the lion's share of national defense contracts, which in turn spawned related industries in durable consumer goods and the emerging high-technology economy. The creation of vast industrial landscapes and the influx of hundreds of thousands of new workers soon led to systematic urban planning, often for the first time; the modernization of government; and the passage of municipal reforms, some of which responded to the demands of emerging civil rights movements.[10]

In the decades since, western cities have been further transformed by the boom in foreign trade, expanded immigration from Asia and Latin America for the first time in more than forty years, and continued U.S. military involvement in Asian Pacific wars. Strategically positioned to act as gateways to the Pacific Rim, the West's cities have become fully networked into the national and world economies. The metropolitan U.S. West coordinates the long-distance exchange of products, services, ideas, and labor, and plays a particularly important role in the contemporary information services and high-tech economy. Certainly, not all western cities participate equally in this phenomenon, nor do they have a monopoly on it, sharing administrative control with Tokyo, London, Mexico City, and other places linked in a scaled and nested hierarchy of local, regional, and global production, consumption, and regulation. But certain problems are shared: widening economic inequality, environmental degradation, infrastructural decline, and political disenfranchisement, among others. These transformations have posed a crisis of sorts for many people living within the U.S. West's cities, who struggle to balance their investments in mythic constructions of the frontier, which have been critically important to the region's culture and self-definition, with their position as skilled and globally networked urban actors within an increasingly uncertain economy.

As the region's cities grow, expand, and change, looking more and more like cities elsewhere in the United States and around the world, it perhaps becomes easy to forget the crucial role that western cities played, and continue to play, in facilitating Anglo-American conquest of the region. However, it is my assumption in this book that conquest is never fully secured and must be maintained through ongoing acts of nation building and the production of hegemonic consent through cultural, ideological, and political-economic means to uphold an unequal social order. Processes of rural urbanism are one such means; struggles to preserve "rural" landscapes are invested with material and symbolic meanings linking whiteness, middle-class status, and American identity. Across shifting racial formations and articulations of racial politics, rural landscapes have been a crucial locus for the production and reproduction of white economic and social privilege in the urban West because they naturalize and make invisible inequalities and relationships of power, all in the name of regional and national heritage.

According to sociologist Howard Winant, modern notions of race were produced in the historical moment during which three macro-scale forces converged: "the making of new forms of empire, the organization of new systems of capital and labor, and the articulation of new concepts of culture and identity," each of which intertwined in the circular and cumulative causation of modernity.[11] White supremacy was a constitutive and central element of this newly racialized world, organized by the structures of empire. As Winant argues, "In the ruling circles — the metropoles, the world's capitals both imperial and peripheral — it was taken for granted as natural, ineluctable, an 'objective' reality, that to be white (however that is defined) conferred a *deserved* advantage on those so identified, while a dark skin *properly* signified inferiority. The name for this set of beliefs, this racial ideology, is white supremacy," which is produced through an ongoing process of racial formation, in which the "key element is the link between signification and structure, between what race means in a particular discursive practice and how, based upon such interpretations, social structures are racially organized."[12] White supremacy has been a central structuring element of social life, political economies, and racial formations within and between emerging nation-states in the global transition to modernity and beyond.

Yet, as geographer Wendy Shaw has observed, the transdisciplinary field of critical whiteness studies has rarely engaged with the production of whiteness through empire, past and present. Shaw contends that this elision has much to do with how the field has been dominated, both geographically and epistemologically, by U.S. scholars, who have tended to privilege a black/white binary while overlooking the ways in which whiteness is constituted in relationship to indigeneity and without necessarily situating U.S. slavery within histories of British and American empire. Shaw's study of gentrification in Sydney, Australia, theorizes the production of whiteness through new forms of urbanism, particularly gentrification, as part of the ongoing colonization of aboriginal people. She argues that mundane urban processes and policies both take whiteness for granted and reinforce the supremacy of white people.[13] I am interested in similar processes here. Like Shaw, I am convinced that the critical study of whiteness must engage with its production through empire. I approach Southern California as a white settler society in which urban policy, especially concerning land use, facilitated American conquest on lands acquired from Mexico at the end of the Mexican-American War. I am interested not only in how this process unfolded historically in the San Fernando Valley during the late nineteenth and twentieth centuries, but also in how it proceeds in contemporary urban politics and everyday life in the early twenty-first century.

Accordingly, I follow historian Maria Montoya in relying on "a paradigm that sees the United States for what it was — an imperial, colonizing state that incorporated the western half of its present-day territory under some rather unequal terms of entry."[14] The negotiation of competing land-use regimes was, and is, a central element of this process. In her study of how different ways of thinking about land collided on the Maxwell Land Grant in northern New Mexico and southern Colorado, Montoya observes that the American West "was a region that reflected the broader trends of nineteenth-century imperial and colonial endeavors throughout the rest of the world."[15] These trends included the philosophical conviction among Europeans and Americans that the lands they conquered were "empty" spaces, when in fact those places were occupied and used by diverse indigenous, Mexican, American, and other inhabitants. As Montoya explains, "the U.S. government acted in imperial and colonial ways that mimicked its European counterparts," particularly to support capitalist interests and landowners.[16] But the connections between the imperial United States and other imperial powers were more than philosophical; they were also political and economic, enabled by dense social networks among landowners, politicians, and bureaucrats in the United States and around the world, who had vested interests in the outcome of land-use contests and who shared among themselves concrete strategies for how to achieve their goals.

> Contestations over territory and property in the U.S. West became central to the material and political structuring of white supremacy. For example, the U.S. Land Commission of 1850, which was established to facilitate the settlement of competing claims in the territories seized during the Mexican-American War, played a crucial role in redistributing land to white Americans. Similarly, the Homestead Act of 1862 transferred more than 270 million acres of land — approximately 10 percent of the acreage of the United States — from indigenous nations to Anglo-American settlers and, to a much smaller degree, freed slaves.[17] Other federal policies such as the 1862 Morrill Land Grant Act, which established state agricultural colleges, and the 1886 Dawes General Allotment Act, which individualized federal Indian reservations into privately owned property (thereby making them more vulnerable to individualized sales), accomplished similar ends of racialized redistribution. At a more local level, exclusionary land-use policies such as alien land laws (which prevented "aliens ineligible for citizenship," or nonwhites and nonblacks, from owning land) and restrictive covenants (written restrictions in property deeds that prohibited an owner from selling his or her property to a nonwhite person) ensured that property transferred to Anglos in the American West would *remain* in white hands across generations.[18] These processes and practices created the foundations of whiteness, linked firmly to empire and to material privilege, in the American West. Access to land was a marker of freedom and citizenship; these were and are constitutive elements of whiteness. They also had profound ideological and political effects, ensuring that expectations to property and upward mobility, protected and subsidized by the state, would become central to white identity. Legal scholar Cheryl Harris has captured these expectations as instances of "whiteness as property."[19] Spatial practices of empire thus fused whiteness with national identity and state-sanctioned material privilege in ways that have far-reaching consequences to the present day.

However, these histories of conquest, dispossession, and exploitation in the American West — and the vast state-sponsored and state-coordinated redistribution of land to whites — are obscured, normalized, and celebrated by the myth of the western frontier posing as national history. The western frontier myth is an example of an imperial "transition narrative," which political philosopher Laura Brace defines and conceptualizes as a story "about the shift from the primitive to the civilized and from feudalism to capitalism."[20] Transition narratives explain territorial expansion in ways that minimize violence, highlight the reason and order associated with the rule of colonial law, and emphasize the social and ideological benefits of expansion for the colonizers *and* for the colonized. Transition narratives are common to virtually all white settler societies formed through European and American imperialism, where they perform a vital ideological role in generating a shared national identity. Sherene Razack elaborates:

> A white settler society is one established by Europeans on non-European soil. Its origins lie in the dispossession and near extermination of Indigenous populations by the conquering Europeans. As it evolves, a white settler society continues to be structured by a racial hierarchy. In the national mythologies of such societies, it is believed that white people came first and that it is they who principally developed the land; Aboriginal peoples are assumed to be mostly dead or assimilated. European settlers thus become the original inhabitants and the group most entitled to the fruits of citizenship. A quintessential feature of white settler mythologies is, therefore, the disavowal of conquest, genocide, slavery, and the exploitation of the labour of peoples of colour.[21]

Essentially, transition narratives reframe the experience of conquest in a way that recuperates the legitimacy of the colonizing force and its social and cultural precepts, thus securing hegemonic rule in conquered territories through appeals to a shared heritage. Frieda Knobloch identifies two related historiographical tropes in such mythologies of transition: the present emerging, as if inevitably, from the past; and the inevitable emergence of culture, over time, from nature. Both tropes rest on notions of a purportedly inevitable "progress," which obscures the tremendous social will that has coaxed these manifest destinies into being. Such social will is, at its heart, spatially operative, occurring through patterns of dispossession, exploitation, and removal that were simultaneously exercises in conquest and race making. [22]

Narratives of rural land in the U.S. West, organized predominantly around myths of the frontier, perform centrally as imperial transition narratives.

Popular representations of the frontier tell us that the U.S. West is the nation's "heartland," a place where purported national values of independence, self-reliance, and hard work are thought to be cultivated through a unique and special relationship with rural land. This idea has been developed through centuries of American political and popular culture, from Thomas Jefferson's homage to yeoman farming in the late 1700s through the contemporary popularity of country-western music.[23] In these representations, the frontier is a liminal space that represents the shifting boundary demarcating spaces of reason, virtue, and civility from spaces of savagery, irrationality, and anticivilization.[24]

Historian Frederick Jackson Turner is most often credited with cultivating myths of the frontier, among both an academic and a popular audience. Turner first articulated his frontier thesis in 1893 at the Chicago World's Fair. Drawing on data from the 1890 U.S. census, Turner proclaimed the American frontier "closed" and used that proclamation to reflect upon and theorize the role of the frontier in the American experience. He argued that a unique American subjectivity had been constituted through the process of subduing and creating order out of the "wild" and "savage" frontier, contending that the process of transforming the frontier's "primitive economic and political conditions . . . into the complexity of city life" had been essential to creating unique American democratic institutions.[25] Turner hypothesized that the conquest of the "savage" frontier proceeded through a series of rural middle landscapes associated with assorted western characters including miners, hunters, and farmers, and ultimately leading to village and later city life. It was with these middle landscapes that Turner was most enamored, because it was there, he claimed, that the American character was produced. He argued that westward expansion, and the necessity incumbent upon settlers to set up social institutions such as schools, churches, and infrastructure, inculcated individualism, self-sufficiency, and antipathy toward despotic control. These characteristics, in turn, created an allegiance to national values and investment in American political institutions. Turner's vision was explicitly, unabashedly imperialist and white supremacist. For Turner, the American character was a white male subjectivity. He argued that in the process of westward migration a composite American nationality formed from the fusion of mixed European races, specifically from English stock and their former indentured servants, Germans and the Scotch-Irish. He rarely mentioned indigenous Americans explicitly in his portraits of the frontier experience, instead folding them into the "beastly" and "savage" forces against which the mettle of white settlers could be tested and measured. Ethnic Mexicans, too, were villains and bandits whose conquest and erasure defined both the white, masculine hero and the inevitable "progress" of American civilization. Indeed, it was precisely through the conquest of indigenous and Mexican peoples and their lands that the (white, male) American was created. Turner's work echoed many of the discursive tropes associated with Enlightenment philosophers and colonial administrators in their interpretations of imperial encounters; his thesis is a classic imperial transition narrative.

Turner's thesis has been largely discredited by academics, including historians of western cities such as Abbott, Reps, and Cronon. Their research challenges Turner's idea that cities emerged organically from the increasingly complex social lives of rugged frontiersmen and women, showing instead that these characters, and the rural places where they lived, were produced by urban corporate, bureaucratic, and cultural interests. But Turner's grip on the field of western history remains pronounced and must be reckoned with, not so much because his work was good history — it wasn't — but because, as Knobloch argues, his prose captured the fantasies and colonial anxieties of his contemporaries, both inside and outside the academy, and influenced the material enactments of American empire throughout the region. Preoccupations with the purported "end" of American empire in the early 1890s, when the large-scale Indian wars were over, guided the work of poets such as Rudyard Kipling, politicians such as Theodore Roosevelt, and agricultural extension agents. For these diverse social actors, Turner's thesis captured a crisis in imperialism, and thus of American identity, that had been built on more than three centuries of aggressive expansion and exploitation of the land, people, and resources.[26] It is also significant that Turner articulated his thesis about rural land and the frontier at the turn of the twentieth century, during the height of industrial urbanization, a period in which cities like Los Angeles were experiencing their most dramatic growth. Within this context, urban planners, capitalists, cultural producers, and everyday activists — who were simultaneously invested in urban growth and anxious about the decline of rural America — incorporated the ideas that Turner expressed about the frontier, rural land, indigenous savagery, and white masculinity into their decisions and actions. Thus, Turner's system of ideas about rural land shaped the cultures, political economies, land-use patterns, and racial regimes of urban places throughout the West. It matters little, then, whether Turner was "right" or "wrong" in his explanation of the frontier's significance. What matters is that ideologies of the frontier — as imperial transition narrative — have been a real and powerful political force in the region's cities and beyond, shaping the development of individual and collective identities, the organization of social movements, and the formulation of urban policy.

In the U.S. Southwest, American imperial expansion across the frontier collided with the efforts of another imperial power: the Spanish colonial system of missions, presidios, and pueblos. The transition narratives developed to explain and justify conquest in this part of the United States thus required engagement with the Spanish colonial past. The web of cultural practices that scholars call the "Spanish fantasy past" exemplify the discursive and ideological merging of narratives of the frontier West with narratives of the Spanish colonial period. Both transition narratives effectively work together to explain American occupation and conquest of the region. Historian Carey McWilliams, who first coined and elaborated the concept, characterizes the Spanish fantasy past as a regional legend depicting the Spanish missions as "havens of happiness and contentment for the Indians, places of song, laughter, good food, beautiful languor, and mystical adoration of the Christ."[27] Such representations elide the reality of indigenous captivity, compulsory religious conversion, forced labor, dispossession, disease and death, and cultural genocide that were part and parcel of life in the Spanish missions.[28] The Spanish fantasy past functioned (and continues to function) through a diverse array of cultural practices, including Helen Hunt Jackson's novella *Ramona* and one of its many manifestations, the Ramona pageant, held annually in Hemet, California; John Steven McGroarty's *Mission Play*, which enjoyed a long run at the San Gabriel Mission; the Mission restoration movement, led by Charles Fletcher Lummis's Landmarks Club; the staging of "Spanish fiestas" in Los Angeles, Santa Barbara, and other California cities; and the popularity of Spanish colonial architecture and "Mission-style" furniture.[29] The Spanish past was put to similar uses throughout the U.S. Southwest in cities such as San Antonio, Texas, and Santa Fe, New Mexico; traces of its influence are everywhere in the region to this day.[30] These activities were hugely profitable, particularly in the first half of the twentieth century and especially in the tourist industry. They contributed to the booming urban economies of Southern California and other metropolitan regions and helped to lure new settlers and investors. Yet the Spanish fantasy past also served a crucial symbolic function by cultivating a sense of place and history among newcomers. In McWilliams's formulation, "the newness of the land itself seems, in fact, to have compelled, to have demanded, the evocation of a mythology which could give people a sense of continuity in a region long characterized by social dislocations."[31] Constructions of the Spanish fantasy past helped give legitimacy to Anglo-American settlement of the region, cohering newcomers around a shared sense of their position in the unfolding drama of American conquest.

Together, imperial land-use practices and the transition narratives that justify them constitute racial projects, linking structure and signification and generating white supremacy in the U.S. West. Land-use practices such as the Homestead Act, the court proceedings of the U.S. Land Commission, alien land laws, and imposition of a grid system remade the social structures in newly conquered territories through the racialized redistribution of land and the establishment of racially exclusive regimes of private property. Transition narratives of the frontier, the Spanish fantasy past, and agriculture explained and legitimated the imperial and racialized social structures thus created. These processes produced the cultural meanings and material experiences of whiteness in the American West, centered on the ownership and control of rural land that had been acquired and regulated by urban political-economic interests and romanticized by urban artists and cultural producers. Whiteness, like all racial categories, has thus achieved its meaning through a particular relationship to land and its resources — in this case, a relationship characterized by entitlement, state subsidy, and histories and contemporary practices of conquest and exclusion.

One of my primary objectives in this book is to contribute to an emerging scholarly discussion, developed mostly by human geographers, concerning the spatial construction of race and specifically whiteness. I find David Delaney's explanation of how racial categories and identities are spatially formed to be particularly helpful. He explains that "space [is] an enabling technology through which race is produced. . . . The territorial division of continuous social space into dichotomous 'insides' and 'outsides' facilitates the polarization of a continuous range of colors (browns, beiges, tans, and pinks) into 'white and black' and hence the freezing of identities into 'we' and 'they.'"[32] Normative state-sanctioned spatial practices, and the qualitative nature of the places that they produce, are a primary force that collectively give meaning — specifically, a spatial referent — to the systems of socially constructed human differences that we recognize as race. Seemingly mundane land-use practices such as zoning, community plans, infrastructure development, and heritage designations actively construct racial categories by producing unequal places and systems of places into which phenotypically distinct bodies are sorted.[33]

My approach in this book treats urban land-use policy as a manifestation of what Michael Omi and Howard Winant conceptualize as the racial state. Omi and Winant argue that the state is never neutral, but rather, "the racial order is equilibrated by the state — encoded in law, organized through policy-making, and enforced by a repressive apparatus."[34] They observe that "through policies which are explicitly or implicitly racial, state institutions organize and enforce the racial politics of everyday life," enabling and constraining the possibilities of human action and the quality of social life.[35] From this perspective, urban-planning practices and land-use policy do not merely reflect but rather are generative of racial identity categories by constructing, maintaining, or dismantling the spatiality of the dominant racial order. Urban land-use policies create a highly particularized relationship to land and its resources among differently categorized racial groups, and structure relationships of power and inequality through the social organization of physical space. On the basis of existing racial, economic, and political relationships, resources are channeled to some neighborhoods, enabling the accumulation of wealth and power, while environmental hazards and unwanted land uses are channeled to others, propelling the concentration of poverty, poor health, and other dangers. Such processes simultaneously define the boundaries of the racial group in question, spatially and corporeally, and create the material and experiential meaning of the category thus defined.[36] My approach to urban policy thus incorporates a social constructivist perspective that treats the urban political arena as a key site for the generation of meaning and identity. In this book, I am centrally concerned with how discursive representations of rural land and the frontier influence the urban policy-making process, and how, in turn, the landscapes created through urban policy affirm and/or tweak those same representations, construct material inequalities, and shape the negotiation of identity within a hierarchical social structure.

In this respect, theories of landscape are particularly useful for understanding how race, especially whiteness, is spatially produced. Cultural geographers define landscape as the fusion of physical, material space and cultural or discursive representations of it. For Denis Cosgrove, the landscape concept "denotes the external world mediated through subjective human experience." Humans give meaning to the physical, material circumstances and spatial arrangement of a place, creating a sense of totality or holism. But landscape is also, simultaneously, a "social product, the consequence of a collective human transformation of nature."[37] That is, the way that a physical place looks, at any given moment, is the result of the choices and actions that individuals and groups engage in as they attempt to shape the world according to their norms and values. Thus, the landscape is both subject and object of human agency; in dialectical fashion, the landscape both shapes and is shaped by social norms and values, including but not limited to those concerning race, class, and nation.

The production of space and of landscape is a fully relational process. All systems of racial categorization are produced through the ongoing reproduction of racialized places and landscapes that are related to — indeed, dependent on — one another.[38] A primary implication of understanding racialization relationally is that the production of a specific place does not just shape the experience of the racial group with which it is most associated, but instead participates in the reproduction of the entire system of racisms, past and present. As

Delaney argues, each physical location "may refer back to or implicate a number of social relations — actually, a network of relations of power."[39] This means, for example, that what appears to be a "black place" is thoroughly marked by historical and contemporary structures of white supremacy such as restrictive covenants, redlining, mob violence, and institutionalized environmental racism. Simultaneously, in the same way that literary scholar Toni Morrison argues for an Africanist presence in the canon of (white) "American literature," "white places" (though they are rarely marked as such) are fully inscribed — or, more appropriately, haunted — by racial Others through the constant practices of exclusion and exploitation upon which they depend for their literal and symbolic value.[40] Every landscape is thus marked by and offers clues to not just its own history but also, and more profoundly, the layered accumulation of historical racial formations that are simultaneously local, regional, national, and global.

Moreover, it is in their interactions with landscapes (both physical and representational) that people learn who they are in relationship to others. One's identity grows out of a way of viewing the world that is fundamentally rooted in a particular relationship to landscape and access to the land's resources. It is also in relationship to landscapes that social groups actively work to reproduce their identities and statuses, both in the way that they work to organize physical space and how they explain why a physical place looks the way that it does. This process involves not only conscious political action but also the unintended consequences of collective action based on taken-for-granted values.[41] As geographers James Duncan and Nancy Duncan explain, "As the visible, material surfaces of places, landscapes can evoke powerful images and sentiments, helping to constitute community values and playing a central role in the performance of place-based social identities and distinction."[42] Thus, through such mundane, everyday acts as gardening or home decorating, people communicate a message about who they are and who they are not. When suburban homeowners in the San Fernando Valley's contemporary rural neighborhoods don a cowboy hat and put a wagon wheel on their front lawn as decoration, they are claiming and performing their identity as characters in the drama of the frontier experience. And when they organize as political movements of suburban homeowners who demand the urban state's protection of their rural landscapes and lifestyle, they embed mythologies of the frontier in the landscapes of their own neighborhoods, where individual and group identities then develop dialectically in relationship to myths and symbols of rural land.

Yet, despite all the work involved in its ongoing creation, the greatest power of landscape is that it seems to be a neutral construction, simply a reflection of the desires, dreams, values, and habits of its inhabitants. In this respect, landscape effectively naturalizes and normalizes systems of power. Don Mitchell has argued that landscape is best seen as both *a work* and as something that *does work*. That is, the landscape is simultaneously the product of human labor, dreams, and social injustices *and* a social agent that acts in the further development of a place by disguising the histories of struggle, resistance, and labor through which the landscape has been produced.[43] It is difficult to see, as one looks at the world, the policy decisions and political-economic forces that have shaped a place, often from afar and in seemingly immaterial or truly invisible ways. Rather, because the built environment reflects histories of investment and disinvestment, human creation and neglect that are invisibly authored, the landscape seems to merely "reflect" the natural attributes, wishes, or desires of the human agents who live within it. The root forces creating inequality are made invisible in the landscape, thereby deflecting critique and containing dissent by suggesting that only those who occupy and use the landscape are responsible for the way it looks.[44] In this way, the landscape shapes ideologies, political standpoints, social movements, and the formulation of policy in such a way as to secure hegemonic consent in support of the legitimacy of the existing social order.[45] Thus, the rural landscapes produced in Los Angeles and throughout the American West seem to naturally reflect the progress of the American frontier experience as the nation's origin story, divorced from processes of illegal expansion, conquest, dispossession, and displacement.

The work that landscape does to disguise and naturalize relationships of power is especially important in the post–civil rights era. Because landscapes obscure the systemic and structural process through which they are produced, and because they appear to be the work of individuals and materially ungrounded and unchanging "cultures," landscapes are crucial grounds for the negotiation of whiteness in the transition from explicit white supremacy to "color-blind" neoconservatism, a transition still very much in process. At stake in this transition — which is roughly simultaneous with the fall of colonialism, or what Winant calls the "postwar break" — are the links between white supremacy, nationalism, and capital accumulation first sutured in the experiences of American and European imperialism. Winant suggests that, at this historical moment, "for the U.S. to come to terms with its own history of conquest and enslavement would have involved a deep national reckoning. It would have severely threatened the foundations of the nation-state."[46] The notion of "color-blindness" has emerged to resolve the crises that Winant identifies. Color-blindness essentially declares that race no longer matters in American life and should not be the basis for decision making among either individuals or institutions. In some respects, the adoption of a color-blind stance ameliorated the worst violations of civil rights and declared that, in theory, individual talent and effort alone would guarantee prosperity. Through the passage of nondiscrimination laws in housing, education, employment, the awarding of government contracts, voting, and political representation, the U.S. state has declared an official position of racial neutrality and mandated that all American citizens do so as well. However, these policies do not address the material and ideological legacies of centuries of legalized segregation, discrimination, and exploitation, instead leaving firmly intact the structures and institutional processes creating white supremacy.[47] As a result, while progress in some areas has doubtlessly been achieved, many indicators of racial inequality remain virtually unchanged and in some cases have worsened. Within this context, imperial transition narratives — such as those celebrating the frontier, the Spanish fantasy past, rural agriculture, and other constructions of rural land in the imperial project — are critically important civic myths through which the basic tenets of American nationalism, as well as historic structures of white supremacy protected by the state, are recuperated and upheld, but in ways that conform and maneuver flexibly in the context of color-blind racial politics.

The book is organized around two chronological pivots — the years 1960 and 2000 — that mark fundamental transformations in the ways whiteness has been and continues to be produced through the dynamics of rural urbanism in Los Angeles and the U.S. West. The three chapters in part 1 explore the ways in which the San Fernando Valley was deliberately planned as a white settler society from 1900 to 1960. Chapter 1 analyzes visions and practices of gentleman farming (small-scale suburban agriculture), which was intended to regenerate the "essential" characteristics of the white race through the strategic combination of rural and urban lifestyles, and produced many of the Valley's iconic citrus groves, poultry ranches, and other kinds of rural districts that would be celebrated by later generations of residents, planners, and activists. Chapter 2 examines the discursive tropes and strategies of the San Fernando Valley's first written histories — all of them produced by urban capitalists and elite social groups — which narrated, explained, and ultimately justified Anglo-American conquest and settlement of the Valley through gentleman farming and, later, suburban subdivision. Chapter 3 considers the multiple roles that the San Fernando Valley played, as both cinematic subject and production location, in the western film and television industry; it demonstrates that the physical landscapes and industrial relations of western film production, which coincided with the San Fernando Valley's massive postwar suburbanization, powerfully shaped new suburbanites' developing interpretations of land and community.

Part 2 chronicles the transition from explicit white supremacy to the era of "color-blind" multiculturalism from 1960 to 2000, illustrating how rural land-scapes have guided and eased this transition while maintaining white privilege intact. In the San Fernando Valley after 1960, urban encroachment (or, more properly, widespread suburbanization) into areas that had previously been imagined and constructed as "rural" coincided with the worldwide fall of colo-nialism and increasingly intense and militant challenges to national racialized social and economic orders, both in the United States and globally, that were very often premised on demands for a reorganization of physical spaces. For many white Americans, these shifts became linked, such that landscape change became associated with undesirable social (especially demographic) change; more pointedly, urbanization and suburbanization in the U.S. West were widely interpreted among some urban planners, reformers, and white homeowners as leading to the decline of Anglo-American civilization. The chapters in part 2 examine how ordinary suburban homeowners in the San Fernando Valley responded to these changes by forming grassroots movements focused on pres-ervation of the rural past. In chapter 4, I analyze the movement to create Los Angeles's first "horse-keeping district" in the neighborhood of Shadow Hills, where activists drew upon the symbolism of the horse as a representation of western heritage to secure privileged land-use policies that protect the rural landscape indefinitely. In chapter 5, I examine the work of grassroots organiza-tions in the west San Fernando Valley that successfully turned the area's historic western movie ranches into regional parks. Amid the major structural changes under way in Los Angeles since the 1960s, the policies created to protect rural landscapes were positioned as racially neutral but drew upon deeply racialized ideological constructions and effectively reproduced rural whites' economic, social, and political privileges.

Part 3 documents the contemporary dynamics of racial formation and the ongoing production of whiteness since 2000, in which a dominant discourse of "color-blindness" coexists uneasily with a celebratory, often uncritical multi-culturalism within an increasingly uncertain urban political economy. In 2000, Latinos became the demographic majority in Los Angeles, and whites became a racial minority. Symbolized by the election of the city's first Mexican American mayor since the late nineteenth century, Antonio Villaraigosa, this demograph-ic shift has propelled new dynamics of engagement with historical processes of rural urbanism, which continue unabated but in more complex and racially ambiguous ways that nonetheless reproduce the key contours of whiteness. To document these nuanced negotiations, part 3 shifts from archival research to my ethnographic fieldwork in the northeast San Fernando Valley's rural communities. Chapter 6 analyzes the scope and extent of rural whites' privileges within the context of the city's economic restructuring, diversification, and globalization in the past four decades. Chapter 7 examines how contemporary rural residents interpret their social positions in the changing city through reference to their beliefs about rural, suburban, and urban landscapes. Chapter 8 investigates how rural residents' beliefs about landscape and their anxieties about social change inform their land-use activism, as well as how they interpret their interactions with growing numbers of immigrants and people of color.

The conclusion links developments in the San Fernando Valley with the contemporary reorganization of rural places and the regeneration of whiteness throughout the U.S. West and Europe. In these places, the production of rural landscapes through the intersections of culture, policy, and everyday life has been and continues to be a means of securing conquest and generating white supremacy. Thus, the central dynamic of rural urbanism that has been critical to the San Fernando Valley's history also has a broader relevance. Indeed, rural urbanism, along with other social processes, to be sure, is reshaping the meanings and experiences of whiteness on a global scale.

PART ONE

Creating the Foundations of Rural Whiteness, 1900–1960

CHAPTER ONE

Creating Whiteness through Gentleman Farming

From the first decades of Anglo-American control after 1848 well into the twentieth century, Los Angeles was an explicitly and unabashedly white supremacist place. The choices that planners, real-estate developers, capitalists, and other city builders made about land use in the developing region were intended not only to attract investment and generate profit but also to solidify Anglo-American control and achieve white racial supremacy. "Gentleman farming," or small-scale suburban agriculture, was an important part of their urban development strategy. Through gentleman farming, planners and policy makers intended to create in Los Angeles a new model of urbanism, one that uniquely combined selective elements of rural and urban life to restore national values and regenerate the white race. Their goal was to enable middle-class white landowners to enjoy and benefit from the moral superiority and political commitments to republican democracy that rural life was thought to inculcate, but within close proximity to the employment opportunities and cultural offerings of downtown. Beginning in the early 1900s, urban planners, real-estate developers, and community builders collaborated to produce semiagricultural districts of "little farms near the city," inhabited by economically prosperous, culturally sophisticated, white gentleman farmers. The production of landscape and the construction of Los Angeles's emerging racial formation thus went hand in hand, linking race, class, and nation through the social and spatial development of the metropolitan region.

Throughout the U.S. West, agriculture had long been a critical way in which Anglo-American settlement and conquest was achieved. Frieda Knobloch argues that agriculture and colonization in the American West worked together as material and ideological practices. She notes that agriculture, defined as "the science and art of cultivating the soil," is fundamentally about changing the land by "improving" it, a concept that she argues rests on the imposition of state power through bureaucratic regulation and policy, institutional knowledge production by "experts" and natural scientists, the consolidation of military power, and the development of tools and methods through which the land can be domesticated.[1] These impositions were and are intended to bring conquered or unsettled territories under the stable, settled control of the state and into a productive and profitable regime of property ownership. She demonstrates that this process has taken place through not only spectacular acts of territorial dispossession but also what appear to be the rather mundane operations of such agencies as the U.S. Forestry Service, innovations in plowing equipment and technique, the development of livestock ranging practices, and the control of weeds. For Knobloch, these practices together enabled colonization, which she understands to be "about enforcing landownership through a new, agricultural occupation of lands once used differently."[2]

The various land-use policies that federal, state, and local governments adopted in the U.S. Southwest were intended to create a secure white settler society on lands acquired through the U.S. war with Mexico, territory that had remained sparsely settled well into the late 1800s. Before the war, Americans (as well as German, French, Scottish, and other European settlers) had applied for and received land grants from the Mexican government. Simultaneously, Anglo-American men had married into elite Mexican families, from which they stood to inherit windfalls of acreage. Thus, already by the launch of the war in 1846, white Americans were relatively integrated into elite Mexican society in the Southwest and had a foothold in Mexican systems of landownership.[3] After the end of the war and the cession of what is now the U.S. Southwest to the Americans, several interlocking processes hastened the mass transfer of land from Mexicans to Anglo-Americans and European immigrants. Foremost among these was the establishment of the U.S. Land Commission in 1851 to settle competing land claims in the ceded territories. Although the Treaty of Guadalupe Hidalgo expressly provided for the legal respect of Mexicans' property rights, a combination of ideological, fiscal, and bureaucratic forces nonetheless led to widespread Mexican dispossession. Conflicts arose between the systems of land tenure and ownership that Americans and Mexicans used. Mexican land grants — typically thousands of acres in size — rarely had clear, legally defined boundaries and instead used natural geographic features of the landscape such as trees, rivers, and mountains to demarcate ownership lines. The enforcement of this system rested upon social relationships of mutual respect embedded in complex kinship structures. In contrast, American claims rested on highly bureaucratic, modernist systems of land distribution, specifically the survey and the grid, which were in most instances privileged over the frequently undocumented, loosely demarcated land claims presented by Mexicans. Economic and demographic factors — including the sheer costliness of defending ownership in court, the relative shortage of cash among Mexican ranchers, the high interest rates and legal fees charged by speculators and lawyers, and Mexican unfamiliarity with the English language — all exacerbated Mexican land loss.[4] Simultaneously, Anglo-American applicants were awarded vast tracts of land by making claims under the U.S. Homestead Act, passed in 1862. By the 1880s, the majority of Mexican landowners in the San Fernando Valley and Southern California had lost their land through a combination of these forces, so that by the close of the nineteenth century, most land in the Valley was owned by a small group of elite Anglo-American capitalists, who planted it in wheat or wine grapes, used it for sheep grazing, or speculated in land subdivision. Their names — Van Nuys, Lankershim, Porter — are indelibly marked in the San Fernando Valley's landscapes, on street signs, neighborhoods, schools, and buildings.[5]

During this period, Los Angeles was popularly conceived as the homeland of the Anglo-Saxon race. Historian William Deverell argues that widely touted promotions of Los Angeles as an "urban destiny in the making" during this period rested on explicit white supremacy. He writes that "Los Angeles was the spot — city leaders of the 1920s liked to call it, without a trace of irony, the 'white spot' — where prophecy met history, where a place inherited millennial destiny."[6] Los Angeles was imagined as the end of a long trek of westward settlement through which white Americans had allegedly met and surpassed the tests of brutal nature and American Indian violence. Los Angeles was, in these interpretations, the Anglo-Saxons' rightful home. Charles Fletcher Lummis, an influential booster, frequently wrote of the region as "the new Eden of the Saxon home-seeker," and many of his peers shared his vision of Southern California as the site of a reinvigorated Anglo-Saxon culture.[7] Mark Wild suggests that the "white spot" idea conflates the ideals of Los Angeles as a morally pure city with the absence of foreigners, who were assumed to bring with them crime and political radicalism, particularly labor activism. In positioning the city as a "white spot," boosters both denied the presence of ethnic minorities and immigrants in the region and presumed their inherent criminality and subversive character. By representing Los Angeles as "white," boosters such as Harry Chandler of the *Los Angeles Times* intoned that the city "possessed none of the blight, decay, civic corruption, or criminal activity that plagued other urban areas."[8] By contrast, such boosters argued, "the city of homes was simultaneously beautiful, ethical, prosperous, and, by implication, white."[9]

Notions of Los Angeles as both a white spot and a new kind of city, pioneering a new kind of urbanism, developed in tandem. Planned decentralization, featuring low-density and semirural landscapes, was a major element of this

land-use vision. Real-estate developers, community builders, and urban planners embraced a model of urban development that conceived of the region as
a patchwork quilt of relatively independent decentralized communities complete with industry, commerce, and home lots, as well as social and cultural
activities.[10] This vision was conceptualized in explicit opposition to the centrist
model of urbanization that had dominated East Coast cities, which planners
and community builders in Los Angeles believed led to undesirable social patterns. Cities such as New York, Philadelphia, and Chicago had recently become
centers of two distinct and related phenomena — large-scale immigration,
particularly from eastern Europe, and industrialization — which together led
to an increase in poverty and the spread of political radicalism, particularly
through widespread labor organizing and unionization. Gordon Whitnall, who
would later become director of the Los Angeles City Planning Commission,
explained the "mistakes" of East Coast urban planners to attendees at the
Sixteenth National Conference on Planning, held in Los Angeles in 1924. He
argued, "[We have] an obligation to prevent the recurrence of those mistakes
which have happened in the growth of metropolitan areas in the east. . . . We
still have our chance, if we live up to our opportunities, of showing the right
way of doing things. It will not be the west looking back to the east to learn . . .
but the east looking to the west to see how it should be done."[11] For Whitnall
and other advocates of what Greg Hise terms suburbanization as urbanization,
manipulation of the physical landscape in Los Angeles offered the opportunity
to develop a new future for humankind based not on centralization but on the
efficient and rational planning of the entire metropolitan region as a collection of independent, comprehensive, low-density suburban clusters. Thus, Los
Angeles planners envisioned their growing city as a place where a new model of
urbanism could be developed and tested as part and parcel of a racialized social
experiment.

In many places, decentralization rested on the creative combination of
selective elements of rural and urban lifestyles. These articulations of rural
urbanism took different forms depending on the class, race, and citizenship
status of the neighborhood in question. In working-class white neighborhoods,
as Becky Nicolaides has shown, planners and community builders left roads
unpaved, provided minimal infrastructure, and created zoning codes that allowed working-class homeowners to raise animals and vegetable gardens on
their properties. These strategies kept taxes low and thereby enabled working-
class whites to benefit from homeownership for the first time; the effect was
the production of semirural, working-class white landscapes in the suburbs of
Los Angeles, usually clustered around manufacturing hubs. Civic leaders also

hoped to keep working-class white homeowners focused on their own private properties and their prospects of upward mobility, so that they would be less likely to inhabit the collective public spaces where the seeds of a multiethnic labor movement might be sown.[12]

Despite boosters' fantasies of Los Angeles as a "white spot," the city was always home to small but important communities of blacks, Mexicans, and Asian Americans. However, land-use policies such as restrictive covenants, redlining, and alien land laws confined immigrants and nonwhites to the central city neighborhoods where, by virtue of industrial and commercial zoning, most simply did not have access to rural lifestyles.[13] Where nonwhite rural neighborhoods did exist, they were the result of civic neglect and abandonment rather than deliberate planning, as in Watts, often called Mudtown because of its dirt roads and the southern roots of its inhabitants; Chavez Ravine, which lacked paved roads, running water, and electricity well into the 1940s; Pacoima, the unofficial "minority district" of the San Fernando Valley, where the vast majority of blacks and Latinos lived; or any of the Mexican *colonias* dotting the suburban gentleman-farming districts.

In the San Fernando and San Gabriel valleys, rural urbanism took the form of gentleman farming, which was envisioned as the foundation of a middle-class white settler society. The creation of gentleman-farming districts redistributed land from the hands of wealthy, elite Anglo-American investors who had benefited from earlier acts of dispossession to the white middle class, who would, it was hoped, settle the suburban valleys and contribute to Los Angeles's growth and prosperity as the "white spot of America." Boosters and planners appealed selectively to American ideologies of yeoman farming espoused by such national icons as Thomas Jefferson and St. John de Crèvecouer. Specifically, they embraced the idea that individual, privatized land ownership on agricultural homesteads would cultivate republican virtue. Jefferson had argued that farmers were "the chosen people of God, if ever he had a chosen people, whose breasts he has made his particular deposit for substantial and genuine virtue."[14] Jefferson believed that a nation of family farmers who owned their own land and performed their own labor, providing for virtually all their own needs with little intervention from the state, would create a strong commitment to a participatory democracy and republican institutions.[15] As Matt Garcia notes in his study of citrus culture in Los Angeles's San Gabriel Valley, "the agricultural settlement was universally recognized as the line separating civilization from savagery—the domestication of the 'Wild West' and the creation of a 'civilized' and 'productive' society."[16] Apart from the romantic elements of the ideal, city leaders embraced gentleman farming for practical reasons; they recognized that individual property ownership on suburban farms would counteract tendencies towards unionization and labor radicalism.

They could not and did not embrace rural life *in totum*, however, because by the late nineteenth century family farms in the U.S. Midwest were experiencing a host of problems that exposed the limitations of Jefferson's vision when practiced in a rapidly industrializing, increasingly corporate world. Farm foreclosures and bankruptcies were common on account of difficulties with pests, floods and drought, and competition with the growing agribusiness industry. Children of family farmers were loathe to re-create the lives of poverty and desperation that their parents had known, and increasingly few were interested in agricultural work. In addition to economic concerns, popular dissatisfaction with the drudgery and isolation of rural life had gripped many agricultural communities, particularly in the U.S. Midwest. Most immigrants who moved to urban centers did so not to achieve greater economic success but to enjoy a more relaxed and culturally varied life.[17] For these reasons, rural-to-urban migration was at its height, and Progressives, who believed in the value of rural life to the American character, knew that something had to be done to make the rural life more attractive to middle-class white families. O. F. Cook, a eugenicist employed by the U.S. Department of Agriculture, argued that "agriculture is not only the basis of our civilization in the mere economic sense of affording food to support our physical existence, but in a still more fundamental biological sense. It is only in an agricultural state that the human individual attains a normal acquaintance with his environment and a full endowment of the intellectual and social faculties of this race."[18] Thus, boosters and planners in Los Angeles were keen to embrace the theories and promises of Jefferson's and Turner's rural, pastoral vision while avoiding its pitfalls.

Gentleman farming was their solution. It would combine the "best of both worlds" — of urban and rural life — for a middle-class white population, for whom the experience of semirural living would cultivate both cultural sophistication and political conservatism. Boosters in Los Angeles promised that, owing to the ideal Mediterranean climate of the region, crops (especially citrus) would grow relatively easily after the initial tasks of irrigation and planting and did not require a large acreage to yield a middle-class income. According to historian Kevin Starr, "Southern California's first self-image after the passing of the frontier was that of the American farm perfected, saved from loneliness and backbreaking labor, graced with some degree of aesthetic satisfaction."[19] As a result, gentleman farmers could devote a good amount of their time to the pursuits of republican democracy and the "civilized" rural life — perhaps attending a play, sponsoring lectures, or helping to create schools, churches, and concert halls in any one of the semirural, suburban community centers scattered throughout the region. In doing so, they would perpetuate the process so valorized by Turner — establishing democratic, locally governed institutions and thereby creating the essential American character. This vision was extremely attractive to migrants who sought to escape the drudgery of midwestern rural life. As Garcia observes, unlike in other farming societies, "in Southern California, a return to the farm did not require a choice between the luxuries of the city and the social and biological advantages of an agrarian life."[20]

These visions took shape as early as the 1880s, during Southern California's first major real-estate boom, although they were most popular in the second and third decades of the twentieth century. An 1883 promotional text titled *A Southern California Paradise (In the Suburbs of Los Angeles)* highlighted the distinct combination of rural and urban living to be had in Los Angeles's suburban valleys and foothills, and the ways in which rural residents could selectively engage with the city.

> By a short and easy journey one can see the homes, orchards, vineyards, gardens, flowers, hedge-lined streets, live-oak groves, the picturesque Arroyo, the round hills and rugged mountains, the great ranches, the cactus hedges, the Old Mission, a touch of the Mexican dominion, and the very best samples of Southern California. These attractions, with a multitude of varying drives and charming picnic resorts, all so near to Los Angeles, are of untold value to the residents of that city. The city in turn is of equal value to these suburban inhabitants. . . . Few cities in the world will have ampler, grander, and more varied and convenient suburban advantages than Los Angeles, and certainly none will have those which are more healthful and invigorating.[21]

Beginning in 1888 and throughout the 1920s, the Los Angeles Chamber of Commerce published a promotional booklet titled *Los Angeles: The City and the County*, which celebrated the strategic combination of rural and urban life to be had in the city's suburbs. Author Harry Ellington Book wrote, "Here may be found beautiful rural homes, whose owners are within touch of social life, and enjoy the best features of the city and country combined."[22] The anonymous wife of one such gentleman farmer shared her story with the *Los Angeles Times*, contrasting the rural times of old with the new style of semirural living in Southern California. She wrote, "In this California country, at least, a trek back to the land does not mean a downward trend in living conditions. On the small farms scattered all around Los Angeles, the family has health, food, comfort, beauty, work, sanitation, education, and safety. What more is to be desired?" She continued by directly addressing the popular dissatisfaction with rural communities elsewhere in the country. "In times past the ranchers were out of reach of schools and social activities, but automobiles and school busses have solved these problems. In nearly every rural community at the present time there are good schools, fire protection, libraries and practically every advantage that can be had in cities. Add to these fresh air, quietness, healthful exercise, freedom, and a saving on food bills, if even one member of the family is willing to take an active interest in agriculture and poultry-raising, and you have quite an argument for this sort of life."[23] She concluded that "the little-lander has every advantage over his city brother." In 1932, the Los Angeles Chamber of Commerce similarly described the community of Roscoe, in the foothills of the Verdugo Mountains: "Citrus orchards near the foothills, poultry ranches, home garden acres and suburban homes predominate. Many prominent business and professional men own homes in the canyons that are famous for their rustic beauty."[24] The report situated Roscoe's landscape within a distinctly Angeleno tradition of small suburban farms in close proximity to the city. "The small farm home is its [Los Angeles's] best offering to those seeking a full life in a rural atmosphere. These little places of from a half to two acres, within commuting distance of the city, are a distinct contribution to better living, and as such, are drawing hundreds of families each year. . . . [Most small farms are] largely developed by families supported by employment in the city."[25] Growth-machine interests thus conceived of the combination of rural and urban life as a new form of urbanism that would be attractive to settlers and could ensure the prosperity of the burgeoning city of Los Angeles, the nation, and the white race.

Promoters of rural urbanism targeted a particular class of people — middle-class, upwardly mobile, and culturally sophisticated whites, often from urban origins in the Midwest and the East — to populate the semirural communities. They made it clear that the region's ideal suburban farmers were not experienced farmers (which would imply rural origins and associations with white rural poverty and cultural backwardness) but rather urban sophisticates, perhaps one generation removed from farming, who could now enjoy semirural life with all the benefits, but none of the disadvantages, of the city. Russell Richardson, a columnist for the *Los Angeles Times*, described the suburban farmer in 1929: "These new farmers are different from the old-time farmers of the '60s or the peasant immigrant of the '70s and '80s, who came looking for large tracts of land. The new type of soil worker is not a professional farmer. Usually he comes after having made a success in some other vocation. Artisans, tradesmen, bankers, mechanics, engineers and lawyers — these are the new farmers on the 'little lands' of California. They are proving the wisdom of Lincoln's words, 'The most valuable of all arts will be the art of deriving a comfortable subsistence from the smallest area of soil.'"[26] Richardson advocated for the power of gentleman farmers, often called "Little Landers," to restore greatness to American democracy, which, he claimed, was threatened by industrialization and urbanization. He argued: "These 'Little Landers' of the Southland are self-employing proprietors. Their loving labor contrasts with the grudging labor of the hireling, and the wasteful exploitation of the tenant farmer. America needs the upbuilding of such a rural democracy to counterbalance the ever-increasing mass of great cities."[27] Boosters extolled the symbolic and ideological importance of independent, middle-class white gentleman farmers who, according to a 1925 article in the *Los Angeles Times*, "take a welcome place in our agricultural scheme."[28]

City and county elites were invested in the success of gentleman farmers to provide proof of the region's multilayered and interlocking promotions as a "garden city," a "city of homes," and a "white spot." In fact, the symbolism of gentleman farming seems more important to its boosters than its economic possibilities. Despite promotions that gentleman farmers could achieve independence on one acre of land, most attention focused on the quality of life that a uniquely rural-urban homestead enabled. A 1928 article written by a staff member of the Los Angeles Chamber of Commerce's Agricultural Bureau and published in the *Los Angeles Times* opined, "While a small farm in the Southland is often a sustaining unit when two or more acres in extent, it is as a home place that these little farms are particularly attractive to the city worker. They combine the ideal rural environment with the conveniences of the city, permit indulgence in home beautification, offer the economies of a continual home-grown food supply and make possible a standard of living that is found in few other sections of the country."[29]

As a result, most residents of the San Fernando Valley at the turn of the twentieth century were white midwestern transplants who dreamed of creating a comfortable and civilized upper-middle-class existence through a Jeffersonian model of life on the land, applied and adapted to suburbia, in close proximity to urban centers of refined cultural sophistication and opportunities for investment and employment. In addition to native-born white U.S. citizens, a good number of European (primarily Armenian, Italian, German, and English) and Canadian immigrants came to call the San Fernando Valley home during this period. Most of these immigrants had lived elsewhere in the United States for at least a few years, some of them for decades; thus most spoke English and had already accrued some capital in their prior home. The early Anglo-American population of the San Fernando Valley was, on balance, racially homogenous but ethnically diverse and middle class. These residents shared substantial economic resources, urban backgrounds, a desire for a less arduous life in Los

Angeles, and a nearly unanimous commitment to the ideals of suburban farming in a booming metropolitan region.[30]

Most gentleman farmers combined a recreational interest in agriculture with full-time employment in Southern California's urban industries, including oil, railroad work, structural engineering, real estate, construction, and hospitality.[31] For example, Mr. and Mrs. F. F. Meyer, who owned five acres in the northeast San Fernando Valley neighborhood of Hansen Heights, grew persimmons as their primary crop but also raised quinces, prunes, pomegranates, nectarines, peaches, pears, almonds, cherries, oranges, lemons, and grapefruits. They set up a roadside stand to sell their spare eggs, milk, honey, and fruit. However, explaining that they had learned it was not wise to carry all their eggs in one basket, the Meyers earned their primary income through a real-estate business.[32] Similarly, John Harns, a contractor born in Iowa who had come to California after a stint in Oregon, raised similar crops for supplementary income as well as eggs, dairy cows, bees, and a vegetable garden for household goods.[33] Mr. and Mrs. Charles Bender, prior residents of Illinois who owned a printing press as their primary occupation, named their one and one-half acre ranch "Atlasta Ranch," because they had at last achieved their dream of owning a ranch in Southern California. Multiplied by the thousands, gentleman farmers such as these migrated to the San Fernando Valley, where they invested their accumulated capital in the growing urban region while enjoying the recreational and symbolic promises of "a little land and a living."

The state invested tremendous public resources — fiscal, legal, bureaucratic, and infrastructural — to transform the San Fernando Valley's landscapes into gentleman-farming districts. According to Frank Keffer, by 1910 there were "millions of dollars budgeted to transfer the valley from a great grain field to the most desirable place in the world for the establishment of suburban farm homes, where settlers might enjoy country life and at the same time have all the conveniences that a city could offer."[34] One of the greatest examples of civic investment in suburban farming is the construction of the Los Angeles Aqueduct. The owners of the *Los Angeles Times* — who were also, as partners in the Los Angeles Suburban Homes Corporation, the San Fernando Valley's largest landowners — initiated a ballot proposal to construct the massive aqueduct from the Owens Valley to the San Fernando Valley. The initiative proposed to pay for the construction of the aqueduct through the issuance of municipal bonds. Their plan, unbeknown to voters, was to subdivide their own newly irrigated lands and pocket tremendous profits. Los Angeles voters passed the initiative by a wide margin. Most historical accounts narrate the tale of the aqueduct in terms of the enormous swindle that Chandler and his cronies orchestrated to profit from the city's subsidization of their own agricultural lands.[35] Yet it is also important to note that the completion of the aqueduct was a vital first step without which middle-class gentleman farming simply could not proceed. Gentleman farmers purchased and then cultivated smaller tracts of land carved out of the elites' enormous holdings after the aqueduct's completion, and their suburban farms benefited in untold ways from access to a cheap, seemingly endless water supply paid for by taxpayers throughout the city.

The urban state's support for the Valley's agricultural development proceeded in other ways, too. City and county governments were keen to provide moral and practical support for incoming gentleman farmers, particularly since most had little or no farming experience. According to George P. Clements, director of the Los Angeles Chamber of Commerce's Agricultural Bureau, "When Mr. and Mrs. John Smith, late of Iowa, arrive in Los Angeles bent on developing a small home place with 'a few chickens and such,' we are morally responsible for their future success and happiness."[36] Government agencies, research groups, chambers of commerce, and local universities (prominently, the University of California) sponsored scientific studies intended to endow gentleman farmers with the most cutting-edge information about crops, climate, soil, and irrigation techniques. Also, the *Los Angeles Times* and other local newspapers featured frequent instructional articles and advice columns. Usually these essays were penned by Clements or other agricultural department staff and were very well illustrated. Articles focused on such topics as which crops to prioritize on a one-acre parcel, how best to use the land for planting and livestock, how to avoid typical diseases, and the importance of culling "bad hens" from poultry stock or of pruning deciduous trees.[37] University professors and agricultural experts gave frequent lectures and workshops on site in the Valley's emerging agricultural districts, often at local schools and community centers, sponsored by the County Agricultural Extension Service, the Los Angeles County Farm Bureau, and the Los Angeles Chamber of Commerce.[38] And, these same organizations sponsored outlets for gentleman farmers to sell their products, while celebrating their lifestyle and the tremendous agricultural productivity of the county as a whole. The Los Angeles County Fair is perhaps the clearest example. First held in Pomona in 1922, the fair was initiated by a board of corporate directors from throughout the gentleman-farming districts. They sold shares, made personal loans, and garnered fiscal support from the Los Angeles County Board of Supervisors to achieve the fair's purpose of promoting "the agricultural, horticultural and animal husbandry interests of the great Southwest."[39]

Much of the semirural vision centered on instructing children, who constituted the future of both the city and the Anglo-Saxon race. Celebratory articles in the local news media, especially the *Los Angeles Times*, regularly highlighted Valley youth's involvement in 4-H clubs, egg production, poultry and calf raising, landscape gardening, and other agricultural specialties.[40] Social groups arranged for schoolchildren to visit local commercial farmers, where they might learn from and be inspired by successful farmers who modeled the combination of agricultural contentment with urban sophistication. City-sponsored egg, poultry, and vegetable contests were common throughout the San Fernando Valley's agricultural districts. These contests brought together diverse constituents — city agencies, local social institutions such as schools and churches, and individual families — in support of training children in proper agricultural methods and, by extension, republican values and virtues. These commitments were also embedded in the San Fernando Valley's newly established educational facilities. The Valley's new public schools included agricultural facilities on their campuses and developed agricultural departments to instruct students in methods of horticulture and animal husbandry. In 1923, for example, the Los Angeles Board of Education approved construction of a modern poultry plant at Van Nuys High School, constructed through consultation with local poultry farmers and with the pro bono design and engineering services of a Valley architect. The poultry plant was intended primarily as an educational rather than a financial enterprise, although in every year of its operation it turned a profit.[41] And in 1924 the Los Angeles County Agricultural Extension Service partnered with the new Owensmouth High School's Agricultural Department to sponsor an egg-production contest. Although theoretically open to all students who attended the school, all the entrants were children from the nearby Weeks Poultry Colony at Winnetka, including first-place winner Mildred Smith and the runner-up, her brother Harold.[42]

Civic leaders and promoters of gentleman farming publicized the testimonials of those who had made a success of their little farms as a way to spread their secrets, folk wisdoms, and tried-and-true tactics. In 1928, the *Times* partnered with the Los Angeles Chamber of Commerce to sponsor an essay contest with this aim in mind. Entries consisted of short essays accompanied by sketches of the property. Figure 2 features a winning sketch submitted by Joseph Weston of El Monte, in the San Gabriel Valley, for the 1930 contest. The sponsors acknowledged that competition for the cash prizes would likely be keen, but that the real motivation would be the desire to help others. They coaxed suburban farmers to "take up your pencil, and tell us about your small farm home, so that we may make your experiences a guidance to the hundreds of persons who annually seek the ideal mode of living you enjoy."[43] A few months later the *Times* featured one of their winning essays, submitted by Chicago natives Mr. and Mrs. J. W.

Milnor, who had purchased a one-acre farm in Elsinore, near Riverside. Mrs. Milnor wrote:

> In July, 1924, we left Chicago in a Ford touring car equipped with a camping outfit and started to tour to the land of sunshine — California. After spending two months sightseeing we were very glad to see Los Angeles. We spent the next few months taking real estate trips and finally a supersalesman sold us an acre in Elsinore. We had no intention of locating permanently, as we have a home in Chicago. It was a beautiful picture that this salesman painted for us on this raw land, covered with sagebrush, land not even level and with no water at that time. We knew nothing about California farming.[44]

Like many vacationers to Southern California in the 1920s, however, the Milnors decided to stay. Despite being duped by real-estate salespersons — a common exploitative practice that threatened to soil Southern California's reputation for would-be migrants — Milnor tells of planting a few trees each year and working for larger farmers nearby to raise money to buy a tractor and other farm equipment. Soon her husband was able to serve as a mentor to newer gentleman farmers. For the Milnors, the sunny California lifestyle of suburban farming was literally a dream come true. As Mrs. Milnor testified, "We like our home very much and have often wondered why other people do not take advantage of a place like this." For the *Los Angeles Times* and the Los Angeles Chamber of Commerce, such stories and illustrations were pure gold, because they confirmed the power of hard work and persistence (along with continuous investment) to turn the vision of gentleman farming into a reality.

Within Mrs. Milnor's sunny story, however, lies a tension that was fundamental to the practice of gentleman farming. Migrants came to the San Fernando Valley expecting to sustain themselves on an acre of land and to enjoy the benefits of rural life, with little effort and minimal capital investment. In reality, however, few were able to achieve that life. Most gentleman farmers ultimately did not and could not achieve self-sufficiency on the land as boosters had promised because of their inexperience with citriculture, the long period of waiting for plant maturity before any profits could be made, and competition from Asian (especially Japanese) farmers.[45] But the most important factor confounding their economic success was the dominance of California agriculture by corporate firms and distribution and marketing cooperatives such as Sunkist. Land monopolies had plagued California agriculture since the earliest days of statehood, and they persisted in the San Fernando Valley despite boosters' and planners' promotions of "little lands" and "gentleman farms." During Spanish and Mexican days, land grants had been enormous, often hundreds of

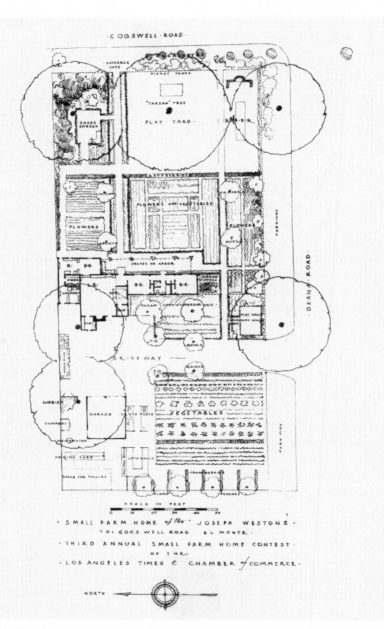

FIGURE 2 The winning architectural sketch submitted by Joseph Weston of El Monte for the third annual Small Farm Home Contest conducted by the *Los Angeles Times* and the Los Angeles Chamber of Commerce in 1930. Courtesy of the Los Angeles Public Library.

thousands of acres. Many of these tremendous parcels had passed to American hands undisturbed in size. The U.S. federal government also participated in the consolidation of land in the hands of a few elites through its grants to the Central Pacific and Southern Pacific Railroad Companies. By the 1870s, much of California land had fallen into the hands of a few individuals or corporations, owners who saw farming first and foremost as a business rather than as an arena for the cultivation of republican virtue. Throughout the state, a plutocracy of agribusiness interests controlled the majority of acreage, employed the majority of workers, and received most of the profits. By 1900, 7 percent of California's farm owners controlled 63 percent of the agricultural land.[46] And within the citrus industry, 3.7 percent of growers owned roughly 41 percent of the orange acreage, while 3.8 percent of lemon producers controlled nearly 58 percent of the land devoted to that crop. Such patterns of land monopoly equally plagued the San Fernando Valley. For example, the 4,100-acre Sunshine Ranch, owned by the Edwards and Wiley Company, contained the Valley's largest citrus orchard of approximately 1,000 acres, alongside other crops. The firm had accumulated tremendous profits through the application of "power farming" methods, including the use of tractors and subsoilers. Edwards and Wiley subdivided the future community of Granada Hills on a chunk of the property in 1928.[47]

These large landed interests — corporations, rather than individual gentleman farmers — controlled the agricultural industry through tightly organized cooperatives, which set prices, wages, and production conditions. By 1920, one-half of California's total agricultural yield was controlled by nearly sixty voluntary cooperatives that handled harvesting, processing, shipping, and marketing. In many cases, the agricultural cooperatives successfully turned what had been luxury foods — such as walnuts, almonds, or in the most famous case, citrus — into foods for daily consumption. But the marketing and distribution cooperatives did not counteract the concentration of wealth and power in California agriculture; in fact, they had the opposite effect. Historian Gilbert Gonzalez argues that "while the cooperative method was considered a democratic system with voting rights allocated equally among the members, in practice it was the larger and more successful growers who dominated the local associations and the central exchange."[48] Voting rights within the associations, for example, were based on the fiscal value of each grower's contribution to the co-op. Large growers thus led the membership in setting prices, formulating marketing and distribution strategies, and squashing labor strikes. As Gonzalez reminds us, "One may deplore the concentration and imbalance in the cooperative system, but the fact is that citrus growing was not a common farming enterprise. Investments in groves required sufficient capital that the average person lacked."[49] A handful of gentleman farmers and Little Landers who joined such cooperatives might achieve a degree of success by pooling their products with agribusiness interests, but they lacked decision-making power and were subject to the whims of large-scale agribusiness with regard to such issues as wages, working conditions, and worker housing. Those who chose not to join a cooperative, perhaps out of a belief in the importance of self-sufficiency and subsistence farming, were at a fierce disadvantage in the sale and distribution of their products; most were literally forced out of the market.

Within this context, the San Fernando Valley's individual gentleman farmers were poorly positioned to compete. Starr argues that land monopoly, coupled with high interest rates, "made it extremely difficult for individual Californians to gain ownership of a self-supporting family farm."[50] Rates of tenancy were high to begin with — nearly 18 percent in 1890 — and rose consistently through the decades, to 35.6 percent in 1925. Those who nominally owned their land relied on long lines of bank credit until their crops matured — up to seven years for citrus — meaning that one-third to one-half of those who "owned" their lands actually were deeply indebted to the bank. Many small farmers worked full time for the larger ranches or for other regional industries such as oil drilling and railroad construction while they waited for crops to mature; in many cases, these second jobs became permanent occupations.[51] In short, many soon found that gentleman farming was not quite as easy, quick, or profitable as they had been promised, and most turned to other pursuits in Los Angeles's expanding industrial economy as their primary activity.

Some civic leaders tried to rein in the popular misconception among many migrants, cultivated by boosters and real-estate salespersons, that little work would be required of them to enjoy self-sufficient garden homes. While popular promotions generally touted the idea that independence could be had on one acre of land, Clements warned newcomers that land parcels smaller than two acres were rarely self-sustaining, and that "independence on an acre" was a misleading slogan that they should investigate with great care. Most small farmers, he said, obtained their primary income from other sources, and newcomers should not expect to do otherwise, particularly with little agricultural experience or horticultural knowledge. For those who wanted to farm for subsistence rather than as a supplementary pastime, Clements recommended a lot size of at least four acres dedicated primarily to poultry farming with no fewer than two thousand hens, and preferably up to three thousand. He coaxed potential migrants to personally inspect potential lots rather than to trust in the promises of real-estate salespeople and developers, and to make sure that plenty of water was available. Without ample capital, he warned that those who wanted to make their entire living from the land would be "hampered seriously in [their] enterprise." He wrote, "The small farm home in Southern California represents a mode of living that is luxuriate, yet economic, and such environment can be found nowhere else in the world. Yet success and happiness in developing these small places are dependent on wise initial investment. The newcomer owes it to himself, his family and the community he elects to live in to make an intelligent investigation of all offers, so that he can become a real economic unit in his new home land."[52] Nor should gentleman farmers expect to be completely self-sufficient. Clements advised that during picking season for berries and vegetables, hired help would be needed. Above all, Clements encouraged potential suburban farmers to approach their migration, land purchase, and farming not as a recreational pastime but as a business. In this way, he attempted to reel in the fantastic promotions of boosters who promised gargantuan crop yields — and thus independence — with little labor or investment.

Agricultural colonies offered one way for smaller farmers to achieve a degree of self-sufficiency and competitiveness because they enabled members to pool their financial and social resources through the tough early years of agricultural production. Indeed, agricultural colonies sprouted up throughout Southern California in the first few decades of the twentieth century as migrants tested new crops and farming strategies. The agricultural colonies were intended to eliminate the social hierarchies that were everywhere apparent in the practice of gentleman farming and corporate agribusiness. By making it possible for landowners to achieve prosperity without hired help, the colonies also excluded social undesirables — namely, immigrant and working-class laborers — from the suburban farming districts. As Garcia writes in his study of the agricultural colony at Ontario, in Riverside County, "By basing the colony on the equal distribution of land among financially independent, white property owners, poor whites and African Americans would not find a place in the community."[53] The biggest and best-known colonies in Southern California are those at Anaheim and San Bernardino. However, the San Fernando Valley hosted several agricultural colonies from 1913 through the 1930s that attracted a great deal of public interest, and some achieved success for a short while. Still, the San Fernando Valley's colonies ultimately failed on account of the same forces that complicated the practice of individualized gentleman farming more generally. Two of these colonies — the Little Landers Colony in Tujunga (established in 1913) and the Weeks Poultry Colony in Owensmouth, now Winnetka (established in 1922) — illuminate how and why agricultural colonies took shape in the Valley, as well as a greater sense of the realities of those who lived there — and illustrate the larger contradictions of gentleman farming as a means of creating a white settler society.

William Elsworth Smythe founded the Little Landers Colony at Tujunga, in the northeast San Fernando Valley, in 1913. Smythe, the son of a wealthy shoe manufacturer, was born in 1861 in Worcester, Massachusetts. A national irrigation advocate with a background in journalism, he gave speeches across the United States, in which he promoted the "back to the land" movement and the virtues of the small family farm. Smythe contributed regularly to the nation's largest popular magazines, including *Atlantic Monthly* and *Harpers*, and was the twentieth-century West correspondent for Charles Fletcher Lummis's *Land of Sunshine* magazine. Smythe was a firm believer that small farms bred both a strong sense of community and active democratic participation. He lectured widely that an American family could fully support itself on an acre of well-irrigated earth, with a goat for milk and some chickens and pigeons for eggs and meat. The key, he argued, was to work in cooperation with other families. Smythe also advocated passionately for government-sponsored irrigation projects as the crucial and necessary first step in ensuring the success of family farms, especially by enabling them to compete with corporate agribusiness. He devoted much of his career to lobbying on behalf of irrigation, creating the *Irrigation Journal* in 1891 and the National Irrigation Congress in 1893. State intervention on behalf of farmers through massive irrigation did not, apparently, confound the promise of self-sufficiency promised by Jeffersonian visions of yeoman farming. As Matthew Bokovoy explains, "According to Smythe, irrigation and profitable agricultural production were primary ingredients for inventing a new rural social order that allowed collective community life compliant with individualism."[54] Until his death in 1922, Smythe remained an advocate of "country living" in close proximity to the city—a construct he promoted far and wide from his apartment on Fifth Avenue in New York City.[55]

Smythe organized his first Little Landers Colony in 1908 at San Ysidro, in San Diego County. That venture attracted three hundred families at its height and boasted a cooperative store and marketing to sell the colony's products. Smythe then teamed up with Los Angeles–based subdivider Marshall Hartranft to organize a second Little Landers Colony in Los Angeles County. They chose a spot at Tujunga, in the rocky foothills of the northeast San Fernando Valley. Hartranft and Smythe promoted the community as "La Ciuadad [*sic*] de los Terrenitos" in a series of advertisements in the *Los Angeles Tribune* in April 1913. For one dollar, they offered daily auto tours from their office at Ninth and Figueroa streets in downtown Los Angeles, where Smythe also gave lectures each afternoon on the virtues of going "back to the land." The colony's mission, penned by Smythe, was marked on a plaque at Bolton Hall, the colony's administrative and social center. Titled "The Hope of the Little Lands," it reads:

> That individual independence shall be achieved by millions of men and women, walking in the sunshine without fear of want. That in response to the loving labor of their hands, the earth shall answer their prayer: "Give us this day our daily bread." That they and their children shall be proprietors rather than tenants, working not for others but for themselves. That theirs shall be the life of the open — the open sky and the open heart — fragrant with the breath of flowers, more fragrant with the spirit of fellowship which makes the good of one the concern of all, and raises the individual by raising the mass.[56]

The Little Landers colony embraced key dimensions of the ideal of gentleman farming — emphasis on self-sufficiency and individualism, the cultivation of republican virtue through communion with the land, and the selective incorporation of urban culture — but with a decidedly cooperative spirit intended to bolster farmers' success in the face of California's corporate agribusiness oligarchy.

Like most gentleman-farming communities in Southern California, the Little Landers colony at Tujunga intended to combine the best of rural life with urban investment, employment, and cultural opportunities. In the colony's advertisements and lectures, the leaders extolled the values of "a little land and a living, surely, with all the joys of life in Los Angeles, too," and described how they intended to achieve their vision:

First, find the VERY BEST PLACE.

Second, dedicate all land profits, above original cost, selling and administrative expense, to an Improvement Fund, to be used in "Raising the Individual by Raising the Mass."

Third, bring the light of world-wide experience and knowledge upon each individual problem in correspondence, personal interview, and lecture room.

Fourth, select expert gardeners and poultrymen to demonstrate the best methods and results on their own places, and teach beginners "how to do it."

Fifth, organize co-operative store to effect every possible saving in purchase of supplies, with co-operative marketing direct to consumer to get best-possible results for producers.

Sixth, create highest conditions of social and intellectual life, that our people may have books, music, art, and entertainment of every kind, and keep step with the march of events throughout the world ("A full, rich life.")[57]

For Smythe, therefore, the city served a triple function for the Little Landers. First, the city would supply intelligent and refined settlers. An advertisement for the colony in the *Los Angeles Tribune* in 1913 claimed that the colony would be made up of "the finest citizens of Los Angeles," elaborating that "a scheme of life that [gave] them the cream of city and country combined — that is both urban and suburban — appeal[ed] to the forehanded folk of high ideals."[58] Second, the city enabled the Little Landers to access cultural events when desired. Smythe wrote, "To deny the people who are to till the land in the future the advantages of the city — social, educational, and commercial — is to deprive them of the best advantages of our civilization."[59] Centered around Bolton Hall, the colony itself had minimal services including a post office, electric lights, and a phone system. Yet it was close to the urban centers at Glendale and San Fernando, reached by daily transit service, and downtown Los Angeles was widely promoted as a resource that Little Landers might take advantage of but for which they would have little responsibility. Third, the city provided a market for the colony's agricultural products. The 1913 ad in the *Times* featured a map of Los Angeles County with an arrow pointing to Los Angeles and the notation, "Los Angeles, 500,000: the Market for Little Landers products." Alongside the map was a promotional essay, subtitled "Of the City, But Not in the City."[60]

This was a racially and economically exclusive vision that, upon closer inspection, was at least somewhat dependent on the labor of nonwhites and immigrants in Los Angeles's urban core. Smythe's colonies in both San Ysidro and Tujunga relied on racially restrictive covenants that excluded Asians, Mexicans, and blacks from access to land ownership. Additionally, Chinese, Japanese, and other Asian Americans were restricted from property ownership by California's Alien Land Laws passed in 1913 and 1920. However, Japanese immigrant grocers served the produce needs of the community through semiweekly truck service well into the 1930s. Mabel Tsumori Abe, a Japanese American resident of Sunland-Tujunga whose family was interned during World War II, remembers that her father operated three produce stands in the San Fernando Valley during this period, one of them on Commerce Avenue in Tujunga, from which he served the Little Landers; and he purchased his goods from both Japanese and Italian tenant farmers in nearby Hansen Heights and Sunland.[61] Her father's experience suggests that the Little Landers and their descendants were not, in fact, able to provide for all their own agricultural needs, and that immigrant labor and commerce, especially among Japanese American tenant farmers, were important for the colony's sustenance.

The Little Landers struggled to make their vision work in an area plagued by remoteness, lack of infrastructure, and rocky soil. Access to water was a particular problem because Tujunga was not yet part of the city of Los Angeles. Although the Los Angeles Aqueduct had been completed in 1913, bringing a massive, secured water source to the San Fernando Valley from the Owens Valley, unannexed territories such as the Little Landers colony could not access it. In 1917, the Little Landers at Tujunga sued the Western Empire Suburban Farms Association for failing to provide adequate water to the colony, despite the fact that colonists had paid more than eight thousand dollars to the association for construction of a complete and independent irrigation system.[62] Tujunga finally annexed to the city of Los Angeles in 1923, and only then because of desperation for access to a cheap, guaranteed water supply. By then, however, the colony had more or less dissipated. At its height, the Little Landers colony had consisted of five hundred families, but by 1925 there was only one Little Landers family in Tujunga.

Similar fortunes befell residents of the Weeks Poultry Colony, in the west San Fernando Valley. The Weeks colony was envisioned and established by renowned poultry specialist Charles Weeks. Born on an Indiana farm in 1873, he was an active promoter of the "back to the land" movement. His magazine, *Intensive Little Farm*, and his many books sold the idea of "one acre and independence" to a national audience. Weeks believed that "getting back to nature" was the solution to modern ills. He argued that urban life cultivated greed, depression, and violence, and if not for the pursuit of money, which urban life facilitated, few would tolerate it. He describes the day he arrived at his newly constructed home in Owensmouth (now Winnetka) in the west San Fernando Valley, after living temporarily in an urban apartment building in Los Angeles: "Pending the time of building our home we had been stopping at a flat in the city where the foul air, noise and grind, and lack of freedom had left an effect that no words can describe. Perhaps this short imprisonment in a city flat was ordained that we might be the more able to appreciate the wonderful peace and freedom of our own little garden home and thus have the power to contrast more clearly the great difference between the artificial, restless, unsatisfying city life with that of the quiet, peaceful, healthful life of the country."[63] As a solution to the ills of modern urbanism, Weeks advocated ownership of rural garden homes, but with all the amenities of modern civilization. In his semiautobiographical collection of essays, *One Acre and Independence, or, My One-Acre Farm*, Weeks promoted the idea that gentleman farming was the centerpiece of a new way of life that could salvage the white race and the American nation:

> The new art of living of which Lincoln foretold is coming — it has come! Men are beginning to see that the life of the land must be revolutionized — that instead of big holdings in lonely places they must have small places near to the heart of civilization; that instead of using the land wastefully they must use the land intensively and scientifically, first, to supply a luxurious table for their families; then, to furnish an ample income for other needs.
>
> That isn't all!
>
> There must be Social Satisfaction, with neighbors close at hand; with organized life of every sort; with opportunities for intellectual and spiritual growth.
>
> I am living this life today, have been doing so for years, and I can show YOU and hundreds of others HOW TO DO IT.
>
> I ask you to give a fair hearing to the claims of that new and bigger Life of the Land which I honestly believe is the biggest thing in the world today, and the thing that means most to the future welfare and happiness of the race.[64]

Weeks emphasized that his vision of the rural garden home included all the amenities of modern civilization and urban culture — as in his exclamation, "We cook with electricity!" — but without the dense and noxious land-use patterns of the city and the racial, class, sexual, and political mixing that urban areas enabled. He argued that science, art, literature, and poetry were just as accessible within the country setting as within the city, especially if one was surrounded by sophisticated and refined neighbors. In his view, through the rational, scientific planning of rural communities within close proximity to the city, the Anglo-Saxon race and the American political experiment could be restored and rejuvenated.

Weeks was famed for his methods of raising poultry and especially for his ideas about the social and economic organization of poultry colonies. He innovated the idea of keeping laying hens in coops, rather than allowing them to roam free, and promoted the idea that careful husbandry on an acre of land with 2,500 hens would lead to a life of prosperity. In 1916, Weeks consulted with William Elsworth Smythe, whose Little Landers colonies at San Ysidro and Tujunga were then doing quite well. Drawing on Smythe's advice, Weeks established the Weeks Poultry Colony (also known as Runnymead) on land near his ranch in Palo Alto, California. By 1922, the Weeks colony in Runnymead had attracted four hundred families with a peak population of one thousand residents.[65]

Shortly thereafter, the Los Angeles Chamber of Commerce invited Weeks to launch a similar community in the San Fernando Valley at Owensmouth (see figure 3). As with gentleman farming generally, the Weeks colony was imbued with a larger symbolic significance beyond its potential economic production. Weeks explained his vision to the *Los Angeles Times* in 1923: "I have a far greater work than the mere subdivision of land. I am building an ideal community made up of successful people who wish to live this natural healthy life close to Nature in a neighborhood of uniform, symmetrical, harmonious garden homes."[66] Weeks promoted the idea far and wide that Southern California was the ideal location for the achievement of his vision. He idealized the region for its high-quality soil, nearly perfect weather, and seemingly endless supply of cheap water, writing, "No place in all the world is better adapted to the intensive Little Farm than Southern California where rich, sediment soil, plenty of irrigating water, finest all the year growing climate, and unlimited home markets, furnish all the essentials for success. . . . The Charles Weeks Poultry Colony in the beautiful San Fernando Valley near Owensmouth is a revelation to the wonderful possibilities on an intensive LITTLE FARM."[67]

Weeks's strategy paid off exactly as the Los Angeles Chamber of Commerce had hoped. By 1922, the Weeks colony at Winnetka had become as popular as the Runnymead community, attracting forty-one families; by the end of the decade the colony included over five hundred families. Within just a few years of its founding, the colony had its own egg-grading and packing plant, a warehouse for mixing feeds, a cold-storage plant, and a "large hatchery for the incubation of the best eggs from the highest quality hens in the colony."[68] It also owned a series of egg trucks used to deliver eggs to hotels, restaurants, and retailers throughout Los Angeles County. In its first eight months, the cooperative organization had done more than two hundred thousand dollars worth of business and had plans to develop other cooperative industries, including an oil station and auto service station.[69] In 1923, the colony opened a retail outlet at Third and Fairfax streets at what would become the Los Angeles Farmer's Market. Although the colony experienced some setbacks in the early years, including the complete destruction of the egg packing plant by fire in May 1925, on the whole it was very prosperous.[70]

Despite its promotions of independent life, however, the Weeks colony, like the Tujunga colony and all of the San Fernando Valley's rural communities, depended heavily on the city's willingness and ability to provide adequate infrastructure, especially for irrigation. The ironies of this dependency are clear in a 1924 report from the *Los Angeles Times*, which assessed the likelihood of

FIGURE 3 Office building of the Weeks Poultry Colony on Sherman Way in Owensmouth (now Winnetka), July 1927. Courtesy of the Los Angeles Public Library.

the colony's success: "Great activity among the class of little landers who are ambitious to possess an acre and independence is certain to follow closely upon the heels of the decision of the electors of the Lankershim annexation district to provide water mains and laterals for 6000 acres, included within the boundaries of the zone."[71] The county engineer estimated the costs of the infrastructure outlay to be in excess of $750,000, one of many subsidies paid by taxpayers from throughout Los Angeles in support of the semirural lifestyle from which many were excluded by racially restrictive land-use policies. Still, rural dwellers' dependence on the urban state did not seem to confound the idea of "independence" at all; on the contrary, urban services and infrastructural development were promoted as essential to the Little Landers movement and a right to which suburban farmers were entitled.

Like the San Fernando Valley's other semirural communities, Weeks's vision of rural life rested on explicit racial, economic, and cultural biases. As a point of pride, Weeks explained that "in the building of the Charles Weeks community only high class people [were] selected, those living as nearly as possible on the same plane, all belonging to the Caucasian race."[72] He insisted that the people living in his colonies were intellectual, cultured, contented, happy, healthy, social, and moral people who could be counted on to maintain the highest levels of civilization and refined culture within a country setting. Weeks also made it very clear that his vision involved a lot size large enough to provide for a family's needs, usually one acre, but small enough that the owner would not have to hire outside help. In an undated recollection, he explained, "We don't want a fram [*sic*] so big that a man has to hire help. A man must earn his bread by the sweat of his brow." Weeks believed that a man who worked his own land to meet his family's basic needs experienced a psychological, cultural, and economic transformation that was essential to leaving behind the sick realities of urban life. In his monograph, *One Acre and Independence*, Weeks explained, "My purpose is not so much to farm my acre as to cultivate myself, and by using only so much land as I can farm intensely without hiring help, I get the full pleasure of doing the thing myself, in my own way, without rush or irritation."[73]

Celeste Dameron was one of those who joined the Weeks colony in Winnetka in the 1920s. A native of Texas, she moved to the San Fernando Valley to join her husband, a widower who had purchased a one-acre lot in the Weeks colony in 1925. She explained, "What Charlie Weeks wanted to do was to prove that they could make a living on one acre . . . if you had about 2500 or 3000 chickens. . . . On top of his chicken units, he had bees and then they had a cow and they had a garden. And Mrs. Weeks had a big bird aviary. She sold birds too, so . . . you could make a living on an acre if you had that many chickens. Of course, we always had a big garden and we had a cow and we had hogs."[74] However, Celeste's husband also worked for Weeks on his model one-acre property, which was used to promote the concept of the colony and sell new lots. When asked about the apparent contradictions between Weeks's claim to take great joy in performing all the work himself while actually relying heavily on employees, Celeste replied, "Well, he [Charles Weeks] was in real estate too, you know. He has . . . I think there were 500 acres like that that he had started, and he was kept busy doing things like that. And then if you've got 3000 chickens to keep the units clean, feed, and run 'em, it's a lot of work."[75] Pushed on this contradiction, Celeste noted that some of the families in the Weeks colony were able to be economically self-sufficient from the products of their land, but only if they had three thousand chickens or more; in these cases, she noted, they would almost certainly require hired labor.

The Weeks colony was active and productive until the early years of the Great Depression, when it proved unsustainable. According to Dameron, the colony failed because Charles Weeks had lent money to families who were not able to repay their loans. But the failures of the Little Landers and Weeks colonies within a relatively short period — just over a decade, in both cases — suggests that the ideal of "gentleman farming" was rather more difficult to achieve than boosters acknowledged, even in instances where members pooled their resources and toughed out the hard times. Land monopolies, the control of cooperatives by agribusiness, and uneven access to water constrained the possibilities for individual gentleman farmers, as well as colonies, to truly achieve "one acre and independence." The Great Depression only made these difficulties more apparent and more painful.

Gentleman farmers typically expressed their thwarted economic and cultural aspirations in racial terms, most often by blaming low-wage immigrant laborers and by scapegoating Japanese agricultural competitors. Indeed, in both the central districts of Los Angeles and the suburban farming districts of the San Gabriel and San Fernando valleys, Asian American and Mexican American laborers were the engine of economic growth. It was their labor, not merely or even primarily that of the gentleman farmers, that turned Los Angeles County's arid land into its famed agricultural empire. Thus, fantasies of cultivating white supremacy in the San Fernando Valley's gentleman-farming districts, and indeed throughout Los Angeles, rested on an impossible contradiction: wholesale dependency on nonwhite and immigrant labor, employed by gentleman farmers but also, and more importantly, corporate agribusiness. According to Mark Wild, "The very success of Los Angeles depended precisely on an image, cultivated by a phalanx of dedicated boosters, of the city as a refuge from the industrial and racial 'pollution' of modern industrializing urban America. . . . [Yet] building such a city required a labor force far too extensive and varied to be staffed solely by Anglos."[76] Though rarely acknowledged in dominant historical narratives, gentleman farming would not have been possible without the dispossession of indigenous and Mexican land; the use of Asian, Mexican, and native laborers to construct the physical infrastructure of the Valley; the hiring of nonwhite and immigrant laborers as agricultural workers to make suburban farms productive; and the exclusion of nonwhites from access to land ownership and from competing on equal terms with white farmers through union busting and policing.[77]

The construction of the Valley's physical infrastructure in the late nineteenth century had been carried out largely by Chinese labor. Chinese workers constructed the railroads that connected Los Angeles to San Francisco and the Western interior, which allowed gentleman farmers and agribusiness elites to ship their goods to a national market. Chinese also labored on many of the other infrastructural developments in the San Fernando Valley, including tunnels, roads, and sidewalks, as well as the Valley's expanding commercial districts, for example, by building hotels, stores, and schools. Yet Chinese immigrants were despised in California, resented for their position within local labor markets as cheap labor, and feared as "alien, despotic, and backward" based on perceptions of their cultural unassimilability. According to Claire Jean Kim, although Chinese immigrant labor was critical to the growth of the state, "it raised the specter of a second form of slavery that would create yet another permanent class of degraded non-Whites" and threatened the "ideal of a pristine White polity."[78] Such fears and anxieties, coupled with demands for cheap labor, propelled the passage of numerous anti-Chinese laws and ordinances, culminating finally in the Chinese Exclusion Act of 1882.[79]

After the exclusion of most Chinese workers, Japanese laborers quickly took their place, fulfilling demands for cheap immigrant labor in the San Fernando Valley. Japanese agricultural workers and tenant farmers were the key racial threat to the goal of regenerating whiteness through gentleman farming. As early as 1905, twenty-three Japanese immigrants were counted in the San Fernando Valley, but over three hundred were concentrated in the nearby Tropico (Glendale) district.[80] However, the Japanese, many of whom came from agricultural backgrounds, were more likely than the Chinese to establish themselves as independent farmers, and they soon dominated the berry, flower, and vegetable industries. They did so through a tremendous degree of intra-ethnic solidarity. Japanese workers often organized themselves into associations led by a "boss" who negotiated terms with an employer. These gangs refused to com-

pete with one another or break strikes. This approach allowed them to monopo-
lize certain sectors of the agricultural labor market within a very short time.[81]
Their practices stand in marked contrast to the determined individualism of
gentleman farmers embracing the ideal of "one acre and independence."

Throughout Southern California, this degree of Japanese land ownership,
success in farming, and interethnic cooperation was typically interpreted as a
direct economic and cultural threat to the promise of idyllic suburban farming promoted to midwestern white migrants. As Starr has argued, the Japanese
"had shown themselves eminently capable of the Jeffersonian ideal of the self-
subsistent family farm, to such a degree, in fact, that they were exciting the envy
of many whites." As we have seen, there were many reasons why Anglo gentleman
farmers struggled to achieve self-sufficiency on their land; however, Japanese
farmers bore the brunt of suburban farmers' political frustrations because, as
Starr explains, they "cut to the core of a dream that was just not working: small
family farms for white California."[82] To contain the perceived threat of Japanese
farmers while deflecting attention from the structural issues of land monopoly
that it exposed, agribusiness interests and suburban farmers supported the passage, first, of land ownership restrictions in the form of California's Alien Land
Laws in 1913 and 1920 and then immigration restrictions in the 1920s.

Furthermore, civic leaders' instructional manuals were framed explicitly as
efforts to make Anglo farmers more competitive with the Japanese. They instructed white American growers how to best bundle crops such as spinach,
which had become dominated by Japanese growers, in part because of their
superior bundling techniques. A 1924 article in the *Times* highlighted the pre-
dicament faced by "leading vegetable growers" in the San Fernando Valley, one
of whom "told of losing a considerable sum on a crop of spinach simply because
he did not know how to bundle it properly for market. . . . He hired Mexican
laborers to bunch the stuff, but said that the result was a sorry mess which
would not sell in competition with the same product brought in by Japanese
gardeners."[83] Ross Gast, of the Agricultural Bureau of the Los Angeles Chamber
of Commerce, lamented that "white men [had] given up the production of
bunched vegetables for the Los Angeles markets" on account of Japanese success, but urged them to reconsider the bunched crops because while it was true
that "they require a great deal of hard labor . . . the returns, on an average, are
better than those received for any other vegetable-growing activity."[84] He provided careful instructions on washing and packing the bunched vegetables for
quick and profitable sale. He also advised farmers to use raffia, as the Japanese
were doing, instead of twine, and featured a step-by-step photograph tutorial of
the best tying technique, called the "Jap tie."

The local media mobilized concerns about the Japanese threat to white supremacy to argue that local consumers should support white gentleman farmers, against the odds, in a sort of agricultural race war. As a 1925 editorial in the *Los Angeles Times* opined,

> In the first place, the new growers [gentleman farmers] are Americans, and in their activities they are building up the start of a new vegetable and berry-producing industry for Americans. While it is true that alien growers of these crops have not relinquished their hold on the Southland industry, the time will probably come when they will, and it is then that the American growers, who are now really serving their apprenticeship in the berry and vegetable-growing "game," will step into the activity, experienced and ready to handle larger acreages. . . . They are demonstrating that they can raise vegetables and berries with profit on comparatively high-priced land just as the orientals have been doing.[85]

City leaders invested in middle-class, Anglo suburban farmers to overcome the agricultural superiority of Japanese farmers. As this writer exclaimed, "We need these little growers and are glad for their prosperity. More power to them!" Boosters argued that if "American" farmers — a term that included European ethnics who could, on account of their whiteness, become citizens — were successful, all whites would benefit because they would not be forced to buy their produce from "alien" farmers. The future of the entire white Angeleno population was thus riding on the success of white gentleman farmers. The writer of this article continued, "Usually, consumers in the smaller towns, persons who are more in touch with agricultural conditions, and who believe that California agriculture should be dominated by Americans, are anxious to buy from local American growers. For this reason, the production of berries and vegetables in the outlying towns of the Southland is being stimulated."[86] The urban state thus coordinated a host of supportive mechanisms that, when combined with exclusionary land-use and immigration policies, were intended to elevate the production and livelihoods of white gentleman farmers by restricting competition from nonwhites and immigrants. These included immigration restrictions, alien land laws, and restrictive covenants as well as other mechanisms of residential segregation. In turn, the Japanese competitive threat was largely erased during World War II by the ultimate exclusionary land-use policy — the almost complete removal of ethnic Japanese — when the Valley's Japanese population was detained at Santa Anita Race Track and a California Conservation Corps camp in La Tuna Canyon, in the east Valley, prior to being interned at permanent camps throughout the American West. At that time, there were 3,177 people of Japanese descent in the Valley, half of whom were citizens; enough San Fernando Valley

Japanese Americans were held at Manzanar to form their own baseball team, the San Fernando Aces.[87]

As Asian ethnic groups were boxed out, Mexican laborers increasingly came to dominate the San Fernando Valley's low-wage, hired labor force. During the Mexican Revolution, hundreds of thousands of Mexican immigrants migrated to Los Angeles and other cities near the border. Large-scale agricultural interests as well as gentleman farmers preferred Mexican laborers to Asian ethnic groups because they were thought to show little inclination toward organizing or unionization, at least in the early years. By the 1920s, Mexican workers dominated the picking and packing industries. Mexican pickers for all crops, along with their families, numbered between seventy-five thousand and one hundred thousand people throughout Southern California. They were particularly concentrated in the citrus industry, where, by 1940, approximately ten thousand Mexican citrus pickers statewide constituted nearly 100 percent of the picking labor force; this number, in turn, represented approximately one-quarter of all agricultural workers in California.[88] By the early 1930s, approximately fifteen hundred Mexicans lived in the San Fernando Valley alone.

In the San Fernando Valley's gentleman-farming districts, the ladder of ownership, management, and labor became distinctly racialized. At each stage on the ladder, land-use policy intersected with other social policies (such as immigration and naturalization laws) to craft white supremacy. Harry Chandler's farm in Glendale was typical. Chandler, the owner of the *Los Angeles Times*, leased his land to Frank Kuwahara, who in turn supervised general manager Shinobu Mashika; both were Japanese immigrants who had resided in the San Fernando Valley and had worked at that particular farm for years. The labor force cutting flowers at Chandler's farm was almost exclusively Mexican, as was true on a statewide level by the 1920s. Such patterns — white absentee ownership, leases to Japanese immigrant tenant farmers, and Mexican manual labor — defined the racial and labor realities of gentleman farming in the San Fernando Valley, though these hierarchies were hammered out through several decades of experimentation, violence, and restriction.[89]

Residential segregation, enforced through legal exclusion and social custom, was central to the maintenance of these hierarchies, particularly for the Mexican workers, who needed to be housed close to the farms but not actually within white residential areas. The result was a patchwork quilt of sorts that suggests not residential integration, but carefully monitored separation to achieve the twin goals of economic productivity and white exclusion. By 1940, at least two hundred distinctive Mexican communities of varying sizes could be found throughout Central and Southern California, some as large as the urban barrios of Los Angeles and San Diego, but also including the many small, semirural *colonias* scattered throughout the region's agricultural districts. Mexican communities in the San Fernando Valley and elsewhere took a variety of forms: full-fledged company towns, company-owned tracts within residential communities, and private residential communities characterized by intra-ethnic leasing and labor. Yet historical studies by Gonzalez, Garcia, and Jose Alamillo have demonstrated that the Mexican villages in Southern California were almost universally marked by concentrated poverty, segregation, substandard housing, and civic neglect.[90] Renowned scholar of the region Carey McWilliams describes the Mexican "Jim-towns," as they were termed in the local parlance, as "lack[ing] governmental services; the streets [were] dusty unpaved lanes, the plumbing [was] primitive, and the water supply [was] usually obtained from outdoor hydrants."[91] For example, in 1918, the American Sugar Beet Company, representing growers in Van Nuys, Marian, and Zelzah, announced plans to construct 150 model cottages for its beet workers because the quality of existing housing was of such poor quality that the company, facing a public relations nightmare, could no longer ignore it. Even the *Times*, which typically only noticed the Valley's Mexican residents to report their alleged crimes, admitted, "The bulk of the rough labor in the beet fields is done by Mexicans and the conditions under which the families of these men have lived can no longer be tolerated. . . . It has been a common sight to see a whole family living in a ragged tent, without floor or any covering for the earth. The water used for domestic purposes was often obtained from the irrigation ditch. Hundreds of these people have lived in the past under conditions which a farmer would not permit for cattle." Though the American Sugar Beet Company, likely under pressure from government agencies (especially the California Commission on Immigration and Housing), had agreed to pay for and construct 150 cottages, given the many thousands of seasonal and migratory workers in the beet fields, their impact was likely minimal.[92]

Although small worker camps could be found scattered throughout the San Fernando Valley, adjacent to gentleman farms and the fields of corporate agribusiness, the commercial and recreational activities of the Valley's nonwhite populations were concentrated in the northeastern Valley neighborhoods of San Fernando and Pacoima. These neighborhoods together constituted the Valley's unofficial minority district. Despite their poverty, Pacoima and San Fernando together constituted a unique, multiethnic place, bringing together Japanese, Mexican, and a small population of black residents amid the San Fernando Valley's intentionally structured white supremacy. Service and recreational organizations flourished there. For example, the San Fernando Valley Japanese

Language Institute opened in Pacoima in 1924 to serve the Nisei (American-born) children of immigrant vegetable farmers and flower growers. Sports teams were common, too; for example, the San Fernando Nippons competed with other Japanese baseball teams throughout Southern California, and the Rotary Club of San Fernando sponsored a women's baseball team in the 1940s.[93] Pacoima also became one of the few places in the San Fernando Valley where African Americans and ethnic Mexicans could own property because restrictive covenants were not enforced there.[94] Yet clues to the poverty of Pacoima and San Fernando are rampant. Despite the fact that Mexican workers labored in some of the most productive fields in the world, hunger seems to have been a persistent problem. In 1917, the *Times* reported that three Mexicans had looted the Southern Pacific Railroad cars at the San Fernando station, stealing sugar, flour, shoes, lard, and khaki, which they sold to members of the Mexican colony at San Fernando. In fact, the men took orders from the community for groceries and clothing, complete with delivery plans for Tuesday and Wednesday of the following week, indicating their intentions to loot from other railroad cars on a regular basis.[95]

Signs of poverty and desperation can also be glimpsed in otherwise celebratory promotions of "Spanish" history performed by the Valley's Mexican inhabitants. Beginning in 1927, acting on the inspiration of Anglo-American teachers and school administrators, Mexican American schoolchildren in San Fernando began to stage an annual "Spanish fiesta" as a fund-raiser for their neighborhood's poor residents. Promoters of the festival lauded its authenticity as a romantic representation of the Spanish past. Yet the Mexican participants had to be instructed in the "proper" ways to look and act their parts. Under the direction of an all-white teaching staff, nine hundred Mexican children were "trained for their parts in the festival and presentation of the legendary romance of the beautiful Senorita Dolores and the bandit Vasquez." Additionally, the school's Anglo-American sewing teacher instructed Mexican mothers in how to make appropriately colorful costumes. During the festival's fourth year, the festival was moved to the nearby Mission San Fernando to increase seating capacity and claims to authenticity. In the *Los Angeles Times'* description, the festival's move to the mission allowed "brown-clad padres once more [to] instruct their dusky neophytes as in the days when the mission was a haven for weary travelers."[96] For the first four years, the proceeds from the annual fiesta were apportioned to the area's impoverished Mexican families for food and clothing. However, in the fifth year of the fiesta, a group of community leaders took over the production from the San Fernando Elementary School, although the principal, Mrs. Della Tarbell, stayed on as president of the new planning committee. The new group of leaders, including playwright Charles Pressley, director of the Santa Barbara Fiesta, reconceived the event as a tourist attraction. Proceeds were now directed away from the community's poor Mexican families and instead dedicated to continuation of the event as an annual enterprise.[97]

The San Fernando Valley's ethnic Mexican laborers were especially hard hit by the Depression. University of Southern California graduate student Laura Lucile Lyon noted in her 1933 master's thesis that Valley schools attempted to respond to Mexican students' poverty by arranging for female students to take cooking and home economics classes just before lunch, so that they might have something to eat. Other schools arranged for their Mexican American students to work in the school cafeteria.[98] By 1938, when the Los Angeles County Relief Association conducted a study of 188 Mexican families in the San Fernando Valley, it found that the average family consisted of six people dependent on public agencies 84 percent of the time, with only brief breaks from public assistance when they were able to find short-term agricultural employment.[99] A 1939 report by the United States Senate reported that Mexican citrus workers were poorly paid, usually earning just 30 to 35 cents per hour, or $423 per year on average, and were unable to achieve what would be considered a fair standard of living for the average American family.[100]

Such conditions sowed the seeds of a nascent labor movement, although organized worker resistance in the San Fernando Valley appears to have been less frequent and less effective than in California's other agricultural districts. The Industrial Workers of the World (iww) began to organize agricultural and industrial workers in the San Gabriel Valley and, to a lesser extent, the San Fernando Valley beginning in the spring of 1919. They demanded a four-dollar daily wage and an eight-hour workday for packinghouse workers. The mainstream press denounced the iww's organizing in the San Fernando Valley as the work of Bolshevist outsiders attempting to inflame and harass otherwise content, loyal workers. The *Los Angeles Times* adopted a paternalistic posture, arguing that iww "agitators," after being ignored by "regular" (presumably white) workers, "began to try to intimidate the Japanese and the Mexicans by efforts to frighten them away from the orchards."[101] Dismissing the possibility that Japanese and Mexican workers might have determined their own genuine motivations for going on strike, the *Times* argued that "Bolshevik propaganda caused a temporary strike in the packing-house," which was quickly suppressed.[102]

Labor organizing throughout California became more frequent and more effective, but also more violently repressed, during the Great Depression, as poverty and unemployment, already bad, became worse.[103] In August 1938, the Congress of Industrial Organizations (cio) attempted to organize Mexican packers at both the San Fernando Lemon Association and the San Fernando Heights Lemon Association's packinghouses. Plant officials at the Heights packinghouse closed the plant and sent its 150 workers home "pending a quieting of an agitated situation."[104] Growers refused to deal with the CIO organizers, however, and instead demanded a "responsible committee" of employees to handle the settlement. While CIO leadership had demanded an hourly wage of twenty-five cents, plus seven cents per box, the final settlement included a rate of twenty cents per hour plus nine cents per box. Those workers who had participated in the strike, about one hundred in total, were effectively denied the right to return to their jobs under the agreement, which stated that they might be hired back as work was available but that none of the scabs who had been hired to replace them would be let go.[105]

A year later, the CIO's United Cannery, Agricultural, Packinghouse, and Allied Workers took on Runnymede Poultry Farms, with whom its workers had a contract. When the contract expired in October 1939, the union demanded that the farm operate as a closed shop, hiring only union workers, and that members be accorded vested rights in their jobs according to seniority. Runnymede leadership refused, and 190 of the Farm's 230 employees walked out on strike, leaving half a million chickens "in a precarious situation."[106] Farm leadership quickly filled all of the positions with non-CIO members and stationed a police guard to protect the poultry and equipment from strikers' potential violence. Eventually, more than 500 farm workers joined the struggle, which included mass meetings in front of the poultry farms and pickets of grocery stores that sold Runnymede products. They were supported by a citizens committee of Reseda, made up of local merchants, and the Longshoremen's Union.[107] Still, after more than two months of pickets and protests, most of the strikers began to lose hope and applied for relief from local agencies. J. Hartley Taylor, owner of Runnymede Farms, adamantly refused to rehire the striking workers, even though Reseda's merchant citizens community tried to negotiate a settlement between the two factions.[108]

Labor organizing exposed the clear centrality of nonwhite and immigrant labor to the San Fernando Valley's entire agricultural enterprise, including not only corporate agribusiness but also gentleman farming. Gentleman farming was intended to restore the purported essential greatness and inherent virtue of the white race. But what if, as Garcia queries, "the labor that produces this virtue is performed by someone other than the farmer?"[109] And if so, why couldn't immigrant and nonwhite workers achieve the independence, self-sufficiency, and upward mobility guaranteed to Anglo-American gentleman farmers? These

contradictions and interdependencies were central to the socio-spatial construction of whiteness in the San Fernando Valley during this period, and the
foundation upon which future articulations of whiteness in the Valley would
be developed.

The history of urban planning for gentleman farming demonstrates the
complex ways in which whiteness was created and given meaning in the San
Fernando Valley from the early 1900s through the late 1930s. At the most basic
level, urban planning, media representations, popular culture, and practices of
social distinction embedded in gentleman farming made rural landscapes crucial to the cultural meanings and values attached to whiteness and middle-class
status in the San Fernando Valley. Gentleman farming consolidated whiteness
among diverse European ethnic groups who "became white" through their participation in gentleman farming, an activity designed to create the "white spot"
of America. And as whiteness is formed through exclusion, so too was rurality
crafted through the exclusion of people and landscapes suggestive of urbanity.[110] The semirural landscapes created in the San Fernando Valley's gentleman-
farming districts and the people who occupied them were valued in reference
to the people and land uses associated with urban landscapes, even though
gentleman farmers depended completely on the support of the urban state and
the labor of excluded populations to realize their visions. These processes were
grounded in the physical geography of the San Fernando Valley's gentleman-
farming districts, which together created a complex, interconnected geography of rural, suburban, and urban places that were deeply interdependent yet
unequal.

Through gentleman farming, whiteness also came to be defined through a
dependence on the state and nonwhite labor to generate economic and geographic privilege. Rural white gentleman farmers could profit economically
from the city and engage selectively in urban life without having to be responsible to the city or its denizens. This view was explicitly embraced in virtually
all the promotional materials espousing "life on the land" with all the benefits
of urban life. This is fundamentally a relationship of privilege and inequality.
Moreover, civic elites, boosters, and government agencies invested heavily in
the success of Anglo-American gentleman farmers in the San Fernando Valley's
semirural districts. Semirural whites came to believe that such state support was
not only crucial to their success but also their entitlement and their due as white
Americans. Although individual gentleman farmers might not experience the
ideals of rural urbanism in quite the way that boosters promoted, their expecta-
tion was that they *should* be able to do so. Gentleman farming thus cultivated

a collective sense of entitlement among whites to live a rural lifestyle with the urban state's subsidy and protection, with few strings attached, that remains meaningful to this day.

The promotional materials that the urban state and corporate community builders distributed were a major force attracting gentleman farmers to the San Fernando Valley, and they shaped migrants' expectations about the possibilities of enjoying rural life with all the advantages of the city. Frequently, such promotional materials included narratives of the San Fernando Valley's history. They are the earliest historical materials created about the San Fernando Valley, and they indelibly shaped the collective historical consciousness of those who settled in the Valley's suburban gentleman-farming districts and then, after World War II, its suburban subdivisions. In the next chapter, I examine how the writing of local history explained and justified American conquest in the San Fernando Valley through reference to the layering of landscape.

CHAPTER TWO

Narrating Conquest
in Local History

Storytelling, through the writing of local history, was a crucial dimension of the Anglo-American conquest of Southern California and the U.S. West. From the 1920s through the 1960s, real-estate developers and community builders, often working in tandem with middle-class social groups, commissioned local professionals to write histories of the San Fernando Valley, which they then distributed to potential home buyers and tourists. The local history texts produced about the Valley during this period are the first written histories of the Valley, but like all histories, they reflect the ideologies and political-economic interests of their creators. Overwhelmingly, these history texts highlight the disjuncture between indigenous waste and barbarity, the romantic but prematurely terminated Spanish mission period, the inefficient and wasteful use of land under Mexican rule, and the verdant, extraordinarily productive use of land by Anglo-Americans. In these interpretations, the Anglo-American presence in the San Fernando Valley returned the land to its natural state, rescuing it from its dormancy under Mexican rule during which the Valley's land had cried out for its properly rational, efficient, and industrious owners. For both authors and readers, such descriptions of layered landscapes were closely linked to eugenicist ideas and ideologies of manifest destiny; indeed, the Valley's semirural landscapes were the spatial embodiment, the geographic evidence, of an inherent process of cultural and scientific evolution that ultimately and rightfully culminated in Anglo-American rule. Produced, widely distributed, and institutionalized in conquered territories, these new historical narratives helped to establish the legitimacy of American economic, political, and social systems.

In the San Fernando Valley, these history texts provided the ideological glue binding white settlers — both an older generation of gentleman farmers and a newer generation of postwar suburbanites — together around a shared sense of the righteousness of American conquest, their occupation of formerly indigenous and Mexican land, and the racial and national hierarchies of an emerging social order. The first such historical narratives were produced during the era of

TABLE 1 Population growth of the San Fernando Valley, 1930–1960

YEAR	POPULATION OF SAN FERNANDO VALLEY	PERCENTAGE INCREASE
1930	78,467	—
1940	155,443	198
1950	402,538	259
1960	840,500	209

Adapted from Preston, *Changing Landscape*.

gentleman farming in the 1920s and 1930s, but they served their most important function after 1941, amid the Valley's massive wartime and postwar suburbanization. California's wartime boom in defense production lured hundreds of thousands of workers with the promise of blue-collar, unionized, and well-paid manufacturing and assembly jobs. Black and white workers from the U.S. South and Midwest, as well as Mexican workers contracted through the Bracero program, migrated to Southern California en masse beginning in the early 1940s. Los Angeles County's population quadrupled between 1920 and 1950, growing from less than one million to over four million people in the span of just three decades. The region's population growth had a particularly pronounced impact on the San Fernando Valley, which — because of its existing low-density and rural landscapes, embedded in the practice of gentleman farming — proved an ideal location for housing and industry.[1] Aided by advances in mass housing construction technologies and federal financing, developers and community builders carved countless tracts of affordable single-family homes out of the Valley's gentleman farms and agricultural colonies. Between 1930 and 1960, the Valley's population more than doubled each decade, accounting for more than half of the demographic growth of the city as a whole.[2] The vast majority of the Valley's housing stock was constructed in just two decades: 24 percent was built between 1940 and 1950, and another whopping 62.6 percent of units were built between 1950 and 1960 (see table 1).[3]

Because of the preferences of federal agencies, federally insured lenders, and real-estate developers, the suburban migrants who bought property and made lives in the San Fernando Valley during this period shared several characteristics: they were newly middle class, of working-class origins; well educated, professional, and white. The federal housing loans that made possible the Valley's rapid subdivision were based on the racial classifications and biases of the Home Owners Loan Corporation's redlining system and practice of systematically denying financing in integrated neighborhoods or to people of color.[4] As in other suburbanizing communities in Los Angeles and throughout American metropolitan areas, developers and community builders followed the well-established practice of instituting racially restrictive covenants in new suburban developments, protected by property owners associations, to safeguard property values by maintaining racial exclusivity. These practices ensured that homes in the San Fernando Valley's rapidly expanding suburban subdivisions would qualify for federal funds, but only by embracing racial exclusion. As a result, according to Mike Davis, only 3.3 percent of federally subsidized suburban housing units constructed in Southern California's 1950s housing boom were made available to nonwhites.[5] These real-estate and lending practices coexisted with, compounded, and extended the earlier social hierarchies and patterns of segregation associated with gentleman farming. By 1960, while non-Hispanic whites represented 82 percent of the population of Southern California, they constituted well over 90 percent of the San Fernando Valley's population, and the vast majority of the Valley's African Americans, Latinos, and Asian Americans lived in San Fernando and Pacoima.[6] The Valley's new white homeowners were economically privileged as well by postwar programs such as Veterans Administration grants for college and small business loans. Designed to boost American workers into the middle class, these federal programs were administered almost exclusively to whites.[7] In 1964, the San Fernando Valley Area Welfare Planning Council reported that more men in the Valley (50 percent) had white-collar jobs than in the county as a whole (43.3 percent), and that they were particularly concentrated in aerospace engineering and film production.[8] These were the people who received and read the historical materials produced by their mortgage lenders, title and escrow companies, and chambers of commerce. For the hundreds of thousands of white, middle-class migrants who came to the San Fernando Valley during this period, local histories gave them a sense of the past to grab onto and a vision of the future in which to invest. Furthermore, a shared sense of rural history alleviated tensions among an older generation of gentleman farmers and a newer generation of suburban property owners, who had different ideas about how land in the Valley should be used, by providing a common ground rooted in local history.

The production of historical narratives about the San Fernando Valley was overwhelmingly an urban phenomenon, coordinated by corporate capital concentrated in central Los Angeles. Los Angeles–based banks, title companies, and chambers of commerce wrote and distributed histories of the San Fernando Valley and its distinctive communities as a way to lure potential home buyers and tourists. Frequently, they worked in collaboration with elite social groups such as the Daughters of the American Revolution (DAR) and the First Families club. The first published history of the San Fernando Valley, titled *A Daughter of the Snows*, is representative. It was produced by the Publicity Department of the Security Trust and Savings Bank's Lankershim Branch in 1923. The bank's explanation of its publication of *A Daughter of the Snows* is instructive: "As further evidence of its desire to serve the Community and the Valley it offers this little booklet, 'A Daughter of the Snows,' for free distribution to all who desire it. We trust that you will feel it worthy of mailing to your friends and relatives in the East as a good advertisement of Lankershim and the whole Valley. That is its purpose."[9] Thus, the first written histories of the San Fernando Valley produced by American interests were deliberately and explicitly aimed at promoting the area's growth and generating profit. The images, historical interpretations, and descriptions of landscape that these authors included reflect choices made with these aims in mind. Like other historical texts, *A Daughter of the Snows* is very well illustrated with photographs donated from the *Los Angeles Times* and *Los Angeles Examiner* as well as the publicity bureaus of the Pacific Electric Railway, the California Walnut Growers Association, the Los Angeles Water Department, Universal Pictures Corporation, and the Union Oil Company. Each of these urban interests had an explicit stake in the writing of local history to justify expanding investments and settlement.

Most booster historians were quite explicit that their histories were meant to be promotional; indeed, they made no claims to objectivity. Instead, they relied on and cultivated the idea that the landscape itself was a neutral record of history. Title companies and community builders used the perceived neutrality of land-use records to position themselves as authoritative experts on the legal history of San Fernando Valley land. In doing so, they affirmed the legitimacy of their ownership and their rights to profit from land speculation and real-estate subdivision.

In this respect, no one person was better regarded or more influential than W. W. Robinson, a historian and writer who, for nearly thirty years, produced historical booklets about Southern California on behalf of Title Insurance and Trust. His biography attests to the familial background, personal influences, and ideological perspectives that dominated the writing of history in the San Fernando Valley, and Southern California more generally, from the 1920s through the 1960s. Robinson was born and raised in Trinidad, Colorado, a mining town entering the global economy, in the 1890s. His father was a banker who moved throughout the U.S. West following oil booms; his mother was a member of the DAR. His brother-in-law was well connected with the citrus industry in Riverside, California, where Robinson's father bought five acres in the late 1890s. Like other "gentleman farmers" who combined urban employment with a rural lifestyle, Robinson's father rose through the ranks at the Riverside branch of Bank of America, eventually becoming vice president, and was simultaneously active in Riverside's citrus associations, including a twenty-year stint as president of the Victoria Avenue Citrus Association. Through his family relations, Robinson was thus directly connected to Southern California's signature industries, which were a hallmark of life in suburban Los Angeles before World War II.[10]

After two years at the University of Southern California, Robinson eventually graduated with a degree in English from UC Berkeley. He held a series of intermittent jobs writing short stories and working for title companies before joining Title Insurance and Trust Company after World War I. To maintain his twin loves of writing and researching local history amid the practical work of managing land-use records, Robinson pitched the idea of creating a series of short historical booklets drawn from the company's title records to his superiors, who enthusiastically agreed. Robinson's first booklet, a narrative of Long Beach land-use history produced for a real-estate agents' meeting there in 1931, was so successful that Title Insurance commissioned him to produce a whole series of historical booklets for individual communities in Los Angeles. The choice of subjects was generally determined by company policy — that is, communities where Title Insurance and Trust already did heavy business or wanted to increase business.[11] Throughout the 1930s, Robinson produced booklets on Southern California's fastest-growing cities, including Santa Monica, Whittier, Pasadena, Glendale, Monrovia, Pomona, San Pedro, Wilmington, Inglewood, Beverly Hills, and Culver City. The booklets were distributed free of charge and were especially popular with chambers of commerce and civic groups but also with students and teachers, who used them in their classrooms to learn about local history.[12] In 1939, Robinson combined many of his shorter essays into a larger monograph, titled *Ranchos Become Cities*, which was widely applauded as "a valuable contribution to the great field of Californiana."[13] Beginning in the late 1930s, Title Insurance also sponsored a weekly half-hour radio program called *Romance of the Ranchos*, based on Robinson's books, which featured dramatic events of early California history; Robinson served as the program's historical consultant until its termination in 1948.

Robinson's texts soon became the definitive versions of Southern California history, lauded for their neutrality and authority based on Robinson's purportedly objective interpretations of land-use records. Reviewers celebrated the neutrality and authenticity of his 1939 edited collection, noting that "for the first time a book of absolutely authentic information [had] been written on the early Mexican land grants and Ranchos of any part of California."[14] Richard G. Lillard reviewed Robinson's 1948 volume, *Land in California*, for the *Pacific Spectator*. Lillard wrote, "The author is not an idealist, not a philosopher; he is a top official in the largest title insurance company in the world. Taking a fresh thematic approach to state history and writing from firsthand study of source materials, he is careful and impersonal."[15] Years later, Robert Kirsch wrote in the *Los Angeles Times*, "W. W. Robinson is the best regional historian Southern California has yet produced. His work has become an important part of Westerniana. He works with meticulous, responsible scholarship. He writes with vigor and style and has a deep understanding of this area and its peoples."[16] The perceived objectivity of land-use records — representing the neutrality of the law, more generally — thus became a key instrument through which Robinson, Title Insurance, and other boosters represented the authority of their histories.[17]

Robinson's historical booklet on the San Fernando Valley was first published in 1938 and reissued with updates in 1951 and 1961. In the 1961 edition, titled *The Story of San Fernando Valley*, Robinson explained,

> In telling this story of a fabulous valley, and its more than twenty communities, the written records of the past have been drawn upon — early deeds, the files of court battles, old maps, histories. This is material out of which a title insurance company builds the "title plant" by which it functions and which enables it to furnish the ownership story of every Valley lot and parcel through Spanish, Mexican, and American periods. In addition, the descendants of pioneer settlers and subdividers, along with men and women playing active parts today in the Valley's development, have made contributions to the story.[18]

In their dependence on the biographical contributions of the San Fernando Valley's "pioneers" and real-estate developers, Robinson's histories reflect a highly particular racial, economic, and nationalist perspective that necessarily privileges the winners and the conquerors. Yet by appealing to the neutrality of land-use records in creating an "ownership story," Robinson's narrative positioned Title Insurance and Trust Company as the legitimate and depoliticized keeper of the Valley's land records. He deployed this sense of legitimacy toward the building of a credible and authoritative history that has remained largely unquestioned.

Because of his respected authority as a historian, Robinson was invited to join the region's most important historical societies and civic groups, including the Historical Society of Southern California and the Southwest Museum's board of trustees. He was a founding member of the Los Angeles

Corral of Westerners and served as the associate editor on the Publications Committee, for which he solicited and edited historical essays. These groups sponsored regular social programs, such as the First Families Luncheons, that celebrated Anglo-American conquest of the San Fernando Valley in the name of pioneer history. Robinson also wrote the book review column of *Westways Magazine*, published by the Automobile Club of Southern California. After his retirement in 1956, Robinson continued to write historical booklets on contract with Title Insurance and Trust. In total, he researched and wrote nearly 150 publications for the company, with distribution of more than one million copies.[19]

Thus, Robinson's impact on the entire Southern California region, including the San Fernando Valley, cannot be overestimated. His narratives of the Valley's history have indelibly shaped the collective historical memory, political culture, and social movements of later generations. But Robinson was merely an especially important figure around which cultural production narrating the Anglo-American conquest of the San Fernando Valley and Southern California pivoted. A diverse range of growth-machine interests including banks, title companies, insurance agencies, and real-estate developers collaborated with elite social groups and "pioneer families" to write local histories that were, at once, promotional materials and historical texts accepted as truth. Their work inscribed a romantic and celebratory history of Anglo-American rule into the San Fernando Valley's physical landscape and its cultural representations through the construction of two simultaneous narratives: one about the past, and another about the future; both were fundamentally grounded in ideas about land.

A crucial first step in explaining and justifying the American conquest of the San Fernando Valley was the reinterpretation of its indigenous, Spanish, and Mexican pasts. Without exception, the San Fernando Valley's indigenous populations are represented as romantic but primitive savages, as barbaric people devoid of civilization. Accordingly, the Spanish mission period — beginning with the establishment of the Mission San Diego in 1769, but with particular focus on the era since the establishment of the Mission San Fernando Rey de España, in the San Fernando Valley, in 1797 — is represented as a welcome and necessary introduction of European civilization. American narrators lauded the Spanish for establishing sedentary agriculture, fixed settlements, and a disciplined work life. By contrast, Mexican independence and secularization of the missions are treated as disastrous and chaotic, an abandonment of the cultural gains achieved by the Spanish and upon which California Indians purportedly depended for their economic and spiritual salvation. These narratives of the past effectively legitimate American conquest of the U.S. Southwest in the war with Mexico.

Booster histories overwhelmingly represent the San Fernando Valley's indigenous communities prior to the era of the Spanish missions as uncivilized and dirty but peaceful people, if only because of their inherent laziness. According to the San Fernando Valley chapter of the DAR, which published one of the first written histories of the Valley in 1924,

> The Indians found in this Valley were of a far lower type than those gathered in the Missions of South and Central America. They were rather peaceful, as may be judged from the fact that two soldiers were considered a sufficient number of protectors. But they were lazy and dirty, the men did as little work as possible, and no ambition for a higher life troubled them at all. They could understand hunger, however, and of this their lazy and improvident ways gave them some experience. The men fished and hunted, eating anything and everything that would support life, even snakes, except rattlers, often without cooking. . . . The padres gave them plenty of grain and beef; this kindness and plenty were what won them.[20]

Such denunciations of indigenous vulgarity and barbarity are frequent in early histories of the San Fernando Valley. The DAR also chastised indigenous methods of housing and land use, again congratulating the Spanish missionaries for introducing more "civilized" methods. "For shelter they used houses of brush, which they made no attempt whatever to keep clean, throwing all sorts of refuse on the dirt floors. When the fleas, mice, lizards, and ants became so numerous as to be really annoying, they set fire to the house and built another in a couple of hours. After a time the Indians learned to build adobe houses but at the founding of the Missions the housing problem offered no difficulties whatever."[21] Analyses such as these wholly disregarded well-developed and time-tested indigenous methods for handling disease (such as fire), instead interpreting them as evidence of Indians' barbarity. On this basis, Spanish approaches to housing and land use were interpreted and narrated as major advances.

Though indigenous peoples were purportedly instructed in proper methods of land use and social hierarchy at the missions, it appears that they rarely, if ever, satisfied Spanish and European standards. According to the DAR, "The Mission lands were regarded as held in trust for the Indians, to be delivered to them as soon as they had learned to live and work like white men. But as the Missions grew and prospered, the Indians became no more independent. They fell easily into the habit of being directed and a white man who understood them could make their labor very profitable and at the same time give them better care, including security from cold and hunger, than they had ever enjoyed."[22]

This description suggests that California Indians in the San Fernando Valley were inherently incapable of taking care of themselves; such portraits justified the enduring treatment of mission neophytes as wards who benefited greatly from the care of the Spanish missionaries.

From the DAR's perspective, the period of Spanish colonization and indigenous captivity in the missions was marked by progress, contentment, and prosperity for all involved. "Doubtless there were cases of abuse," the DAR acknowledged, "but the growth and prosperity of the Missions proves the success of the system and the contentment of the majority of the Indians."[23] Consider the DAR's description of the daily schedule at the Mission San Fernando:

> Life at the Mission does not seem to have been very strenuous, save for the Fathers, on whom the whole responsibility rested. At sunrise a bell called to Mass to whom all came washed and combed. This was in itself a wonderful lesson in the first principles of decent living and good citizenship. Then forty-five minutes were allowed for an abundant breakfast of mush, made of corn instead of acorns, which seemed a feast to the Indians. Then, the men went to the fields, the women to their grinding of grain, their sewing and other light work, the children to school. . . . At noon two hours were allowed for dinner which consisted of stew with whatever vegetables they had. Then work again until five when all stopped and went to the church for prayers. Another ample meal and the Indians could use the evening for their own games or for rest. . . . Thus in many ways helping with work was really play.[24]

This characterization of mission life emphasizes abundance, recreation, and ease. Alternative historical sources suggest quite the opposite. Decades later, a retired schoolteacher who was part Chumash and who identified herself as Bright Star offered an alternative perspective on the mission experience. She wrote, "My people didn't know anything about the god of the Spaniards or understand why they should be converted to receive better living conditions and enough food. Some of us remained in the 'heathen category' and worked at the Mission because they needed food for their family."[25] Death, disease, and small acts of rebellion were common at the Mission San Fernando and throughout California's mission system. Characterizations of the mission experience as a peaceful, abundant existence full of "play" elide the captivity, forced labor, and compulsory conversion that characterized life at the missions for indigenous peoples, and ignore the only other option available to most coastal indigenous communities: the hunger and poverty wrought by the theft of their lands.[26] As such, these representations fall fully in line with the Spanish fantasy past's romanticization of the mission experience and conform broadly with the ideological functions of transition narratives more generally in explaining and justifying conquest.

American writers were particularly appreciative of the Spanish contributions to the Southern California landscape. Booster histories credit the Spanish missions with introducing sedentary agriculture to the San Fernando Valley, thus inculcating basic elements of civilization that would allow American land-use practices, such as gentleman farming, to flourish under a still-higher order of civilization. According to the historical narrative commissioned by Los Angeles's centennial committee in 1881, "The orange orchard of San Gabriel, and a fragment of the vineyard and olive grove of San Fernando, still remain, as living witnesses of the energy and untiring industry of those zealous Friars who, coming into a country full to overflowing with ignorant, savage barbarians, changed them into patient, docile laborers, and in less than fifty years filled the country with fruitfulness."[27] An undated brochure promoting the restoration and preservation of the Mission San Fernando, likely printed in the 1950s, painted a similarly celebratory portrait. Note the utter passivity of the landscape and the lack of any active agents in making the San Fernando Valley's agricultural land productive.

> Before the end of 1797, 56 Indians joined the Mission community and a church and quarters for the two priests and their escolta of six soldiers were built of adobe. Grain fields, orchards and vineyards were planted. The huge valley rancho was explored and sources of lime and clay were found. Additional water was located and an elaborate irrigation system was built. Workshops, granaries, stables, and houses for the rapidly increasing number of Indian converts were constructed. . . . The mission was soon producing abundant harvests of wheat, corn, beans and olives. Metalwork, feathergoods, cloth, soap and candles began pouring from its workshops. Its herds of cattle, sheep and hogs grew.[28]

These descriptions suggest that the land is somehow naturally productive and fecund, wholly obfuscating the importance of captive, forced indigenous labor working for the productivity of the Spanish Crown and the Catholic Church.

But why would Anglo-Americans celebrate the period of Spanish rule this way, when Spain had been an imperial rival in the not-so-distant past? Historian James Rawls has argued that glowing representations of Spanish mission life were unprecedented before the 1880s, and that earlier representations of the Spanish mission system were almost universally critical. In the late 1700s and early 1800s, French and English travelers described and criticized the missions as hostile and inhumane institutions, similar to slave plantations in the

U.S. South. Rawls advises that such comparisons be taken with a grain of salt, since French and English writers (as representatives of imperial competitors) were more concerned with repudiating Spain's worthiness to rule the region than with illuminating the plight of American Indians. "Their hostile views of the missions served to show the failure, the inadequacies, the backwardness of Spanish efforts in California."[29] Despite their potential exaggerations, however, such outside observers offer an important and unique perspective on daily life in the missions and rates of abuse. Until the 1880s, Americans shared this perspective; more commonly, they ignored the Spanish past altogether. In the decades immediately following American conquest of the Southwest, the Spanish missions were allowed to fall into ruins because new American migrants passively sought to repudiate any evidence of prior occupation by the United States' imperial rival. It was only in the 1880s that the missions and the Spanish colonial era began to be romanticized in Los Angeles; in the San Fernando Valley, efforts at mission preservation and celebratory narratives of the Spanish past did not emerge in earnest until the 1920s. By that time, Spain had been vanquished as an imperial competitor in the Spanish-American War. Enough chronological and symbolic distance now intervened, enough vestiges of Spanish influence had been rooted out, and the Anglo-American population was sufficiently established and growing rapidly in Southern California. Under these conditions, the decaying Spanish missions became an attractive regional symbol to lure more settlers and capital and to craft a regional identity based on reinterpretations of its history.

While life in Southern California under the authority of the Spanish missions is painted in romantic terms, Mexican rule is represented as the downfall of civilization. This portrait was crucial to the self-identification of Anglo-Americans. Deverell has argued that "narratives about Mexico and Mexicans are integral to the city's cultural and economic rise during the period between the Mexican American War and World War II."[30] Local histories produced during this period overwhelmingly degrade the era of Mexican rule, both because of the temporal proximity of Mexican rule and the persistence of living, breathing Mexican people who retained limited control of political and economic institutions and made their presence well known through, for example, the labor strikes described in the previous chapter. History writers focused on two dimensions of Mexican rule that they perceived to be wholly catastrophic: secularization and the "abandonment" of mission Indians, and the purported waste of Spanish advances in agriculture and land use. According to the Security Trust and Savings Bank's *Daughter of the Snows*, "With Mexican independence came secularization, and with that, the greedy plundering and pillaging of Mission wealth, the scattering of neophytes and the final decay and ruin of the whole Franciscan system."[31] The DAR agreed, arguing that

> because, to California, Spain had turned her softer side, the entire population was filled with loyal patriotism to the mother country. Mexico, on the other hand, was to prove but a brutal, indifferent step-mother. Her rule in California for more than twenty years was marked by conflict, unrest and deterioration. . . . Under this new regime, the Mission Indians gradually drifted to the mountains and desert. Lifted from the lowest depths of ignorance, they had been much benefited by Christianity. They had been taught obedience but not self-reliance; industry but not initiative. . . . They were children suddenly orphaned.[32]

Building on their interpretations that the Spanish missions had saved California Indians from their inherent cultural barbarity, American historical writers thus lambasted Mexico's secularization of the missions for inhumanely abandoning mission neophytes.

Historical writers were also incensed by the abandonment of Spanish gains in sedentary agriculture. According to a promotional brochure for the restoration of the Mission San Fernando, upon transition to Mexican rule, "the Indians soon began leaving and production fell as crops rotted in the fields and unattended livestock were stolen or perished. . . . In the years following secularization, the mission buildings suffered from abuse and neglect."[33] Or in the words of Palmer Connor, writing a history of the San Fernando Valley in 1941 on behalf of the Title Insurance and Trust Company, "Spain encouraged and protected the Missions of California and granted to them great tracts of land — Mexico plundered and destroyed the Missions and seized their lands. Among these Mission lands seized by the Mexican government was the prize of them all, the Mission de San Fernando. For years chaos reigned at the Mission. The government drove off many of the Indians, others left and the herds of cattle became legitimate prey alike for 'Gentlemen of Mexico' and Mexican bandits not claiming the distinction."[34] Within these treatments, the expansion of the Mexican land-grant system after Mexican independence in 1821 allowed bandits and social undesirables to "prey upon" the gains achieved by the Spanish through the missions. Conveniently ignored is the fact that French, British, and American settlers were primary beneficiaries of the Mexican land-grant system, which in fact awarded grants to a range of applicants from diverse national origins.[35]

For American observers, Mexican approaches to land distribution and use were evidence of Mexicans' bureaucratic and technological inferiority and cultural backwardness. Many Anglo-Americans believed these "inherent" cultural characteristics inevitably led to waste, greed, and decadence. According to the DAR, "The Mexican government gave land to any one who had money to stock it, from one to eleven square leagues, with the most careless of surveys. When forty or fifty thousand acres of land could be had for nothing, with not even taxes to be paid, when cheap labor was abundant and styles changed not more than once in fifty years, it is no wonder the cattle ranchers grew rich."[36] Portraits of the purported decadence of Mexicans are frequent. Historical writers consistently point to their silver saddles, velvet clothing, and abundant fiestas as evidence of their purportedly wasteful approach to the land and its riches.

Such representations of Mexican land-use systems and the cultural characteristics they were thought to represent justified the widespread dispossession of Mexican landowners after American conquest. Howard Kegley painted a story of the passing of the rancho days in a lengthy 1922 feature article for the *Los Angeles Times*. His descriptions of the Mexican rancheros supported the popular conviction that their territorial dispossession was both inevitable and justified on account of Mexican cultural characteristics, especially their attitudes toward land. "In those olden, golden days, farming was a matter of herding cattle and sheep. The Dons rode magnificent horses, kept countless casks of sparkling wine in their cellars, wore gorgeous garments, and took life easy. But the old order changed. With most of the old land barons it was a case of come easy, go easy. Their land cost them but little, if anything, and it slipped through their fingers, in many cases, over a game of cards. Many of those who once counted their acres by hundreds of thousands died in abject poverty."[37] Similarly, for Palmer Connor, writing for Title Insurance in 1941, the fate of Pio Pico, the last governor of Mexico, was an excellent example of how romantic but ultimately misguided and premodern concepts of honor prevented Mexicans from using their land appropriately and thus justified their land loss. He wrote, "While Pio Pico, who once counted his acres in hundreds of thousands, spent his last days in abject poverty—his ranchos, his city property, his hotel and his home all sold for a mortgage—nothing was left—nothing but his medals of honor and his memories of the past."[38] In historical narratives of the San Fernando Valley, the mass transfer of land from Mexicans to Americans is represented as the rightful reclaiming of an era of frugality, productivity, and sacrifice associated with the Spanish past from the greed, decadence, and wastefulness of Mexican rule. References to Mexican hospitality and honor compliment these portraits by suggesting that Mexican land was freely available for the taking, as in this characterization: "Picture a map of California cut up into Ranchos like a crazy quilt, dotted with twenty-one Missions and a handful of Pueblos. Picture a people browned by the sun, happy, prosperous, and carefree.

Picture a white-walled hacienda on each of the ranchos, every one open with a never failing hospitality and welcome. That was California when the Americans took it."[39] Such narrations rested on cultural characterizations of Mexicans as romantic, gracious, and charismatic people who were not particularly good at business and therefore gave up their land willingly, even gratefully, in recognition of the bureaucratic and technological superiority of American landowners. These narratives represent the widespread dispossession of Mexican landowners in the second half of the nineteenth century as the outcome of a natural and righteous cultural progression, from the quaint and ineffective land-use systems that Mexicans used to the modern, progressive land bureaucracies, dependent on modern instruments such as the survey and the grid, employed by the Americans.[40]

In many cases, however, historical storytellers were careful to distinguish between local Mexican Americans and the character of Mexicans generally. While portraits of Mexicans elsewhere highlight their corruption, inefficiency, greed, and decadence, Mexicans in the San Fernando Valley are represented as warm, generous, hospitable, and — most importantly — voluntarily yielding to the essential rightness of American control. As a result, a kind of San Fernando Valley exceptionalism emerges in historical treatments of the Mexican period. Boosters and social elites insisted that, even as other places may have been fraught with the interethnic tensions wrought by the American conquest, the San Fernando Valley was not one of them. The general strategy was to argue that all the missions had been productive and peaceful enterprises; when that was not possible, they insisted that, even if abuse or corruption had occurred at other missions, that had not been the case at the Mission San Fernando. According to the DAR, "In happy contrast to this [the purported disasters wrought by secularization] is the story of our own San Fernando Mission. The first majordomo appointed was the kind and efficient Don Antonio del Valle, who took charge of the estate in 1834. In 1837, Don Pedro Lopez, a capable, intelligent man, was appointed majordomo or superintendent of the Mission."[41] Similarly, writing for Title Insurance and Trust Company in 1961, W. W. Robinson wrote that "while Mexico was revolting against Spain, life in the San Fernando Valley continued its pastoral way, centering about the Mission and prospering. . . . In that year the broad San Fernando plain supported 7000 cattle, 6500 sheep, 40 goats, 50 pigs, 1320 horses, and 80 mules, all Mission-owned."[42] The DAR concurred, writing, "[The] San Fernando Valley, happily free from strife, occupies little space in our histories."[43] The DAR history repudiated the critiques lodged by other contemporary sources, notably Helen Hunt Jackson's novel *Ramona*, by arguing that the mission at San Fernando was an exception to the tensions between Spanish-speaking Californios and English-speaking Americans: "The bitter resentment shown in 'Ramona' toward the Americans found no duplicate on our Valley; not only harmony prevailed, but many warm personal relationships were formed between the Spanish and English speaking people, friendships which still endure to the succeeding generations, notwithstanding the larger social opportunities of the present time."[44] The Mission San Fernando's purported exceptionalism, including relatively complimentary narratives of the "Mexican character," was a discursive strategy used to explain contemporary social relations in the Valley, which were still very much in flux.

Stories of "friendship" between Mexicans and Americans abound in promotional materials, and the land transfers, dispossessions, and subdivisions that besieged the San Fernando Valley's Mexican ranchos in the decades following American conquest are usually described as a series of peaceable agreements made among friends. For example, W. W. Robinson describes how the San Fernando Farm Homestead Association "brought a *friendly action* for partition against the heirs of Eugelio de Celis [the owner of the Ex-Mission de San Fernando Rancho] and got full title to the southerly portion of the Valley."[45] Californios and Mexican Americans in the San Fernando Valley were represented as loyal and romantic dons who cared more about their dignity and honor than about practical matters of land ownership, business efficiency, and productivity. Americans could appreciate such characteristics of their "friends" but ultimately referenced these qualities to justify the dispossession of their land. In his history of the Valley, Palmer Conner explained that "it was a period of rare honor. Don Abel Stearns refused to take advantage of a technicality in his favor and lost a 29,000 acre rancho. Juan Matias Sanchez to help his friends, William Workman and F. P. F. Temple, signed their mortgage to 'Lucky' Baldwin and lost his own rancho in the San Gabriel Valley, wholly without consideration."[46]

The treatment of Geronimo Lopez, son-in-law of the majordomo at the Mission San Fernando after secularization, and his wife, Catalina Lopez, is similarly instructive. Their residence at Lopez Station was the Valley's first Mexican settlement after the closure of the mission. The Lopez Adobe was a rest stop for travelers and housed the Valley's only general store and the post office for the entire surrounding area. According to the DAR, "Both Mr. and Mrs. Lopez having enjoyed the best educational advantages of their time, the instruction of Don Coronel, were earnest advocates of education" and opened the Valley's first public school in 1860. Geronimo Lopez is described in booster histories as "landlord, postmaster, merchant, rancher, school trustee . . . easily the most progressive of [the Valley's] early pioneers in all the activities that pertain to modern life."[47] Nearly all the Valley's early histories devote much attention to Catalina Lopez, who is described as a gracious hostess with a penchant for gardening, dancing, and entertaining. Together, Geronimo and Catalina Lopez are applauded for bringing civilization and romance to the Valley's early social life. In spite of the Lopezes' alleged importance to the Valley's early American history, however, their lifestyle is represented as part of a bygone era that must necessarily succumb to the march of American progress. The DAR wistfully proclaimed that Geronimo Lopez "saw the changing epochs of the Valley; the sheep ranges turn to golden grain, the grain in turn giving place to orchards and finally bursting with yet greater development, the Valley dotted with cities. In the span of his own life he saw the medieval pass into the modern."[48] Ultimately, those changes would claim his own property in the name of progress, as in the following unromantic summary statement: "The Lopez Adobe was finally removed to make way for the reservoir."[49]

Although they went out of their way to paint glowing portraits of elite Californios and warm friendships between Mexicans and Americans, boosters had no similar concern with California's indigenous populations, whom they assumed to be wholly obliterated. This too is a common element of white settler mythologies, which across contexts assume the always-impending extinction of aboriginal or indigenous peoples. According to *A Daughter of the Snows*, "In the end, all of the Indians died or disappeared until now only old Zetimo is left. When there is work in the harvest Zetimo comes down from the hills for a time, only to return later to his cabin to dream over the days when as a boy he saw General Fremont and his Americans come streaming across the great green sun-swept plain below, on their way from the camp near Newhall to the Mission. That was back in 1847."[50] This narrative suggests that the San Fernando Valley's remaining Indians, having been abandoned by Mexican secularization of the missions, had been patiently waiting for the "return of civilization"; upon American conquest, their wishes have been granted and they can retire, peacefully, to extinction.

Still, contradictions can be found even within booster histories. Although apparently all the Indians except Zetimo had died or disappeared, the DAR described an incident in 1875, long after secularization and squarely within the American period, in which "there was little rain, and the Indians finally in anger took the image of San Fernando down to the ditch in back of the Church and there immersed it. They dragged it up and down the stream, cursed it for not sending rain and, in fact, abused it in every way they could think of. So successful were their efforts that a few days afterward there came a heavy downpour. This was the first instance of anyone making it rain in Southern California."[51] The DAR used the story as evidence of the neophytes' alleged commitments to Christianity, sedentary agriculture, and the missions. The DAR interpreted the event in a lighthearted way that thoroughly disavowed the possibility of legitimate grounds for resistance among the San Fernando Valley's indigenous people. Though there is no way to be certain, it is possible that the 1875 incident constituted an indigenous rebellion against the forced conversion to Christianity or the tremendous repression and exploitation that California Indians faced under American rule.[52] Drought and the coming of rain might have been but a coincidence, or perhaps the former mission Indians told this story to avoid punishment.

Such historical narratives about San Fernando Valley exceptionalism, friendship, the romantic but impracticable virtues of Mexican honor, and presumptions of indigenous extinction all served to justify and legitimate the American conquest. In the hearts and minds of the San Fernando Valley's American boosters and elite social groups, the seeds sown by the Spanish missions cleared the way for American migrants and institutions to take the land to ever-higher states of fertility and productivity. According to these visions, American settlers reclaimed the land from a period of Mexican chaos and charted the way forward for the progress of civilization, led by an industrious, rational, prosperous Anglo-American elite. It was within this context that the gentleman-farming districts and suburban subdivisions could be, and were, promoted as creating the "white spot of America."

If the era of the Spanish missions and Mexican ranchos was interpreted as a romantic but wasteful approach to land and its resources, then gentleman farming and suburbia under Anglo-American rule were represented as channeling the best elements of conquered societies — the romance and hazy peacefulness of rural life under the Spanish missions — into the bustling productivity of American society. A very common trend in the promotional history texts is to portray the Anglo-American country towns and gentleman-farming districts as the inevitable and righteous outcome of waves of progress, which have finally unearthed a glorious landscape and united it with its rightful (Anglo-American) owners. The DAR's historical description is symptomatic of this trend.

San Fernando Valley was once an apparent desert, chosen by the Mission fathers, who were keen-eyed to see below the surface, as a field rich in promise of future harvests whether material or spiritual; later a vast cattle and sheep ranch; then

divided into large ranches of waving grain where hospitable warm-hearted proprietors welcomed the casual stranger; and then, suddenly, a wide green expanse
of orchards and cultivated fields of vegetables and fruit, dotted with thriving little
cities and *predestined* to become the home of thousands living in abundant content on small home acreages.[53]

Similarly, Palmer Connor narrates the purportedly inevitable result of the
Valley's transition from rancho society to American agriculture and gentleman farming: "With progress and development the ranchos gave way to the
towns and farming communities. Many of these towns, now grown to cities,
were named for the ranchos on which they were built."[54] In this narrative, place
names and mildly flattering yet simultaneously disparaging historical references
are consolation prizes for widespread Mexican dispossession, which in turn is
a necessary stage in the march of progress.

Descriptions of layered landscapes were especially common in historical characterizations of Southern California's citrus industry. According to
Douglas Sackman, Southern California's citrus myth suggested that the land
had once been rich and naturally productive, flourishing under the Spanish
missions but destroyed by the lazy and idle Mexicans after independence,
then rightfully reclaimed by white Christian hands but temporarily soiled
by the greedy extravagance of mining and wheat farming. In this narrative, citrus culture coaxed the return of the landscape's natural beauty and
the productivity of the soil and sunny climate, returning the region to its
original promise as an Edenic garden. "In this potent vision," Sackman argues, "California as cornucopia would be the highest and most perfect stage
in the succession, a landscape that would manifest the American dream
itself."[55] Through this duplicitous storytelling, which coupled reinterpretations of the past with projections about the future, rural landscapes in the San
Fernando Valley were portrayed as the exclusive and rightful province of white
Americans.

Often, boosters, planners, and civic elites described the semirural landscape
itself as "white," referencing connotations of purity, cleanliness, sophistication,
and progress. In 1923, the Lankershim Branch of Security Trust and Savings
Bank described how the Los Angeles Suburban Home Company, the syndi-
cate of businessmen who purchased San Fernando Valley land in anticipation of the Los Angeles Aqueduct's completion, had transformed the Valley's
landscape: "Wide streets, great white schools and excellent railway facilities,
enough to accommodate a population of 50,000, were there waiting almost before the people came."[56] And then, within just a few years, the entire Valley had

been transformed into a collection of sophisticated country towns, brilliant in their whiteness:

> Ten new towns, centering around the *great gleaming white school buildings* sprang up like magic. And with the towns came gas and electricity, manufacturing plants, banks, canneries, golf courses, packing houses, over-subscribed Liberty Loan Drives, warehouses, Ebell Clubs, more paved boulevards, American Legion posts, community churches, public libraries, women's clubhouses, picture theaters, chambers of commerce, sanitariums, Easter Sunrise services, Boy Scout troops, University Extension Courses, Kiwanis Clubs, and all other known appurtenances and attachments that make country life attractive without being metropolitan.[57]

Similarly, the San Fernando Valley chapter of the DAR, in its calls for restoration and preservation of the mission, noted the gleaming white qualities of the landscape as an exemplar of its moral virtue:

> San Fernando Valley, in its setting of wondrous beauty, with its background of rugged mountains whose tree-draped canyons tinkle in season with the music of limpid streams, its towns with their pleasant homes, *their clean, white streets*, bordered by graceful fronds of pepper or palm, though now thriving exemplifications of modern progress, is still, in the last analysis, the seat of the gray old Mission, whose crumbling walls ever remind us that material things are transitory, that high ideals survive in spite of time, that motivation and character and self-sacrifice are, after all, of supreme value.[58]

Whiteness, in these vivid descriptions, was used stylistically to mean both material and cultural progress and the advent of modernity, with associated characteristics of efficiency and rationality, situating the San Fernando Valley as an integral place within the "white spot" of America.

Such arguments hinged on presumptions of Americans' bureaucratic, technological, and cultural superiority, especially with regard to land law. The DAR contrasted Mexicans' purportedly wasteful and inefficient ways of using land with American systems by arguing that "as the Americans began to come in, from the North and East, the . . . wasteful extravagance of the early ranchers was replaced by more business-like methods. . . . When this country came into the hands of the United States after the Mexican War, it was found that the land titles were in dire confusion. . . . The Federal Government in 1851 appointed a Claims Commission to straighten out the tangle so that secure title could be given and their work took five years." In fact, the settlement of competing land claims through the U.S. Land Commission took more than thirty years; many cases were not settled until the late 1880s, and a complex range of factors — equally geographical, social, and economic — were involved. However, the cleanliness and simplicity of this narrative suggests that the legal cases were straightforward, easily handled by the rational and efficient American legal system, and thus devoid of conflict. A different passage further iterates the ease of the transition, owing to the bureaucratic superiority of the American government: "The wonderful climate, the scenery, the natural attractiveness of Southern California would probably have remained almost unknown to the world for another hundred years if it had not been for the enterprise of the railroad builders and also the firm and business-like management of our Federal Government as soon as it became the owner of this part of the country."[59] American land policies and systems are thus represented as manifestations of Anglo-American superiority that will pragmatically and efficiently lead the march of civilization forward.

The texts also pointed to technological innovations, especially in agriculture and irrigation, as evidence of the application of Anglo-American cultural superiority to the San Fernando Valley's physical landscapes. As one book claimed, "Meanwhile, the Americans were learning that this new possession of ours was a land full of surprises. Wonderful results were obtained where water could be secured, so that expensive irrigation systems and elaborate agricultural experiments were amply justified."[60] Landscape photography was one such technological innovation. In her study of the use of photography in Southern California booster magazines at the turn of the twentieth century, Jennifer Watts argues that photography provided visual evidence of Southern California's natural fecundity, coaxed to greatness through American technological and bureaucratic superiority. She argues, "The domestic landscape of the homeowner set the Los Angeles of the Anglo tenderfoot definitively apart from the dusty pueblo town of her Mexican predecessors."[61] Boosters promoted the idea of Southern California land as blessed by a climate so perfect that its products would flourish year-round and with minimal effort, and they supported these promotions with ample, often hyperbolic photography. In the 1923 history of the San Fernando Valley, *A Daughter of the Snows*, the Lankershim Branch of the Security Trust and Savings Bank emphasized the sheer size of virtually every aspect of life in the San Fernando Valley: "Back of these towns stand a million laying hens, 100 dairies, the world's largest olive grove, the world's largest chicken hatchery, the world's largest motion picture plant, the world's largest combined fruit, stock, and poultry farm, the world's largest rose and fresia [*sic*] nurseries, state highways, interurban electric service, a transcontinental railroad, water transportation but two hours away, and the largest contiguous market enjoyed by any agricultural district in America." *A Daughter of the Snows* included numerous photos designed to illustrate the largeness of everything about the San

Fernando Valley, such as a photo of "A Good Citizen of Lankershim: Norma Korndyke" whose cow "Cornucopia has produced more milk and butter than any other cow in the world!" A second photo described the decline of the wheat industry and its replacement with gentleman farming by featuring a man in suit, tie, and top hat standing waist-deep in green foliage. Still another photo, captioned "Lankershim's best product" showed several hundred white children standing in a field, grinning at the camera, just a few pages after an almost identical photo of thousands of white laying hens grouped together in a similar field.[62] Together, the magazine's text and accompanying photographs emphasize the fertility of San Fernando Valley land to improve virtually everything that grows there — plants, animals, and humans — with little effort. Simultaneously, it implied that only under rational, efficient land-use systems could such results be realized.

In these narratives, then, a persistent contradiction emerges between the purported "natural" fecundity and prosperity of the Southern California landscape and the requirement for application of Anglo-American knowledge, technology, and regulation to bring that natural landscape to fruition. That is, even as booster publications insisted on the natural qualities of the landscape, they also insinuated that only Anglo settlers, through their prodigious use of rational and scientific knowledge, had been able to coax the landscape to its fullest and richest state of productive glory. As portrayed by the DAR, that potential had been glimpsed in the era of Spanish colonization but buried during Mexican rule:

> As we consider Southern California today, with its many flourishing cities and prosperous country districts, it is hard to realize how little progress had been made in developing this garden spot of our country only a half century ago. . . . The fifty years that have passed since this group of cities was planned have seen marvelous changes. The growth and development of Southern California has been so much greater than in the 105 years of the white man's rule that preceded it, that the chance observer is at first puzzled to explain it. A very slight study of Southern California history explains this and makes the country far more interesting.[63]

A fundamental element of this history, according to the authors, is the fact that there were only six thousand inhabitants of Los Angeles prior to 1874, "most of them Mexican," who regarded technological advances such as the railroad a "wild extravagance."[64]

In the local histories produced during this period, boosters and civic elites go out of their way to deny the crucial role that nonwhite and immigrant labor played in the region's rapidly expanding agricultural industries, often by once again appealing to the "natural" productivity of the land. Some descriptions consist of an entirely passive description of landscape, utterly devoid of human effort and the agency of laborers. At times, their efforts are downright awkward. Note the passivity of landscape and the obfuscation of labor in the following passage, which describes the gentleman-farming districts.

> Surrounded by foothills the hundreds of green acres of varied natural products attest the permanence of her sources of wealth for generations yet unborn. Walnuts raise their green and stately trunks. Olives toss their gray-green waves that give the great orchard north of San Fernando its fitting name, Sylmar, "sea of green." Oranges lavish their golden fruit and fragrant white blossoms at once among the deep, glossy foliage; lemon and grapefruit, pale gold apricot, crimson cheeked peaches; purple, red, and green plums; heavy pendants of grapes, like so many luscious, many-hued drops of jeweled dew, lend their riot of color and fragrance to the scene. . . . Down the Valley a soft, green expanse shows how acres and acres of alfalfa, beans, sugar beets, lettuce, or even the prosaic potato and cabbage, all combine to tell the tale of happy, prosperous labor.[65]

This description is remarkably similar to portraits of life at the Spanish missions. The implication of such narratives is that labor is contented because the landscape itself makes work so easy. Natural fecundity, coupled with legal and technological mastery, makes the land productive, rather than the physical toil of planting, pruning, harvesting, and packing borne overwhelmingly by immigrant and nonwhite labor.[66] As a result, labor is imagined to be content, and the tensions among ethnic and racial groups in the Valley — evidenced by the strikes and widespread poverty explored in the previous chapter — can be summarily dismissed as evidence of either the moral and cultural inferiority of immigrant and nonwhite peoples or the work of outside agitators.

When acknowledged at all, labor relationships in the San Fernando Valley are treated in such a way as to provide further evidence of American progress and the essential righteousness of Anglo-American rule. References to Chinese labor, for example, exhibit a kind of pride in mastery similar to the status accorded to the owner of many slaves and a large plantation in the antebellum U.S. South.[67] Consider the Security Trust and Savings Bank's description of the completion of the tunnel linking the northern and southern branches of the Southern Pacific Railroad in 1876: "Then, too, there were 1500 Chinamen used in the construction of the big tunnel. . . . The 1500 Chinamen were lined up with shovels at 'present arms' during the ceremonies."[68] The bank described the settlement of the Lankershim tract and the city of Burbank in similar terms, noting that subdivider W. H. Andrews "had a force of 120 Chinamen and 200 mules to cut roads through the brush and stubble of the Lankershim Ranch. He used this same force in laying out the new town of Burbank also. Those were historic days!"[69] In describing the subdivision of Pacoima, the DAR narrated that "in laying out the new town, Chinamen were hired with mule teams to grade the streets, etc., and white men did all the carpenter and cement work."[70] While acknowledging the labor of Chinese workers, this description makes a clear distinction between those who did the skilled work — white men — and those who did the menial labor — Chinese immigrants — in order to preserve the mythology of Anglo-American supremacy and the idea that whites had built the city.

In some cases, the arduous labor of constructing the necessary infrastructure for gentleman farming could have deathly consequences, as in the following chilling account, which exposes the cruel labor practices upon which American settlement of the San Fernando Valley depended.

> As the work [in San Fernando] was practically done by Chinese coolie labor, the groceries brought up consisted of rice, fish, and tea. Perhaps the most difficult obstacle encountered were the shifting quicksands which had to be combated. There were often terrific slides, causing great loss of life. . . . Rumors of large numbers of coolies being killed and hurt would be heard, but no one had any definite information. The only person who knew how many died was A. B. Moffitt, then coroner, and he never told. He did this so that the work might go forward without delay, to prevent the coolies striking and leaving the task unfinished.[71]

Injury and death were common in the construction of a vast infrastructure to support the productivity and livability of urban centers throughout the American West. The San Fernando Valley was no exception. Locked out of positions of ownership and suppressed from organizing to improve their lot, the nonwhite and immigrant workers who built the Valley were disproportionately vulnerable to disease, illness, and death. Early accounts of the San Fernando Valley's history either ignored these incidents or represented them as necessary to the march of progress under American rule.

The narratives that growth-machine interests produced from the 1920s through the 1960s are steeped in white supremacist ideology and reflect eugenicist notions of the "natural" evolution of civilization into Anglo-American hands. Through their representations of the past, present, and future, these historical texts situated gentleman farming and, later, postwar suburbanization as the fulfillment of an inevitable march of progress. Although initially used to attract home buyers, local history books were also embedded within the San Fernando Valley's social life in the decades just before and after World War II.

They were distributed to property owners, taught in schools, read on the radio, and used as the basis for social activities. As such, these historical texts instilled in new suburbanites a mythologized version of the history of their new communities and socialized them to embrace their role in extending that history into the future.

Upon their arrival in the San Fernando Valley, new suburbanites also encountered and engaged with another equally important narrative of history: stories about the western frontier, produced in and around the Valley by the film and television industry. In the next chapter, I consider how local western film production shaped the development of the San Fernando Valley's postwar political culture, with particular attention to how mythologies of the western frontier were embedded in — and interacted with — the Valley's semirural landscapes.

CHAPTER THREE

Producing Western Heritage in the Postwar Suburb

In 1998, Tinsley Yarbrough, professor of politics at East Carolina University and western film aficionado, set out to document the production locations of western films throughout California. Financed and edited by Albuquerque-based VideoWest productions, Yarbrough's cinematic tour included landmarks of western filmmaking in the San Fernando Valley and its outskirts, such as the Iverson Ranch in Chatsworth and Corriganville in Simi Valley; Monogram/Melody Ranch, the Andy Jauregui Ranch, and Walker Ranch, all in Placerita Canyon; as well as other sites throughout California's Central Valley and deserts. In painstaking detail, Yarbrough shows his viewers every rock, road, and tree from literally dozens of angles, carefully explaining how directors, producers, and actors used elements of the physical landscape to craft plots and develop characters. He juxtaposes his footage with black-and-white, action-packed clips from various western films and television shows shot in those same locations and from the same angles. In the opening to the first volume of his five-volume videocassette series, Yarbrough remarks, "When I was a boy, I assumed that the movie companies went away thousands of miles to Texas and Colorado to make their films, but when I was older I realized that most of the films that interested me most were made within a 200 mile radius of Hollywood, and often only a 30 to 40 minute drive to the studios of the San Fernando Valley."[1] Yarbrough's documentary series testifies to the persistent fascination with mythological western landscapes among the American public, as well as the starring role that the San Fernando Valley played in western film production.

Indeed, while western film production traversed the U.S. Southwest, nowhere was the western myth-making machine more powerful than in the San Fernando Valley, where production coincided exactly with the Valley's most explosive growth phase during and just after World War II. Film was Los Angeles's third largest industry in the immediate postwar period, second only to defense and oil, and westerns constituted a significant share of the films produced by both the major studios and the Poverty Row studios, such as Republic, that made B westerns. All the major studios owned large parcels of land in the San Fernando Valley and north Los Angeles County that served as adjunct lots for westerns and other genres. Countless western actors and actresses, directors, producers, stunt doubles, stock contractors, and production-ranch owners made their home in the Valley, where they built ranch-style homes with a rural western aesthetic. The Valley's many production ranches, stock contractors, feed and tack stores, and riding schools further supported western cinematic and television production and constituted an important economic subsector that was fully invested in the continued success of the western myth. As a result, for many residents of the San Fernando Valley, western mythmaking was literally woven into the fabric of their everyday lives, shaping their political consciousness and developing suburban identities.

In its many articulations — and the western film genre is but one — the American frontier myth is a narrative of white imperialism and conquest. It is the American version of the white settler mythologies that are common to European, especially British, postcolonial societies. The main function of such transition narratives is to explain and justify social hierarchies as natural, inevitable, and even desirable. "Classic" westerns, which achieved their height of production and popularity from the late 1930s to the mid-1950s, were particularly important in this regard. Classics echo the Turnerian vision of the settlement of the frontier. They are usually set in the late nineteenth century and feature archetypical frontier characters including cowboys, ranchers, saloon keepers, prostitutes, Indians, and military men. Classics tend to be centered on a clear-cut set of binaries between good and evil, right and wrong, and white and Indian or Mexican, which are in turn mapped onto geographical distinctions between West and East coasts and between rural and urban areas. Classics were extraordinarily popular because they interpreted major demographic, economic, and political alignments in such a way as to affirm basic American values. During World War II and the cold war, westerns extended a sense of American exceptionalism that justified the United States' preeminent role in world politics, its interventions in communist and socialist states around the world, and its suppression of domestic rebellions lodged by the growing civil rights movement. Within this context, Stanley Corkin argues that classic westerns inculcated broad loyalties to American foreign policy, celebrated the nation's ability to face down the evils of communism and global instability, and demonized those who questioned the nation's commitments to capitalism.[2]

This ideological labor was particularly important in the San Fernando Valley. For one thing, the majority of San Fernando Valley residents worked in some capacity on behalf of national defense, whether in an aircraft or spacecraft firm contracted by the federal government or in an engineering firm that indirectly supported such aims. Thus, westerns affirmed the values and labor of people who had a direct economic investment as workers in defense of what were perceived to be fundamental American ideals. Westerns also justified American interventions in socialist and left-leaning states around the globe. They did so through stylistic and technical choices that affirmed an imperialist agenda on behalf of free-market ideologies based on the presumption of individual choice. Corkin notes that westerns typically feature extremely wide or long shots that emphasize "the openness of the land, a geographical condition that creates the terms of freedom as it invites the exercise of individual will." Such shots reflect notions of imperialism and conquest because "for the viewer to apprehend the process of conquest in a thorough and effective manner, he/she must fully comprehend the scale of the territory that must be tamed."[3] Corkin argues that such scenes virtually beg their viewers to bring properly American notions of social order to the landscape, as the main (white male) characters do.[4]

Classic westerns also cultivated nationalism and deep allegiances to traditional American values through their portrayal of rural land and small-town communities as the centerpiece of the American experience. Westerns powerfully argued in favor of local control among socially and economically homogeneous communities as a defense against the essentially corrupt nature of (urban, federal) government. Film historian Scott Simmon has argued that, "the Hollywood Western begins and apparently ends with praise for small-community democracy," and that postwar classic westerns often engaged themes of escape from urbanity and the restoration of family and small-town community.[5] Implicit in this narrative of rural land, small community, and local control were the racial and class biases underlying housing policy, property law, and land-use zoning. This was particularly important amid federally sponsored and racially excusive suburbanization, which subsidized whites' upward and outward mobility while neglecting urban areas and communities of color. Westerns affirmed the basic righteousness of the separation of the races and the assumptions of white supremacy upon which these divisions were founded. Corkin has observed that one of the reasons western films were so popular in the years just before and after World War II is because they narrated a kind of social Darwinism and natural selection that offered an explanation for widespread social disparities made worse by federally sponsored postwar suburbanization and urban renewal. Western films helped white suburbanites to explain and rationalize their experiences by interpreting them through the cloak of national and imperial progress.

Moreover, westerns were in ideological conversation with other genres of postwar film that offered relational portraits of rural, urban, and suburban landscapes. Geographer Chris Lukinbeal argues that American film is marked by a long tradition of antiurbanism; across genres, urban landscapes are repeatedly used as metaphors for chaos, corruption, impersonal human relationships, and dirtiness. Conversely, he finds, rural and country landscapes are used as visual metaphors for happiness, redemption, and core American values.[6] These contrasts were amplified in film during the postwar era, when many people were anxious about the social and spatial changes under way. And nowhere was the urban setting more pathologized than in film noir, which achieved its height of popularity at the same time as westerns did — both during the era of massive middle-class white suburbanization. One of the defining characteristics of film noir is the use of the modern city as both setting and subject. According to cultural historian Eric Avila, "film noir emphasized the social and psychological consequences of urban modernity" through repeated use of those spaces most associated with urban malaise, including tenement houses and nightclubs. Noir linked urban spaces and landscapes with themes of moral, and particularly racial, depravity, most frequently through portrayals of the dangers of heterogeneity — political, sexual, economic, and racial. In particular, noir reflected a long-standing American fear of racial mixing as leading to the decline of the white race and the fundamental American character.[7]

In spite of its racial, class, gender, and national specificity, however, the power of the western frontier myth is that it poses as national history. Therefore, although it celebrates white supremacy and Anglo-American conquest through the figure of the white male, the frontier myth has historically been and continues to be attractive to diverse audiences. According to Yardena Rand, who conducted an innovative study of audience reception among western film viewers, "At the heart of the Western lie ideals that appeal to and validate the perspectives of a broad base of people — the right to live life on your own terms, the right to stand up and fight for what you believe in, survival against overwhelming odds, loyalty, honor, self-reliance, independence, personal courage, strength, skill."[8] Indeed, the frontier myth celebrates these values in a simultaneously generic and specific way: as the embodiment of the general American character, which is specifically personified as white and male. As frontier myths are consistently reaffirmed and naturalized as national history, the West's actual social histories of violence, dispossession, exploitation, and exclusion are erased. Abstracted from its historical context in this way, the myth of the western frontier is flexible enough to allow even those people who were and are subjected to its actual histories of conquest — American Indians, blacks, Mexicans, and Asian Americans — to embrace it.

Nonetheless, although westerns have long been popular among a wide range of audiences, white Americans are most likely to interpret western films as accurate chronicles of history. In the early 1990s, JoEllen Shively conducted a series of innovative focus group interviews with both Anglos and American Indians who watched western films. She found that diverse ethnic and racial groups enjoyed westerns, but for very different reasons. Whites interpreted westerns as accurate chronicles of national history and the roles played by Anglo-Americans in that history. In her study, Anglos reported that they liked westerns for reasons such as "My grandparents were immigrants and westerns show us the hard life they had"; "Westerns are about my heritage and how we settled the frontier and about all the problems they had"; "Westerns give us an idea about how things were in the old days"; and "Westerns are true to life." American Indians, by contrast, enjoyed westerns for their landscapes, humor, and stunts, as well as for the acting talents of American Indian actors and actresses, but they did not interpret westerns as accurate historical representations. While Anglo participants interpreted the white male characters in western films as representations of their connection to the American past, American Indian participants were highly unlikely to identify with the Indian characters in western films, both because of tribal and regional distinctions (which are usually glossed over in western films) and because of the shallow stereotypes inherent to most portrayals. Shively concluded that for white viewers alone, western films are like primitive myths that affirm and justify the righteousness and necessity of their ancestors' actions.[9] Similarly, for new suburbanites in the San Fernando Valley, locally produced western films helped them to justify the foundation of racial, economic, and geographic exclusions on which their new homes and communities were based.

For many new suburbanites, their beliefs about what kind of place the San Fernando Valley should be had been cultivated long before they ever arrived in the Valley, both by promotional materials narrating local history and by western films and television shows that explicitly celebrated the San Fernando Valley as subject. Films and songs titled "San Fernando Valley" proliferated in the 1930s and 1940s, broadcasting the manufactured link between the San Fernando Valley and the "authentic" West to a national audience. For example, Tex Ritter, "America's Singing Cowboy," recorded his song "San Fernando Valley" in 1941. Ritter was a native of Texas and a resident of Van Nuys, one of the Valley's older communities, when the song was released. His lyrics bring together the multiple kinds of rural mythologies that intersected in the San Fernando Valley.

I long to re-turn to the val-ley . . . That for years was my home . . .
I long to stay there for-ev-er . . . Nev-er more to roam . . .

CHORUS
Take me back to the San Fer-nan-do val-ley . . .
To my old mis-sion home by the hills . . .
Let me stroll when the moon comes o'er the val-ley . . .
With the one for whom my heart ev-er thrills . . .
Take me back to the San Fer-nan-do val-ley . . .
Let me dream by the cool val-ley stream . . .
It is there that my heart is ev-er go-ing . . .
Take me back to my San Fer-nan-do home.[10]

Ritter's lyrics capture the idea of the San Fernando Valley as the end of a journey ("never more roam"), a peaceful place where one's troubles can be left behind. At the same time, he reassures migrants that the Valley has a deep and rich history rooted in the Spanish past ("my old mission home"). Repeated references to my "San Fernando home" further emphasize the importance of the home and the domestic sphere as a link between western and suburban ideals. In the iconography of western popular culture, the settled home represents the ultimate objective of westward expansion and the signpost of imperial conquest.

Even more popular was a song written by Gordon Jenkins, also titled "San Fernando Valley," which Roy Rogers and Dale Evans made famous when they sang it in Republic Pictures' 1944 film *San Fernando Valley*. Jenkins's lyrics highlight the Valley's unique combination of western and suburban living.

Oh! I'm pack-in' my grip
And I'm leav-in' to-day,
Cause I'm tak-in' a trip
Cal-i-for-nia way.
I'm gon-na set-tle down and nev-er more roam
And make the SAN FER-NAN-DO VAL-LEY my home.

I'll for-get my sins,
I'll be mak-in' new friends
Where the West be-gins
And the sun-set ends,

'Cause I've de-cid-ed where "yours truly" should be
And it's the SAN FER-NAN-DO VAL-LEY for me.

I think that I'm safe in stat-in'
{She/He} will be wait-in'
When my lone-ly jour-ney is done
And kind-ly old Rev-'rend Thom-as
Made us a pro-mise
He will make the two of us one.

So, I'm hit-tin' the trail
To the cow coun-try.
You can forward my mail
Care of R. F. D.
I'm gon-na set-tle down and nev-er more roam
And make the SAN FER-NAN-DO VAL-LEY my home.[11]

Jenkins's song emphasizes similar tropes and visual imagery as Ritter's version but is more explicit about how the San Fernando Valley embodied the best values of both the American West and the American suburb. References to "the trail" and the "cow country" are iconographic references to the frontier West, while the references to domesticity capture the ideals of suburbia and property rights. Like Ritter, Jenkins emphasized the importance of "never more roaming," promoting the San Fernando Valley as the end of a journey but also as a place where one could start afresh. The theme of starting over in a new place ("where the West begins, and the sunset ends") is classic western Americana, but also classic real-estate technique.

When Bing Crosby (a resident of the San Fernando Valley's Toluca Lake neighborhood) remade the song, it soared to the top of the Billboard charts, where it stayed for twenty-two weeks. The song's author, Gordon Jenkins, considered the song one of his least memorable and was perplexed by its popularity. He recalled, "One night I had the hives and couldn't sleep. . . . It was a melody, if you can call it that, that people liked. Made more money than it really deserved. . . . The strange thing is that in the song lyrics I never say anything good about the San Fernando Valley. All I say is, I want to go. . . . It could be a sewer."[12] In fact, Jenkins said all the right things. San Fernando Valley suburbanites believed that they would, and should, be able to combine the very best of the frontier West and the all-American suburb in their own backyards. As W. W. Robinson explained, "Sung, whistled, and played throughout the nation, the song helped — like the presence of movie stars, glamorous estates, and kidney shaped swimming pools — to make more and more people do something about making their Valley dream come true."[13]

Similar themes abound in Republic Pictures' *San Fernando Valley* (1944), directed by John English, which catapulted Jenkins's song to national popularity. The film is set largely at the fictional Kenyon Ranch operated by the elderly Cyclone Kenyon, a migrant from Maryland, although his oldest granddaughter, Dale Kenyon (played by Dale Evans), makes most major decisions. In the film's opening sequence, we learn that Dale's younger sister, Betty Lou, is a boy-crazy teenager who constantly distracts the male ranch hands with her flirtations, especially by engaging them in song. When the Kenyon Ranch horses get out through a broken fence because the ranch hands aren't paying attention, Dale fires them and decides to hire an all-female group of ranch hands to prevent Betty Lou from getting into "more serious trouble." Dale drives into the nearby town of Pendleford, which just happens to be hosting its "Days of '49" celebration, to find her new crew. There, she meets Roy Rogers (played by Roy Rogers), who becomes instantly enamored of her and invites her to the evening's dance. Brushing him off, Dale gives him a fake address, and when he goes to meet her that night, he is robbed. Looking for work, Roy ends up at the Kenyon Ranch, where he takes a job as a cook. Not once in the film does he go near the kitchen, however. Instead, he spends all his time riding Trigger and courting Dale.

Meanwhile, Betty Lou concocts a plot to bring the male ranch hands back. She conspires with them by convincing them to steal her grandfather's horses. By her scheme, the former ranch hands can then look like heroes — and get their jobs back — when they "find" the stolen horses. The ranch hands reluctantly agree, but two of their group (the two who are dark skinned and ethnically ambiguous) actually do steal the horses and sell them to a third party. Roy Rogers discovers the plot and returns all the horses. Betty Lou confesses her role, and the male ranch hands return to their jobs, though Cyclone Kenyon agrees to keep the women on since there is plenty of work for all.

Tales of the nuclear family, domesticity, and heterosexual courtship are central to the film and are enacted most directly in a subplot involving Dale, Betty Lou, and Roy. Throughout the second half of the film, Betty Lou develops a crush on Roy, who is at least ten to fifteen years her senior. To show Betty Lou the foolishness of the crush, Dale pretends to be developing a relationship with Roy. Predictably, she ends up falling in love. The closing sequence of the film features Roy and Dale driving out of Pendleford in a brand-new, shiny car pulling a horse trailer with Trigger in the back, singing Jenkins's version of "San Fernando Valley." The film closes with a close-up of the horse trailer's rear fender, painted with "The End," and Rogers and Evans singing in duet: "We're going to settle down and never more roam, and make the San Fernando Valley our home."

Filmed at Kentucky Park Farms in Thousand Oaks, in the western foothills of the San Fernando Valley close to the Ventura County line, *San Fernando Valley* combines elements of the Old West and suburban modernity, often in nonsensical ways, for its wartime audiences. Though never explicitly engaged in the film as a real place (that is, it is never clear where the Valley is — is it the site of the Kenyon Ranch? the place where Roy comes from? the place where the newly married couple is moving?), the Valley is presumably the ranch land outside the town of Pendleford. Pendleford's landscape consists of storefronts and businesses associated with the Old West, such as a Wells Fargo bank, multiple saloons, and a saddle and harness shop, though it is ambiguous whether this is how the town looks on an everyday basis or if it has just been decorated that way for the "Days of '49" celebration. During every town sequence, extras costumed in pioneer attire or Indian headdresses wander through the streets. In all likelihood, many of these extras were San Fernando Valley residents recruited to participate in the shoot. Familiar narrative elements of the western genre (such as fistfights, runaway horses, and gunshots in the air) are incorporated almost randomly and for their own sake, not because they advance the plot in any significant way. Cars and horses coexist in the film; indeed, while the Kenyon Ranch is apparently within riding distance of Pendleford, Dale always makes the trip by car.

The Kenyon Ranch itself explicitly combines elements of suburbia and western ranch life. Dirt roads and white fences lead up to the suburban ranch-style home, which is furnished with the latest kitchen appliances. Outside, a swimming pool abuts the horse corrals, shaded by citrus and oak trees. In one memorable scene, the expelled male ranch hands serenade the female ranch hands on the deck of the swimming pool; the women recline on chaise longues in swimsuits, while the men, dressed in jeans, boots, and cowboy hats, play fiddles and harmonicas. As we shall see in the next chapter, these are exactly the kind of semirural, suburban landscapes that newcomers to the San Fernando Valley tried to create through urban policy. The film sometimes, but only indirectly, engages the San Fernando Valley's actual social history. For example, at the very end of the film, over a stack of Sunkist orange crates piled in front of the ranch house, we observe Roy, Dale, and the supporting characters in front of a stage set of a Spanish-style mission. There they sing the closing song, get into their shiny new car with horse trailer, and drive off into the sunset — toward the San Fernando Valley, of course. This moment stands out as unique amid the film's overwhelming treatment of the Valley as a generic, quintessential western suburb.

The film was not among the most popular or memorable of westerns; critics, too, dismissed it as ineffective. *Variety* reviewed the film with gentle disparagement: "*San Fernando Valley* will be pleasant entertainment for Roy Rogers fans . . . but it is just about time for somebody to give screenwriters an ultimatum to turn out decent material or get out of town."[14] Despite its quirky plotlines and underdeveloped characters, however, the film "works" because it relies on shared understandings about the meanings of the West and American suburbia, which could be blurred together in ambiguous — and therefore flexible — historical and geographic ways. It also performed a powerful function in shaping popular ideas about the San Fernando Valley as subject. By the time of the film's release, the San Fernando Valley had achieved national renown as the home of western film and television celebrities. For viewers, the film (as well as the Jenkins song that it made famous) wasn't supposed to "make sense" so much as to celebrate the unique combination of western and suburban lifestyles available in the San Fernando Valley. Consuming these representations of place, landscape, and community, new migrants to the Valley invested in a vision of rural and western land use within suburbia before they even arrived.

The San Fernando Valley was not just the subject of western film production, however, but an active production location. As Lukinbeal reminds us, "Cinematic landscapes are not mere representations but are working landscapes involved with cultural production and reproduction."[15] Similarly, geographer Don Mitchell argues that "landscape representations . . . do not stand apart from landscape production. . . . Hence it is important to explore the ways that landscapes . . . come to be made, not just in contested representations but also through social processes working themselves out, quite literally, on the ground."[16] As one of the Valley's key industries, western film production profoundly influenced the directions and aesthetics of suburbanization in the San Fernando Valley and ensured that Valley suburbanites did not merely absorb the messages that western films communicated but actively shaped them.

Through their economic activities at the city's outer limits, western film studios brought the fringes of Los Angeles County fully within the reach of regional industrial production. Thus, western film production has had nearly as important an influence on Los Angeles's sprawling form as gentleman farming and other processes noted by the region's historians, such as Henry Huntington's electric railway, the Los Angeles Aqueduct, the power of the real-estate industry, and automobile and highway lobbyists such as the Automobile Club of Southern California.[17] Indeed, all the studios owned large tracts of land on the outskirts of the county that could be used for filming, especially for westerns. For example, in 1915, Universal Studios purchased a 410-acre chicken ranch in North Hollywood and later developed the major tourist attraction and production facility that stands today. Warner Brothers owned thousands of acres of land in Los Angeles and the San Fernando Valley, including a 2,800-acre studio ranch in Calabasas and a 135-acre lot in Burbank. Henry Warner, one of the studio chiefs, used a corner of the Calabasas ranch to raise Thoroughbred racehorses. Fox Studios owned a 6,600-acre ranch in the Calabasas/Thousand Oaks area but sold the property in the mid-1960s, at the height of the Valley's subdivision boom.[18] In this way, western film production exerted a very strong influence on the region's economic geography, pulling development outward well before World War II.

Individual western celebrities also shaped the region's emerging physical geography through their personal and business decisions about real estate, architecture, and land use. According to W. W. Robinson, "The Valley was still in its small-farm, fruit-orchard phase when movie stars felt the pull and began buying acreage there, to be transformed into horse ranches, polo fields, and ranch-style hideaways that enabled their owners to lead less conspicuous lives than in Bel-Air or Beverly Hills mansions."[19] Many western directors and producers preferred to live on large ranches in the San Fernando Valley and north and west Los Angeles County that emulated the on-screen rural western landscapes their films depicted. For example, director John Ford shot many of his most popular western films, starring Harry Carey, on Carey's ranch in Saugus, where "although there was a three-room house on the property, the two men wanted to emulate real pioneers while they worked and slept in bedrolls out in an alfalfa patch."[20] William S. Hart, well known for demanding "dusty, bleak, and harsh settings for his stories," owned a ranch in Newhall where he moved upon retirement.[21] After filming *Birth of a Nation*, D. W. Griffith purchased a ranch in Sylmar, against the foothills of the San Gabriel Mountains northeast of San Fernando, which soon became a hangout for Lillian Gish and other actor friends. Cecil B. DeMille's Paradise Ranch was located in Little Tujunga Canyon, where he built numerous cabins and a redwood guesthouse as a retreat from Hollywood.[22] Northridge, dubbed the Horse Capital of the West, boasted dozens of working ranches and attracted celebrities who liked to ride or to breed horses, such as actress Barbara Stanwyck, who owned a 140-acre thoroughbred breeding facility there with her manager, Zeppo Marx. Actor Robert Taylor, with whom Stanwyck had a relationship, owned the ranch next door.[23] Pat Brady, who appeared on the *Roy Rogers Show*, was also a Northridge resident. Gary Cooper owned 10 acres in Van Nuys, while Tom Mix owned a ranch at Canterbury Avenue and Osborne Street in Arleta. Sidekick actor Chill Wills, best known for his western series with George O'Brien in 1938 and 1939, lived in Encino, and Smiley Burnette, Gene Autry's sidekick, lived in Studio City.[24] And John Wayne, who grew up on a ranch in the Antelope Valley homesteaded by his grandfather, lived in Glendale beginning in 1916 and later owned 5 acres in Encino with his family.[25] The San Fernando Valley could thus boast a veritable colony of western film stars as one of its primary attractions.

Many western actors, producers, and writers had second careers as real-estate agents and developers. They took keen advantage of their own and the genre's popularity to promote suburban development. Al "Fuzzy" St. John, an established sidekick actor who worked with numerous popular western film heroes, "had a lot of money tied up in real estate out in the Valley," and another sidekick, "Arkansas" Slim Andrews, bought and sold twenty-three houses in the Valley during his career. Tom Mix, a noted western film star, owned multiple homes not only in the Valley but also in Beverly Hills, Newhall, and Avalon on Santa Catalina Island. Jimmy Ellison, who had played Hopalong Cassidy's side-kick, became a full-time real-estate developer after quitting show business.[26]

Equally important to the physical geography of western film and television production were the many stock contractors, clothing shops, tack and feed stores, and riding schools located throughout the Valley. These businesses supported western cinematic production as well as the idea of the Valley as a uniquely western suburb. They helped to give the cultural notion of western heritage both economic clout and political influence that extended far beyond the film industry. For example, the Fat Jones Stable, located first in North Hollywood and then at Devonshire Downs in Northridge, rented the first horses to the studios in 1912, just after the studios had relocated to Hollywood from the East Coast. Fat Jones was perhaps the most respected trainer and stock contractor working in the industry, and his ranch functioned as both a production facility and a noted social center for real and on-screen cowboys.[27] Devonshire Downs opened in the mid-1940s at Devonshire and Zelzah boulevards in Northridge, with a track for training racehorses. In 1946, the San Fernando Valley Trotting Association hosted Sunday-afternoon harness races there. In 1948, the state bought Devonshire Downs and used the property for the San Fernando Valley Fair for the next three decades.[28] Golden State Rodeo Company, located in Chatsworth, was the largest rodeo stock contracting company west of the Rockies. Golden State supplied cattle, horses, stagecoaches, wagons, and assorted equipment and paraphernalia to western film studios.[29] One of the partners of Golden State was Lex Connelly, a popular sports announcer who worked to get the first rodeos televised. Tom Mitchell, a movie stock contractor, owned two large ranches in Southern California, one in Simi Valley and another near Riverside.[30] Also, many feed and equipment stores as well as training facilities sprang up to meet the demands of western film production, such as the Spanish riding school established in North Hollywood in 1959 where actors like Gene Autry and Roy Rogers improved their horseback-riding skills. Many of the stock contractors who supplied cattle and horses to the studios also trained the animals and the actors. Especially in the later years of western films' popularity, many of the actors who played cowboys had, in fact, never been on a horse; as a result, doubles were often used but actors nonetheless had to be trained in basic horsemanship. Andy Jauregui, who owned a large production facility in Newhall, trained the horses used by Will Rogers and Jack Warner and taught Clark Gable to rope calves.[31] All these people were San Fernando Valley residents, business owners, employers, taxpayers, and voters. It would be difficult to overestimate their political, economic, and cultural influence in the years during and just after World War II.

The western production ranches peppered throughout the San Fernando Valley and north Los Angeles County deserve special attention for their influence on the city's real and imagined rural landscapes. As tangible, physical places, the San Fernando Valley's production ranches were palimpsests of Southern California's layers of conquest, most particularly the territorial dispossession of indigenous and Californio owners and reallocation of property to white American settlers. Some ranches had been initially acquired through the Homestead Act; some had been working ranches that later rented their facilities to the studios; still others were deliberately created as moneymaking ventures by people who were experienced with the western film industry, familiar with the studios' needs, and hopeful about capitalizing on those needs to generate profits.

The San Fernando Valley's production-ranch owners merged fantasy and fiction to craft rural frontier landscapes that would generate lots of cash. They did so in part by capitalizing on audience expectations about what western landscapes should look like, cultivated by previous generations of western popular culture. As a result, all the western production ranches had certain landscape elements in common. All had a ranch house or cabin, and most had a barn as well as several outbuildings that could function variously as bunkhouses, tool sheds, or simply background scenery. Most had dirt roads winding through groves of trees that could be used for chase scenes, and some boasted majestic, awe-inspiring rock formations. The larger ranches all had western-themed streets, with either false fronts or fully functional buildings, which were used for the scenes representing town life, and many had a Mexican or Spanish village of some kind. Their choices reflect decisions about which iconographic elements they thought the western experience *should* include. By physically creating those landscapes in the San Fernando Valley and north Los Angeles County, they reaffirmed the basic legitimacy of the western heritage narrative as well as its aesthetic and ideological dimensions.

The production ranches tended to concentrate on the northern and western fringes of Los Angeles County, in the foothills of the San Fernando Valley, both because of physical proximity to the studios in Hollywood, Burbank, and Glendale and because of union rules that workers be paid extra if they traveled more than thirty-five miles out of town for a shoot. In north Los Angeles, three production ranches were literally neighbors on Placerita Canyon Road just east of Newhall. The first, the Andy Jauregui Ranch, was owned by a rodeo cowboy who began renting horses and cattle to the film studios during the silent era and then leased his personal ranch property for western filmmaking in the early sound era. Just next door was Walt Disney's Golden Oaks Ranch. Disney purchased the ranch in 1959 as an adjunct to his Burbank studio because he "saw that many of the movie location ranches were being sacrificed to the bulldozer for housing developments or were being sliced up by the construction of new super highways and were consequently becoming unavailable for filming. . . . Thus the Golden Oak Ranch became part of the Disney Studio."[32] On the same road, about a half mile away, was the Walker Ranch, which featured almost no structures and was used almost exclusively for chase scenes by Monogram Studios. Across the 14 Freeway, in Newhall, was the Melody Ranch, which was leased to Monogram Studios beginning in the 1930s and then sold to Gene Autry in 1952.

The production ranches located in Chatsworth and Simi Valley, at the far western end of Los Angeles County and spilling over into Ventura County, were the most famous and extensively used of the city's forty-odd ranches, largely because of the area's majestic topography. The Iverson Ranch, where over two thousand western films and numerous television serials were filmed, was especially beloved. The Iverson Ranch belonged to Swedish immigrant Augusta Wagman and Norwegian Karl Iverson, who had separately homesteaded adjacent 160-acre plots in Chatsworth and consolidated their holdings upon marriage. Eventually, their ranch grew to approximately 500 acres.[33] Director Bill Witney of Republic Studios called Iverson Ranch the "armpit" of western film locations, perhaps because, as Tinsley Yarbrough notes, "actors and crew members complained of the sweltering Iverson summers, the bitter cold winters and the gale-force Santa Ana winds that regularly challenged the most securely attached hairpieces of our stalwart western heroes." Nonetheless, Yarbrough reminds us that, "for location fans, Iverson — with its cliffs, chase roads, enormous rock formations and elaborate sets — was the premiere filming site of the western/serial era."[34] The Iverson Ranch was particularly noted for its unusual red rock formations, such as the "Garden of the Gods" and the "Indian Head" rocks, which formed a desertlike background more reminiscent of the nineteenth-century U.S. Southwest than the mid-twentieth-century suburban San Fernando Valley. At the height of western film production in the mid-1940s, up to eight crews filmed at Iverson at once, with each paying a minimum of one hundred dollars per day.

Among the many films shot at Iverson's was the popular *Tarzan* series, based on the writings of Edgar Rice Burroughs, author of *Tarzan: King of the Apes*. Nine *Tarzan*-themed films were shot at Iverson's over a thirty-five-year period, beginning in 1919.[35] In the series, the ranch's dramatic rocks and cliffs became sub-Saharan Africa and a village named Waziri. Simultaneously, elsewhere in the Valley, Burroughs was developing the suburban community of Tarzana on the site of his personal estate, where he had once dressed up in colonial garb and hunted rabbits and other game. The new neighborhood's advertising drew on the themes of British imperialism and white supremacy, promoted by both the novel and the film series, to create a racially exclusive and elite subdivision, enforced by racially restrictive covenants.[36] Burroughs's simultaneous activities in real-estate development and cultural production linked the San Fernando Valley to American and global processes of European conquest through unabashed promotion of white superiority, coupled with the use of land to realize that ideal.

Corriganville, straddling Chatsworth in Los Angeles County and what would become the independent city of Simi Valley in Ventura County, was second only to Iverson Ranch as the busiest western production location of the golden era. It was widely acclaimed for its fantastical and varied landscapes. A native of Milwaukee, Ray "Crash" Corrigan had been a body builder who trained stars for MGM pictures and then did stunt double work, most famously in a gorilla suit for the jungle-theme movies that were popular in the 1930s. One day while shooting on location at nearby Iverson's, Corrigan visited the Jonathan Scott cattle ranch in Chatsworth and immediately saw its potential for film production. He bought the ranch for $11,354 in 1937 and immediately hired contractors to create a major production facility that could compete with Iverson's.[37]

Corrigan invested his money in the construction of the western-themed Silvertown Street, bunkhouses, a livery stable, and a rodeo arena. He also kept thirty-five head of Hereford cattle at the ranch as a convenience for the studios. Corrigan's investments in these standard tropes of western films — cattle ranching, bunkhouses, and a generic western Main Street — point to the homogeneity of western landscapes that would become inextricably linked with the genre. At its height, Corriganville hosted up to five film production companies at a time, charging each of them a minimum of $650 per day for the use of his property and extensive sets. Corrigan lived on the ranch full time with his family in the westernmost building of Silvertown Street. His young children attended public schools in the San Fernando Valley and, as adults, became involved in the Valley's emerging slow-growth and historic preservation movements, explored in the next two chapters.

One of Corrigan's many successful business strategies was to contract with the studios to construct semipermanent sets that materialized the rural western landscapes that directors, producers, and ranch owners considered authentic and profitable. After constructing a set, the studios had exclusive rights to use it for one year, after which Corrigan could rent it out to other studios. As William Ehrheart has noted, "With a little help from the studios, different parts of the ranch could resemble almost any location in the World: an island in the South Seas, an African jungle, the Burma Road, the Northwest woods, a Sonoran desert, the American West, a European forest, or a vista of green meadows by a sylvan lake."[38] Through such agreements, Columbia Studios constructed a lagoon with diving rock, bridges, and waterfall; John Ford constructed a "Fort Apache" set for $65,000; Warner Brothers trimmed the trees of a five-acre forest; and Howard Hughes constructed an extensive "Corsican village" for $103,000 that was later transformed into various "third world" locations.[39]

The production ranches' physical landscapes empowered western film actors and crews, many of whom were urban born and raised, to "play frontier" during production. Pierce Lyden, a retired self-identified "Western film heavy," recalls how cinematic and physical landscapes intersected in magical ways for those working at Melody Ranch.

> Melody Ranch was one of the close locations where we often stayed overnight. They had a very few crude shacks or "outhouses" that were about the same size. It was doubling up, army cots and community festivities with everything else. Roughing it, it was, but far superior to riding back to Hollywood each night and out again in the morning. The nights were great fun. There was always music, a guitar or mouth organ, and the café had games of chance going. Some would sit

on the porches swapping stories of the "old days" or having a drink while new boys were shown the fast draw by an old cowboy. All this took place on a dimly lit street on a dark night with only a make believe setting. But it was our town, and that night it was real.[40]

Similarly, many actors and actresses considered Corriganville to be an excellent representation of western life and a retreat from the hustle and bustle of Hollywood. Early in the ranch's history, Corrigan offered a sort of dude ranch club membership to one hundred select members "who had the use of sleeping facilities, a well equipped private gymnasium, and an indoor barbecue pit and kitchen. . . . Members could ride horses, swim, go hunting, or use archery, rifle or skeet shooting ranges. These activities attracted Hollywood actors who wanted to 'disappear' for awhile."[41] Western celebrities developed a personal attachment to Corriganville, and in later years many went on to advocate for the ranch's preservation when it was no longer being used for filming.

The production ranches — more than forty altogether — collectively cultivated a widespread ideological and practical commitment to rural landscapes in the San Fernando Valley and its exurbs. They did so by actively shaping the physical landscape through the construction of large ranches and low-density residential development with a deliberately rural aesthetic and by presenting their business motives — to make money by selling the western landscape as an attractive product — as benign cultural imperatives. These were first and foremost business decisions, based equally on what production-ranch owners and directors thought the "real West" had looked like, drawn from prior generations of western popular culture; the kinds of imagery they thought would be attractive to audiences, who were similarly invested in representations of the "real" West; and finally by practical matters of which land could be secured to meet the studios' often tight schedules and limited budgets. Given these constraints, the most useful and profitable western production landscapes were those that were generic enough to be recognized as western, yet abstracted from the specific historical context of Los Angeles or the West. Working under the direction of studio executives and directors, production-ranch owners and staff were as quick to assemble a set as to destroy it or move it to a new location in order to meet the needs of whatever plot sequence was being filmed. Studios would build false-front buildings and towns just to blow them up or set them on fire during an important scene, and ranch owners built false cliffs, rocks, and other "natural" elements to make production easier and more comfortable. And at Corriganville, as we have seen, Ray Corrigan worked with the studios to create a different set of environmental possibilities than the western San Fernando Valley's dry, dusty climate would allow.

Furthermore, despite the popular association of the western with "wide open spaces," Tinsley Yarbrough's documentary series reveals that many of the western production ranches were extraordinarily compact. Even on the largest ranches, the areas used for production were typically quite small. At the Walker Ranch, for example, the road used for chase scenes only allowed rides of twelve to thirteen seconds. The chase scenes that were filmed there thus required skillful camera direction, set design, and editing. Camera operators would shoot from different angles on each thirteen-second stretch of a chase scene to capture different backgrounds, while the whitewashed cabin on the property had a camouflage tent that could be draped over it to prevent it from being recognized repeatedly in the background and thereby ruining the shoot. Similarly, Yarbrough shows that the chase roads at Corriganville all had several small trails alongside to allow shooting from different angles that would make film sequences look different from one another.[42] Its three inset roads were arguably the best in the business for this reason.[43]

Thus, despite their suburban locations and the creativity required of filmmakers in these contexts, western cinematic production conveyed impressions about the size, expanse, and undeveloped nature of rural western landscapes that were accepted as authentic by most viewers. Despite (or perhaps because of) their camera tricks, the westerns shot in the San Fernando Valley were highly effective not only in narrating regional and national history but also in promoting a generic and highly romanticized vision of rural landscapes that could be easily translated into suburban contexts. The production of western films in the San Fernando Valley complicates the purported divide between "real" and "reel" life noted by western historians.[44] The visions of western life portrayed on-screen *were* real to Valley suburbanites because they could see the impacts of the industry on the physical landscapes of their neighborhoods. Viewers in the San Fernando Valley witnessed the materiality of rural western landscapes adjacent to their new suburban tract homes, and most saw no contradiction; moreover, they were actively involved in the production of western film and television even as they carved out postwar suburban livelihoods.

This was particularly so in Chatsworth, on the far western end of the San Fernando Valley, near both Iverson's Ranch and Corriganville. Anna "Queenie" Billings remembered that, when she was growing up in Chatsworth, "every kid went up there to watch" the studios make movies nearby. In earlier years, her family had hosted the surveyors of the Southern Pacific Railroad in their five-bedroom house, one of the few dwellings in the area. Beginning in the 1930s and

1940s, her family's home became a resting place for western film crews. Billings recalled, "Later on in years, we had . . . as many as forty movie characters staying overnight with us for a week at a time or two weeks." The cast and production staff "slept in the front room on the floor, they slept on the porch, anything, then go back to Los Angeles."[45] Her family's friends, Pearl and Romeo, owned a catering truck and brought coffee and sandwiches to the production crews for many years.

Before the automobile became widely available, film studios frequently hired local teenagers to drive wagons and carriages from the train depot at Chatsworth to remote filming locations. Queenie Billings's older brother, Jess Graves, often met arriving film crews this way. As Graves recalled, "The movie people, they came in and the stars all came out in big limousines and others come out on a train. We had nine flatbed wagons that we used to haul all these extras up there . . . and then we'd haul them back and be out there the next day and get 'em." They performed this task for two or three pictures until automobiles became widely available. In an oral history conducted in 1978, Graves recalled an incident in which he played a direct role in the success of a western film.

> I remember one time I was standing out watching them, you know, and they had somebody riding off in the hills . . . some cowboy riding up a hill and he couldn't . . . he wasn't much of a cowboy. And I went down there and I said to the director, I said, "Do you want me to go up there and show him how to come off there?" He looked at me and he said, "Can you do any better that that?" I says, "You're damn right." Well, I climbed up there, whipped the horse up and away we come down, just big jumps right off that thing, you know. And the director says to the actor, he says, "Now that's the way I want you to come off of there." I got a big kick out of it.[46]

This experience no doubt confirmed to Graves that he was more authentically western than the western film stars.

Even for suburbanites who did not participate directly in western filmmaking, there were ample opportunities to interact and mingle with western celebrities. The San Fernando Valley's resident western celebrities could be counted on to sanction and bless suburban growth. They frequently appeared, in full western costume, to mark developments in suburban progress, even when those developments directly threatened the future of western filming (see figures 4 and 5). For example, in 1940, Gene Autry was on hand to mark the opening of the Cahuenga Pass into the San Fernando Valley. In March 1959, Corriganville's western actors appeared at the grand opening of the Ralph's grocery store in Canoga Park.[47] And in 1966, they mingled with suburban homeowners and

FIGURE 4 Western film stars Gene Autry (center) and Tom Keene (far left) are on hand to participate in the Opening Day Ceremonies at Cahuenga Pass in June 1940. Keene was then honorary mayor of the Valley community of Sherman Oaks. Also present are, from left to right, Governor Culbert Olson; John B. Kingsley, president of the Hollywood Chamber of Commerce; Los Angeles mayor Fletcher Bowron; Mayor Frank Gillson of Burbank; and Richard Arlen. Courtesy of the Herald Examiner Collection, Los Angeles Public Library.

county officials at the groundbreaking of the new Simi Valley–San Fernando Valley Freeway (State Highway 118), which had ironically bisected Iverson's Ranch and virtually destroyed film production both there and at nearby Corriganville.[48] Like earlier cultural productions such as Gordon Jenkins's song "San Fernando Valley" and the Republic Pictures film of the same name, the active participation of western film stars in everyday suburban life fused the mythology of the American West with the physical landscapes of the suburban San Fernando Valley.

Corriganville, in Chatsworth, played a crucial role in bringing the Wild West into suburban daily life. Ever the entrepreneur, Ray Corrigan looked for ways to maintain the viability of his tremendous real-estate investment as western film production began to decline in the late 1940s and early 1950s. His solution was to open the ranch to the public as an amusement park. Guests could

FIGURE 5 Los Angeles mayor Norris Poulson, cowboy star and Chatsworth resident Roy Rogers, and Don McMahon, president of the Chatsworth Chamber of Commerce, at the Chatsworth cleanup campaign in 1961. Courtesy of the Hollywood Citizen News/Valley Times Collection of the Los Angeles Public Library.

visit their favorite movie locations while also watching the filming of western television shows, which increasingly came to replace feature-length films on the ranch. Corriganville was the only production ranch in Southern California that opened its operations to public viewing. After its official opening on May 1, 1949, Corriganville became as famous as Disneyland or Knott's Berry Farm, attracting as many as ten thousand visitors on a typical Sunday, with upwards of twenty thousand during special events. At the height of its popularity, Corriganville was listed as one of the ten most popular amusement parks in the world.[49]

Corrigan's vision of the Wild West theme park was ambitious and future oriented. He constantly sought out new land and new sales strategies to keep the ranch attractive and fresh to suburban visitors. In May 1953, he purchased the neighboring Touvin Ranch, increasing the overall ranch size to two thousand acres. He built an entrance gate, additional parking, a rodeo arena, grandstand seating for four thousand, and a food concession. Such improvements expanded the range of possibilities and moneymaking opportunities beyond western film production to encompass the wide variety of western-themed recreational activities that flourished in Southern California during the 1950s. According to the ranch's historian, William Ehrheart, "The arena scheduled not only rodeos, but also Wild West, equestrian stunt and horse shows. Ray would have celebrity Western actors appear as Grand Marshals for each rodeo parade." Corriganville's financial success was so great that, in 1955, Corrigan contracted with Outdoor Entertainments, Inc., to manage operations at the ranch, while he stayed on as an advisor and technical consultant.[50]

Corriganville promised that visitors to the ranch would have the chance to interact with their favorite western film stars — a tangible promise given the ranch's still-functional role as a frequently used location for film production. The ranch was advertised as the "Last of the Old West," and the sign at its entrance read, "Through these gates pass the world's most famous people."[51] A page in Corriganville's pictorial souvenir booklet featured western film actors and actresses such as Max Terhune, Elaine DuPont, Jack McElroy, Charlie Aldrich, "Lucky" Schliep, Chief Thundercloud, and Chief White Eagle. The booklet promised that these "familiar faces" would "act as your hosts and see that you have a grand time."[52] The last page of the booklet was reserved as a special autograph page, and visitors were encouraged to get all their favorites. Throughout the day, stunt actors performed short skits drawn from the repertoire of western film plots, such as the "Dalton Brothers Bank Hold-Up," "Billy the Kid Becomes an Outlaw," the "Johnson County Cattle War," and the "OK Corral Gunbattle." According to Ehrheart, these skits, performed every half hour to a taped narration, soon became the model for western historic reenactments.[53]

Corriganville's primary attraction, in addition to the promise of interacting with western film stars, was the physical landscape itself. A map distributed to visitors in the pictorial souvenir book directed guests to famous filming locations including Silvertown, Robin Hood Lake and Forest, Fort Apache, Burma Road, and Vendetta Village — all of which had been constructed in elaborate collaborations between Corrigan, studio directors, and urban financiers. The ranch had eleven miles of hiking and riding trails, caves for children to explore, picnic areas, and places for overnight camping. Visitors could rent horses from the livery stable used in countless western films and ride throughout the ranch's scenic acreage. While some of the buildings in Silvertown had false fronts, the interiors of many buildings were used to sell thematic merchandise, such as the Country Auction, Leather Tooling Shop, Frontier Store, Mexican Store, and Chinese Store.

For visitors, fact blended into fiction as they experienced and consumed the American West at Corriganville. In the *Corriganville Gazette*, Corrigan explained why he had chosen to open the production ranch to the public and how visitors responded to the site. He wrote, "You know, folks who come to Corriganville say that this place is timeless, and I guess they're right. It stands as an epitaph to an era, so rich in romance, so wild in adventure, that it has captured the hearts of many. Jesse James, General Custer, William H. Bonney (Alias Billy the Kid) are all gone, but Corriganville is still one place that exists to remind us of those days."[54] Corriganville's souvenir booklet billed the movie ranch as an authentic and fun-filled representation of the nation's mythical past — a place that merged representation with reality in the shaping of historical memory. According to the introductory remarks, "This is truly the Old West's Last Frontier. . . . On entering the vast expanse of Corriganville's two thousand acres, it is thrilling to stand and look about you as far as the eye can see and realize that in this very spot Father Serra traveled on the original El Camino Real 'The Highway of Kings.' Corriganville is a land of realism and yet make-believe. . . . Everywhere, at Corriganville, there is history, romance, and glamour combined to make your visit a thrilling and memorable one."[55] Corrigan well understood the powerful blend of fact and fiction, blended in the physical landscape of the San Fernando Valley, for a new generation of suburban families.

Corriganville explicitly targeted a local, suburban demographic. The back page of the souvenir book advertised Corriganville as "just 29 miles Northwest of Hollywood — 5 miles north of Chatsworth on scenic Hiway [sic] 118 through beautiful Santa Susanna Pass. Just a half hour's drive from most points in San Fernando Valley." In 1951 and 1952, the *Los Angeles Times* featured an automobile tour of historic attractions in the San Fernando Valley, with brand-new cars prominently provided by the Hudson Commodore and Pontiac Dealers of Southern California (the *Times* regularly promoted tours of city attractions to local families, many of whom were new to the area). Corriganville was included on the tour along with the Lopez Adobe and the Mission San Fernando; the ranch received by far the most textual attention. Automobile and outdoor editor Lynn Rogers described Corriganville's attractions and extensive production facilities before noting, "Corriganville is the sightseers' conception of Hollywood and scenic Southern California wrapped into one big outdoor package."[56]

Furthermore, Corriganville was thoroughly and deliberately woven into the San Fernando Valley's recreational life in the postwar period, especially that of children. Valley-based benevolent societies, fraternal and social organizations, historic preservation groups, and recreational equestrian associations frequently rented Corriganville for their meetings, events, and annual reunions. In 1951, the Kiwanis Clubs of Southern California sponsored a National Kids Day observance including a picnic and western celebration there. For many of the children, who had grown up watching western movies, horseback rides were the highlight of the day. Four-year-old Diane Hymes was especially lucky because she got to ride with Crash Corrigan on his trained horse.[57] Five hundred young members of the Camp Fire Girls and Bluebirds of Compton—then a solidly white, working-class community—also visited Corriganville in fall 1952 on a trip sponsored by the Compton Council, which arranged for the girls to see a rodeo, Silvertown, and Indian caves.[58] In May 1960, the Glendale YMCA's Summer Adventure Club included a visit to Corriganville as one of its excursions, as did the Orange County Association for Retarded Children and the Monterey Park Recreation Department in the summer of 1963.[59] Nor did young boys and girls have to travel all the way to Chatsworth, at the far end of the San Fernando Valley, to enjoy the Corriganville experience. Corriganville's actors and employees frequently appeared at civic events throughout the city. As a feature of Boy Scout Week at the Shrine Auditorium in downtown Los Angeles in 1957, for example, Rex Allen and stunt men from Corriganville "brought the house down" when they staged a reenactment of the famed "Fight at the OK Corral."[60]

The fantasy of western-themed recreation was not equally available to everyone, however. Corriganville, like most recreational areas in the United States at that time including other theme parks such as Disneyland, was a segregated, whites-only facility. Murray's Dude Ranch in Apple Valley attempted to fill this void and catered specifically to African American celebrities and vacationing black families, who were barred from other dude ranches in the area like Corriganville and faced segregated recreational facilities throughout the city. Owners Nolie and Lela Murray, who had lived in central Los Angeles, bought the thirty-five-acre ranch for one hundred dollars in 1922 and opened the dude ranch as a retreat for underprivileged and troubled urban children. Murray's Dude Ranch became extraordinarily popular after Herb Jeffries filmed two black musical westerns, *The Bronze Buckaroo* and *Harlem Rides the Range*, there in 1938. Over the years, African American entertainers, professionals, and athletes including Lena Horne, Bill "Bojangles" Robinson, architect Paul Williams, and boxer Joe Louis stayed at the ranch for rest, relaxation, and in Louis's case, training for upcoming matches. During World War II, when the Victorville USO refused to admit an African American National Guard unit, the Murrays began to host entertainment at their ranch and, in Lela Murray's words, "promptly killed business at the USO." Singer Pearl Bailey was one of those brought to entertain at the ranch, and she purchased it from the Murrays in 1955.[61] The Murrays' ranch was an important exception, however, to a larger pattern whereby the rural western lifestyle was enacted as the exclusive province of suburban whites in the San Fernando Valley through housing restrictions and legal segregation. As a result, although people of all racial backgrounds watched and delighted in western films, white suburbanites alone could claim legitimate symbolic as well as literal ownership of the mythic West produced in their backyards.

Locally based western cultural producers played a key role in this emerging political culture. For all its celebration of the working-class and rural cowboy or homesteader hero, the people who actually crafted the western myth in Los Angeles were decidedly elite and politically powerful. Western actors, actresses, directors, and producers were consistently among the most highly paid and influential people in the country — but they lived, worked, played, and invested in suburban Los Angeles. As a result, their influence operated on at least two geographic scales, national and local. Western celebrities and the iconography and ideology they espoused played a critical role in the San Fernando Valley's developing postwar political culture and especially its conservative social movements.

For one thing, the economic influence of western film stars was tremendous, and resident western celebrities typically invested their profits locally. For example, the economic conglomerate Roy Rogers Enterprises, owned by Chatsworth residents Roy Rogers and Dale Evans, grossed $35 million annually during the mid-1950s. They invested their fortune in such moneymaking ventures as the Roy Rogers Theme Park, located in Victorville, California, on the outskirts of Los Angeles; and Rogersdale, a western-themed entertainment and retail project in Temecula, approximately sixty miles southeast of Los Angeles.[62] Between 1947 and 1954, Roy Rogers and Gene Autry both topped the list of the *Motion Picture Herald*'s wealthiest movie stars. Gene Autry was also consistently included on *Fortune* magazine's "Wealthiest Men in America" list, and by the mid-1990s his net worth was estimated at $300 million. A renowned philanthropist, Autry regularly donated to social causes such as the Red Cross and provided millions for the construction of the Autry Museum of Western Heritage (now the Autry National Center) in Griffith Park, California. In his two biggest ventures, Autry also purchased the Los Angeles Angels (later the California Angels) baseball team franchise and the local television station KTLA in 1961.[63]

The political influence of western film stars on electoral politics and the directions of American domestic and foreign policy since the 1960s have been equally profound. The Autry National Center even devoted a 2008 exhibit, titled "Cowboys and Presidents," to the topic. The exhibit's curators explained that American presidents, from Teddy Roosevelt to George W. Bush, have long used the iconographic symbol of the cowboy to define themselves and their administrations to the nation and the world. While the cowboy character has a nearly universal and bipartisan appeal, it has been a particularly powerful vehicle for the rise of the New Right beginning in the 1960s.[64] Perhaps the most renowned of these "cowboy presidents" is Ronald Reagan. Although he played the cowboy role in only a few of his forty-odd films, it was in that role that he made the biggest impression. He capitalized on his association with the cowboy in his successful 1966 bid for governor of California and again in his 1980 presidential campaign. Indeed, Reagan's entire political career spanned the period when fascination with the American West reached its height among the baby boomer generation. As historian Gary Wills has noted in his cultural history of Reagan's life and appeal, one reason Reagan was so popular was his great talent as a storyteller, which enabled him to bring Americans together under a comforting mythology of the past and an optimistic vision of the future.[65] In this regard, he was particularly successful in narrating the frontier West as the nation's origin story. In March 1983, Reagan was invited to open the exhibit The American Cowboy at the Library of Congress. During his speech, Reagan remarked that the exhibit contained elements of fact and fantasy, both of which, he claimed, were equally important to the development of American culture. Reagan observed, "Among the horse-hair lassos and Remington sculptures and Gene Autry songs is a part of our national identity. Tales of Wild West men and women from Kit Carson to Wild Bill Hickok to Calamity Jane to Annie Oakley are woven into the dreams of our youth and the standards we aim to live by in our adult lives. Ideals of courageous and self-reliant heroes, both men and women, are the stuff of Western lore."[66] Reagan personally embodied the mythology of the U.S. West through his ideological pronouncements in support of rugged individualism and against big government, even as his actual policy decisions reflect a more mixed record.

Reagan's influence and cowboy appeal was not only national but also decidedly local. Throughout his career, Ronald Reagan was very active in California politics and cultural life. As governor and then president, he spent much of his time at his Santa Barbara ranch, where he was an avid horseback rider (see figure 6). He even used the ranch in 1981 to sign the biggest tax cut in American history. Local activist groups in the San Fernando Valley also frequently requested his support. In 1972, for example, the Santa Susana Mountain Parks Association extended a personalized invitation to Reagan to attend their two-day country fair in Chatsworth, the proceeds of which would be used to purchase the land surrounding the Old Stagecoach Trail for a regional park (see chapter 5).

Other popular western stars — virtually all of them full-time residents of the San Fernando Valley — supported and guided the development of an emergent conservatism based on anticommunism, resistance to big government, and

FIGURE 6 Ronald and Nancy Reagan horseback riding, probably on their Santa Barbara ranch, in January 1981, shortly before his inauguration as U.S. president. Courtesy of the Los Angeles Public Library.

derision toward racial and sexual minorities and feminists.[67] In 1961, Roy Rogers, John Wayne, and Ronald Reagan (then employed as an actor in Hollywood) together supported the Southern California School of Anti-Communism during a televised six-night program at the Los Angeles Memorial Sports Arena. During Reagan's candidacy for governor, Autry and Rogers appeared at ballgames, rallies, and fund-raisers, and Andy Devine, Roy Rogers's sidekick, accompanied Reagan to several of his speeches in Orange County. Roy Rogers and Dale Evans, evangelists with a Disciples of Christ background, similarly touted their beliefs on radio, on television, and in a series of evangelical books meant to inspire conservative lifestyles and political activism. They used their media access to lend their support for Nixon's escalation of the war in Vietnam, televangelist Pat Robertson's presidential bid, and Ronald Reagan's campaigns for governor and president.[68]

Singing cowboys, who bridged the visual media of western film and television with the auditory culture of country music, played an especially important role as leaders of the conservative movement because of their multimedia exposure to the children of the baby boom generation. Such figures were, according to historian Peter La Chappelle, "endowed with deep financial pockets and the ability to easily generate publicity," which enabled them to use their cultural influence in the name of local, regional, and national politics.[69] Gene Autry had particularly expansive power to promote conservatism through his television empire, earning him George H. W. Bush's designation as one of the "stars of the GOP galaxy." The *Gene Autry Show*, on the CBS network, was wildly popular among baby boomers. Through his ownership of KTLA, Autry gave future Orange County congressman Bob Dornan his start as a talk show host, telling the *Washington Post*, "He's a great spokesman for conservatism." Dornan was a leader of the New Right who would later virulently attack "lesbian spearchuckers" and "betraying little Jews." Singing cowboy Tex Ritter campaigned for Ronald Reagan during his campaign for the California governor seat and for presidential hopefuls Barry Goldwater and Richard Nixon. Ritter also befriended and vocally supported strict segregationist George Wallace, arguing on one occasion that while Wallace may have been farther right than he was, at least Wallace and his fellow conservative hardliners hadn't shot any policemen. Ritter attacked Democrats in general as "socialists" and believed the New Left to be a cancer. He argued, "America is soiled, and she can't be cleaned up by kowtowing to any small, destructive minority voice."[70] After relocating to Tennessee for a radio job, Ritter campaigned unsuccessfully for a seat in the U.S. Senate, during which he emphasized his support for school prayer and Nixon's foreign war-making policies in Southeast Asia.

Finally, western celebrities exerted political influence at the local level through honorary political positions in the San Fernando Valley. Beginning in the early 1940s, community boosters established a tradition of naming celebrities as honorary mayors of their developing communities, likely as a way to lure would-be home buyers and commercial investors. Gene Autry was honorary mayor of North Hollywood, while Andy Devine was mayor of Van Nuys from 1940 to 1956. Sunland resident Arthur "Slim" Vaughn, a western film star dubbed the "Southwest Tumbleweed" who also played the gold prospector at Knott's Berry Farm for ten years, was the honorary mayor of Sunland in 1958.[71] Cowboy rider Montie Montana was the San Fernando Valley's honorary sheriff.[72] In 1961, no fewer than twenty movie stars held such positions.[73]

In each of these ways, the Valley's resident western celebrities provided the framework and leadership for an emergent political conservatism that soon became dominant in national politics. And at a broader level, ideologies of the western frontier were embedded within the everyday life of a generation of suburbanites in the San Fernando Valley who were almost exclusively white, newly property owners, and upwardly mobile. Together, these conditions generated the growth of a grassroots suburban conservatism, centered on the preservation of the rural past and all that it signified — nationally, racially, economically, and culturally. The San Fernando Valley's grassroots suburban conservatism manifested itself in social movements focused on the preservation of the Valley's rural landscapes. I examine two such movements in the next two chapters.

PART TWO

Consolidating Rural Whiteness, 1960–2000

CHAPTER FOUR

Protecting Rurality through Horse-Keeping in the Northeast Valley

In 1966, Glenn Haschenburger, an activist from the semirural community of Shadow Hills at the northeast end of the San Fernando Valley, explained the reasons for his neighborhood's activism to a reporter from the *Los Angeles Times*. Just a few years earlier, Shadow Hills had been designated the city's first "horse-raising zone," which guaranteed minimum lot sizes of twenty thousand square feet (approximately one-half acre), zoning for horses and other livestock on suburban lots, and the indefinite protection of the neighborhood's "rural atmosphere." Activists there were struggling to preserve their new zoning in the face of the San Fernando Valley's tremendous population growth and pressures for housing, industry, and services. As Haschenburger explained, "We should be able to keep and ride horses in designated areas of the city. And we shouldn't have to live 30 miles out of the city to pursue our interests. That's what our fight is all about — just a little corner of Los Angeles."[1]

Haschenburger was one of many suburbanites who mobilized in the postwar era to preserve the San Fernando Valley's rural landscapes. His biography and path to activism is typical. A native of Nebraska, Haschenburger had moved to the Valley in 1948, when he was transferred to Los Angeles by the pharmaceutical company for which he worked supervising defense contracts. He had learned about horsemanship in the countryside near his parents' farm in Nebraska. In Los Angeles, he became involved in equestrian activities, first at the local level in Shadow Hills and then, after his retirement in 1970, in national organizations such as Equestrian Trails, Inc., for which he served as president from 1975 to 1976.[2] Like his neighbors and peers, Haschenburger perceived the Valley's rapid development and growing density as threats to his social status and quality of life, and he sought to protect the rural landscapes in which he and so many others had invested, both materially and symbolically. Organizing in property owners associations, equestrian clubs, historic preservation groups, and parks and recreation task forces, he and thousands like him articulated the importance of preserving the Valley's mythical and material rural past.

Their arguments drew directly from — indeed, had been cultivated by — the historic investments in rurality made by the urban state, capital, and cultural producers during the first half of the twentieth century, explored in the previous three chapters. Along with resistance to school and residential integration, support for freezing property tax revenues through California's Proposition 13, and repeated attempts to secede from the city of Los Angeles, mobilization to protect the Valley's rural landscapes constituted a collective — and largely successful — attempt by suburban homeowners to ward off many dimensions of unwanted social change.[3]

Rural land-use activism in the San Fernando Valley during this period illustrates the ways in which the social and spatial construction of whiteness changed in the 1960s and 1970s, from explicit discrimination to the "color-blind" production of racial privilege and inequality. During this period, in response to pressures from civil rights movements, the racial state shifted toward a position of discursive, if not fully substantive, nondiscrimination in the allocation of social goods and resources.[4] At the local level, white suburban activists responded to the federal state's shifting position in kind. In such diverse American metropolitan regions as Baltimore, Charlotte, Detroit, Atlanta, and Orange County, white suburban activists — often called the Silent Majority — mobilized to resist school and residential integration, the construction of public housing, efforts to increase taxes, and other forms of liberal government intervention.[5] Thomas Sugrue argues that these political movements were a logical outgrowth of racially exclusive New Deal policies in housing, education, and transportation, which had collectively bred an unprecedented sense of white entitlement — part of what he calls a "rights revolution" — to the state's protection of personal welfare, segregation, and continued upward mobility.[6] As Matt Lassiter observes, "Through the populist revolt of the Silent Majority, millions of white homeowners who had achieved a residentially segregated and federally subsidized version of the American Dream forcefully rejected race-conscious liberalism as an unconstitutional exercise in social engineering and an unprecedented violation of free-market meritocracy."[7] However, from the 1940s onward, suburban activists, too, increasingly incorporated the language of "color-blindness" into their campaigns, often emphasizing the protection of "lifestyle" instead of explicit white supremacy. Explicit discrimination gave way to a color-blind discourse that emphasized the defense of families, schools, and neighborhoods and the protection of "individual rights" (in contrast to "civil rights" and "special interests"). Kevin Kruse aptly characterizes this political development as "the decline of white supremacy and the rise of white suburbia."[8]

Yet the evolution of postwar racial politics proceeded in regionally specific ways. Postwar grassroots suburban activism looked and functioned differently in diverse parts of the country depending on the ways in which regional racial formations had been historically constructed and spatially produced. In the U.S. South, as Lassiter argues, the growth of the metropolitan Sunbelt replaced the rural Black Belt as the center of southern political power, ensuring that the interests of corporate capital and white suburbs took precedence over the traditional culture of white supremacy, and contributing to a color-blind, middle-class outlook of individual consumer rights and meritocratic individualism; these developments, in turn, "played a crucial role in the fading of southern distinctiveness" and the evolution of the New South.[9] In the U.S. West, ideologies about rural land and the frontier myth, which positioned the West as regenerative of basic characteristics of whiteness and American identity, were critical to the growth of the region's cities before World War II; these same mythologies and ideologies indelibly shaped the region's shifting political culture, including the rise of suburban grassroots politics, in the postwar period. Narratives of the western frontier and of rural land provided a powerful vehicle within which suburban white activists successfully mobilized to preserve historic patterns of white privilege, while conforming to — and helping to shape — the emerging discursive mandates of color-blind racial politics. Among the San Fernando Valley's rural land-use activists, rights-based rhetoric and discourses of victimization were articulated in reference to ideologies of the frontier West, the Spanish fantasy past, and gentleman farming that were everywhere visible in white suburbanites' lives.

In Shadow Hills as well as the other communities that went on to create horse-keeping districts, these multiple linked ideologies merged in the body and symbolism of the horse, which represented to activists a threatened rural way of life. Horses are a central symbolic element of the western frontier experience. For example, in her study of the symbolic white mustang that appears in countless novels, films, and other genres of western Americana, anthropologist Elizabeth Lawrence argues that "the story of the White Mustang expresses the freedom-captivity or savagery-civilization dichotomy that is intimately tied to the Western frontier mystique and seems to take on the universality of the nature-culture dilemma in a wider sense."[10] By taming the mythical white mustang stallion, the frontiersmen of diverse cultural representations were symbolically assured of their success in conquering the West's harsh climate, Indian opponents, and "wild" land.[11]

Because of their centrality to myths of the West, horses were critical to western film production. Cinematic horses helped cowboys to escape from antagonists or save women and children in distress. Moreover, an on-screen cowboy's relationship with his horse helped to define his character and ultimately determined whether a film would be successful. H. F. Hintz argues that "western movies would never have been successful without the horses," and that horses were especially important in attracting the young audiences upon which B westerns, in particular, depended.[12] Often horses received equal billing alongside their human counterparts. Roy Rogers's Trigger, deemed "the smartest horse in the movies," is perhaps the best-known example of this trend. Horses were so important to western films that many studios had separate horse casting directors, who were typically experienced horse trainers, like Bill Jones at Republic Studios.[13] The stables and ranches that supplied these horses to the studios were all located in the San Fernando Valley and its outskirts. These included the Fat Jones Stable in North Hollywood and later Northridge; the Hudkins Brothers Stable and the Spanish riding school, both in North Hollywood; Golden State Rodeo Company in Chatsworth; Tom Mitchell's ranch in Simi Valley; and Andy Jauregui's facility in Newhall, among others.[14]

Yet the horse is a contradictory figure. Alongside its centrality to myths of the frontier West, the horse has also long been a marker of status, wealth, and nobility. As anthropologist Stephen Budiansky argues, "The nature of the horse and its special role in human society guaranteed that, alone among domesticated animals, it would be a consumptive rather than a productive resource."[15] Although horses have been extensively used for transportation, freight, and agriculture, their role in ancient societies was generally more consumptive and performative, ensuring that only those with disposable income would be able to own and care for them. As early as 1250, a knight-farrier wrote to Emperor Frederick the Second that "no animal is more noble than the horse, since it is by horses that princes, magnates, and knights are separated from lesser people."[16] In diverse human societies, from medieval Europe to the Plains Indians in North America, the horse — and especially the possession of large numbers of horses — has been used to construct distinctions among social classes. Images of armed foremen on horseback guarding plantation slaves, prisoners working the fields in the shadow of a mounted guard under the auspices of the convict lease system in the U.S. South, and efforts to minimize access to horses among indigenous neophytes in the Spanish missions throughout the U.S. Southwest, except for a privileged few who served as models for conversion, all attest to how the horse has been used as a tool of power and social control. The contemporary practice of thoroughbred racehorse breeding further indicates the association of the horse with a wealthy and powerful social elite.[17]

Thus, the horse is simultaneously a symbol of the American frontier experience and a marker of wealth, status, and political power. These symbolic contradictions were embedded in the San Fernando Valley's postwar horse-oriented leisure culture. The horse shows, rodeos, and other events that saturated recreational life in Los Angeles County in the 1950s and 1960s encouraged participants to engage in fantasies of the frontier, which rest on constructions of working-class cowboys and rugged frontiermen. Yet equestrian-themed recreation was also the province of a newly prosperous middle class with time and money to spare. As we shall see in this and future chapters, such contradictions also emerged in the social movements, past and present, that were intent on protecting and institutionalizing horse-keeping in the San Fernando Valley.

Horse-oriented recreation was extremely popular in Los Angeles's postwar leisure and tourism industries and engaged both locals and visitors equally. For example, the weekly horse auctions held on Friday nights in Downey were popular places not just to purchase horses but also as places where Angelenos could dress up in western clothes and "just go to look — and maybe be looked at — playing like they're back in the old days of the West."[18] A 1947 issue of *Equestrian* magazine, published in Van Nuys, featured a contest with the top prize of an all-expense-paid trip to "Movieland, entertainment and excursions with the stars, including visits to the scenes of great pictures in the making; OR, ten days of rest and roughing it on a California ranch, in the custom and famous hospitality of old California ranch tradition."[19] The horse shows held at the Kellogg Ranch in Pomona were deemed "must-see" tourist attractions; it was estimated that nearly ten thousand visitors attended the Arabian horse demonstrations and competitions in October and November 1958 alone.[20]

Rodeos, which narrate through performance the conquest of the frontier, were especially popular with suburban audiences. The first documented rodeo took place in Los Angeles in 1922, when Tex Ritter (who also penned the first song titled "San Fernando Valley," examined in chapter 3) hosted the first "cowboy contest" in Hollywood. In 1938, the Rodeo Association of America held numerous contests in Southern California, with the biggest events in Palm Springs, Saugus, El Monte, and downtown Los Angeles. Around the same time, Ray Beach, a Canadian rodeo rider and jockey, built a permanent arena in the working-class white suburb of Southgate and held weekly rodeos there for many years. At other times, Beach hosted rodeos up and down Pacific Coast Highway, sometimes right on the sand. Throughout the 1940s and 1950s, participants and spectators flocked to the amateur and professional rodeos held both within the city and on its desert outskirts (see figure 7). Los Angeles was such an important center of rodeo competition that the city was chosen to host the National Finals Rodeo for three years, from 1962 to 1964, just a few years after the national organization was founded.[21]

Horse shows, too, were a major part of Los Angeles's postwar leisure culture. Nearly every weekend throughout the 1950s, equestrian organizations and saddle clubs hosted competitions. Frequently, these events were fund-raisers for local charities. The Flintridge Riding Club, for example, hosted some of the oldest and also the most prestigious horse shows for children beginning in 1922. Many of their shows drew horses and riders from throughout California and the West. By 1960, a national horse show held at the Sports Arena was expected to surpass even the annual equestrian classic at Madison Square Garden in New York, awarding prize money totaling nearly seventy-seven thousand dollars and sponsored by a corporation organized specifically to coordinate the event.[22] Horse shows were held at the Pan Pacific Auditorium, the Los Angeles Sports Arena, and Devonshire Downs in the San Fernando Valley (which would

FIGURE 7 Sheriff's Rodeo at the Los Angeles Coliseum in August 1955. More than seventy-one thousand spectators were present. Equestrian events such as rodeos and horse shows were extremely popular in Los Angeles during the late 1940s and 1950s. Courtesy of the Herald Examiner Collection, Los Angeles Public Library.

later become part of the campus of California State University, Northridge), as well as other smaller venues around the city and in unlikely places such as the Sawtelle Baseball Fields.[23] These horse shows increasingly had corporate backing as well as cosponsorship by civic organizations, and some solicited the participation of movie and television stars from Hollywood westerns. In 1947, for instance, the Los Angeles Horse Show featured more than five hundred competitors and promised the event would be "a mecca for those of prominence in civic, stage, screen, and radio activities."[24] Similarly, the Devonshire Horse Show held in June 1961 at Devonshire Downs in Northridge featured not just competitive events but also entertainment by "noted horsemen and horsewomen, Western television and film stars and public officials."[25] A few months later, John Wayne presented the top prize to the winner of the Junior Western Pleasure Horse Championship at the Long Beach Community Hospital auxiliary benefit horse show.[26]

These activities both drew from and expanded a widespread investment in horses as a symbol of the western frontier experience, but they occurred in Los Angeles's expanding postwar suburbs, and their participants were upwardly mobile suburban homeowners and their children. By 1960, the California Outdoor Recreation Committee estimated that there were 267,326 horses in the state — a number it assumed to be a vast undercount — with 33,000 in the San Fernando Valley alone.[27] While some of these were TV and film horses, the majority were "backyard horses" — those kept on suburban property, sometimes illegally, or stabled at any of the many commercial stables popping up throughout the Southland. And just as the massive wartime human migration to Los Angeles strained the city's housing supply and infrastructure, the city was equally unprepared for the booming suburban horse population. News stories about horses that escaped from stables around the city and created various types of social chaos, causing traffic jams and running into cars on busy streets and even freeways, flooded newspapers in the 1950s.[28] In 1954, the Public Health and Welfare Committee of the Los Angeles City Council initiated a study of horse-keeping conditions in the city, responding to traffic caused by horses and wagons competing with cars on city streets and to the dangers of runaway horses being hit by cars.[29] Horses and stables could be found in almost every suburban community across the city, even where there was no "official" zoning for horses, so that in 1962, the Regional Planning Commission of Los Angeles County singled out the stabling of horses in residential zones as a major problem. A concern to provide proper infrastructure and land-use designations for the city's growing equestrian population, therefore, had already emerged among city agencies by the mid-1950s.

Suburban horse owners from throughout Los Angeles County created numerous local and statewide equestrian organizations to represent and pursue their interests. By the mid-1950s, equestrian groups had sprung up in places across Southern California as diverse as Pomona, Flintridge, Malibu, Sawtelle, West Hills, and Compton. Many of the new equestrian clubs were organized specifically for children, reflecting the commonly held and long-standing belief that children's exposure to and care for animals would help them to become democratic, responsible, and independent adults. Such organizations ran the gamut from elite associations for children who owned and competed with their own horses, such as the Flintridge Children's Riding Club, to groups for middle-class kids who did not own their own horses and rented them from local stables. The *Los Angeles Times* featured a story on girls and horses, which noted the many horseback riding opportunities available in the city for female youth of different class backgrounds such as Beaumarie St. Clair, a Malibu resident who rode her horse, Snookie, on the beaches every day; Ellen Senn of Thousand Oaks, who had received her horse, Swamp Fox, as a Christmas present; and Linda Weldon, who rented a horse from the Flintridge Riding Club or borrowed one from a friend almost every week; at age twenty-four, Weldon was called a "girl" and gently chastised in the article for focusing on horse-keeping instead of housekeeping.[30] Sometimes, these youth organizations incorporated military structures, symbols, and practices. For example, the California Rangers, a paramilitary organization founded in 1945, was modeled on the equestrian cavalry of the late 1800s, especially Teddy Roosevelt's Rough Riders, which played a central role in the Spanish-American War. The organization remains active to this day; since its founding, California Rangers has held weekly practices at stables in Shadow Hills and Lakeview Terrace, where children rent horses for the night or ride their own, riding in from the surrounding neighborhoods as I did on my pony Tara for nearly ten years. Rangers wear military-style uniforms and progress through ranks with such names as "Trooper" and "Stable Sergeant" as they learn how to ride and take care of horses.[31] A similar organization, the Blue Shadows, was organized in 1957; like the California Rangers, it remains active and still attracts young people interested in horses to its stables in Lakeview Terrace and Agua Dulce, on the northern edge of Santa Clarita.[32] The Glory Riders, a youth organization in Whittier, taught children ages six to sixteen how to care for and ride horses. Members attended lectures on Mondays and participated in mounted drills on Fridays.[33]

The growth of these youth organizations points to a commonly held belief that horseback riding and horse care led directly to a decline in youth delinquency and, by extension, the cultivation of the ideals and values of democratic citizenship.[34] In February 1947, the *Los Angeles Times* profiled fourteen-year-old Johnny McFadden, from Shadow Hills, who took "complete care of Buddy [his horse], feeding and grooming him, and every month [rode] him at the Shadow Hills Saddle Club show, where youngsters stage[d] their own shows." The author mused, "It's a wonderful thing for a youngster to associate himself with animals, and Johnny exemplifies the result of character building from the companionship with his pets."[35] Similarly, Casey Tibbs, a rodeo champion in the saddle bronc competition, was quoted by Bill Brown, reporter for the *Los Angeles Examiner*, as saying, "If every kid could own a horse we'd have little juvenile delinquency."[36] Brown himself reached the same conclusion, though he realized that horse ownership was an economically biased opportunity: "Nobody has ever suggested with any sincerity owning a horse is not expensive. But neither is keeping a boat, a summer cabin, or supporting a golf habit. . . . And one more point: Feeding and currying a horse at dawn and dusk is not calculated to produce juvenile delinquency."[37] For Brown, as well as for the countless suburban parents who invested in a horse or pony for their child or perhaps paid for weekly riding lessons, the costs involved were well worth the rewards of creating disciplined young citizens.

Whether aimed at children or adults, many of the Southland's new equestrian organizations performed and celebrated elements of the Spanish fantasy past. Their recreational activities complemented the historical narratives examined in chapter 2, which were being published at approximately the same time and used tropes of the romantic Spanish mission experience to lure suburban home buyers and inculcate them with an appropriate sense of local history. One such organization was the El Camino Real Horse Trails Association. The majority of the club's membership claimed to trace their ancestry to "pioneer" California.[38] Their main priority was to establish a statewide trail system that would closely follow the historic path between the Spanish missions in California. In a profile of the organization and its objectives, the *Los Angeles Examiner* predicted that the "romantic days in early California, when colorfully costumed riders galloped up and down El Camino Real, [would] again become part of the Southland scene."[39] In March 1948, the San Fernando Valley Horse Owners Association (SFVHOA) sponsored a "Restoration Ride" to raise funds for the restoration of Mission San Fernando. Members dressed in "the costumes of early California" and ate an "authentic early California dinner" on the mission grounds, accompanied by civic officials and officers of the Friends of the San Fernando Mission.[40] Both the SFVHOA and the El Camino Real Horse Trails Association sponsored regular sermons on horseback, "as . . . given by the padres decades ago," followed by barbecues and picnics, with the proceeds typically donated to local charitable organizations such as the orthopedic hospital.[41] An elite Palm Springs organization, Vaqueros del Desierto, was comprised of Anglo-American urban businessmen from Los Angeles who turned their three-to-five-day overnight horseback rides into luxury affairs. Joking that members would not be as effective at their business desks after completion of their five-day ride in October 1941, the *Los Angeles Examiner* described the ride as follows: "Unbounded in their zest for the outdoor life as the pioneers lived it — barring certain small comforts like air mattresses, music and entertainment, chefs de cuisine and other trivia — Los Vaqueros del Desierto comprise a list of legal, business, and social leaders who every year ride from ranch to ranch for a wholesome and often hilarious vacation."[42] The daily tribulations of the Vaqueros del Desierto were frequently highlighted in the *Examiner* as members completed their luxurious multiday rides. As members of equestrian organizations such as these performed the Spanish fantasy narrative on horseback, they participated in the larger project of justifying the Anglo-American conquest of Spanish, Mexican, and indigenous land and peoples.

Los Angeles's equestrian organizations were not merely recreational or social associations, however. Rather, they constituted a well-organized and influential political constituency with a distinctive land-use agenda. For example, the California State Horsemen's Association, founded in 1944, counted twenty-seven thousand members in 1950.[43] One of the more active regional chapters of this statewide organization was the San Fernando Valley Horse Owners Association, which was devoted to developing horseback riding trails in Los Angeles County as well as sponsoring recreational equestrian events for its booming membership. Similarly, Equestrian Trails, Inc. (ETI), was founded in 1944 with a charter "dedicated to the acquisition and preservation of trails, good horsemanship, and equine legislation."[44] ETI is a national organization that in the postwar period had chapters (or "corrals," as they are called) in Glendale, Altadena, Griffith Park, Shadow Hills, Glendora, and Compton — all of which were solidly middle-class and white suburban communities through the end of the 1950s, and which self-consciously blended elements of rural and suburban life into their landscapes and local cultures.

One of the primary missions of these groups was the creation of a statewide equestrian trail system. By 1945, the El Camino Real Horse Trails Association and ETI had garnered support for the statewide trail project among elected representatives at both the city and the state level. In March of that year, California Supreme Court justice Jesse Carter appeared at a meeting of the California State Horsemen's Association to announce that Assembly Bill 630, which would authorize funds for the construction of a statewide trail system, was pending before the state legislature and had the full support of Governor Earl Warren and the state parks commissioner. The trail system was imagined as both a tourist attraction and an employment opportunity for workers laid off from defense industries during peacetime demobilization.[45] On February 1, 1946, the California State Park Commission met and gave strong support to the proposed $1.5 million Master Loop Riding and Hiking Trail, and appointed the special Hiking and Riding Trails Project Committee to secure three hundred thousand dollars from the state legislature to begin work on construction of the trail.[46] Los Angeles County by this time had already begun drafting plans for a countywide trail system that would include two hundred miles of trails.[47] In 1951, regional groups of the California State Horsemen's Association agreed to work together to coordinate the trail system through thirty-seven of the state's fifty-two counties.[48]

The construction of a statewide trail system was no small financial or bureaucratic matter, however, and by the late 1950s the project still appeared to be in its infancy, pointing to the difficulties of preserving open space in booming metropolitan areas, working across political jurisdictions, and carving trails through occasionally resistant communities. Apparently, the proposed trail system encountered resistance from areas where horseback riding clashed with other forms of suburban recreation and outdoor living. For example, residents in Arcadia and Monrovia (both located in the foothills of eastern Los Angeles County) opposed the trail system, which would cross through their neighborhoods, on the grounds that the proposed trails passed too close to homes, that horses could be dangerous to small children playing in suburban yards, and that riders had already torn up landscaping. They also argued that cigarettes dropped by horseback riders constituted a fire hazard and that dust and flies posed a health hazard. The Los Angeles County Board of Supervisors ordered a restudy of the proposed trail system and required the Los Angeles County Regional Planning Commission to hold public hearings on the matter.[49] But the trails project more or less evaporated amid the exigencies of postwar planning. In 1968, when the Department of City Planning and the Department of Recreation and Parks issued a joint report on equestrian and hiking trails, only sixty-three miles of official trails had been constructed in the county, forty-five miles of which were within city limits — a far cry from the two hundred miles originally proposed for the county.

Despite the slow pace and limitations of the statewide trails project, the willingness of government agencies at various levels to support the equestrian agenda suggests that recreational horse-owner groups had become an organized and formidable political constituency. The editors of *Equestrian Magazine* acknowledged the potential political power of Los Angeles's equestrian associations: "With added incomes, and financial stability, [equestrian] association leaders lean towards channels that will make their individual position more secure and, at the same time, solidify the popularity of the breed of animals they happen to be sponsoring." In order for that power to be maximized, the writers encouraged solidarity among diverse horse owners in the face of pending social change. In particular, they urged readers to work across some of the differences within the horse-keeping world that, importantly, represented the multiple symbolisms of the horse, such as western-style riding (with its associations with the frontier and the U.S. West) and English-style riding (which is associated with an East Coast fox-hunting tradition and thoroughbred horse racing). The magazine opined: "It should be the aim and object of every association, whether fostering horses or comprised of horsemen, to further the interest of *all* horsemen. There is too much controversy between the English rider and the Western rider, the Saddlebred owner and the Stock Horse enthusiast, the Trail Club and the Hunt Club. Only as a whole can we combat the negative forces that are constantly seeking to tear our beloved horses from our hearts, to rid our country of the most noble of all animals."[50] For the staff of *Equestrian Magazine*, writing in the aftermath of World War II and amid the cold war, horses symbolized American values, and the practice of horse-keeping was a patriotic exercise in supporting those values. These links had been cultivated by the long-standing association of horses with the myth of western heritage and the lived social history of conquest and expansion into the U.S. West.

Among the most worrisome of those "negative forces" identified by the magazine as a major threat to horse-keeping and, by extension, to national values, was the rezoning of agricultural land for residential use to accommodate relatively high-density subdivisions and commercial properties. This process was taking place throughout the San Fernando Valley, as builders, developers, and planners struggled to accommodate a rapidly growing population. *Equestrian Magazine* offered as an example of these forces a case pending in a white section of Pacoima, where home and horse owners were witnessing the demise of their lifestyle along with the neighborhood's population expansion and racial transition. The editors characterized the Pacoima Saddle Club as "a group of earnest and honest horsemen and women who have developed and fostered their club so that their children might be kept from the ways of evil by cultivating a sport which is not only healthful but all consuming of spare time. This group of California citizens constructed their own arena for their amateur (non-profit) shows and through the past two years this arena has been the gathering place of the children of Pacoima and surrounding areas." The editors' narrative echoes common rhetorical themes among horse owners, particularly the appeal to the horse as a symbol of virtuous, republican citizenship that is, in turn, linked to myths of the rural frontier West. These virtues were endangered because, according to the magazine's coverage, "Now our Los Angeles zoning office has informed the club that they must dispose of their ring! Pacoima citizens want this club to continue. They know the fine work it has done to make their citizens good ones and, at the present time, the matter is before the city planning commission and a change of zone is being contemplated. It is to be hoped our city leaders will act wisely and for the good of the citizens rather than the individual who might have a commercial reasons for wishing the zoning restrictive to the Pacoima club ring." The editors offered this story as "a small example of why horsemen should stick together to preserve the younger generation and foster their love of horseflesh."[51]

In response to incidents such as these, as well as the broader changes they portended, equestrian organizations focused their energies on the preservation of the San Fernando Valley's historic rural landscapes. Though first and foremost recreational associations, these organizations also cohered white middle-class and elite suburban residents around a distinctive rural land-use agenda. Through their involvement in equestrian organizations, many members became involved in more explicitly political activities, particularly as they saw their way of life increasingly threatened by land-use and other changes. Equestrian recreational groups fused members' concerns as horse owners and property owners, empowering them to push for land-use policies that would preserve the historic privileges of rural life within an urban context. During the 1960s and 1970s, four officially designated "horse-raising zones" were created in the city of Los Angeles: Shadow Hills, La Tuna Canyon, and Lakeview Terrace, all in the northeast end of the San Fernando Valley, and Chatsworth, in the west Valley. Equestrian areas were also established elsewhere in Los Angeles County, such as Burbank and Rancho Palos Verdes, during the same period. In the remainder of this chapter, I examine activism and the development of horse-oriented land-use policy in Shadow Hills, the first and oldest of these horse-raising districts, where activism to create and institutionalize horse-keeping points to significant changes in how whiteness was produced in and through the rural landscape in the San Fernando Valley after 1960.

Prior to World War II, Shadow Hills was a prototypical gentleman-farming community. In 1907, plots of land in Shadow Hills (then know as Hansen Heights) were advertised as "little farms near the city" and sold for $150 per acre.[52] The vast majority of incoming gentleman farmers were white migrants from the U.S. Midwest. Ethnically diverse but racially homogeneous, they tended to be middle aged or close to retirement and to bring with them substantial resources that they wanted to invest in Southern California.

As in other gentleman-farming communities in the San Fernando Valley before World War II, suburban agriculture in Hansen Heights rested on ethnic and racial distinctions that were, in turn, sustained by racialized land-use policies. A large Mexican American and Mexican immigrant *colonia* was located directly adjacent to Hansen Heights in the area now known as Sun Valley. Although many of Sun Valley's Mexican residents were listed as railroad workers in the 1920 census, some also likely worked for Hansen Heights farmers or in the olive-canning factories located just past Hansen Heights, in Sunland.[53] Manuel Machado was one of the only Mexican Americans to actually reside in Hansen Heights; he rented a house on Sunland Boulevard and hired himself out to local farmers.[54] By 1920, Hansen Heights was also home to a handful of Japanese farmers, although because of California's Alien Land Laws, most were tenants rather than landowners. Many of the Japanese farmers in Hansen Heights were flower growers, and some of them had distinctly large land holdings. The Kawakami family, for instance, grew fruit and carnations on their twenty-five acres, a holding significantly larger than the one to five acres owned or rented by most midwestern Anglo migrants.[55] Hansen Heights' Japanese farmers generally worked cooperatively among co-ethnics. Japanese truck farmers frequently rented rooms to other Japanese immigrants who worked for them as field laborers. Natangi and Termuo Takimoto, for example, immigrated from Japan in 1912 and raised four children in their rented house on Helen Street. Yahiora Kasa, who had immigrated much earlier, in 1899, worked for them as a general laborer.[56] Hansen Heights' Japanese Americans were also bound into the larger ethnic Japanese community in Los Angeles, which dominated the produce and flower industries during the 1920s and 1930s. For instance, Aiko Tsuneishi's father owned a grocery store in downtown Los Angeles near Union Station in the early 1930s, and once per week he rented a wagon to deliver staples such as beans and rice to Japanese grocers in the Sunland area.[57] By 1942, Japanese farmers owned or leased 115 ranches in the Tujunga Valley, which included the communities of Sunland, Tujunga, and Hansen Heights. In that year, they were ordered to vacate their farms under the auspices of Executive Order 9066 and were held at a Conservation Corps facility in Lakeview Terrace before being sent to permanent camps throughout the U.S. West. After the war, they were resettled in a trailer park in Sunland. Japanese Americans never regained the agricultural preeminence they had once enjoyed in the east Valley, but they did return to and expand their historic commercial and cultural centers in Pacoima and San Fernando.[58] Thus, as in the San Fernando Valley's other gentleman-farming districts, whites, Japanese Americans, and ethnic Mexican lived in ad-jacent but distinct communities in the north San Fernando Valley, structured by unequal possibilities and life chances.

For their part, like so many other new suburbanites in the San Fernando Valley, white Shadow Hills residents were deeply invested in the myth of the rural frontier. Numerous films, including some westerns, had been shot in the neighboring Sunland-Tujunga area, particularly at Sunland Park.[59] By the 1940s, an older generation of gentleman farmers and a new cadre of suburban hom-eowners together supported several local equestrian organizations. The Shadow Hills Saddle Club hosted frequent horse shows at its arena near the corner of Sunland and Wheatland boulevards, which attracted a local crowd, if not the re-gional and sometimes national audiences that a show at Flintridge could bring. Shadow Hills also had its own polo club, which competed often with the team from Beverly Hills, among others; as well as a local corral of ETI, which remains a popular group to this day. Many Shadow Hills residents were production peo-ple who worked in the film industry as creative directors, casting agents, and production assistants. Others were contractors, lawyers, defense workers, and engineers — all typical occupations for white Valley residents in the postwar period, and which gave activists a crucial level of technological and legal literacy that they would soon mobilize in the land-use planning process. As they saw the San Fernando Valley changing around them, these rural-urban profession-als successfully translated their professional expertise and film-industry con-nections into land-use policies that preserved the Valley's much-mythologized rural landscapes.

By the late 1940s, Shadow Hills had begun to experience substantial subur-ban development, although — owing to its remote location in the foothills of the northeast Valley and its hilly topography — not as rapidly or extensively as other places on the Valley floor. Local residents were worried by the rapid den-sification of the San Fernando Valley's former gentleman-farming districts and cinematic landscapes, which they believed would soon affect their neighbor-hood. They were particularly anxious because Shadow Hills was relatively close to the San Fernando Valley's historic minority district at San Fernando and Pacoima, which expanded rapidly in the postwar period, and which symbolized to Shadow Hills residents the linked nature of urbanization, integration, and decline.[60] The San Fernando Valley's first and only integrated public housing project, the Basilone Homes, was constructed in Pacoima in 1945 and housed returning GIs of diverse backgrounds. Afterward, in the private housing market some real-estate developers deliberately exploited the potential for creating a black enclave in Pacoima. The Joe Louis Homes, for example, catered to returning African American veterans and other members of the black middle class, who had difficulty finding sufficient housing in the overcrowded, segregated districts of South Los Angeles. Mexican Americans, too, created expanding residential districts around the historic *colonia* at San Fernando.[61]

Nonetheless, the nonwhite population of the Valley remained tiny. According to the 1950 U.S. Census, out of 402,538 Valley residents, only 2,654 (approximately 7/10 of 1 percent) were black and 2,189 (about 1/2 of 1 percent) were other nonwhites.[62] Even by 1964, the San Fernando Valley Welfare Council reported that Pacoima was the only neighborhood in the Valley with a black population larger than 1 percent.[63] Although blacks who moved to the Valley tended to be better educated and to have higher incomes than African Americans elsewhere in the city, those who attempted to buy homes in the Valley outside Pacoima were fiercely resisted. Sid Thompson, future superintendent of the Los Angeles Unified School District, was blocked from moving to Mission Hills to be closer to his job as a math teacher at Pacoima Junior High. He eventually managed to purchase property in Pacoima only because of the efforts of real-estate agent James Robinson, who sold homes to the area's new black teachers and business people. In 1962, Robinson became the first African American admitted to the San Fernando Valley Association of Realtors.[64]

Even within Pacoima, tensions flared between the growing black middle-class community and an established section of working-class and middle-class whites. Journalist Reuben Borough highlighted the social tensions surrounding a wealthy, mixed-race woman who had moved to Pacoima from Hawaii. She and her husband owned four adjacent house lots in Pacoima; they rented out three of the houses and lived in the fourth. In 1945, Mrs. Walker — who was half white, one-quarter American Indian, and one-quarter black — was evicted from a dance hosted by the Pacoima Saddle Club after she was seen dancing with several white men from the neighborhood, including her tenants; an angry white woman slapped one of her dance partners in the face, telling him he should be ashamed to dance with a colored woman. According to Borough, the Walkers' move to Pacoima symbolized the neighborhood's shift to a middle-class black enclave, and local whites were anxiously seeking to institute racially restrictive covenants in their community.[65] They were unsuccessful, however, and as the 1960s and 1970s wore on, the neighborhoods immediately adjacent to Pacoima and San Fernando — the communities of Sylmar, Arleta, Lakeview Terrace, and Sun Valley — began to transition from resolutely white and working class or middle class to majority black and Latino. Whites fled these neighborhoods during this period, moving to places where the rural landscape was legally protected. Increasingly, those places were outside the city of Los Angeles altogether, especially on the northern fringes of Los Angeles County — the communities of Palmdale, Lancaster, Santa Clarita, Antelope Valley, and beyond — the same places where western films had been produced in the 1950s.

Residents of Shadow Hills were worried by these transformations because of their geographical proximity to San Fernando and Pacoima and the adjacent "spillover" neighborhoods. They feared that the changes under way there would soon spread to their community. Their concerns were not without reason. The leaders of the northeast Valley's expanding black and Latino communities were trying hard to attract expanded commercial and industrial opportunities to create local jobs and shopping opportunities.[66] Also, Shadow Hills residents shared political districts (and thus political representatives) as well as a public school catchment area with Pacoima. Los Angeles City Council District 1 brought Pacoima together with the solidly white communities of Shadow Hills, Sunland, Tujunga, Sun Valley, and Lakeview Terrace. The district was remarkable during this period for having the highest percentage of owner-occupied dwellings (72 percent compared with 52 percent citywide) but also the youngest average age, lowest income levels, most affordable rental properties, and the only minority population of any significant size anywhere in the Valley.[67] Within the district, however, minority residents were considered a political throwaway, since they voted in very low numbers and rarely gave campaign contributions, and thus their needs were often overshadowed by the more vocal and politically empowered white residents of Shadow Hills and Sunland. Nonetheless, Shadow Hills residents worried that the election of a city council or school board representative who was committed to meeting Pacoima's needs would not support their own. They sought to create various kinds of rural land-use policy so that rurality would be institutionalized rather than subjected to the whims or commitments of political representatives, who could change with the seasons. The threats of urbanization, integration, and decline were fused in their minds and in the discourses they mobilized in their land-use activism.

Fewer than half of Shadow Hills residents owned horses at this time, but they universally recognized that the horse was a useful way to preserve the semirural landscape in which they had invested.[68] Shadow Hills residents mobilized the iconography of the horse as a symbol of western Americana, downplaying its elite associations, in the hopes of creating a "horse-keeping district" where large lot sizes and rural character would be indefinitely protected against the incursions of urbanity and the possible election of civil rights–minded political leaders. In the early 1960s, a coalition of local attorneys and members of ETI Corral 20 pushed the Los Angeles City Council to establish special "horse-raising" zones in neighborhoods with at least 1 million square feet of agricultural zoning and where 90 percent of property owners voted for it. The new horse districts would have a minimum lot size of 20,000 square feet. The proposal included a revision to the health code that would permit horses to be stabled as close as 35 feet from dwellings, rather than the 75 feet on the books in areas not zoned for horses. Commercial stables and training facilities were deliberately prohibited — a crucial qualification, because it demonstrates that residents were concerned not only with the preservation of horse-keeping but with creating a rural, low-density landscape of individual horse owners on large, privately owned lots.[69] The proposal capitalized upon and responded to public anxiety about unregulated horse-keeping and suburban growth; it promised to instill order while protecting horse-keeping as a symbol of rural western heritage.

Robert S. Butts, the main lawyer representing area property owners in their case and presumably a Shadow Hills resident, offered practical reasons to support the creation of a horse-keeping zone in Shadow Hills. In his letter of September 1961 to Councilman Everett Burkhalter, he argued,

> There is no question . . . that the establishment of such a zone would be beneficial to the city at large. Persons presently maintaining horses in areas of the city where such a zone does not exist would no longer have excuse for violating present zoning since they would have a place where they could move, acquire property and maintain their horses. . . . From health and sanitation standpoints the matter would be greatly simplified through concentration of horses in one area. . . . Under the registration fee provision there would be revenue for the City of Los Angeles. For instance, in the first area, which is proposed to be created in the Shadow Hills–Sunland Tujunga area, there are presently approximately 1,700 horses. Furthermore, property values in the areas created would increase with the result that the city's tax revenue would likely increase. In short, there is every advantage through the adoption of the ordinance and the creation of the zone and there are no disadvantages.[70]

Butts's arguments appealed to the practical difficulties wrought by the widespread popular interest in horses throughout Los Angeles County, while subtly pointing to the economic and political power of suburban horse owners.

A whopping 98 percent of Shadow Hills residents signed the petition. The matter was referred to the Los Angeles City Council's Public Health and Welfare Committee, which did not immediately agree with the necessity for such a horse-keeping district. The committee correctly reported that existing agricultural zoning regulations already allowed the keeping of horses. Since the majority of Shadow Hills was still agriculturally zoned by 1962, the committee was not convinced of the need to create a special district there. However, the committee did agree to amend the health codes to allow horses to be kept within 35 feet of dwellings, rather than 75 feet. In response, pointing to the rapid subdivision of large farms and agriculturally zoned land throughout the Valley, horse owners from Shadow Hills argued that the minimum lot size and special "rural" designation were essential to protecting their rights as horse owners in the future. They were willing to accept a lot size of 20,000 square feet — which was smaller than agricultural zoning of 40,000 square feet, but still substantially larger than the typical suburban lot of 7,500 square feet — if it would be legally guaranteed for an indefinite period.

The Public Health Committee eventually agreed, and on September 20, 1962, the city council approved the horse-keeping ordinance by unanimous vote of the thirteen members present.[71] Six months later, on March 24, 1963, more than two hundred equestrian residents of Shadow Hills participated in a dedication ceremony to mark the zoning designation of the first horse-keeping district in Los Angeles. The ceremony was followed by a horse show featuring many of the recreational equestrian organizations established over the last two decades such as the Trail Dusters Drill Team, the San Fernando Rangers, and several local chapters of ETI.[72]

Despite the heavy support of Shadow Hills homeowners for special horse zoning, however, at least a few local residents opposed the zoning change for reasons that illustrate the class and political tensions within the neighborhood as well as the horse's competing symbolisms. Within a few years of the zoning change, some homeowners expressed unhappiness with the way that increases in horse-keeping had, in their eyes, negatively affected their community. In a letter ominously concluded with "For our protection, we sign only as Property Owners," a small group complained about the smell, dust, and lack of cleanliness of horse-keeping facilities in tight quarters.

> Some of us longtime residents regret that our steep hills were designated a horse area because here even 75 feet is too close to the nearest dwelling when a corral is seldom and sometimes never cleaned and when sometimes 5 horses are kept on a half acre with dwellings etc. We feel that a minimum annual license fee of $50.00 placed on every horse stabled in this area will provide funds with which to police their owners healthwise, safetywise, and against damage to private and public property. Since the boarding of horses here has become a profitable business a registration of ownership and responsibility might curb some of the violations.[73]

In another anonymous letter, the owner of a very large land parcel and many horses expanded upon these sentiments by distinguishing between horse owners and *real* horsemen.

It should be understood that the Shadow Hills area has many more horseowners than it does horsemen. It should also be understood that much of the area is filthy and poorly kept, that many of the property owners fail to recognize their obligations to themselves, their animals, their neighbors and their community. I would be delighted to show you or your designated representative exactly what I mean. If the horsekeeping does not improve it is my intention to begin shortly an organization of non-horse-owners and real horsemen to urge the city to crack down. We already have a serious odor and fly problem and it will get worse if the housekeeping does not improve. . . . So that my position is totally clear I would like to point out that I have one of the larger property investments in the area and one of the two or three largest investments in horses.[74]

These two letters express class tensions between the diverse residents of Shadow Hills — perhaps between those who kept recreational horses in their own backyards, had little experience with horses, and took care of the animals themselves; and those who considered themselves professional or "real" horsemen, kept animals for breeding or competition, and employed at least one hired person to care and clean for their horses. These letters also suggest a differing set of opinions toward the city's role in preserving and maintaining horse-keeping districts. Some residents, clearly in the minority, expected that the city would be actively involved in regulating the distance between horse facilities and dwellings, the condition of trails, and the bans on commercial horse facilities expressly outlined in the zoning ordinance. On the other hand, the residents and horse owners who had signed the petition in favor of the zoning ordinance quite likely hoped the city would interfere little once the change had been effected. The fact that both letters were signed anonymously suggests some of the pressure their writers must have felt to conform to the overwhelming support for horse zoning in Shadow Hills.

Immediately after the horse-keeping zone was created, however, residents faced a series of residential and commercial development proposals, propelling them into continued activism to tighten and modify their community's new rural, horse-oriented land-use policies. For example, in April 1965, two years after the horse-keeping ordinance was adopted, residents and Councilman Louis Nowell opposed an application for manufacturing rezoning on one parcel on the edge of Shadow Hills. Nowell argued that the rural agricultural zoning should be maintained and the application denied, because residents had spent a great deal of money to improve their lots by adding corrals, barns, and other horse facilities. According to Nowell, "They have made these investments in good faith that the horse district would be maintained and protected for this

type of living. This is the only area of this kind within the city and the only specifically zoned horse district. As long as the people wish to maintain the horse
district and their rural atmosphere, I will support them to the fullest degree and
vigorously oppose any zone change which would jeopardize their status."[75] The
city planning commission agreed with Nowell and rejected the application for
rezoning for manufacturing use on the grounds of preserving the newly created horse districts amid the rapid development of the San Fernando Valley as
a whole.[76]

In some cases, Shadow Hills residents opposed even specifically equestrian-
themed residential subdivisions, such as the Shadow Hills Hacienda project that
was proposed in 1966. The Hacienda development would include 154 homes,
some on lots only seven thousand square feet in size, built in a "cluster concept"
south and east of Hansen Dam, a flood-control channel that by the 1950s had
become a major recreational area for the San Fernando Valley. The project also
proposed to feature a central equestrian center jointly owned by all the property
owners, a network of horse trails winding throughout the area and connecting
to the trail system in Hansen Dam, and a small commercial center oriented
toward horse owners with such services as a blacksmith, a veterinary office, and
a gas station. Existing Shadow Hills residents, led by the Shadow Hills Property
Owners Association and ETI, opposed the project because they claimed it was a
gimmick to raise the population density of the area. Furthermore, they claimed
that the central stable concept did not fit with a rural landscape or lifestyle, because it precluded the possibility of keeping horses in individual backyards. The
lawyer representing the developer countered with the claim that the Hacienda
development would enable a person with a more modest income to keep horses
by removing the prerequisite of purchasing a very large lot.[77]

In August 1966, the planning commission unanimously approved the residential subdivision but rejected the commercial center.[78] The developer resub-
mitted the commercial center as a separate project, this time applying for a
conditional use permit rather than rezoning. Again, homeowners came out in
opposition to the project, citing problems such as inadequate hay storage, lack
of need for a gas station, and the threat the project would pose to neighborhood
character. At the same time, homeowners filed an appeal on the residential project, forcing the planning commission to postpone the commercial center fight
until the residential project could be settled. Effectively, they tied up both pieces
of the project. Residents then staged a community trail ride through the proposed development area as a form of protest.[79] Even Councilman Nowell, who
until this point had sided with Shadow Hills residents in most of their development battles, encouraged his constituents to accept this particular project

because it would strengthen the area as a horse-keeping community. He cautioned that "the only way to keep horses [was] to bring horses into that area" and warned them that any non-horse-keeping project would be far more damaging because new residents who did not own horses would soon complain of flies and demand street paving.[80] Eventually, the application for the conditional use permit for the commercial center was denied, on the grounds that it was doubtful that the project satisfied the conditions for such a permit.[81] Residents then turned their attention back to appeal of the residential development. Finally, in November 1966 the city council rejected the homeowners' appeal, allowing the builder to proceed with the residential project.[82]

Although homeowners lost the fight for the residential part of the Hacienda project, they nonetheless were able to delay the construction for at least six months and to remove those parts of the proposal that they found most objectionable, such as the commercial center. This type of victory has been typical of their activism. That is, even when developments are approved, they are limited in scale and scope and often deliberately incorporate or reinforce elements of rurality and horse-keeping when none had been originally proposed. The result is generally a low-density, residential development with provisions for horse-keeping that further consolidates the rural landscape.

As a result of the long and protracted battle over the Hacienda project, Councilman Nowell lobbied the City Planning Department to initiate a detailed study of horse-keeping districts. Nowell argued that the hilly nature of some lots in the Shadow Hills area made it difficult if not impossible for residents to keep horses while satisfying the clause of the horse-keeping ordinance that required horses to be kept at least 35 feet from dwellings. He asked the planning department to consider five proposals related to preserving the rural and horse-keeping nature of the community. Most important among these proposals were requests that bridle trails be established on existing public property wherever practicable and that commercial development follow an architectural theme that would conform to and enhance the rural atmosphere.[83] In response, the city planning commission unanimously approved an amendment to the horse-keeping ordinance that set the minimum lot size in these districts at 17,000 square feet net or 20,000 square feet gross area, thus enabling horse-keeping even on the neighborhood's hillier parcels.[84] Nowell's other proposals would be incorporated into the Shadow Hills Community Plan, adopted in 1968 and to be discussed shortly.

As they engaged in these efforts to uphold the newly created horse-keeping ordinance, address its loopholes, and secure further protections, Shadow Hills activists and their supporters frequently appealed to the San Fernando Valley's multiple, interlocking myths of rural heritage. They capitalized on their neighborhood's history of gentleman farming and their connections to western film production to attract urban planners, elected officials, and sympathetic media to their cause. During the 1960s, the *Los Angeles Times* regularly promoted the rural lifestyle through extended profiles of Shadow Hills' historic tradition of gentleman farming — though the *Times* was far more likely to celebrate the stories of Anglo-American landowners than immigrant or nonwhite workers. In 1960, the *Times* featured a story on seventy-year-old Frank Palomara, who had purchased thirteen acres of land in Shadow Hills upon his retirement in 1955. Palomara farmed cucumbers, corn, squash, tomatoes, melons, and fruit, which he sold at a roadside stand to supplement his pension. According to the *Times*, "Although the word farming may ring a nostalgic note to many an urban dweller, it means hours of long labor to Frank Palomara, a man new to the fields but one who has worked hard all of his life."[85] Palomara's previous occupation was not mentioned, nor was there any reference to how he was able to buy such a large, expensive parcel of land. Another story in December 1966 profiled Don Shively, a Shadow Hills homeowner who kept eleven horses and other animals on his one-acre property, where he had invested approximately thirty-five thousand dollars into his hobby; and Glenn Haschenburger, the president of the Shadow Hills Property Owners Association whom we met earlier in the chapter, who described Shadow Hills as the epitome of the suburban good life.[86] Such portraits helped Shadow Hills activists to position their community as a last bastion of the city's rapidly disappearing rural heritage.

The Shadow Hills Community Plan, completed in 1968 as part of the citywide master-planning process, reflects the success of such ideological positioning and the collaboration of grassroots activists, the media, and the urban state around the preservation of rural heritage. Pulling together input gathered during nearly three years of community meetings in which hundreds of activists participated, the Shadow Hills Community Plan explicitly encouraged the indefinite protection of the area's "rural atmosphere."[87] The plan retained the single-family residential zoning and minimum half-acre lot sizes. Commercial uses were minor, and no industrial land uses of any kind were allowed. One reason given for the lack of industrial zoning was the availability of land already zoned for industry in nearby Sun Valley, San Fernando, and Pacoima — the Valley's minority districts.[88] Despite complaints from some residents about the particular burden the lack of drug and grocery stores would place on the community's disproportionately elderly population, the city planning commission adopted the proposed plan without revision on October 3, 1968.[89] Though the Shadow Hills Community Plan has been revisited every decade since then, few substantive changes have been made, and the city has consistently reaffirmed its commitment to maintain and preserve the rural lifestyle in at least a few corners of the San Fernando Valley.

Shadow Hills activists used these two key legislative protections — the horse-keeping ordinance and the community plan — to oppose virtually all proposed developments that were not single-family homes on minimum half-acre lots with provisions for horse-keeping. From the late 1960s through the 1980s, Louis Nowell and later city council representatives Bob Ronka and Howard Finn led residents in successfully opposing a pool hall, an equestrian-themed trailer park, a gas station, a health spa, a landfill, and a foster home, to name just a few of the proposed but ultimately unsuccessful developments.[90] Much of the Shadow Hills homeowners' activism took place literally on horseback, a politically strategic move that relied on the symbolism of the horse to link the northeast San Fernando Valley's rural neighborhoods to the mythical western heritage. In 1979, over two hundred activists from Los Angeles's horse neighborhoods gathered in Hansen Dam to protest proposed changes to the community plan that would have allowed higher-density development in two parcels on the edges of the neighborhood. Mounted protesters held signs with appeals such as "Don't fence me *out!*" and "Every city needs a little country: Save L.A.'s rural land!"[91] In large part because of local protests, the proposed changes for the community plan were not approved, and higher-density housing and industrial projects have been consistently located in the black and Latino neighborhoods of the northeast San Fernando Valley.

Shadow Hills activists often expressed a sense of entitlement to urban services and to the urban state's subsidization of infrastructure on behalf of the horse-keeping lifestyle. They were particularly incensed by a 1972 proposal that they pay a special services tax for manure pickup, trail maintenance, and other horse-related services. Although a special tax had been suggested as part of the draft horse zoning in 1962, it was not implemented until July 1, 1972, and only then because of a new city council policy requiring recipients of special city services to pay their fair share of costs. Of the proposed $10 annual fee, $6 were intended to cover Department of Animal Regulation costs for servicing the horse population (including costs associated with handling dead, stray, and loose horses) and the remaining $4 were supposed to be used for developing riding trails and new equestrian facilities. Several Shadow Hills horse owners formed a new organization to fight the tax. Rose Zufelt, publicity chairperson for the new organization, complained, "It looks like they're trying to make us pay for everything." Claiming that the expense might force her and other horse owners to sell their animals, Zufelt argued, "We're not rich people out here.

We give up everything else just to have a couple horses." The group presented a petition, which was signed by 170 people, asking the city council to repeal or lower the tax. In rebuttal, city administrator C. Erwin Piper argued that the fee should in fact be increased to $16 per year, in order to cover the actual annual maintenance costs of $186,000 paid by the Department of Recreation and Parks for bridle trails in the city. At this point, Councilman Nowell came out in support of the Shadow Hills homeowners. He asked his city council colleagues, "Tennis and other facilities are made available to the public without charge so why should horse riders have to underwrite this burden?"[92] His argument was that individual horse owners should not have to pay for the costs of facilities and trail upkeep because these were public resources.[93] Eventually, the annual fee was reduced from $10 to $6. Nowadays, the fee remains linked to horse registration, a legal requirement that is not enforced (the vast majority of contemporary horse owners in Shadow Hills, for example, do not register their horses with the city). Moreover, although in theory the horseback-riding trails in the north San Fernando Valley were and are publicly available, in fact they are unlikely to be used by non–horse owners and, as we shall see in chapter 8, tensions between white horseback riders and other trail users, who tend to be Latinos, have occasionally erupted into arguments and physical altercations.

The result of such protracted activism among white suburban horse- and homeowners and their political representatives since the 1960s is a complex legal infrastructure that protects horse-keeping indefinitely and signals the formal commitment of urban-planning agencies to preserve traditions of rural urbanism. Table 2 illustrates the most important land-use policies implemented in Shadow Hills since 1963. They range from minor amendments, including a policy that allowed property owners to keep up to two horses that didn't belong to them on their lots (thus slightly modifying the ban on commercial horse-keeping in the original zoning) to major revisions, including the expansion of the Shadow Hills horse district by 315 acres in 1978.

Activists have been particularly effective in controlling the development of open space in the hills within and surrounding Shadow Hills. Their arguments and tactics became all the more persuasive as the San Fernando Valley became more densely developed and crowded throughout the 1980s and 1990s. In early January 1989, residents began to collect signatures for an amendment to the community plan that would further restrict density on the area's adjacent mountains and hillsides. Land on these hillsides was, at the time, zoned for low (lot size of 5,000 to 9,000 square feet) and very low (11,000 to 20,000 square feet lots) density; activists hoped that the area would be rezoned for minimum density, which would allow only one single-family home per acre. In

TABLE 2 Major land-use policies implemented in Shadow Hills from 1963 to 2006 that collectively protect and institutionalize the rural landscape

1963	"Horse-raising" district implemented in Shadow Hills.
1965	City Planning Commission adopts "Open Space Maintenance District" in mountainous areas of the city, including Shadow Hills, to reduce density.
1968	Sunland Tujunga-Lakeview Terrace-Shadow Hills-La Tuna Canyon Community Plan adopted; advocates for protection of "rural" atmosphere.
1972	Special City Services Tax of $10 annually is imposed on Shadow Hills Horse-Keeping District to pay for trail maintenance and special services; upon protest by horse owners, the fee is reduced to $6.
1973	Horse-Keeping Ordinance amended to allow property owners to keep up to two additional horses (such as those belonging to a friend or neighbor) on their lots, provided there is no more than one horse per 5,000 square feet.
1973	City council reduces agreement needed to create a new "horse-keeping" district from 90 percent to 75 percent.
1978	Shadow Hills Horse-Keeping District is expanded by 315 acres.
1982	City Council passes "landmark" ordinance requiring developers to obtain special permits before constructing next to a horse owner's property.
1990	City Planning Commission amends Shadow Hills Community Plan to decrease density in hillside areas from "extremely low" (one home per 20,000 square feet) to "minimum" (one home per 40,000 square feet).
1997	City Planning Commission amends Shadow Hills Community Plan to cluster development in flat areas.
2002	Scenic Corridor Plan passes; severely restricts development within a designated "scenic corridor" that includes Shadow Hills hillsides.
2006	Councilmember Wendy Greuel introduces motion to Los Angeles City Council to study possibility of increasing minimum lot size to 40,000 square feet on all future development.

Created by author.

extremely mountainous areas, only one home would be allowed for every five acres. Activists argued for the necessity of the zoning change by pointing to the urbanization of hillsides in neighboring Valley communities such as Glendale. The director of the Sunland-Tujunga Association of Residents, Sylvia Gross, said, "This is the last open land in the whole city. We're trying to stop here what's happened in Woodland Hills and Glendale. You look at the hillsides there and you see nothing but bad. We can't let that happen here."[94] For Gross, "nothing but bad" refers to the dense, often very expensive tract-style homes that line the hills in these formerly semirural, semiagricultural communities.

Clearly, many members of the local communities agreed with her — the first public hearing on the matter had to be rescheduled because there were too many people to safely fit in the meeting room. When the hearing was held at the Verdugo Hills High School auditorium in July 1989, more than eight hundred people attended. Then-councilman Joel Wachs was also supportive, arguing that the hillside slope-density ordinance would protect a rare commodity in Los Angeles — the "'California Dream' of hillside neighborhoods of natural beauty that are affordable to the person of average means."[95] The "California Dream" to which Wachs refers is a particularly Los Angeles dream — the idea of rural communities in close proximity to the city. Still, some people who owned property in the affected areas (but typically lived elsewhere) opposed the amendment on the grounds that it would restrict their right as property owners to develop and profit from their land. They also claimed that the rezoning for one home per acre would effectively limit residency in the new homes to millionaires. Charlyne Pleasant, the president of a competing property owners group, Foothill Alliance for Informed Residents, told the *Los Angeles Times* that the plan would "restrict the opportunities for minorities to own single-family homes in the foothills" by making the new homes prohibitively expensive.[96] Nonetheless, in 1990 the Los Angeles City Planning Commission gave tentative approval, by a 4–0 vote, to the amendment, expressing its support for the preservation of a semirural environment somewhere in Los Angeles. As Commissioner Fernando Torres stated, "I do feel there needs to be some part of Los Angeles that preserves its country atmosphere."[97] Two weeks later, the amendment was presented to and approved by the city council. Although seven developments already in process were exempted from the slope-density ordinance, Wachs confirmed that he would work to reduce the residential density of each project when it came up before the city council. In 1997, the area's community plan was further updated to encourage the preservation of ridgelines and steep slopes as open space, and to concentrate and cluster development on the level portions of the foothills.

According to Wachs, "We're making sure that what's developed there is compatible to the equestrian way of life and to protect open space."[98]

The battle to protect hillsides and open space through low- and minimum-density zoning remains a centerpiece of activism in Shadow Hills, Lakeview Terrace, and La Tuna Canyon. A recent example is the San Gabriel/Verdugo Mountains Scenic Preservation Specific Plan, passed in December 2003, which drastically restricts development on the area's foothills. The culmination of more than a decade of activism, the plan prevents grading or development along prominent ridgelines that are visible from several scenic corridors in the area (especially the 210 Interstate Freeway), protects oak trees and native plants, and establishes standards for site design, landscaping, and signage to assure that projects and improvements preserve, complement, and/or enhance the existing aesthetic. The scenic plan also contains a fourth area of regulation, aimed specifically at protecting horse-keeping, which "define[s] minimum standards for subdivisions located within existing and future 'K' Equinekeeping Districts within the Plan area; provide[s] for the designation and development of existing and future equestrian trails; re-establish[es] the right of property owners to keep domestic livestock in conjunction with residential uses . . . and protect[s] non-conforming equine uses in 'K' Districts in order to preserve the historic use of the area for equestrian and domestic livestock."[99] This element of the plan further associates horse-keeping with the privatized, residential rural landscape in Shadow Hills and the surrounding communities of Lakeview Terrace and La Tuna Canyon and recommits the urban state to the rural land-use protections developed in earlier years. It is the capstone of forty years of rural land-use activism in the northeast San Fernando Valley.

When viewed on its own terms, the effort to create and maintain the city's first horse-keeping district in Shadow Hills might appear to be simply a case of dedicated and successful civic activism among horse lovers. However, when considered in the context of changes within the San Fernando Valley and Los Angeles County more broadly since the 1960s, clear patterns of racial, economic, and geographic privilege emerge. Even as the urban state was working to protect rurality in the northeast Valley, it was simultaneously engaged in massive campaigns of urban renewal and highway construction that decimated neighborhoods in Los Angeles's urban core. Throughout the 1950s and especially in the 1960s, civic boosters who were intent on turning Los Angeles into a "world-class city" persistently targeted working-class and immigrant neighborhoods such as Bunker Hill, Chavez Ravine, and the Broadway District for demolition, using the cleared land to construct a civic center, music and art facilities, and office complexes in the hopes of attracting national and, increasingly, global investment.

As a point of comparison that illustrates the racial and economic inflections of urban renewal and rural preservation, in 1962, the same year that Shadow Hills activists began to lobby for horse zoning, Dodger Stadium opened in Chavez Ravine. Chavez Ravine had been a primarily Mexican community with dirt roads, goats, pigs, and chickens, as well as a tightly knit sense of community. Its rural aesthetic was nearly identical to that in Shadow Hills, though its residents were decidedly poorer and more likely to be immigrants. Yet the rural landscape in Chavez Ravine was considered blighted, uncivilized, and backward enough to be completely razed in the name of urban renewal and a failed public housing scheme. Certainly, Chavez Ravine's location close to downtown, compared with the suburban location of Shadow Hills, offers a partial explanation for its destruction. However, the concentration of ethnic Mexicans in the central parts of the city was no accident, having been mandated by generations of residential exclusion. Furthermore, the residents of Chavez Ravine were not connected to the political and economic interests that made rural landscapes meaningful in the larger context of suburban Los Angeles history or regional western heritage. Although Mexican immigrants and Mexican Americans worked in the western film industry, they did so in segregated work crews and stereotyped roles. Ethnic Mexicans represented not the heroes of western films, but the villains and bandits whose conquest and erasure defined both the white, masculine hero and the inevitable "progress" of American civilization. Seen in this light, the fate of Chavez Ravine is exactly what the western cultural narrative mandates for indigenous and Latino communities: removal in the name of progress and the public good.[100] Meanwhile, the rural neighborhoods populated almost exclusively by white people, on the fringes of Los Angeles County, were protected on the basis of their cultural and symbolic merit.

Like grassroots suburban activists around the country who were engaged in similar defenses of "rights" and "traditional values," Shadow Hills activists articulated their rights to keep horses in their backyards, to be sheltered from unwanted industrial and commercial land uses, and to enjoy city subsidization of equestrian trails and horse-oriented services. The claims they made in their resistance to social change were, more than anything, claims about their "rights" to continue enjoying the privileges of a rural lifestyle within an urban setting — privileges that had been constructed through historic processes of rural urbanism that linked whiteness with expectations of upward mobility and property and an authentic American identity. Moreover, in successfully securing the urban state's continued protection of rurality in the northeast Valley, they effectively consolidated these historic privileges for future generations. As we shall see in the next chapter, similar processes were under way in the west San Fernando Valley, where suburban activists mobilized to protect the area's movie production ranches from the incursions of residential and industrial development, citing the need to preserve rural "open space" within a growing environmental movement but contributing to structural patterns of white social, economic, and environmental privilege.

CHAPTER FIVE

Linking Western Heritage and Environmental Justice in the West Valley

At the same time that horse owners in Shadow Hills were working to create the city's first horse-keeping district, citing the threats that suburban development posed to the San Fernando Valley's rural western heritage, the owners of the Valley's western movie ranches were engaged in a similar struggle. By the late 1950s, the movie ranches and associated production locations had begun to experience a slow but steady decline, because of both the waning popularity of westerns relative to other genres as well as the incursion of suburban infrastructure and population expansion into filming areas. For years, the Valley's production-ranch owners struggled to preserve the look of an authentically western landscape within a rapidly developing suburban region; increasingly, however, they faced a losing battle. Nothing symbolized this threat more than the freeways that linked the San Fernando Valley's suburban workers with employment centers in downtown Los Angeles, Glendale, Burbank, and the Westside. At Walt Disney's Golden Oaks Ranch in Placerita Canyon, for example, a huge backdrop had to be erected to block the sight of busy Highway 14, which connects suburban commuters from Santa Clarita, Palmdale, and Lancaster to their jobs and family members closer to downtown Los Angeles. And in the west Valley, the construction of the 118 Simi Valley Freeway laid bare the difficulties and contradictions of trying to maintain a suburban landscape and lifestyle with western heritage. Many west Valley suburbanites celebrated the 118 Freeway because it would make commuting to their jobs over the hill faster and more comfortable than their current drive over the curvy, rutted old Santa Susana Pass Road. Yet, in a planning meeting with California State Highway department officials in March 1961 to discuss possible routes, Ray Corrigan threatened to assess severance damages of five hundred thousand dollars against the state if the freeway line cut through his property, while Mrs. Iverson argued, "[The freeway] is a disease and it is going to ruin us."[1] In an illuminating portrait, a reporter described the ribbon-cutting ceremony (titled "Open Door to Opportunity") for the Simi Valley Freeway held in April 1966: "In the lush green meadows alongside Kuehner Drive, hundreds of Simi Valley residents and visitors mingled with colorful groups of Sioux and Blackfoot Indians, Old West gunfighters, horsemen." These characters were staff members from Corriganville — who would soon be struggling to keep their jobs. Sure enough, after its completion, the 118 Freeway spoiled numerous camera angles, and the constant sound of traffic made filming virtually impossible.[2]

Thus unable to compete effectively for film contracts, and because of their sheer size, the San Fernando Valley's production ranches became vulnerable to subdivision and development. Many studios simply began traveling further away to more rustic, less developed regions such as Lone Pine, California; Santa Fe, New Mexico; and Tucson, Arizona, which were not yet so encumbered with the blights of suburbanization.[3] Owners often sold their production ranches to mixed-use development projects. These developments, of course, exacerbated the very conditions of their demise, like dominos tumbling down one after another. The Warner Ranch, for example, was developed as the hugely profitable Warner Center in Woodland Hills.[4] And at the Paramount Ranch, owner and manager Dee Cooper resorted to using the western-themed street in films that needed a ghost town rather than a functional social setting, but then sold a sizable parcel of the ranch to the Paramount Development Corporation, which planned to construct 279 homes, in 1979.[5]

In a wholly ironic twist of fate, the west Valley's emerging network of suburban activists — whose own lifestyle decisions had led, in large part, to the ranches' demise — mobilized to protect the western movie ranches by turning them into parks. In Chatsworth, members of Chatsworth Beautiful and the Santa Susana Mountain Parks Association fought for fifteen years (1969–84) to create the Santa Susana Mountain Park on part of the former Iverson's Ranch. Across the county line in Simi Valley, beginning in 1985, activists worked to turn Corriganville into a theme park and recreational area that would rival its 1950s glory days. In both cases, activists invoked the values of western heritage as a nostalgic response to the San Fernando Valley's rapid urbanization. They built coalitions with the urban state and corporate capital, as well as the Valley's emerging network of slow-growth organizations, in order to protect the rural western past.

Yet activism to create parks and recreational space on the fringe of the west San Fernando Valley contributed to regional patterns of environmental injustice in Los Angeles that were already bad and became much worse during this period.

Taken together, the Santa Susana Pass State Historic Park and Corriganville Park constitute more than one thousand contiguous park acres on the western fringes of Los Angeles County. While theoretically open to users from throughout the region, they primarily serve residents of adjacent middle-class, suburban white communities. Moreover, they were created in the aftermath of Proposition 13, amid the slashing of funding for parks and recreational facilities elsewhere in Los Angeles and the state of California. In twenty-first-century Los Angeles, access to open space and exposure to toxicity continues to be strongly mediated by race, class, immigration status, and geography. Environmental hazards are disproportionately concentrated in the eastern and southern parts of the city, which together constitute Los Angeles's older, highly industrialized core and are occupied primarily by immigrants and people of color. Blacks and Latinos in Los Angeles are disproportionately exposed to toxic hazards arising from unwanted land uses. They also have far less access to parks and recreational facilities than do residents of other areas of the city. These factors, in turn, influence myriad poor health conditions such as asthma and other respiratory conditions, inflated blood lead levels, obesity, and more.[6] White people in Los Angeles, by contrast, tend to live on the peripheries of the city, which are cleaner and healthier environments. They enjoy decreased exposure to toxic hazards, better air quality, and superior access to recreational opportunities. Majority-white neighborhoods fare better on indicators of public health and possess a generally higher quality of life.[7] Such patterns collectively situate Los Angeles as an exemplar of environmental injustice.

These correlations are not by chance, nor are they the result of individual malice or intentional racism. Rather, as geographer Laura Pulido has argued, widespread patterns of environmental injustice in Los Angeles are the cumulative result of historical and contemporary structures, practices, and ideologies of white privilege. From this perspective, the persistence of racial disparities is the result not of individual intentions but rather of the macro-scale structural forces that systematically privilege white people and disadvantage people of color, the poor, immigrants, and indigenous communities. Among these structural forces, Pulido identifies racially exclusionary postwar suburban housing and transportation policies, which ensured that whites alone were able to move to cleaner, healthier suburban areas and to enjoy newer housing stock and buildings as well as the opportunity to accumulate home equity–based wealth. Nonwhite immigrants and native-born people of color were overwhelmingly locked out of this process and instead confined to the central neighborhoods that housed the vast majority of the city's manufacturing. Concurrent processes such as highway construction, which enabled suburban whites to reach employment centers in the central city, had the combined effect of carving up inner-city neighborhoods, thus interrupting established communities, social routines, and travel routes, and of exposing those who lived adjacent to the freeway underpasses and off-ramps to toxic emissions, heightening respiratory damage and exposure to toxicity. In the 1960s and 1970s, industry began to decentralize at the same time as limited suburban housing opportunities opened up to people of color in formerly all-white neighborhoods. But with fewer resources and less accumulated wealth, black people and Latinos continue to live in neighborhoods that suffer from inferior access to parks and open space and that have poor public health — even when those neighborhoods are sometimes now located in the suburbs, such as Pacoima, San Fernando, and Sun Valley. Thus, according to Pulido, "although the geography of environmental racism is the result of millions of individual choices, those choices reflect a particular racial formation, and are a response to conditions deliberately created by the state and capital."[8] Historical processes of rural urbanism in the San Fernando Valley were part and parcel of the structures of white privilege and regional racial formations that Pulido and others describe, creating a particular geography of opportunity wherein, by the postwar period, open space was most likely to be located in the places where whiteness and rurality had historically been linked.

Before World War II, planned efforts to create parks and recreational space in Los Angeles were minimal. Although a city park commission was established in 1889 and a playground commission was created in 1904, on the whole, public agencies did little in the way of park provision. Prior to the 1920s, most land dedicated to parks and recreation came through the gifts of private philanthropists, most notably Griffith J. Griffith, who donated the land that became Griffith Park in 1896. Despite his generous donation, by the mid-1920s the city had only about four hundred acres of usable parkland.[9] The city's dramatic population growth in the 1920s briefly led some civic leaders to push for a long-range plan for parks and recreation. Their efforts culminated most famously in a 1930 report, titled *Parks, Playgrounds, and Beaches for the Los Angeles Region*, prepared by the Olmstead Brothers landscape architecture firm in association with the urban-planning firm of Harlan Bartholomew and Associates. Still, little was done with the Olmstead-Bartholomew plan, and parks provision remained sporadic and haphazard through the end of the 1940s.[10]

In part, the shortage of planned open space was a logical outgrowth of Los Angeles's mythic self-promotions, in which the city itself was touted as a playground, a garden city, and a city of homes. Gentleman farming further compounded such imagery through its visions of large, semiagricultural properties on the city's outer fringes. That is, the city's approach to parks and open space planning before World War II mostly equated open space with agriculture. By virtue of its low-density, sprawling, semiagricultural landscape, it was believed that the region would offer sufficient opportunities for exercise, recreation, and communion with nature. These visions were aimed at a population for whom the relationship with agriculture was one of communion, restoration, relaxation, and contemplation — that is, middle-class, white gentleman farmers. The idea of agriculture-as-open space did not account for the needs or perspectives of working-class people of color who lived in the city's industrial districts or for the immigrants and nonwhite laborers who lived and worked in the agricultural belts of the San Fernando and San Gabriel valleys, but who related to agriculture as a job rather than as a pastoral retreat.

Thus, although parks and recreation planning was sporadic, uneven, and inequitable in the city as a whole, it was even more neglected in the San Fernando Valley, where the primarily agricultural character of gentleman-farming districts and experimental colonies precluded the development of planned open space well through the first half of the twentieth century. When Los Angeles adopted its first comprehensive zoning ordinance in 1920, the Valley was excluded from its provisions. Instead, the Valley remained under the Residential District Ordinance that was adopted in 1915 upon annexation.[11] In the immediate aftermath of World War II, however, some urban planners and social reformers, who worried about the short-term and long-term effects of the Valley's transformations, began to push for comprehensive planning. In particular, they worried about the lack of a coherent land-use plan for the Valley and, more specifically, the failure to provide for open space, parkland, and recreational facilities. Even with the growing anxiety about suburbanization, however, it appears that fantasies of the Valley's agricultural past clouded planners' attempts or abilities to plan open space under different terms. In 1946, Charles Bennett and Milton Brievogel created the Valley's first zoning ordinance, which envisioned eighteen distinctive communities that would provide commercial and some industrial services and would be surrounded by agricultural belts of progressively lower density. Immediately surrounding the community settlements would be RA (residential agriculture) zones, with a minimum lot size of twenty thousand square feet. Beyond those would be rings of properties zoned A2 (agriculture, two-acre minimum), and farthest out would be A1 zones (agricultural with a five-acre minimum). Bennett and Brievogel believed that their plan would be sufficient for a population of nine hundred thousand, which they did not expect the Valley to reach until 2000.[12] Actual demographic and geographic growth patterns, however, far surpassed their expectations (see table 1 in chapter 2), and already by 1954 a restudy was ordered.

The 1950s and 1960s were marked by a flurry of civic debate about the city's need to protect or create open space amid rapid growth. Suburban Los Angeles's semiagricultural past proved an ideological heavyweight within these debates, always cast as the foil against which encroaching (sub)urban development was measured — and usually with alarm. Victor Gruen and Associates, a firm hired to write a 1963 report on Southern California's development, captured this tension while trying to assuage anxiety, opening its report by saying, "Within a short ten years, the 150-year-old American dream of city life in the country, the factory in the field, urban centers defined by agricultural belts, will have been shattered for at least ninety-five percent of Southern California's citizens. Though this most surely dispels a myth about the region, it by no means condemns the area to growing, man-made devastation."[13] Postwar development presented a crisis of sorts to the city's self-image, and one that resonated with particular force in the San Fernando Valley. There, the ideals of gentleman farming, though never fully realized, had attracted generations of migrants intent on achieving "one acre and independence." There, too, western films had capitalized on the Valley's semirural agricultural landscape to broadcast the fantasy of rural life to a national audience. Small wonder, then, that the erosion of a deeply romanticized agricultural heritage through the highly visible specter of suburbanization provoked such consternation among a wide array of planners, reformers, and suburbanites who had invested so thoroughly in the dreams of rural urbanism.

The gap between the Valley's image of an idyllic rural heritage and its emerging tract-home suburban reality framed and guided postwar planning efforts for open space and parks. In 1966, the Los Angeles County Regional Planning Commission began its first systematic analysis and long-range planning for the San Fernando Valley. The planning commission convened civic activists, business leaders, and planners for study and analysis to participate in a forum titled "Destination Ninety," which aimed to develop a plan that would guide the Valley's development for the next twenty-five years. The Destination Ninety's Citizens Advisory Committee (CAC) issued its final report in 1968. The report represented the completion of three years of work among six subcommittees with twenty-five study units, led by 150 active citizen leaders and involving 1,000 other citizens in some capacity, in addition to an in-depth survey of two thousand Valley households. In the report's introduction, the CAC

referenced the song made famous by Roy Rogers and Dale Evans in the film
San Fernando Valley.

> A popular ballad of World War II vintage proclaimed of the San Fernando Valley:
> "I'm taking a trip to the cow country, you can forward my mail care of R.F.D."
> Obviously, the Valley's rapidly emerging urban image has rendered this verse ob-
> solete. But with the new image has come new problems — scores of new urban
> problems. City Planners must necessarily address their primary efforts to these
> problems and issues in order to ensure that viable solutions are immediately in-
> corporated into the plan. Perhaps, the most basic issue that must be resolved in
> planning the San Fernando Valley area is: What relationship should the Valley
> bear to the Los Angeles core area? The surrounding environs?[14]

These were difficult questions because they pointed to the shifting relationship
between the San Fernando Valley and the city of Los Angeles in the postwar
period, from a relationship whereby suburban gentleman farmers could have
the "best of both worlds," of rural and urban life, to something new and not yet
intelligible. The members of the CAC understood their effort as one of easing the
Valley's transition through this process. Careful planning for open space was a
vital part of their work. The CAC recommended that 10 percent of the Valley's
land area be dedicated to open space, with facilities available at the neighborhood, community, and regional levels.[15] Together, they argued, these three levels
of parks provision should amount to a standard of ten acres of parkland per one
thousand residents.

At the city level, similar planning efforts were taking place. The City Planning
Department issued its *Open Space Plan*, an element of the master plan, in 1973.
The plan reaffirmed the city's existing recreation standard — which had never
been realized — of six acres of land per one thousand persons. Parkland might
be publicly or privately owned and could take a variety of forms including scenic corridors, cultural heritage sites, or hiking and equestrian trails.[16] In recognition that much of the ideal land for recreational and open space purposes had
already been developed, the *Open Space Plan* proposed the creation of a park
network that would connect small pockets of existing open space across the city
by using flood control channels and rights-of-way under power lines to create
a comprehensive trail system.

By the late 1960s, both the city and the county had devised the first systematic plans for the San Fernando Valley, but the goals they established for open
space were increasingly hard to meet. Richard Alan Watson, who wrote his
1969 master's thesis on the topic of open space in the Valley, observed that the
new community plans, released incrementally throughout the 1960s, showed no

indication that they would preserve agricultural zoning except in two tiny areas, one in the mountains above Sylmar and another tiny enclave in Chatsworth. By 1965, he noted, 42 percent of the Valley's remaining agricultural land was actually in RA zones with lot sizes of around twenty thousand square feet, such as those recently created by the horse-keeping ordinance in Shadow Hills. Watson argued, "Increasingly, this zone is agricultural in name only. Its characteristics are more and more those of the RE or residential estate zone. In fact, on the latest community master plans, the two zones are grouped together as large lot residential uses. Consideration of RA zones as residential rather than agricultural presents a more accurate picture of the declining importance of agricultural zoning as a way of preserving open space in the Valley."[17] Watson warned that "this trend to large nonagricultural residential plots in RA zones may lead to a situation where there is no agriculture except for the keeping of horses in RA areas."[18] Richard Preston, assistant professor of geography at the new San Fernando Valley State College (now California State University Northridge) agreed. He estimated that by 1980, "the transformation from a scene of intensive field and orchard agriculture to a rapidly maturing urban-industrial landscape should be quite complete."[19] Nor was converted agricultural space being replaced with planned parks and recreational facilities. By 1969, Watson's examination of all three categories of park space (neighborhood parks, community parks, and golf courses) showed that all twenty-two Valley communities were markedly deficient — far from the standard of six acres per one thousand people that the city of Los Angeles had delineated in a 1955 ordinance.[20]

Within this context, there emerged a particular geography of opportunity within which communities on the outermost fringes of the San Fernando Valley — particularly in the north and west Valley — were poised to stake their claims to parks and open space. The Destination Ninety Forum's Citizens Advisory Committee had noted that the mountain areas surrounding the Valley presented the best possibilities for regional parks acquisition and specifically recommended that areas with unusual land features, such as the Santa Susana Mountains with their giant red boulders, be preserved through the creation of a regional park. Similarly, the city's *Open Space Plan* noted, "The City, as a whole, is deficient in open space and recreation facilities. Therefore, the establishment of large parks in the Santa Monica and Santa Susana Mountains, and regional parks in the north San Fernando Valley are endorsed. Also endorsed is the creation of a regional park in Baldwin Hills."[21] Communities on the city's outer fringe were the most logical place to create large regional parks, which would — it was hoped — compensate for the relative density of neighborhoods closer in. While not a perfect solution, which would involve the creation of scattered neighborhood parks in an equitable way for communities throughout the Los Angeles region, the idea was that people from denser areas could at least travel to regional parks on the fringes. Yet the regional parks in the west Valley most directly served those who lived adjacent to them and effectively extended historical patterns of white privilege.

The neighborhoods in the west Valley where the regional parks were eventually created had been the beneficiaries of historical practices of racial exclusion in housing, transportation, and employment that were common to virtually all American suburbs. Yet they had also developed through a special relationship to the mythology, social history, and land-use policies of the American West. Like Shadow Hills, Chatsworth and Simi Valley had been settled by Anglo-Americans through processes of legal dispossession, homesteading, and gentleman farming. For example, Swedish immigrants Niels and Ann Wilden Johnson filed a homestead claim for part of Chatsworth in the early 1870s. They came to Chatsworth from Compton, then a solidly white working-class community in South Los Angeles, after earlier stops in Long Beach and, before that, Kansas. Their daughter, Emma Johnson, is heralded as the first American child — that is, the first *white* American child — born in the San Fernando Valley. Another Swedish family, the Williamses, homesteaded a claim beginning in 1878 after moving from Kansas. Mrs. Williams's sister, Augusta Vaugman, later visited from Sweden and decided to file her own claim. Years later, she met fellow homesteader and Norwegian immigrant C. J. Iverson. They combined their acreage, purchased more land, and eventually founded Iverson's Ranch. At approximately the same time, Chatsworth and Simi Valley witnessed their first subdivision and population spurt. In 1887, a group of Chicago investors organized the California Mutual Benefit Company and submitted a tract map to the Los Angeles County Recorders Office for a community called Chatsworth Park, which consisted of ten-acre parcels of small farms. A few years later, English immigrant W. B. Barber, president of the San Fernando Valley Improvement Company, submitted plans for a town site around the planned rail depot. Still, by 1900 only twenty-three people were counted as living in Chatsworth, largely owing to Southern California's real-estate bust in the 1890s. Those who did live there typically grew tomato seeds and walnuts, the area's primary crops, on small farms.

Chatsworth's primary role was service to the stagecoach lines, particularly the Butterfield Coach, which passed daily over the Santa Susana Pass from the San Fernando Valley to Santa Barbara and on to San Francisco. Chatsworth, just on the east side of the mountains, was a good place for stagecoach drivers to rest and change their horses, in order to have a fresh team for the trek over the Santa Susana Mountains. In 1860, working in cooperation with the Ventura County government, the city of Los Angeles had constructed the Santa Susana Pass Road over the stagecoach line to make travel and shipment of goods within its newly acquired territories easier, safer, and more efficient. For nearly fifty years, several stagecoach lines used the road, which was widely noted for its danger and discomfort. Eventually, public support from both urban ends of the stagecoach line — San Francisco and Los Angeles — clamored for a faster and more comfortable transportation option than the treacherous, lurching Santa Susana Pass Road and its infamous Devil's Slide. Beginning in 1901, the Southern Pacific Railroad constructed a rail line along the former stagecoach road, including three tunnels through the Santa Susana Mountains, a monumental and dangerous task that took a crew of fifty men three years to complete. The Southern Pacific's work crew, made up of Chinese and Mexican laborers, lived in camps at the base of the mountains during the construction period, while the engineers and supervisors — including Edward (Jack) Carrillo, brother of Leo Carrillo — stayed in either the Johnson home or at the Santa Susana hotel.[22] With two other men, Niels Johnson opened Graves and Hill General Store to serve the crew as well as travelers along the Santa Susana Pass. Other important social institutions were established at this time as well, such as the Chatsworth Community Church, constructed in 1903. For environmental activists decades later, the stagecoach would become an important symbol of the west Valley's role in the settling, or conquest, of the U.S. West.

It was the area's rural aesthetic, complete with expansive ranches and dramatic red rocks and cliffs — all within relatively close proximity to Hollywood studios — that made it attractive to the western film industry. Rail transportation through the San Fernando Valley created a newfound accessibility that attracted film producers and directors looking for appropriate places to shoot outdoor films. Cecil B. DeMille discovered the Iverson Ranch in 1911 and shot his first film there soon after. Iverson's Ranch dominated western film production until 1935, when Ray "Crash" Corrigan began scouting the area looking for a property that could compete with Iverson's. His ranch, Corriganville, was located just a few miles from Iverson's, but across the county line in what would become the independent city of Simi Valley. Many movie stars purchased homes on small ranches in Chatsworth after working in the area. Roy Rogers and Dale Evans are perhaps the most famous example. Though they were not yet married when they filmed *San Fernando Valley* in 1944, they later purchased a home together in Chatsworth, where they became involved in local politics.[23]

As we saw in chapter 3, the western film industry's positioning of the San Fernando Valley as a place that uniquely combined the values of the Old West with suburban modernity was extraordinarily attractive to suburban migrants. Yet, as geographer Allen Scott has shown, the suburbanization of Los Angeles's postwar high-tech industry was an equally strong pull.[24] In 1951, the Rocketdyne division of North American Aviation selected the Santa Susana area as a test site for its field missiles, and suburban development in Chatsworth and Simi Valley exploded. Vast new subdivisions were created to house Rocketdyne's workers, with modest homes on small lots intended to make housing affordable for the emerging middle class. The Rancho Sinaloa Estates, for example, offered 1,350-square-foot homes on one-third acre lots to defense workers with VA home loans for just under thirteen thousand dollars.[25] The Chatsworth Chamber of Commerce described how urban development had begun to change the community by the mid-1950s: "For many years this historic little community has been passed by in the mad rush to metropolitan centers; but lately it has been 'discovered' by many wealthy and representative people, who, recognizing its many assets, have been buying permanent investments, both for homes and the financial returns made possible by the rich and fertile soil, ample water and ideal climatic conditions."[26] The chamber nonetheless observed, "The community is noted for its fine horses and the miles of picturesque trails and roads make it ideal for saddle parties" and "there is NO SMOG."[27] Such promotions blended the ideals of properly refined rural living bolstered by urban wealth and capital, alongside the much cheaper cost of land in Chatsworth.

Quickly, though, rapid subdivision in Chatsworth pushed established residents and newcomers over the county line. Some San Fernando Valley residents began to move over the hill to Simi Valley, then an unincorporated area in Ventura County, because of a feeling that the San Fernando Valley was becoming too dense, urban, and expensive and that governance by the city of Los Angeles was corrupt and inefficient. For many newcomers, Simi Valley was an attractive place to live simply because it was *not* in Los Angeles. Real-estate developers capitalized on, and helped to cultivate, this sense of antiurbanism in order to lure home buyers over the hill, where land and building costs were up to five times cheaper. Already by 1947, the subdivider of Rancho Simi, a tract of thirty-five homes, explained that homes in the tract were selling well because "San Fernando [Valley] people [are] coming to get away from the crowded conditions and higher taxes which prevail[ed] there."[28] This trend became more pronounced throughout the 1950s. According to press coverage of a community meeting to regulate lot sizes in February 1960, for example, "many said they had moved out of the San Fernando Valley to get out of the crowded city and they [didn't] want houses crowded close together."[29] By 1960, an agent from Tab Realty in Simi Valley remarked, "Home sales in the Simi Valley remind me of the San Fernando Valley in 1952."[30] A suggestive feature on Simi Valley in the *Los Angeles Times* in March 1961 extolled the community's rural virtues, in implicit comparison to the rapidly suburbanizing San Fernando Valley. Al Johns, the *Times'* real-estate editor, noted, "Simi Valley has a rural atmosphere that may well retain its countrified savor for many years to come. This is its charm. And while many houses are being constructed and sold, it does not seem likely that the atmosphere will be sullied by industry, nor by fumes exhaled by far too many automobiles."[31]

The area's apparent ability to hold on to rural heritage, along with comparatively low property taxes and housing prices, appealed to Simi Valley's new home buyers, who were often of working-class origins but upwardly mobile. Most of those who migrated to Simi Valley in the 1970s and 1980s were white, young, middle income, and "house poor," paying a giant share of their paychecks toward housing. According to a 1975 study conducted by the Department of Environmental Affairs of Simi Valley, 95 percent of city residents were white. The median age was twenty-two years, with 44 percent of residents under the age of eighteen. Over 50 percent of residents had some college education; thus, virtually all the city's adult residents were well educated. For these people, life in Simi Valley afforded all the benefits of urban employment, including work at Rocketdyne or one of the Valley's other aerospace plants, but without having to actually be a part of (or pay taxes to support) the city of Los Angeles, which was perceived as being poorly planned and managed.

In short order, however, these conditions created their own set of problems. In 1963, a Ventura County planning report found that the vast majority of Simi Valley residents were employed in Los Angeles, at least in part because of the lack of local employment options (excepting Rocketdyne), and that they had an average commute of 39.8 miles per day.[32] In October 1964, a Los Angeles Regional Traffic Study found that nine of ten vehicles moving eastbound over the Santa Susana Pass every weekday morning were leaving for work or other business in Los Angeles County. More than 75 percent of Simi Valley's population in the mid-1970s worked outside Ventura County, the majority of those just across the county line in the San Fernando Valley.[33] In 1975, Simi Valley was featured in a special issue of the *Ladies Home Journal* as one of the fifteen best suburban communities in the nation. Yet just two years later, it was also ranked the worst violator of air pollution standards in Ventura County.[34] Commuting patterns contributed to the lack of a strong community identity. In a portrait of the changing community in 1977, eight years after cityhood, Art Seidenbaum noted that the city had done a far better job of attracting suburban tract-home developments and golf courses than jobs, and that the community suffered greatly from the lack of relatively mundane institutions such as a major department store or bookstore, which might bind residents to a sense of local community. He remarked, "The second largest city in Ventura County . . . has all those people but not much to occupy them between commutes."[35] In Seidenbaum's words, Simi Valley was a "stringbean of urbanity" with little sense of identity apart from the struggle to maintain a single-family lifestyle, privacy, and open space.[36]

As it would turn out, however, those shared concerns were strong enough to form the basis of a political movement. Given its demographic composition and the reasons why residents moved there — to escape the impacts of urban growth and the demands of urban taxation but still have access to the benefits of urban life, particularly employment — Chatsworth and Simi Valley predictably emerged as conservative strongholds. Residents were overwhelmingly registered as Republicans. State representative Bobbi Fiedler, who achieved local fame through her grassroots organizing work to resist school integration through BUSTOP, represented the area until 1986, when she vacated her seat to run for the U.S. Senate.[37] In later years, the Ronald Reagan Presidential Library was also located in Simi Valley, an indication of the area's importance to the conservative movement.

Antiurbanism was a definitive element of the area's emerging political conservatism. Concern about Simi Valley's rampant subdivision, which mimicked Chatsworth within just a few years, grew quickly, and residents — most of them new to the community — soon began to mobilize against what they perceived to be unregulated suburban development. They were concerned by the small lot sizes of new homes, the inadequacy of local transportation routes serving commuters, and the poor quality of services offered by the county. But they were particularly incensed by proposals to develop the area's western film production ranches — proposals that, to many, threw into sharp relief the ideological contrasts between country and city, rural and urban, old and new, right and wrong. A shared investment in the mythic western past and opposition to its development became the grounds for forging a sense of community and belonging among people who otherwise would have had little reason for coming together. Ultimately, they succeeded in creating two regional parks that ensured access to substantial open space on the fringes of Los Angeles for a population that was almost exclusively white and middle class.

The timing of these campaigns was crucial, particularly for the Santa Susana Mountain Park Association (SSMPA), which began its efforts first and subsequently inspired Corriganville Park activists. The SSMPA lobbied for land acquisition during a period in which interest in protecting open space was high, and in which legislation in two key areas — parks and recreation, and historical preservation — were being formalized and institutionalized at both the statewide and the federal level. Suburban activists in Chatsworth and Simi Valley were fully part of the process, defining the terms of debate about open space in suburban Los Angeles and the legal grounds upon which concrete plans could be developed. Their efforts actually helped to define legislation as it was taking shape, and their ideological and practical arguments informed the positions that their political representatives embraced.

Furthermore, the campaigns to preserve rural and open space in Chatsworth and Simi Valley fundamentally depended on the forging of coalitions with urban interests such as banks, title companies, television media, elected officials, and urban planners. Their work reflects a larger contradiction that is central to the operation of rural urbanism in Los Angeles and in metropolitan regions throughout the U.S. West. That is, the rural landscape has been created and sustained by harnessing the infrastructure and resources of the urban state and increasingly global capital. The money and staff to acquire and restore the area's large ranches for parkland and open space — in the name of protecting rural western heritage — depended on local activists' abilities to frame local history in such a way that would make it attractive to urban interests. Far from remote and isolated rural landscapes, then, the parks of the western San Fernando Valley and eastern Ventura County are thoroughly mediated and protected by urban interests in a complex relationship of interdependency that both reflects and reproduces racialized inequalities.

For everyday suburban activists in the west Valley, however, this larger social context and set of contradictions were invisible, or perhaps simply less important than the issue of protecting the environment from unrestricted development and preserving open space. Their concerns were to create regional parks that would protect plant and animal species, wildlife corridors, and opportunities for passive recreation — and, simultaneously, rural heritage. Hardworking and dedicated to the integrity of their mission as they envisioned it, they paid little attention to the fact that their goals were instituted in ways that reproduced historical patterns of racial, economic, and geographic inequality.

One of these dedicated suburban activists was Janice Hinkston, a teacher who moved to Chatsworth in the mid-1960s. After driving by the Chatsworth Reservoir one day on her way to school, Hinkston recalls that she saw "hundreds of ancient oaks lying severed on the ground" and "couldn't believe such a violent thing could occur in this day and age without warning — for what reason?" Hinkston remembered a newspaper advertisement she had seen for Chatsworth Beautiful, a new organization that was forming committees that very night in May 1969, and she decided to attend. At the meeting, she recalls, "My turn came to voice my concerns about Chatsworth Reservoir and preserving those gorgeous mountains that most of us moved here to be near."[38] Hinkston was appointed chairperson of a committee to study and lobby for the creation of a regional park. This was to be her entry into a rapidly expanding role in Chatsworth community politics. She soon founded the SSMPA and became a master of building coalitions with historical preservation groups, equestrian organizations, and corporations throughout California to preserve Chatsworth's rural landscape and lifestyle.

The regional park that Chatsworth Beautiful and then the SSMPA envisioned would be an "overall mountain preserve offering hiking and wildlife study trails, equestrian trails, picnic and camping facilities" and a green belt to curb the negative impacts of future development. The SSMPA also believed that Chatsworth was a prime location to create a living museum of California's past.[39] Accordingly, Hinkston and the SSMPA built their campaign largely around the historical and ecological significance of Chatsworth. Their initial vision was to create a regional park that would include three culturally significant sites: the Butterfield Stagecoach Trail, the Iverson Movie Ranch, and part of the Corriganville Movie Ranch that fell within Los Angeles County. Thus, their vision blended the lived social history of the western San Fernando Valley with mythic representations of the frontier West created and broadcast through filmmaking. Several of the pieces were already in place. In 1957, the city had passed a recreation and parks bond issue, and in May 1958 the Los Angeles Recreation and Park Commission authorized $95,650 to purchase twenty-four acres for a park and playground in Chatsworth, with facilities construction estimated at an additional $245,000.[40] In the SSMPA's view, this small city park, located in a hilly crevice of the former Iverson Ranch, could become the cornerstone of a major regional park. The SSMPA's first priority was the stagecoach trail, where the Butterfield coach had passed through at the turn of the twentieth century, which had just been approved for a mobile-home park.

The first step was to get local, regional, and national elected officials on board. In April 1970, the parks committee of Chatsworth Beautiful (which would not be folded into the SSMPA until later that year), led by Hinkston, began an aggressive letter-writing campaign to Congressman Barry Goldwater, Los Angeles County Supervisor Warren Dorn, and Senator Alan Cranston, whom Hinkston

remembers as being "most helpful and encouraging."[41] In August 1970, the committee members arranged a tour of the area for Roy Greenaway, field deputy
for Senator Cranston. The tour featured stops at Stoney Point, a spectacular
red rock formation; Iverson's Movie Ranch — especially Garden of the Gods,
one of the production facility's most famous locations; Cactus Gardens; and
Hummingbird Ranch. A few months later, committee members provided
a similar tour for Mervyn Filipponi, park consultant for the State Parks and
Recreation Department, and the next year for members of state and county
historic landmarks committees and the Nature Conservancy. By November
1970, the organization had secured resolutions of support from the Los Angeles
County Regional Planning Commission, the Simi City Council, the Regional
Conservation Committee of the Sierra Club, and the Simi Valley chapter of
the American Association of University Women.[42] Within just six months,
Hinkston and her colleagues had built an extensive political coalition, made
up of representatives from local, state, and federal government, in support of
creating a major regional park. They did so by emphasizing the historical and
ecological significance of Chatsworth and Simi Valley as representations of regional heritage and by strategically situating these communities as remnants of
a romantic past, disappearing amid the rapid urbanization of the San Fernando
Valley.

In January 1971, the zoning variance for the mobile-home development on
the upper stagecoach trail was denied. But although the immediate threat of
development was gone, the SSMPA continued to pursue its larger goal of creating a regional park. Hinkston made a presentation to the Los Angeles County
Regional Planning Commission featuring a slide show of vacant properties that
might be joined together with the existing Chatsworth Park to create a larger
regional park. In response, the planning commission ordered a staff study.[43]
Similar efforts were under way at the statewide level. In April 1971, local state
assemblyman Robert Cline (R-Canoga Park) introduced Assembly Bill 2470
to the state legislature, which would appropriate funds for a California State
Department of Recreation and Parks study on establishing the mountain park.
Cline cited the area straddling the line between Ventura and Los Angeles counties as rich in historical significance, scenic beauty, and ecological value. Cline's
administrative assistant wrote to Hinkston with an update on AB 2470's status.

> During this coming week, Mr. Cline will introduce in the State Assembly, a resolu-
> tion requesting the Director of the State Department of Parks and Recreation to
> include in his proposed programs a feasibility study of the Santa Susana Mountain
> Park. Additionally, Mr. Cline will personally negotiate with the Department of

Parks and Recreation to consider the Santa Susana Mountain Park for acquisition by the State so that its unique historical and ecological attributes can be preserved. Finally, Mr. Cline will introduce a bill for the purpose of accomplishing a feasibility study for the Park.[44]

The Assembly Natural Resources and Conservation Committee approved Cline's bill in June 1971, appropriated $10,000 for the park's feasibility study, and forwarded the bill to the State House Ways and Means Committee for approval.[45] Soon thereafter, Hinkston appeared before the Assembly Natural Resources and Conservation Committee to request funds for the purchase of 175 acres at the site. At that point, lawmakers told her that the state couldn't afford to participate in the request, so the SSMPA changed tactics and took its request to the Los Angeles County Board of Supervisors, where it requested $850,000 in county funds for purchase of the land.[46] In anticipation of her meeting with the supervisors, Hinkston explained to a reporter, "It gives us one of our rare links with the past. It has recently even been determined that El Camino de Santa Susana y Simi used by mission padres and Indians runs near the Stagecoach Trail."[47] In June 1972, the SSMPA gave a tour to Robert Meyer and Emmett Blanchfield, both of the California Department of Recreation and Parks, and representatives from the Simi Valley Recreation and Parks District, who were collaborating on the feasibility study authorized by Assembly Bill 2470. Also present were the land-use consultant to Congressman Barry Goldwater and the wife of County Supervisor Warren Dorn, who was then chair of the County Board of Supervisors. The tour included stops at the Garden of the Gods, Stoney Point, a former Indian village, and the stagecoach trail.[48] In May 1972, the SSMPA even toured the area with *Sunset* magazine's photographer, Walter Houk.

Hinkston and her peers simultaneously developed close collaborations with the San Fernando Valley's emerging network of slow-growth, historical preservation, and equestrian organizations, all of which were pursuing similar agendas of rural landscapes and open space in the 1960s and 1970s. The SSMPA gave slide-show presentations on the history of the Chatsworth area, with particular focus on the stagecoach trail, to groups such as the Canoga Park Coordinating Council.[49] The slide show was also shown on Simi Valley's local Channel 8. In March 1971, Robert Jones, president of the Southern California Horsemen's Council, responded to Hinkston's letter requesting his organization's support. He wrote, "If there is 'ANYTHING' we can do to assist your organization, 'PLEASE' notify me."[50]

While working to create a widespread political coalition, Chatsworth activists pursued legal designation of the site's historic value. Statewide historic preservationists were very supportive. In March 1972, Walter Frame, past president and legislative chairman of the Conference of California Historical Societies, wrote to Hinkston, "[I am] very interested in your desire to preserve the Santa Susana region. I first saw it from the observation platform of the parlor observation car 'Santa Susana' in 1926. I have appreciated the unique beauty of the area ever since. The Conference is composed of all of the historical societies of California acting together to protect and preserve California's history and beauty. You should request our aid in whatever steps you take for preservation."[51] The California Historical Landmarks Committee designated the Santa Susana Stage Road a Point of Historical Interest (no. P227) in September 1971. SSMPA members then began the push to appeal for cultural heritage monument status at the city level. In 1962, Los Angeles had created a cultural heritage board with the authority to designate buildings or landmarks as historical monuments. One of the members of the cultural heritage board was W. W. Robinson, author of many of the San Fernando Valley's historical booklets as well as a member of the Los Angeles Corral of Westerners, the Historical Society of California, and numerous other historical groups in the region. The city declared the Santa Susana Stagecoach Road a historic-cultural monument in January 1972.[52] It was subsequently listed on the National Register of Historic Places in 1974.

By October 1971, the SSMPA had negotiated a purchase option with the existing property owners of the 177-acre parcel that included the stagecoach trail. According to the terms of the agreement, the SSMPA would immediately pay $25,300 and would have one year to raise the total purchase price of $1,263,000 through a combination of state and federal funds.[53] The SSMPA then began an aggressive fund-raising campaign. The organization planned a series of public hike-ins on Sunday mornings beginning in January 1972. Some were specifically for nature enthusiasts, others for families, still others for singles. Flyers for the first hike encouraged residents to "Join the posse," and closed with "See ya thar, Pahdner!"[54] Over eight thousand people attended the first hike-in and donated more than $10,000.[55]

Hinkston also spoke with Laurence Hoge, the publicity director of Wells Fargo Bank, and requested a financial contribution to assist her organization in restoring the Santa Susana Stagecoach Trail. After presenting her proposal to Wells Fargo's budgets and contributions committee, Hoge reported that the bank would not be able to fund the proposal but could make loans to her organization until enough money could be raised through donation. He also offered artwork and posters for the campaign, and wrote, "We might also be able to arrange for one of the coaches to be involved in some type of one-day publicity event that your group might want to initiate to kick-off a fund drive."[56] The irony, of course, is that Wells Fargo likely already had, or soon would, provide construction loans to the area's real-estate developers and home loans to new home buyers. Yet, in one of the key contradictions of rural urbanism, the corporate giant could and would provide a key symbol of western Americana — the stagecoach — to help fund the protection of rural land.

The ssmpa's coalition-building work with corporate interests, political representatives, and grassroots organizations came together quickly and paid off handsomely. In March 1972, the ssmpa cosponsored a two-day country fair and parade celebrating Chatsworth's eighty-fourth birthday, with proceeds donated to the ssmpa's land trust fund for purchase of the stagecoach trail. The parade's grand entry was a stagecoach donated by Wells Fargo and driven by Don Shively of Shadow Hills, whom we met in the previous chapter.[57] State assemblyman Robert Cline, who had long supported the preservation of open space and rural landscapes in the northwest Valley, relayed a personalized invitation to then-governor Ronald Reagan, inviting him to drop by the fair whenever his schedule permitted. Cline wrote,

> The Santa Susana Mountain Park Association formed to save its historical and native beauty from developers is putting on a two-day "fair" in Chatsworth on March 11 and 12. I am relaying to you on their behalf an invitation to drop in at any time which would be suitable for your schedule. This group is raising money to buy an option on the property where the Butterfield Stage passed enroute north, (which has been zoned for mobile homes). I have championed their cause here in the Assembly and your attendance would be a boost in their efforts to raise funds privately to purchase this property.[58]

Although Reagan did not attend, his invitation signals his importance as an icon of western heritage and how grassroots communities in the west San Fernando Valley and Simi Valley fit into the growing conservative movement.

As a major part of its fund-raising campaign, in 1973 the ssmpa published a well-illustrated booklet titled *Santa Susana: Over the Pass . . . Into the Past*. The booklet sold for $3.35 per copy with all funds donated to the land trust. According to the booklet's introduction,

> We hope this publication will not only serve as a shopping guide but as a link to our cultural heritage by bringing out the wonders of the stagecoach trail area, as well as the Santa Susana Mountains and the Simi Hills. Years from now, perhaps nothing will remain of the 178 acres of the old trail which caught the spirit not only of Chatsworth, but the entire San Fernando and Simi Valleys in the early 1970s. On the other hand, perhaps this tiny publication will inspire the many

hungry people, who feel a need to walk into the past and escape the city below, to save the stagecoach trail.[59]

The booklet featured articles on the history of the stagecoach trail, the De la Ossa family, and the indigenous groups that had once lived in the area, as well as information on plant and animal species.[60] Students from the journalism class at Sinaloa Junior High in Simi Valley prepared drawings of the stagecoach trail with a handwritten appeal: "Preserve Our Heritage: it's the only one we have!!" Many of the materials used in the booklet were donated by the same interests that had spurred rapid urban development in the San Fernando Valley for decades. Most of the photographs used in *Over the Pass . . . Into the Past*, for example, were donated by Security Pacific National Bank; Title Insurance and Trust Company donated a map. The booklet also featured a bibliography related to the history of the stagecoach trail and other related events, which pointed readers to early histories written by growth-machine interests and by the San Fernando Valley chapter of the DAR, examined in chapter 2.

The booklet included a history of the SSMPA and explanation of its objectives, penned by Hinkston, who reveals her personal motivations to protect the west San Fernando Valley's rural landscape.

> For over ten years now, from my house and yard, I have seen one of nature's greatest artistic masterpieces . . . with all the elements of art right there — unsurpassed — line, form, color, rhythm, variety, and unity too, as only nature can unify. Each day I see the west end of the San Fernando Valley, and the rugged escarpments above. Each day I feel how lucky I am to live in what still feels like the countryside, and to work within view of the breathtaking and unique rock formations of the Simi Hills. . . . Not only children, but people of all ages, all backgrounds, respond to the freshness, openness, unplanned, *unstructured* beauty in our mountains. With so many millions of us tied to concrete and asphalt, how *crucial* it is for us to have close access to nature and all its works.[61]

The article was accompanied by a photo of Hinkston emerging from a stagecoach, dressed in bonnet and old-fashioned western attire and accompanied by a young girl, perhaps her daughter.

The booklet's advertisements reflect the dense network of historic preservation and slow-growth activists that had emerged as a powerful force in the San Fernando Valley by this time, and whom the SSMPA had woven together through its organizing. Several corrals of Equestrian Trails, Inc., placed ads in the booklet, as did the Rockpointe Homeowners Association, Simi Valley Beautiful, and the Sierra Club. Elected officials, including councilman Joel Wachs and state assemblyman Robert Cline, and the Chatsworth and Simi Valley Chambers of Commerce publicly expressed their support for the SSMPA through funded ads in the booklet. Local businesses that were invested in the preservation of the San Fernando Valley's "Wild West" image and rural lifestyle likewise supported the project, evidenced by advertisements for Wiltsey's Western Wear and Mac's Country Feed Store, as well as Wells Fargo Bank. Clearly, these organizations and businesses perceived that they shared a vision of rural land use and open space that could be mobilized for different purposes — and sometimes cross-purposes — in the rapidly changing city of Los Angeles.

In 1974, an opportunity arose to garner state funds. Proposition 1, which would authorize the state to raise $250 million in bond money for parks, appeared on the statewide ballot. The Los Angeles City Council urged the state to include five municipal parks in the bill, including 876 acres in the Santa Susana Mountains as well as acreage in Griffith Park, the Tujunga Wash, and the Santa Monica Mountains. While the specifics were being worked out, Proposition 1 raised heated debates about the allocation of funds for open space and recreation and, in turn, the city's racial, economic, and geographic inequities. City council members Gilbert Lindsay, John Ferraro, and Billy Mills criticized the locations of the proposed projects, which were overwhelmingly in the San Fernando Valley and northwest Los Angeles County. Lindsay, who represented South Los Angeles, explained, "I'm tired of voting millions and millions for the big park areas and we don't even have peanut parks in the 9th District." Ferraro concurred, calling the supporters of the proposed park sites "greedy, selfish people" who "ought to be ashamed" of themselves.[62] Even after voicing their opposition, however, both Lindsay and Ferraro voted in favor of the measure; Mills was the lone dissenter. For its part, the SSMPA distributed the *Santa Susana: Over the Pass . . . Into the Past* booklets to each of the state park commissioners, continued its hike-ins, and waited for the June 4 vote.

Voters passed Proposition 1 in June 1974, and the funds it authorized quickly became the battleground for a statewide contest over the allocation of scarce resources for recreation and open space. Under the original ballot measure, Los Angeles County was allocated $28 million, or roughly 9 percent, of the total $250 million bond revenue. City and county legislators began lobbying for a greater share, arguing that Los Angeles taxpayers paid 37 percent of state taxes and should therefore receive a roughly equal distribution of park moneys. The Los Angeles City Board of Recreation and Parks Commissioners, the Los Angeles County Regional Planning Commission, and the Simi Valley Recreation and Parks District all endorsed a proposal to request $43 million for Los Angeles; the proposal made its way before the legislature as Senate Bill 907.

Yet, ironically, their claim to a larger share of the state's revenues on the basis of fairness overwhelmingly privileged the San Fernando Valley at the expense of Los Angeles's more densely populated areas. Of the additional $15 million requested through the proposal, $8 million would be devoted to acquisition in the Valley and its exurbs, including $4 million for the proposed Santa Susana Mountain Park, and $4 million for Castaic Lake.[63] Seymoure Greben, director of the Los Angeles County Department of Parks and Recreation, argued that properties in the west Valley such as the Santa Susana Mountain Park were of particular concern and envisioned a network of trails for hiking, cycling, and horseback riding.[64] Still, no money was allocated explicitly to the Santa Susana Mountain Park from Proposition I.

At roughly the same time as city and county representatives in Los Angeles struggled to get their "fair share" of statewide resources, a similar contest was slowly developing in the U.S. Congress. In August 1972, U.S. senator John Tunney had introduced a bill to create a federally funded Santa Monica Mountains and Seashore National Urban Park, which was to include the Chatsworth area.[65] Tunney's bill provoked further debate over the distribution of resources among Los Angeles's urban and rural spaces. Several Los Angeles city councilmen representing inner-city areas charged Tunney, the Sierra Club, and Tunney's grass-roots supporters, including the SSMPA, with elitism and racism. Councilman Robert Farrell passionately argued, "Given priorities in terms of bills getting introduced, in terms of election campaigns and limited funding — if the money constantly goes to the more affluent areas, doesn't it make sense that some of us are going to look at the Sierra Club people as racists for constantly supporting legislation that will put more parks and open space in the communities of the privileged?"[66] Los Angeles city councilmen Robert Wilkinson and Art Snyder agreed. Wilkinson observed that mountain residents "want to keep the mountains only for hikers and open space that the people from the Valley and South Central can't get to. They don't want those types of people to visit, or the East Side (of Los Angeles) people." Snyder, who represented East Los Angeles, wondered how residents of his district would get to remote mountain parks. He noted that parks in his district were "overcrowded with people practically shoulder-to-shoulder," at least in part because — he claimed — official head-counts in his district did not include over one hundred thousand undocumented immigrants.[67]

Representatives from the Sierra Club and middle-class suburban homeowner associations responded with indignation, labeling Farrell a separatist whose polarizing strategy stood in the way of the public good. They argued that the proposed parks would be regional parks, available for use by residents from

throughout Los Angeles County, thereby overlooking the remote mountain locations of the proposed parks and the almost complete lack of public transportation to enable access by nonresidents. Councilman Marvin Braude argued,

> Are we going to say let's not have a park in the Santa Monica Mountains until
> we get everything we want? What kind of separatism is that? Are we going to pit
> blacks against whites because we are advocating a park to serve all the people in
> Southern California? Are we going to pit the people in one area of the city against
> another area because they want a local park that they are not going to get? . . . The
> polarizing of communities in this way leads to separatism and irrationality. It just
> moves in a direction inimical to all our interests. It saddens me very much to hear
> a member of our council talk in that way.[68]

In response, Snyder explained that his comments, and those of Farrell and
Wilkinson, expressed the frustration that existed in Los Angeles's poorest districts. He pointed out that federal funds continued to be allocated for mountain
parks in affluent areas even while money for federally subsidized public housing
projects had eroded. Despite the furor the bill raised, as well as the very real
questions about access to parkland and recreational equity, Tunney's bill was
passed in 1976 as the Urban and Coastal Park Act. One of its provisions was
the creation of the Santa Monica Mountains Conservancy, formally organized
in 1980, a public-private agency whose primary purpose is to assist the state in
acquiring land for parks, recreational facilities, and open space.

While awaiting the conservancy's creation and its potential allocation of
funds, the SSMPA continued to sponsor hike-ins, chicken dinners, and barbecues as fund-raisers for land acquisition. In 1977, the SSMPA entered escrow on
another piece of property, the McDonald-Nichols property, which comprised
265 acres and included a major part of the stagecoach trail. Of the total purchase
price of $570,000, the group was required to pay a $50,000 down payment immediately. They did so by pooling the $15,000 that the SSMPA had raised from
previous efforts with $10,000 from the Foundation for the Preservation of the
Santa Susana Mountains, a private organization, and another $40,000 from the
West Los Angeles County Resource Conservation District. The terms of the sale
called for the balance to be paid over the next seven years.[69]

In the meantime, representative Robert Cline continued to levy his political networks in Sacramento in a last-ditch attempt to allocate public funds for
land acquisition. The SSMPA was particularly concerned because another parcel
that it wanted, the Open Diamond Bar Ranch, had already been approved for
development. The Open Diamond Bar Ranch's owner, Eugene Kilmer, was an
aircraft-parts salesman turned real-estate developer who intended to retain 60

acres of the ranch as his own private estate and subdivide the rest into large, elite "country estates," each approximately 2.5 acres and with a price tag of $250,000 to $500,000. The remainder of the land would be devoted to equestrian activities. Kilmer explained that he was "inclined toward ecology and conservation" and intended to "disturb nothing, create only surface roadways without curbs, sidewalks, or lighting." The rural landscape that he envisioned was part of an elite real-estate package. Kilmer said that he was willing to listen to state proposals for the creation of a regional park but was unconvinced that a public park would impact the environment less than his proposal.[70]

Finally, in August 1977, the California Senate passed SB 448, authored by Senator Lou Cusanovich (R-Woodland Hills), which appropriated $2.5 million from the state budget for acquisition of land in the Santa Susana Mountains. The money was to be allocated from California's receipts of the 1976 Urban and Coastal Park Act that Tunney had championed — and that had provoked so much consternation among city, county, regional, and national representatives. The bill carried an urgency clause, with implementation to be in effect immediately upon signing by the governor. The $2.5 million would cover the purchase of two parcels of land together comprising 745 acres: the McDonald-Nichols property and the Open Diamond Bar Ranch.[71] Cline credited community activists, particularly the SSMPA, for holding the purchase option on the two parcels for nearly nine years while the lengthy legislative process was pursued.

The timing of SB 448's passage, and especially its urgency clause, was crucial. Just one year later, California voters passed Proposition 13, which fundamentally restructured the possibilities for all public services and amenities in the state, including parkland and recreational facilities. A reaction to soaring property taxes, Proposition 13 drastically curtailed allowable property-tax assessments, assigned full responsibility for allocation of property taxes to the state rather than local jurisdictions, and required any special tax to be approved by two-thirds of voters.[72] Proposition 13 effectively slashed state and local budgets and forced local agencies to cut services and facilities and to identify creative revenue sources for basic services such as schools, fire and police protection, and parks. During the early 1980s, the City of Los Angeles was forced to close 24 recreation centers, reduce funding for the remaining 154 centers, and cut the weekly operating hours of many facilities. Acquisition of new parkland was similarly limited. Between 1972 and 1998, the city purchased fewer than one thousand acres of land for parks, pushing Los Angeles to the bottom of West Coast cities and most other major American cities in terms of parkland per capita.[73] All of this occurred even as the SSMPA was purchasing or holding the option to purchase additional properties for the creation of a regional park on the city's fringes, to which the State of California was already legally committed.

According to Stephanie Pincetl, the restructuring of finance and governance mandated by Proposition 13 propelled an increase in environmental nonprofit organizations that were forced to devise creative new solutions to secure parkland and recreation space. Because so little money was available from the state or local general funds after Proposition 13, environmentalist groups took to the state ballot to raise revenues on a parcel-by-parcel basis. Their typical strategy was to craft a package deal of specific projects for parks, recreational facilities, and open space. This strategy required environmental groups to negotiate coalitions that could win at the ballot box. Not surprisingly, they usually focused on developing coalitions among powerful groups such as homeowner associations, private interests, and local governments that were well funded, well organized, and could turn out the vote. According to Pincetl,

> Civil society institutions beyond political parties, such as charitable organizations, participate in attempts to mobilize state resources and/or to influence policymakers and business interests for programs and policies. Much like business coalitions, they lobby local elected officials, work with local bureaucracies, and mobilize both to influence state-level political bodies and to divert public support for projects. They may enter into coalitions with business interests, other nonprofit organizations, or create alliances with the structure of bureaucratic service providers to move their agendas forward. They create competitive funding programs and compete for those funds.[74]

Clearly, this level of coalition building and political networking requires substantial resources and social and political capital. Pincetl's description captures precisely the technical and political sophistication of environmentalist-oriented civic groups since the 1970s. Although the SSMPA began its work well before the passage of Proposition 13, its strategy clearly mirrors the patterns she describes. After Proposition 13's passage, the SSMPA was already well positioned to play what had become a high-stakes game of lobbying for parks and open space in California.

Thus, in June 1979, when the impacts of Proposition 13 were just beginning to be felt, the state began the purchase process for the two properties secured under SB 448. Several additional purchases of large and small tracts would follow over the next few years, as the SSMPA pieced together properties as they became available for sale or were proposed for development.[75] Largely because of the financing and governance changes mandated by Proposition 13, the purchase process was slow, and money was allocated on a case-by-case basis to acquire each of the private parcels that comprised the entire 1,100-acre site the SSMPA envisioned for the park. The SSMPA prioritized the acquisition of land parcels that were threatened with imminent development proposals, moving to the back burner those properties that had not yet been targeted for subdivision.

In November 1980, the SSMPA set its sights on three additional properties near the stagecoach trail, and lying within the proposed park area, that had just been approved for residential development. Two of the parcels were owned by the same person, Sherman Whitmore, who planned to construct fourteen large estates on an eighty-acre parcel and sixty-nine smaller homes on another fifty-five acres. As a condition of his approval, Whitmore agreed not to build homes on the area where the stagecoach trail ended. But Janice Hinkston claimed that the new homes would still come so close to historical artifacts that they would destroy the scenic value of the landscape as a window into the past. She asked, "Suppose you have houses on each side of the trail. How are we going to be able to get the feeling of what it was like by walking between houses? To me, the whole cultural resources are ruined."[76] Whitmore was skeptical. He did not doubt that the trail had existed but wondered whether it was worth saving. "I'm not denying there's a trail there," he said. "As to its historical importance, you could declare all of California a historical monument because people have been walking all over it for 2,000 years."[77] In this particular struggle, the SSMPA merged environmental concerns with claims to heritage. It seized upon the Santa Susana tarweed, an endangered species found only in the Santa Susana Pass and in Malibu, as a new weapon. According to William Fulton, this move — of using endangered species to fight development — was common among suburban "tract-home environmentalists" throughout Southern California in the 1970s and 1980s and constituted an important and tried-and-true tactic for the San Fernando Valley's slow-growth movement.[78] With the tarweed as their method, the SSMPA effectively stalled Whitmore's development proposal and, parcel by parcel, continued their work.

At last, on November 18, 1984, the visitor center at the Santa Susana Mountain Park held its opening ceremonies. The ceremonies included the SSMPA's slide show on the history of the park area, as well as guided hikes led by docents through the 428 acres of parkland that had been acquired so far.[79] And in 1986, Los Angeles city planning director Calvin Hamilton, upon the eve of his retirement from the post he had held for twenty years, called for the annexation to Los Angeles of 15,000 acres of unincorporated land in the Santa Susana Mountains, north of the Simi Valley Freeway, and a smaller 1,000-acre parcel south of the freeway. The meeting at which Hamilton announced his plans was coordinated by Janice Hinkston and held in the Glendale Federal Bank Building in Chatsworth, where the ssMPA had been meeting for over a decade. In 1998, the Santa Susana Mountain Park was designated a state historic park, which attaches an additional layer of protection and permanency to the rural landscape. The ssMPA's Web site maintains that the historic park "is a valuable cultural and biological resource as well as a comforting sanctuary, a place of re-creation for today's harried city-dwellers."[80] The organization continues to host living-history events, community cleanups, archaeological stewardship trainings, and film screenings including, in November 2008, *Susanna Pass*, starring Roy Rogers and Dale Evans.

Almost immediately after the opening of the Santa Susana Mountain Park Visitor Center in 1984, a related struggle began to build steam just over the hill in Simi Valley. There Simi Valley activists worked to transform the abandoned movie ranch at Corriganville, now slated for a suburban tract-home development, into a park that would emphasize the area's unique Wild West heritage. Ultimately they, like the ssMPA, were successful in securing the land in perpetuity as a large park and passive recreation area. They too emphasized the values of open space and rural culture within a dense, complex, and diverse metropolitan region.

Like Iverson's Ranch, Corriganville had been effectively destroyed as a production facility by the mid-1960s and was vulnerable to subdivision and development. This was particularly so after Corriganville's purchase in 1965 by actor and comedian Bob Hope, one of the largest — and, according to Fulton, most unpopular — landowners and real-estate developers in the west San Fernando Valley and Ventura County. Following a series of messy real-estate transactions after Ray Corrigan's divorce from his wife, Rita Stultz, in 1954, Hope bought the Corriganville Ranch property in 1965 for $3.5 million and renamed it Hopetown. According to the ranch's historian, William Ehrheart, "[Hope] had acquired the movie ranch from Corrigan intending to carry on its Hollywood traditions, knowing that other movie ranches in Southern California had been sold, subdivided and forgotten."[81] But although Hope promised to refurbish the western-themed sets and enlarge the recreation areas, he never actually did so and closed the ranch to the public in 1967. In 1970, most of the buildings were destroyed by fire.[82] By 1976, Corriganville/Hopetown was described as "a real ghost town from a real movie set" and was rarely used, except for an annual two-day motorcycle race and a memorial celebration for a teenage rodeo star from Burbank who had died in a car accident.[83] In 1979, another fire destroyed the remaining buildings.[84]

In the mid-1980s, Griffin Homes, a Calabasas-based real-estate development company, purchased most of the former Corriganville/Hopetown property and paid Hope $4.6 million for the option to buy the remaining 212 acres of the ranch. Griffin Homes had already won approval to build 238 single-family houses on the ranch's lower 40 acres as well as an industrial park on another 17-acre parcel. Fully 70 percent of the property would be donated as open space for the creation of a city park.[85] Slow-growth activists were incensed by the proposal, but they were also fully aware of the very recent victory in Chatsworth. Armed with a toolkit of historical and ecological strategies, they set forth to preserve Corriganville in the name of western heritage and rural land from the advent of tract-home-style suburbanization.

Barbara Johnson and Wilma Tomerlin, two self-identified housewives from Simi Valley, led the fight against the proposed development. Though they recognized that most of the land would not be touched, they feared that the initial intrusion of bulldozers would soon bring more of the suburban tract homes and geometric monotony that increasingly characterized Chatsworth and Simi Valley (including, possibly, their own homes). Johnson asked, "Why this place? We have lost so much already, and Hope Town is a treasure of history. Must they standardize everything?" Tomerlin concurred, arguing, "The whole integrity of Hope Town ought to be preserved for the future. The open space won't be a *wilderness* park, it will be a *city* park. There's a difference."[86] Johnson and Tomerlin approached Hope's lawyers, Griffin Homes, environmental organizations, and even Gene Autry to try to persuade him to buy the land for a western museum.

Although Autry didn't bite, other western celebrities played a crucial role in the campaign for Corriganville's preservation. Ray Corrigan had already donated one hundred acres of his property for parkland in 1961.[87] Corrigan's children, both of whom had grown up in a ranch home on the westernmost end of Silvertown Street at Corriganville and still lived in the San Fernando Valley, were actively involved in the ranch's restoration project. The ranch's historian, William Ehrheart, mused that "while the children played, Hollywood was recording their home on film as a stage depot, a telegraph office or a pony express way station, as well as a ranch house."[88] One of the children, Tom Corrigan, had often brought his elementary school and middle school classmates to the ranch on school field trips.[89] During the preservation campaign, he conducted numerous television and radio interviews and filmed a documentary using footage his father had shot at the ranch. He also toured rodeos and county fairs with a team of stuntmen, using old scripts to stage the same reenactments that actors had performed at Corriganville thirty years earlier.[90] In July 1985, the Simi Valley Cultural Association sponsored a weeklong Southern California Classic Film Festival, featuring screenings of films made at Corriganville, to raise money for the former movie ranch's restoration. The festival included a celebrity banquet, guided tours of the old Corriganville production locations, cavalry and stunt demonstrations, pony rides, and concession booths. The festival closed with a chili cook-off, barbecue, and country-western music. Tom Corrigan arranged for stunt men to re-create the "Gunfight at OK Corral" scene, which had been one of the most popular shows at Corriganville during its public heyday.[91]

Numerous political organizations, with suburban residents their core membership, emerged with the shared interest of preserving Corriganville. The Simi Valley Cultural Association, the Corriganville Preservation Committee, the Corriganville Movie Ranch Restoration, and the Trail Riders of the West all organized to prevent development by promoting Corriganville as a historic reminder of Hollywood's early moviemaking days. Ehrheart observes that many of the activists in these organizations were children who had visited Corriganville during its heyday, noting, "Yesterday's child visitors are today's business people, corporate executives and other interested parties."[92] All grown up, with suburban properties and children of their own, Corriganville's preservationists channeled their nostalgia for the rural western past into well-organized land-use activism. These organizations helped to cohere and politicize a generation of middle-class white suburban residents, many of whom had moved into the area within the past five or ten years, around a threatened vision of rural land use.

Typical among the Corriganville preservationists was Jack Harding, who grew up in Ohio in the 1950s and spent Saturday afternoons watching westerns. Harding had moved to Simi Valley in 1979 and retired, at age forty-five, in a house just a few miles from Corriganville, where he took afternoon walks nearly every day. He explained, in January 1986, "It was like going home again. I recognized the rocks and trees. You can still see where the Lone Ranger stood and where the stage coach went through. There's the rock that Lash LaRue always seemed to be on top of when he cracked his whip. You sit there and look out over the horizon and you see the rolling hills and the rock formations. It all comes back again."[93] Harding was concerned that development of the site would erase not only the specific landscape of Corriganville but also the larger social mores that western films represented. He elaborated, "If you sit and watch a Hopalong Cassidy or a Lone Ranger film, there is a simplicity. There's a black and there's a white. There were values. You could always count on the guy in the white hat being there. Those men kept their word."[94]

Not all of those who rallied around Corriganville/Hopetown's preservation were western film buffs like Harding, but they recognized the site's political value as a symbol of western Americana and understood that it was a strategic way to preserve open space and create a park. As Judy Mikels, vice president of the Simi Valley Cultural Association, explained, "As far as value to the cultural history of Simi, Corriganville is very, very important. Culture is the sign of the times and Corriganville was what was happening in Simi. It was big in its heyday." Many of the preservationists hoped that the site could be restored to a Wild West amusement park and thus stave off monotonous tract homes. Mike Stevens, cofounder of Citizens Aware of a Sensible Environment, explained, "I'm not a no-growther but I am afraid of the recent trends that we will be developing in areas that should be preserved or kept as a refuge." Lee Shapiro, Simi Valley resident and chairman of the neighborhood council where Corriganville/ Hopetown was located, explained that many residents were against high-density development, no matter where it was located. "Most of us who live in Simi moved here to escape the traffic and congestion. I'd like to see it all open space or a park. We have so little open space left in Simi Valley." For Stevens, Shapiro, and other activists who were not specifically invested in the preservation of the western cinematic past, Hopetown nonetheless offered the greatest strategic possibilities to resist encroaching (sub)urban development. According to Stevens, "There are more reasons to preserve Hopetown than any other area in the community."[95]

Encountering strong grassroots resistance, Griffin Homes changed its industrial park proposal to build 300 condominiums instead. But the Simi Valley Planning Commission claimed that the new project would require an amendment to the city's general plan, which mandated that all high-density housing be developed on the floor of the Valley rather than on the hillsides where Hopetown was situated. In a unanimous 0–5 vote in March 1986, the planning commission rejected such an amendment, but approved Griffin's proposal to build 219 single family homes on forty acres of the former ranch's lower section.[96] The resulting Hopetown Estates are located along Kuehner Drive in Simi Valley. The subdivision's large homes are of a Spanish mission style, with red tile roofs and arched doorways, and its interior streets feature names such as Bonanza Avenue, Empty Saddle Road, Chaps Court, Gold Dust Court, Cody Avenue, Cowboy Street, and Cowgirl Court.

With the immediate threat of industrial and high-density condominium development gone, but the promise of suburban tract homes on their way, suburban activists in Simi Valley accelerated their efforts to create a park at Corriganville. In 1986, the Santa Monica Mountains Conservancy offered one million dollars as seed money toward the purchase of remaining acreage in the Corriganville/Hopetown property, with the provision that it be used for recreation or to commemorate filmmaking history. The conservancy and local activists recommended the construction of picnic grounds, hiking trails, softball diamonds, and an equestrian center linking horse trails entering Santa Susana Pass.[97] In 1987, the State of California passed Senate Bill 1508, which authorized the City of Simi Valley to purchase 190 acres of land that had comprised the principal working areas of the original Corriganville Ranch, and in 1988 Simi Valley executed the purchase for one million dollars. Again, these purchases took place amid the devastating closures and stalled acquisition of parks and recreational facilities statewide in the aftermath of Proposition 13.

In 1988, a master plan was drafted for Corriganville Park. The master plan noted, "Through the community forum process, it has become apparent that OVERWHELMING community support exists for the restoration of the western town."[98] The plan recognized that the park's history provided a unique opportunity for theming and encouraged the coordination of public events such as living-history days, fairs, and Corriganville filming reenactments with the Simi Valley Historical Society. The plan mapped out in extensive detail the existing areas of the acreage such as Silvertown Street and Sherwood (Robin Hood) Forest. It noted their historical and cultural features and identified suitable ways in which they might be used, pending the availability of funding. The most expensive proposal involved the restoration and significant redevelopment of many of Corriganville's major tourist attractions during its days as an amusement park. This plan speculated that Silvertown Street might house a museum, several themed concessions, an indoor theater, restrooms, a conference room, and staff facilities. The Fort Apache Area might also include equestrian facilities such as a corral, horse-trailer parking, and a barn for the housing of a stagecoach and perhaps horse rentals.

However, development of the land into any kind of western theme park was stymied, much to the chagrin of suburban activists who had envisioned Corriganville's complete rebirth as a living testament to western heritage. Although the City of Simi Valley tried to obtain funding through grant applications to various federal and state agencies, none was approved, and private fund-raising efforts through special events eventually stalled. Land acquisition proceeded in small increments, usually funded by the City of Simi Valley rather than by county, state, or federal agencies. Throughout the early and mid-1990s, small parcels of land were added to the park as they became available, including a seventeen-acre parcel along the tracks of the Southern Pacific Railroad that was acquired between 1990 and 1992.

Corriganville Park now consists of 246 acres comprising the former production ranch's central area. It is governed by the Rancho Simi Recreation and

Parks District. It is a city park that falls within Simi Valley limits in Ventura County, but it abuts the Santa Susana Mountain Park, which is a regional park governed by Los Angeles County. The eastern part of the park is part of the Santa Susana Pass wildlife corridor connecting the Simi Hills with the Santa Susana Mountains.[99] Effectively, the two parks function as one large space and a single ecological corridor.

Taken together, the Santa Susana Mountain Park and Corriganville Park provide more than one thousand acres of parkland for the residents of the west San Fernando Valley and east Ventura County (see figure 8). These communities on the fringes of Los Angeles, occupied overwhelmingly by white and middle-class professionals, benefit from access to substantial open space in those very places where "wide open spaces" had been historically cultivated through both image and policy. The creation of these parks is thus central to the larger context of environmental racism in Los Angeles, illustrating the persistent power of white structural and institutional privilege in ensuring unequal access to open space.

To put things in perspective, during the same period in which the Santa Susana Mountain Park and Corriganville Park were created, activists in South and East Los Angeles were struggling to prevent the development of yet more polluting industrial facilities in their residential neighborhoods. Already disproportionately burdened with the city's waste facilities and toxic industrial plants, South Central Los Angeles was targeted for the construction of a waste-to-energy incinerator in 1983. Dubbed the LANCER project (Los Angeles City Energy Recovery project) and funded by a $535-million municipal bond, the incinerator would process 1,600 tons per day, emitting dioxins, heavy metals, and fly ash into the surrounding neighborhoods, which were overwhelmingly populated by poor and lower-middle-class African Americans. Concerned Citizens of South Central Los Angeles (CCSCLA) organized to fight the project, and through grassroots organization and the building of political networks, they managed to defeat the incinerator. Just a few years later, a similar struggle took place in East Los Angeles. In 1985, California Thermal Treatment Services proposed a hazardous-waste incinerator to be located in the city of Vernon, a purely industrial city that was already dubbed the "dirtiest zip code in California." The City of Vernon welcomed the incinerator, despite the fact that it was expected to burn over 22,500 tons of hazardous waste and thus would add to the region's already acute air pollution. The local regulatory agencies did not require an environmental impact report for the incinerator project, a decision that was seen by working-class Latino communities in adjacent East Los Angeles neighborhoods as a blatant act of environmental racism. The Mothers of East Los Angeles (MELA), which had recently formed to successfully pre-

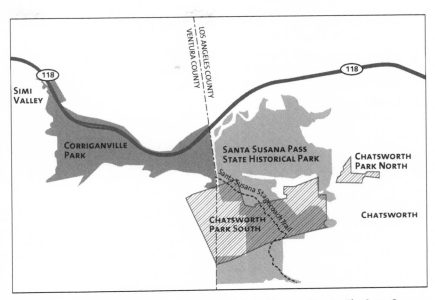

FIGURE 8 Parks in the west San Fernando Valley and east Ventura County. The Santa Susana Pass State Historic Park, Corriganville Park, and Chatsworth Park South essentially function as one large recreational area and wildlife corridor serving the people and animals of the west San Fernando Valley and Simi Valley. Map by Jacky Woolsey.

vent the location of a state prison in their community, organized weekly protests and pursued litigation in cooperation with the National Resource Defense Council.[100] Ultimately, the bid to build the incinerator was withdrawn. However, while working-class black and Latino activists were able to defeat these particular projects, both South Central Los Angeles and East Los Angeles remain saturated with toxic chemical and industrial plants. East Los Angeles, for example, houses both Quemetco Inc., ranked the greatest toxic polluter in Los Angeles County in 2005, in the City of Industry; and Amvac Chemical Corporation, located in Commerce, which manufactures and sells pesticides that have either been banned by the Environmental Protection Agency (EPA) or are on their way to being banned and have been implicated in the sterility of banana workers in Nicaragua.[101]

Clearly, the struggles that working-class and poor people of color and immigrants face in Los Angeles are fundamentally different from the environmentalism pursued by white, middle-class suburban-parks activists in Chatsworth and Simi Valley. The divergent nature of these activist battles in Los Angeles is symptomatic of a larger schism between the mainstream environmental movement and the environmental justice movement that was particularly pronounced in the 1980s but still persists in some ways today. According to Giovanna Di Chiro, the mainstream environmental movement has been premised on the construction of an artificial separation between humans and the natural world. She notes, "Environmentalists are therefore often said to be obsessed with preserving and protecting those 'wild and natural' areas defined as places where humans are not and *should* not be in large numbers."[102] Typically, mainstream environmentalism has been limited to issues such as wilderness preservation and endangered species protection, which means that, in the eyes of working-class environmental justice activists, mainstream environmentalists are "fixated on anti-urban development campaigns (read as 'no jobs for city-dwelling people') or utterly indifferent to the concerns of urban communities."[103] By contrast, environmental justice movements such as those led by CCSCLA and MELA assume that people are an integral part of what should be understood as the environment, and that the daily realities and conditions of people's lives — issues such as human health and sheer survival, workplace poisoning, poverty, and unsafe and unhealthy housing — should be at the center of environmental struggles. Environmental groups such as the SSMPA and the multiple groups that worked to preserve Corriganville Park clearly were part of the mainstream environmental movement. Despite their good intentions, their activism both drew on legacies of white privilege and reinforced them.

Race, class, and geography continue to fundamentally shape disparities in access to parkland and recreational space in Los Angeles. In a 2002 study, Jennifer Wolch, John P. Wilson, and Jed Fehrenbauch found that white neighborhoods in Los Angeles have, far and away, superior access to parks and recreation. White-dominant neighborhoods (where more than 75 percent of the population is white) have 31.8 park acres per 1,000 population and 192.9 park acres per 1,000 children. Conversely, Latino-dominant neighborhoods have just 0.6 park acres per 1,000 population and 1.6 park acres per 1,000 children. Black-dominant neighborhoods have 1.7 park acres per 1,000 population and 6.3 acres per 1,000 children. And Asian–Pacific Islander–dominant neighborhoods (of which there are relatively few) have just 0.3 park acres per 1,000 population and 1.9 acres per 1,000 children. These racial discrepancies are even more striking when levels of need and geography are considered. White neighborhoods are disproportionately low density (that is, they tend to have larger private yards) and have the fewest children, meaning that their need for public park space is much lower than other groups. Predominantly black, Latino, and Asian–Pacific Islander neighborhoods are two to five times as dense as white neighborhoods;

and Latino neighborhoods, which have the fastest-growing population in Los Angeles, have three times as many children both because of higher overall density and higher birth rates.[104] In a 1998 study, Patrick Tierney, Rene Dahl, and Deborah Chavez found that low-income groups, especially blacks, Latinos, and some Asian–Pacific Islanders, are the least likely to use undeveloped natural areas in Los Angeles County. Those who are most likely to visit such areas are white, young, male, and high-income; as well as high-income and highly educated members of other racial groups. Black people in Los Angeles, especially women, are the least likely to visit undeveloped natural areas.[105]

Proposition K, passed by California voters in 1996, seemed to offer an opportunity to ameliorate these racial and economic discrepancies. Prop K generates $25 million per year for acquisition, improvement, construction, and maintenance of city parks and recreation facilities, paid for through a real-property tax assessment.[106] Over the span of its thirty-year lifetime, Prop K will provide almost $300 million for 183 specific projects that were designated in the original language of the bill. An additional $143 million is to be allocated through a competitive process in which community-based organizations, city agencies, or other public entities submit proposals. However, Proposition K's competitive process actually appears to be exacerbating disparities in park access. To qualify, nonprofits must show that they have the internal capacity (especially financial management skills and administrative ability, as well as past experience in similar projects) to manage the amenity over a thirty-year lifetime. These requirements privilege sophisticated, professionalized environmental agencies (such as the Sierra Club, the Trust for Public Land, the Boys and Girls Clubs, local conservation corps, and the Watts Community Labor Action Committee — as well as the SSMPA and the Santa Monica Mountains Conservancy) run by highly educated, paid staff with strong connections to political officials. Neighborhood groups run by experienced, well-connected volunteers also do well. Smaller grassroots groups, run by neighborhood activists who may have fewer skills and economic resources but frequently have a more intimate knowledge of their communities' needs, are not faring as well in competition for Prop K money. According to a recent study, the highest success rates (in terms of proposals approved) have been in neighborhoods with populations that are more than 75 percent white, while the lowest rates of approved proposals are in areas that have the highest shares of Latino residents. In spite of the resources available through Proposition K, then, access to parks and open space in Los Angeles remains severely limited and is unequally available to racially defined communities.

The environmental benefits that communities in the west San Fernando Valley enjoy are but one dimension of their privileges relative to the larger metropolitan region. Indeed, by the turn of the twenty-first century, rural communities in both the northeast and the west Valley came to enjoy a host of economic, social, and environmental privileges compared with the growing poverty and racial diversity of the city as a whole. In the next chapter, I examine the multiple dimensions of rural whites' social-class privilege in the San Fernando Valley, with attention to how legacies of property ownership and social capital enable the reproduction of whiteness across shifting political economies and articulations of racial politics.

PART THREE

Rural Whiteness in the Twenty-first Century

CHAPTER SIX

Urban Restructuring and the Consolidation of Rural Whiteness

The institutionalization and formalization of the San Fernando Valley's rural landscapes examined in the previous two chapters occurred during a period of radical transformation in racial politics at the local, regional, national, and global scales. As we have seen, beginning in the 1960s, explicit white supremacy gave way to a position of official "color blindness," which is now widely regarded to be the dominant racial discourse in the United States. However, this discursive and ideological shift coincided with growing inequality, propelled by the intersections of economic restructuring, demographic change, and political choices to disinvest in social-welfare programs. Together, these changes have created an ever-wider gap between rich and poor in the United States, especially its cities, that is distinctly racialized but that is hidden and ignored by color-blind racial ideologies that proclaim racial inequality to be a thing of the past.[1]

Across these transformations, whiteness and white privilege in the San Fernando Valley have been reproduced through the rural landscape. At the moment in which the racial state at the national level shifted to a position of color blindness, the local urban state in Los Angeles also shifted its position — from explicit production of the rural landscape as an integral part of the "white spot of America" to the protection of "rural heritage" as a presumably racially neutral and universal concept. The urban state institutionalized horse-keeping zoning and historic preservation policies and created vast regional parks on the sites of western film production during the exact period, from the 1960s through the late 1980s, in which deindustrialization, increased immigration, and the emergence of color blindness as the dominant racial discourse intersected to vastly increase urban inequality. Through these practices of rural reproduction and reinvestment, the urban state in Los Angeles recommitted itself to protection of not only rural landscapes but also the historical social relations in which they were embedded.

In this chapter, I contextualize the protection of rurality in Shadow Hills and Chatsworth in relationship to Los Angeles's structural changes over the last half century. I compare indicators of economic, geographic, and social status in Shadow Hills and Chatsworth with Los Angeles County, supplementing my fieldwork with quantitative data from the 2000 census in order to situate rural privilege relative to the metropolitan region as a whole. Beyond standard measures of socioeconomic status (income, wealth, and education), I find that rural white residents benefit from racially unequal legacies of property ownership; possess the highly valuable forms of knowledge, expertise, and social connections that result from whites' overrepresentation in the upper tier of the city's contemporary economy; and enjoy the public health benefits of low-density residential landscapes with significant open space. These dimensions of social-class privilege not only create a higher quality of life for white residents of Los Angeles's semirural neighborhoods but also ensure that they are disproportionately able to protect their status for the long term and for future generations.

In the last five decades, Los Angeles has become a profoundly different city from the metropolis envisioned by urban planners and civic boosters at the turn of the twentieth century. Restructuring of the regional economy and exponential growth — both geographic and demographic — have transformed the middle-class, suburban "city of homes" and gentleman farming into a highly unequal region wracked by poverty, environmental racism, and segregation.[2] Economic restructuring has increased the extent and concentration of poverty in Los Angeles and the spatial, economic, and racial gaps between rich and poor. As in most U.S. cities, Los Angeles's loss of manufacturing began in the 1960s, gained steam throughout the 1970s, and is still in process. Deindustrialization destroyed hundreds of thousands of blue-collar, often unionized, living-wage jobs in manufacturing — especially in defense, automobile production, and durable consumer goods — and devastated the city's middle class. Unlike other cities that have suffered wholesale deindustrialization and high unemployment, however, Los Angeles has retained a significant manufacturing base through nearly simultaneous processes of reindustrialization. Yet the city's new manufacturing no longer guarantees a relatively secure, middle-class existence. Instead, the high-quality jobs once associated with the manufacturing of defense and durable consumer goods have been replaced with low-wage, nonunionized work in the manufacturing and assembly of clothing, furniture, and electronics.[3] During the same period, a bifurcated two-tier service-sector economy has emerged that consists of both high-wage, high-skill jobs and extensive low-wage, low-skill service work. Collectively, these transformations have earned Los Angeles the dubious distinction as national capital of the working poor. Indeed, while overall employment increased by 2 percent in the 1990s, working poverty increased by 34 percent, and the overall poverty population increased by one-third.[4]

The city's macro-scale economic changes are marked by their racially uneven impact. Convulsive bouts of deindustrialization and reindustrialization
coincided with, and have been propelled by, substantial increases in the size of
the city's Asian and Latino immigrant populations. These demographic shifts
are the result of the overhaul of immigration policies in 1965, the globalization
of industry, and U.S. interventions in Latin America and Asia that dislocated
existing economies and civil societies.[5] Simultaneously, the city's non-Hispanic
white population has declined significantly as a result of comparatively lower
birthrates as well as persistent white flight out of the county to the city's exurbs
and out of the state of California altogether. In 1970, Los Angeles was 71 percent
white, 15 percent Latino, 11 percent black, and 2.5 percent Asian American. By
2000, the white population had declined to 31 percent, while the Latino population increased to 37 percent. The Asian American population had grown to 11
percent by 2000; the black population remained stable.[6] Yet the city's growing
diversity has not created a benign multiculturalism; instead, diversity in Los
Angeles is premised on sharp, glaring inequality. African Americans have been
disproportionately affected by the loss of durable manufacturing jobs, suffering
higher rates of unemployment, while Latinos have overwhelmingly filled the
new manufacturing and low-skill service jobs and therefore are overrepresented
among the working poor.[7] Median incomes for African American and Latino
households in Los Angeles trail those of whites by nearly twenty-five thousand
dollars; and in 2000, while Latinos made up 40 percent of the city's workforce,
they accounted for 73 percent of the working poor.[8]

Amid these changes, the material privileges of whiteness in Los Angeles have
been consolidated. Whiteness (and especially white masculinity) in contemporary Los Angeles is associated with disproportionately high levels of education,
concentration in professional occupations, and high incomes. In part, whites'
overrepresentation in the upper levels of the regional economy is a result of their
disproportionate ability to take advantage of racially exclusive federal spending
in higher education, vocational training, and small business loans, most notably
through the GI Bill.[9] But it is also a result of the out-migration of lower-middle-
class, working-class, and poor whites, who were most likely to leave California
from the late 1970s through the early 1990s, the state's most intense years of
deindustrialization. These lower-income whites typically moved to regions of
the country that were less attractive to the immigrants with whom they competed for the new low-skill manufacturing and service jobs. Many of these jobs
were in the rural interior of the country. This phenomenon of white urban-to-
rural migration — which some have termed the "new white flight" — reached
its height in the mid-1990s, although it continues to be observed in the United

States and Europe; it is especially common, according to demographer William Frey, in cities that have experienced economic restructuring in tandem with an influx of immigrant labor.[10] Upper-income whites in Los Angeles, by contrast, have been far less likely to leave the city. They are disproportionately represented in the high-skill, high-wage occupations of the service economy and can typically afford to send their children to private schools and to live in exclusive communities.[11] As a result, while class divisions among white people in Los Angeles certainly persist, in broad terms whiteness there is an economically privileged experience.

These racialized economic divisions are literally mapped onto social space in Los Angeles. As poverty has grown, it has become more spatially concentrated. The proportion of all neighborhoods classified as "extremely poor" (with more than 40 percent of residents in poverty) increased by over 80 percent between 1990 and 2000.[12] As a result, according to 2000 census data, Los Angeles is the most economically segregated region in the country — only 28 percent of its neighborhoods are middle class or mixed income.[13] And since Los Angeles's labor markets are distinctly organized by race, the concentration of poverty is a racialized phenomenon associated with the segregation of people of color, particularly blacks and Latinos, from whites. White people in Los Angeles were actually *more* spatially isolated from blacks, Latinos, and Asians in 2000 than they were in 1940, even though they constitute a far smaller share of the population. The majority of whites in Los Angeles reside in neighborhoods that are predominantly white and wealthy, and these neighborhoods have higher property values, regardless of where they are located.[14] Thus, it appears that the geography of whiteness in Los Angeles, while shifting, remains linked to economic privilege. Majority-white neighborhoods, through their concentration of wealth and other privileges, ensure that future generations of white children and young adults will continue to benefit from the range of opportunities and resources available to their parents.

The San Fernando Valley has changed dramatically in recent years, too, though on balance it is still a wealthier and whiter place than Los Angeles County. In 2006, the U.S. Census Bureau released its first-ever demographic survey of the San Fernando Valley as a distinct unit. Non-Hispanic whites made up 43 percent of the Valley's population, compared with 29 percent in Los Angeles County, while Latinos were 42 percent of the Valley's population, compared with 47 percent in the county. Compared with the county, the Valley also had a lower Asian American population (10 percent versus 13 percent) and a smaller black population (4 percent in the Valley versus 9 percent in the county). Home values were significantly higher in the Valley, at $524,800 versus $480,300 in

Los Angeles, as were median household incomes, at $51,717 in the Valley compared with $48,248 in Los Angeles County.[15] Thus, compared with the larger metropolitan region, the San Fernando Valley is both whiter, though not the "lily white" of its stereotypes, and economically more advantaged, though not markedly so.

Some observers of the Census Bureau's 2006 survey have used the data as a way to distinguish the San Fernando Valley from its oft-cited stereotypical misconceptions as a bastion of white supremacy. Jim Newton, writing for the *Los Angeles Times*, noted that the new data "helps explain the Valley as it is — slightly wealthier than the rest of the city to which it is sometimes uncomfortably attached, but with large numbers of immigrants and a medley of languages."[16] Joel Kotkin and Erika Ozuna, in a joint project of Pepperdine University and the Economic Alliance of the San Fernando Valley, argue that

> few places in America over the past quarter century have undergone as profound a change in its ethnic character than the San Fernando Valley. Back in the 1970s, the region was perceived — and rightly so — as a bastion of predominantly Anglo, middle class residents living adjacent the most cosmopolitan society of Los Angeles. Today that reality has drastically changed. . . . Yet, to many from outside the region, and some within, the Valley still remains a prisoner of old stereotypes. . . . The Valley today is not a bland homogenized middle class suburb; it is an increasingly cosmopolitan, diverse and racially intermixed region united by a common geography, economy and, to a large extent, middle class aspirations.[17]

As a partial explanation for the Valley's demographic change, Kotkin and Ozuna suggest that the middle-class, mostly white migration out of the San Fernando Valley during this period was "not necessarily for racist and nostalgic reasons . . . but for such basic things as better education for their children, excellent parks, and other amenities."[18] The problem with such an interpretation is that, in the San Fernando Valley as in virtually all American suburbs, amenities like schools and parks have never been nonracialized; indeed, perceptions of the quality of schools and parks are based, at least in part, on the racial, social-class, and national status of those who use them. Moreover, meaningful divisions exist *within* the Valley and are important indicators of social difference and latent tensions. According to Newton, "As close observers of the San Fernando Valley know, today's Valley is itself divided, principally by an east-west split that runs along the 405 Freeway. . . . On one end of the Valley [the west side], gated mansions and old ranch houses still preside over well-groomed neighborhoods; on the other [the east side], some residents still don't have sewer hookups or streetlights."[19] On the west side of the Valley, a majority of residents are white,

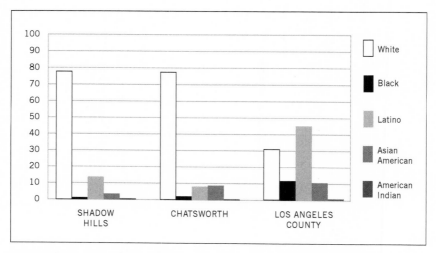

FIGURE 9 Comparison of the racial demographics of Shadow Hills, Chatsworth, and Los Angeles County based on U.S. Census 2000 data.

whereas on the east side, just one-third are; West Valley residents also earn five thousand dollars more per year in household income than East Valley residents. Homeownership rates and educational achievements reflect similar discrepancies. These differences appear to be growing.

Within this context, the San Fernando Valley's rural neighborhoods — on both the east and the west sides of the Valley — have been relatively protected from the region's structural changes and the downward economic spiral affecting so many of the city's residents. They are refuges of open space and a very high quality of life within a globally connected, sharply unequal city. They are also home to a disproportionately white, middle-class, professional population that enjoys high incomes, property values, and levels of education, whether compared with the San Fernando Valley or the city more broadly.

Indeed, the contrasts between the San Fernando Valley's legally protected rural areas and Los Angeles's dense urban core are striking (see figures 9–12). In 2000, in both Shadow Hills and Chatsworth, the white population was much larger and had substantially higher incomes and education levels, and were more concentrated in professional jobs, than in the population of Los Angeles County. Shadow Hills's population in 2000 was 78.6 percent non-Hispanic white, 13.7 percent Hispanic/Latino, 3.3 percent Asian, 1 percent black, and 0.8 percent American Indian, with 3.7 percent of the population identifying

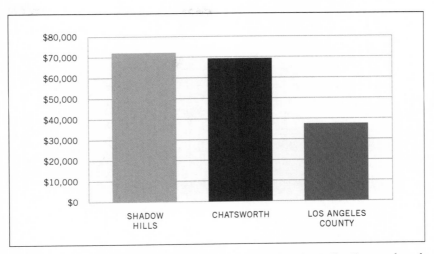

FIGURE 10 Comparison of the median household incomes of Shadow Hills, Chatsworth, and Los Angeles County based on U.S. Census 2000 data.

as mixed-race.[20] Chatsworth exhibits remarkably similar patterns. Chatsworth's population in 2000 was 78 percent non-Hispanic white, 8.4 percent Latino, 8.9 percent Asian American, 2 percent black, and 0.2 percent American Indian. Approximately 3 percent of the population identified as mixed-race. In 2000, by comparison, Los Angeles County was just 31 percent non-Hispanic white, 45.5 percent Hispanic/Latino, 10.9 percent Asian American, 12.1 percent black, and 0.8 percent American Indian, with approximately 5 percent of the population reporting two or more races. Thus, both Shadow Hills and Chatsworth have retained and attracted residential populations that are substantially whiter than the city as a whole. Likewise, rates of poverty and tenancy are much lower in the Valley's rural neighborhoods. The median household income in Shadow Hills was $73,884, and 4.4 percent of families lived below the poverty line; the median household income in Chatsworth was $69,837, and only 2.3 percent of families lived in poverty.[21] By contrast, the median household income of Los Angeles County households was $37,338, approximately half that of rural neighborhoods, and nearly 18 percent of Los Angeles County families — or four to six times those of rural neighborhoods — lived below the poverty line in 2000. These discrepancies between rural areas and the larger metropolitan region are not coincidental; rather, they are the result of complex histories of white privilege embedded in and structured into the rural landscape.

Yet the privileges of rural whiteness in the San Fernando Valley extend far

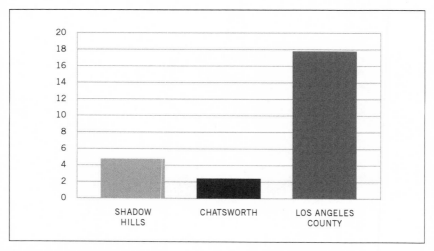

FIGURE 11 Comparison of rates of poverty in Shadow Hills, Chatsworth, and Los Angeles County based on U.S. Census 2000 data.

beyond conventional measures of social class such as income, education, and occupation. Economist Michael Zweig notes, "When people in the United States talk about class, it is often in ways that hide its most important parts. We tend to think about class in terms of income, or the lifestyles that income can buy"; education and occupation also figure prominently in most popular conceptions of social class.[22] Yet this understanding does not adequately capture the complexity of social class or the reasons for its endurance across generations. Class inequalities, according to Paul Sweezy, "are not only or perhaps even primarily a matter of income. . . . More important are a number of other factors which are less well defined, less visible, and impossible to quantify: the advantages of coming from a more 'cultured' home environment, differential access to educational opportunities, the possession of 'connections' in the circles of those holding positions of power and prestige, and self-confidence which children absorb from their parents — the list could be expanded and elaborated."[23] Zweig understands the middle class as a group of professional people who have a degree of autonomy and control over their lives that other people with fewer resources do not have.

I find Zweig's conception of class-as-power useful for understanding the social-class position of Los Angeles's contemporary rural residents. Contemporary residents of Shadow Hills, Chatsworth, and the Valley's other rural neighborhoods are middle class not only because of their incomes and

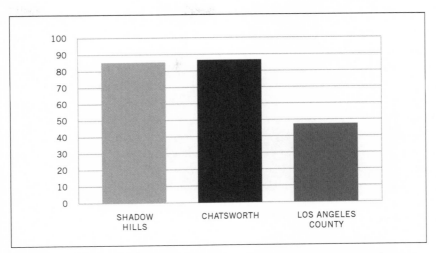

FIGURE 12 Comparison of homeownership rates in Shadow Hills, Chatsworth, and Los Angeles County based on U.S. Census 2000 data.

education levels, which are in fact relatively high compared with the county's workforce as a whole, but also because they possess a level of power and control over their lives unmatched by other workers. Crucially, they have the ability to protect the rural landscapes of their neighborhoods and to preserve and transmit their economic and geographic privileges to future generations. In this respect, two processes are especially important: (1) property ownership and access, including high rates of property ownership, high property values, and the ability to accumulate equity, all of which are enhanced by the rural aesthetic of "wide open spaces"; and (2) social capital, particularly the use of occupational skill sets and networks to reproduce and protect the rural landscape.

Given the city's economic dislocations, the ownership of property has become ever more critical to economic security in the last half century. Moreover, property has long been a crucial dimension of white privilege, central to both the material and the cultural identity of white people. Historically, the exclusionary reservation of property ownership for white people, based on perceptions of their moral and rational superiority as individuals, simultaneously reinforced the meanings of whiteness not only as a social construction but also as a spatially produced category associated with particular landscapes and models of land use deemed superior. According to Laura Brace, "White people were . . . defined as white on the basis that they had the capacity to exclude others, and to exercise despotic dominion over themselves. Whiteness itself was a probationary category with permeable boundaries of belonging and identity. . . . Being white, and being able to exclude others from whiteness, involved being able to prevent yourself from becoming property, to protect yourself from the threat of commodification."[24] Legal scholar Cheryl Harris has argued that whiteness itself shares the critical characteristics of property, namely, the right to exclude, as well as the legal justification of expectations of power and control with state sponsorship. Through these practices, the legally guaranteed entitlement of white people to own and profit from the bodies and labor of others became, and remains, a form of property.[25]

This is particularly true in terms of the racially unequal accumulation of wealth, which is the result of generations of exclusionary policy and legacies of discrimination in access to property. Gaps in wealth accumulation are far more important than income differentials as explanations for enduring racial inequality in the contemporary era. That is, even when individuals from different racial groups make the same income, their wealth portfolios remain highly unequal. The wealth gap is important because assets (in the form of real estate, equities, or retirement funds, for example) act as an economic buffer that can, during economic downturns, make a profound difference in individual and family security. Property ownership also allows for the accumulation of wealth that can be transferred to children and is thus a primary factor in the reproduction of social-class status from generation to generation. Within this context, real property is especially critical, because it is the single largest dimension of most households' wealth portfolios.[26]

In Los Angeles, crises of housing affordability are legion, especially since the 1970s, and rates of real-property ownership among the city's racial groups are highly unequal. In 2000, 51 percent of white households in Los Angeles were homeowners, while only 31 percent of black households and 27 percent of Latino families owned their homes.[27] Homeownership is positively correlated with higher levels of education and higher incomes, as well as U.S. citizenship, and these characteristics are associated with native-born whites in contemporary Los Angeles and disassociated from foreign-born Latinos.[28] In Los Angeles as elsewhere, these patterns are a result not only of the shorter time that immigrants have spent in the country but also of historical policies of housing exclusion that gave white families a head start in the accumulation of home equity, as well as the skewing of the contemporary regional economy in ways that favor middle-class and professional whites.

With their emphasis on large lot sizes, open space, and a rural aesthetic, land-use policies in the San Fernando Valley's rural neighborhoods exacerbate the racialized dynamics of property ownership and wealth accumulation. The zoning in Shadow Hills restricts residential development to single-family homes, ensuring that most residents are homeowners and that those who do rent are living in houses rather than apartments. In Chatsworth, some higher-density condominiums and townhouses (though few apartments) have been allowed, but the community is still dominated by homeowners. In Shadow Hills in 2000, 86 percent of residents were homeowners; in Chatsworth, homeowners comprised 87 percent of the population. By comparison, only 48 percent of Los Angeles County residents owned their homes in 2000.[29] Moreover, scholars have consistently found that the legal protection of open space increases property values in adjacent residential neighborhoods, and that this effect is heightened when the open space is preserved in perpetuity.[30] Thus, residents of Shadow Hills and Chatsworth, both of which have legally protected low-density landscapes and are adjacent to large public recreation areas and regional parks, benefit directly and personally from their access to these resources and the increasingly valuable aesthetic of the rural landscape within the dense, global city (see figures 13 and 14).

Historical developments in Shadow Hills are instructive for understanding the racialized accumulation of wealth through property law and land-use policy that protects open space and the rural aesthetic. The horse-keeping ordinance in Shadow Hills was passed in 1962, during the long era in which fair housing laws were being debated, passed, and implemented. In 1948, the U.S. Supreme Court had made federal enforcement of racially restrictive covenants illegal, although individual property owners could nonetheless adhere to them through mutual agreement; at the height of postwar suburbanization, therefore, residential segregation proceeded apace. In 1963, California passed the Rumford Fair Housing Act in an effort to repeal some of the barriers to housing. However, almost immediately, the California Real Estate Association sponsored a ballot initiative to repeal the Rumford Act, charging that it infringed too heavily on the rights of property owners to sell their homes to whomever they chose and that it represented unwanted and undue influence by government in the lives of everyday people. The initiative, which became Proposition 14, was endorsed by conservative social groups such as the John Birch Society and the California Republican Assembly and ultimately passed by 65 percent of the state electorate in 1964, thus repealing California's early efforts at housing integration and nondiscrimination. In 1968, legal barriers to housing integration were fully removed, though still not adequately enforced, by the federal Fair Housing Act. By

FIGURE 13 Large ranches such as this one are the sites of development battles in contemporary Shadow Hills. Photo by author, 2006.

that time, rural and horse-keeping neighborhoods had been legally created and were already largely off limits to incoming nonwhites because of their expense. Already by February 1964, the director of Equestrian Trails, Inc., reported that new homeowners in Shadow Hills had paid, on average, five thousand dollars more for their lots than they would have paid for the same amount of property elsewhere in the city.[31] Higher housing costs dovetailed with persistent anxieties about integration to maintain and actually increase the white population of Shadow Hills throughout the 1970s.

Those who moved to the neighborhood before its designation as a horse-keeping district have seen the value of their properties increase dramatically since then. This became clear in the life histories of the Shadow Hills residents whom I interviewed. For example, Ann Finn, the wife of former city councilman Howard Finn, now deceased, recalls that they purchased twenty-two acres in Shadow Hills in 1945 for less than fifteen thousand dollars; they later subdivided the property and designed and built custom homes. She still lives in the same house. Evan and Myra Jones purchased their two-bedroom house, which they slowly remodeled and expanded over the years, in 1957 for fifteen thou-

FIGURE 14 Residents can keep horses on relatively small suburban lots because of provisions in the horse-keeping ordinance and the community plan. This property's barn and pipe corrals are typical. Photo by author, 2006.

sand dollars. Both the Finns and the Joneses thus purchased their homes before the matrix of zoning and land-use policies designed to protect open space and rurality was implemented. As older residents, they or their beneficiaries stand to gain a windfall upon the sale of their properties. After the implementation of the horse-keeping ordinance and the community plan during the 1960s, Shadow Hills home values increased steadily, mimicking the overall inflation of Southern California real estate. Eric Franco purchased his home in rural Sun Valley, which is included within the Shadow Hills community plan, in 1977 for twenty-five thousand dollars. But housing prices exploded in the 1980s, tripling or quadrupling in less than a decade. Realtor Elaine Hillsboro recalls that the average price of a home in Shadow Hills was sixty thousand dollars when she began practicing real estate there in 1986, and Richard Eagan purchased his home overlooking Hansen Dam, on 1⅓ acres, for eighty-five thousand dollars in 1985. Although both Hillsboro and Eagan characterized those prices as "cheap," they were nonetheless an increase of more than 200 percent in less than a decade.

The average value of a home in Shadow Hills in 2000 was $330,000. However, during the time I conducted my interviews, in 2005 — at the height of a real-estate boom — most homes on half-acre lots were selling for a minimum of $800,000, with "equestrian estates" on even larger lots selling for upwards of $1 million. Thus, homeowners who purchased their homes as late as the mid-1980s for a median price of $60,000, as real-estate agent Elaine Hillsboro recalls, experienced more than a tenfold increase in the value of their properties. Buyers who purchased property even earlier, in the 1950s or 1960s — before the passage of fair housing laws and the institutionalization of rurality — have benefited from gains of more than fifty times their initial investment. Therefore, even when Shadow Hills' homeowners' income levels are roughly comparable to nonwhites in the immediate surrounding area, what counts is their degree of wealth, because they are occupying pieces of property that have increased greatly in value as a direct result of the land-use policies that protect rurality, as well as the overall inflation of Southern California real-estate values in the past half century.

Even those who purchased homes in Shadow Hills relatively recently, at prices of $800,000 or more, were able to do so because they benefited from the explosion in Southern California real-estate values in other neighborhoods. A few biographies demonstrate this point clearly. Donna Reese and her husband bought their first house in La Crescenta (a nearby suburb in the foothills east of Shadow Hills that was, at the time they lived there, almost exclusively white) in 1973 for $34,000. Four years later, they sold that house for $68,000 and purchased a new house, also in La Crescenta, for $72,000. They raised a family in that home, but after their children had gone to college, Reese pursued her long-standing dream to keep horses on her own property. She and her husband sold their La Crescenta home in 2003 for $640,000 — representing nearly a 900 percent increase in value — and purchased a home on a half-acre lot with a barn in Shadow Hills for over $800,000. Reese is a public school teacher; her husband is an auto mechanic for high-end racecars. Although they earn a solid middle-class income, it is unlikely that they would have been able to purchase a home in Shadow Hills without the boost in real-estate values and corresponding accumulation of home equity and wealth that occurred throughout Southern California from the 1980s until recently, and their ability to purchase a home in a racially exclusive neighborhood that increased in value over time.[32]

Gary McCullough, a commercial real-estate developer specializing in storage facilities, offered a remarkably similar story. McCullough recalled that he and his family moved numerous times throughout the 1970s and 1980s, each time climbing a ladder of ballooning real-estate values to purchase subsequently more expensive homes. He narrated in detail his family's history of real-estate investment:

> I moved to Santa Monica [from Virginia], bought my first piece of property there when I was like twenty-three. And lived there for about five years. . . . That was back in the early eighties. . . . And I eventually moved up here in 1985 and bought our first house in Sunland. . . . It was a fixer; we fixed it, sold it within a year, made a $100,000 profit. And wanted to get a place we could have horses, so we could have our horses at home. . . . So I found this house over on Pearson Place that was a total wreck. So I bought it and then took her [his wife] to show it to her. She was crying. Because we had this house that was all nice, and here we were moving into a bomb again. So over time we fixed it up, and it was a great house on Pearson Place.[33]

In 2003, McCullough purchased a home in the brand-new Rancho Verdugo Estates, a tract-home development in Shadow Hills. He recalled,

> Those homes were advertised at $650,000, [but] nothing in the development sold for under $760,000 because by the time they got them built, the land value had gone up so much. Every time they sold five homes, they'd have a new "phase," they'd call it; prices would go way up. I mean, they were just on fire. And you know, you feel like you were getting stuck at the time, but hindsight being what it is, you got a great deal there. You can't get anything close to that for the money. Nobody paid over a million there, and I don't think there's anything worth under a million now, based on the value of real estate in Shadow Hills.[34]

Thus, rural residents are fully aware of the importance of climbing real-estate values for their own upward mobility. Although they may dismiss the steep increases in property values as unbelievable or as something beyond their control, standard fare in Southern California, they nonetheless stand to materially benefit from the power of the real-estate industry and the shortage of developable land in Los Angeles and are politically invested in their property rights.

The legally protected large lot sizes and horse-keeping aesthetic in Shadow Hills and the state-protected regional parks and open space districts in Chatsworth directly benefit local property owners — even those who make a relatively modest income — by contributing to higher property values and the accumulation of wealth across generations. In this respect, individual property owners, who are disproportionately white, continue to benefit from historical policies and political-economic structures. As the city of Los Angeles becomes more dense, undeveloped land becomes more valuable, and the "open space" and rural aesthetic protected by rural land-use policies benefit existing property owners. As we have seen, these privileged few include those who had earlier, racially exclusive access to the housing market and can convert capital gains into investment in new properties; those who have received large inheritances, often based on the sale of property bought during an earlier era; and those who occupy the upper stratum of the contemporary two-tier service economy. Each of these conditions is associated with white people in the San Fernando Valley, Los Angeles, and most other American cities.

The San Fernando Valley's rural residents are also disproportionately empowered to protect their primary investment — their homes and properties — for future generations, because of their ability to translate their extensive social capital into highly effective land-use activism. Scholars of social movements have shown that higher education levels and higher incomes translate into greater involvement in the local political process, expanded political credibility, and better likelihoods of success in achieving movement goals.[35] These forms of social capital are likewise crucial to the reproduction of social-class status.

The Valley's rural neighborhoods are home to professionals with high levels of education and extensive skill sets. They are also well connected socially to others who have access to resources and who are embedded in the city's political process. According to 2000 census data, 43.2 percent of Shadow Hills residents were employed in management, professional, and related occupations, with another 27.3 percent employed in other service occupations. Chatsworth residents are employed in similar kinds of jobs, with a substantially larger share of the population (54.9 percent) working in management, professional, and related occupations and another 31.1 percent in sales and office jobs. Not a single person in either Shadow Hills or Chatsworth was employed in farming, fishing, or forestry despite both neighborhoods' billing as "rural" places. Comparatively few were employed in construction, transportation, or material-moving occupations.[36]

Most of these jobs are middle-class jobs; they are not the positions of Los Angeles's superelite. Yet the types of jobs that Shadow Hills and Chatsworth residents hold are typical of the relatively high-wage, high-skill occupations produced through Los Angeles's economic restructuring. More importantly for my purposes here, their jobs demand and cultivate skill sets that are extremely useful for protection of the rural landscape. Table 3 lists the occupations of the people I interviewed for this project and their position in community activism at the time of the interview. On account of their occupations, many rural residents are highly proficient with legal, technical, and environmental languages;

TABLE 3 Interviewees' occupations and positions in the northeast San Fernando
Valley's community organizations at the time of interview, summer 2005

NAME (PSEUDONYM)	OCCUPATION	POSITION IN LOCAL ORGANIZATIONS AT TIME OF INTERVIEW
Gillian Black	Self-employed	President of recreational equestrian organization
Edward Burkett	Construction (retired)	Cochair, trails committee of property-owners association
Lisa Burkett	Bookkeeper (retired)	Cochair, trails committee of property-owners association
Michael Castalucci	Public relations consultant	Newsletter editor for property-owners association
Richard Egan	Contractor	N/A
Linda Ellison	Teacher (on leave)	Advertising manager for property-owners association
Leslie Forster	Assistant to real-estate developer	Historian of property-owners association
Eric Franco	Small business owner	Chairman of Neighborhood Watch
Elaine Hillsboro	Real-estate agent	N/A
James Huck	Lawyer	Chair, land-use committee of property-owners association
Evan Jones	Grounds supervisor/ facilities management (retired)	Cochair, membership committee of property-owners association
Gary McCullough	Real-estate developer	President of homeowners association
Donna Reese	Public school teacher	N/A
Patricia Wheat	Ranch owner/operator	Vice president of recreational equestrian organization

Created by author.

they are also unusually familiar with the land-use planning and real-estate development processes.

A few narrative examples will demonstrate the relationship between whites' occupational privilege and their successful land-use activism. Jim Huck is a lawyer who serves as the land-use chairman of the Shadow Hills Property Owners Association. He devotes a substantial amount of time, pro bono, to reading environmental impact reports and dissecting the legalese of proposed developments. At monthly property-owners association meetings, he always has a dedicated place on the agenda, during which he explains and interprets pending developments for those in attendance. Typically, he equips them with specific language and strategies with which to lobby the city council and the planning commission. In our interview, he explained to me how his legal expertise had helped to protect Shadow Hills from encroaching urban development.

> In terms of protecting that area [Hansen Dam], what we've done is the following:
> . . . Because the Los Angeles County Department of Public Works had done pretty
> much unspeakable things, not to the wash but to wetlands, they were required
> to mitigate what they had done. I knew that they had this mitigation problem,
> when that property over in the wash went up for sale. . . . I immediately called
> the Department of Public Works because they had to buy this mitigation bank,
> so I got them to buy basically the Tujunga Wash in the Shadow Hills area [for $2
> million] so that it is now preserved because it has to be a mitigation bank for all
> the other things that they did. So it is now a defined area that's not going to be
> messed with for the most part.[37]

Huck's knowledge of the legal requirements with regard to development and mitigation, as well as his comfort in approaching and negotiating with representatives of the urban state — and the fact that they listened to him and took him seriously — translated directly into the protection of open space and enhancement of the rural landscape in his own neighborhood. He then explained to me one of his most recent successes, the purchase of nearly five hundred acres in the hills northeast of Shadow Hills that will be dedicated to permanent open space:

> There's a foundation . . . [with] substantial amounts of money to purchase open
> space in Los Angeles County and Ventura County and there's three directors.
> I'm one of them and two other people I've known for a long time are directors.
> So we were made aware of this property. We purchased it; we still have to raise
> some additional money to pay off the note, but effectively we have contained and
> surrounded Shadow Hills. . . . Doesn't mean that there won't be infill problems

and infill issues, but from an encroachment area, you're not going to have massive development so that you have a substantially better opportunity to in fact keep the area as a rural horse-keeping community.[38]

Again, Huck's social connections and his position as a director of a major land-acquisition foundation contributed directly to the preservation of the rural landscape adjacent to Shadow Hills.

Similarly, Richard Eagan, a contractor, could be counted on to monitor on-going construction and development activity from his hilltop home in Shadow Hills. He told me of one incident in which he helped to "shut down" someone who was using a residential parcel illegally for commercial sales: "He came in and he discovered that if he called his place a worm farm, then it was legal in that zone. But he was really selling mulch. So we got hip to him real fast and we were taking pictures and video of him, and he took it to every extent of the law. We went to the building and safety commission, the planning commission, and he had a really high-priced lawyer in building and planning issues, and he lost every step of the thing." When I pointed out that activists in other neighborhoods were not likely to have the same degree of legal expertise or knowledge, he replied: "Yeah I'm very familiar with the whole thing. I know building and safety [the commission] very, very well. I know city planning very well. I've been dealing with them for many years, and I know the whole process."[39] These narratives point to the complex nature of social-class privilege among Los Angeles's rural residents — as determined not only by income, education, and occupation but also by patterns of wealth accumulation, social capital, and control over the material conditions of their lives. These stories also illustrate that the contemporary rural landscape is the product of residents' skills and social connections as urban professionals, which are a direct result of whites' privilege in the new urban economy, but also of knowledge gained and social connections built through generations of rural land-use activism.

This point is not lost on rural residents themselves, many of whom are aware that their efficacy as activists rests upon residents' skills, education, and social networks. A retired landscape gardener, who had lived in Shadow Hills for fifty years and was instrumental during the early 1950s in founding the property-owners association (then known as the Shadow Hills Civic Association), told me that over the years the organization had become increasingly powerful. He said, "Then the new group came in, which is a more powerful group because they've got a much more elevated background." When I asked him what he meant, he elaborated, "Well, people who are businessmen themselves, who have a little bit of punch with City Hall." He then pointed to Jim Huck as an example. "He's the land-use attorney, and a good one. People like him and the other membership that we have. . . . They come up with a strong, effective, ongoing body."[40]

Those who are skilled in these areas, like Huck, share their knowledge and expertise with others through formal and informal venues. One of the reasons why activists in Shadow Hills are powerful is because of the geographic concentration of relevant social capital. Lisa Burkett, for example, recounted to me that former city council representative Howard Finn had taught her virtually everything she knows about the land-use planning process. She and her husband, Edward, both retired, now coordinate the trails committee of the Shadow Hills Property Owners Association. They organize trail maintenance and cleanup days and also lead political and legal action to acquire new land for bridle and hiking trails.[41] Concentrated together, activists like them in Shadow Hills and Chatsworth have achieved high rates of success in their neighborhoods because of their ability to translate professional skills into effective land-use activism. Few neighborhoods in Los Angeles possess such a concentration of skilled professionals; those that do can effectively translate their current economic status into political power.

Thus, residents of Los Angeles's legally designated rural neighborhoods are privileged in multiple ways compared with the city as a whole, and they can use those privileges to extend their social and economic status across generations, thus reproducing racialized patterns of economic and geographic inequality. But how do contemporary residents of the San Fernando Valley's rural neighborhoods themselves understand the city's political, economic, and demographic restructuring? How do they interpret and explain their privileged social-class positions relative to the city's increasing poverty, and the relative whiteness of their neighborhood compared with the browning of Los Angeles? And what can we learn from them about the contemporary negotiation of whiteness in the urban U.S. West? These questions inform my analysis in the next two chapters, which draw on my ethnographic research to investigate the construction and negotiation of individual and collective identities, relative to structural change, in the San Fernando Valley's contemporary rural communities.

CHAPTER SEVEN

Beliefs about Landscape, Anxieties about Change

On a sunny March afternoon in 2003, I arrived at the Shadow Hills home of Patricia Wheat. Wheat, a white woman in her mid-sixties, met me in the driveway, wearing her characteristic jeans and cowboy boots, and greeted me warmly in a voice made hoarse by a lifetime of smoking cigarettes. Wheat's property, a sprawling six-acre ranch, is one of the few large parcels that remain in Shadow Hills. Wheat is a fixture in local politics and social life; many other people in the neighborhood had urged me to speak with her. Like so many other residents of the San Fernando Valley, Wheat's life history has been deeply influenced by her participation in the local production of western films and, more broadly, by the city's history of structuring urban life around myths of western heritage. She grew up on film sets with her father, a character actor who worked in westerns and who encouraged her to learn how to take care of horses and other animals instead of staying inside doing domestic chores, as her mother would have liked. As she recollected with enthusiasm early in our conversation, "If you were to get a little tape, you could see me dressed up as an old lady at about thirteen years old, riding a wagon down the road through [the western-themed television series] *Death Valley Days* with Ronnie Reagan!"[1] Wheat now runs a commercial horse-boarding facility on her Shadow Hills property, taking care of others' horses (feeding and watering, cleaning stalls, and turning horses out for exercise) in exchange for a monthly fee. She regularly hosts parties and organizational fund-raisers, such as Equestrian Trails, Inc.'s annual Harvest Moon Festival, at her ranch; her home is both large enough to entertain hundreds of people and powerfully symbolic of the rural western lifestyle that people in the community embrace.

But Wheat's property is also a symbol of the political and economic forces at work in contemporary Los Angeles that make the rural lifestyle increasingly vulnerable. After our interview, Wheat and I walked together through the gently rolling hills of her property. She stopped to introduce me to each of the horses and dogs that live on the ranch, explaining their personalities and daily habits

206 • CHAPTER SEVEN

(and usually those of their owners as well). She then pointed to her neighbor's driveway, which runs along the north side of the property, and explained with some exasperation that her neighbors have been agitating for settlement of a property-line dispute and harassing her boarders. The dispute, she explained, might stand in the way of her ability to renew her conditional use permit, which allows her to run her horse-boarding business despite the parcel's residential zoning and the community plan's prohibition against most forms of commerce. Wheat confided that she has frequently contemplated moving from Los Angeles because of what she considers to be the inefficiency and poor planning sensibilities of city and county governments, and because of recurrent disputes among neighbors who have different visions of what life in the rural community should be like. When I asked her why she stays, she replied: "My property. There's really nothing else that I like about the city of Los Angeles, period." She continued, "There's not much to recommend in any of these areas except the fact that we do, or seem to, have the ability to keep our properties open for horses." But she was pessimistic about the rural community's future, predicting, "We'll be gone, eventually. Sure. This can't be protected forever. This is too close to the American dream."[2]

Wheat's narrative is suggestive of the ways in which contemporary rural dwellers, who identify so strongly with Los Angeles's semirural past and myths of western heritage, are responding to the city's changing political, economic, and demographic dynamics. As in decades past, the rural landscape remains central to their constructions of individual and collective identities and their interpretations of social dynamics. As James Duncan and Nancy Duncan observe in their study of rural Bedford, New York, "People . . . see landscapes as communicative of identities and community values. They speak of landscapes symbolizing — and even inculcating — political and moral values, as well as creating and conveying social distinction."[3] In the northeast San Fernando Valley, residents believe that rural life shapes human character, community dynamics, and the social order in superior ways, instilling in children and adults strong moral character, independence, humility, concern for community, and commitment to democratic participation. By contrast, they believe that urban and suburban lifestyles lead to moral weakness, criminality, greed, corruption, poor decision-making abilities, political apathy, and lack of concern for one's neighbors, animals, and the environment. On the basis of these relational beliefs about landscape, rural residents are anxious about the changes under way in Los Angeles, which they believe threaten not only the materiality of rural landscapes but also the cherished cultural values those landscapes are thought to cultivate.

For many residents of the rural northeast Valley, the rural community is attractive simply because it embodies everything that is not urban. Linda Ellison, a white female Shadow Hills resident and former teacher, told me that she loves living in Shadow Hills because "you don't feel like you're in Los Angeles anymore." A former resident of Atwater Village, a gentrifying neighborhood in north central Los Angeles, Ellison explained that she missed being closer to some of the benefits of urban life, such as cafés, live music, and greater cultural diversity. But she then unwittingly described the highly urbanized neighborhood where I lived at the time of the interview as her "nightmare." She said, "Well when I think of areas like 6th and Western, for example, like that's my nightmare. Everything is paved, you know. It's nice to be able to have some space and I just think more than anything, more than even the horse thing for me, it's having space to breathe. I don't want to be on top of my neighbor."[4]

Apartment buildings symbolized to some rural residents everything that is wrong with urbanity. Many people believed that apartment buildings are a cradle of undesirable and immoral human behavior. I repeatedly observed that semirural residents equate apartment buildings with "low-income housing," regardless of the fact that most apartment buildings currently being constructed in Los Angeles are luxury units that are simply unaffordable for the vast majority of the city's residents and certainly for the working poor. Eric Franco, the owner of an industrial-supply business who also runs the local neighborhood watch group, told me that Shadow Hills is special because "we don't have apartments. We have one apartment in Shadow Hills." When I asked him to elaborate on the difference that apartment buildings make, he explained, "I think a lot of difference, because it's low-income housing. A lot of those people have a million kids, and they don't watch them, and they let them do whatever they want. And that's what happens, kids grow up with no discipline. And they go out and do graffiti and drugs and chaos." Franco then offered a story that related apartment living directly to gang violence. For several years, he had taught free martial arts classes at the recreation center in the local park. He remembered, "We only lost one kid to the gangs. But he lived in the projects. But then years later he came back to me and says, 'I've just got to let you know that I should have stayed with you guys, but I didn't, but I was forced to go with the gang 'cause I lived in that apartment.'" In his narrative, apartment buildings are public housing "projects" that are assumed to be hotbeds of gang-related and criminal activity, as well as undisciplined parents who have too many children and fail to teach them proper discipline and ethics.[5]

Although Franco was more explicit than most about what he considered to be the negative influences of high-density living on the human character, similar undercurrents existed in many of my interviews and in community meetings. Gary McCullough, the owner of a real-estate development company that specializes in the construction of commercial buildings in the San Fernando Valley (though not in Shadow Hills, since zoning prohibits such facilities), drew upon his childhood experiences in suburban Virginia to explain to me his understanding of the values of rural versus urban neighborhoods:

> I'm not from L.A. L.A.'s the kind of city where your kids can die just for making the wrong turn somewhere. You can make a mistake in this city and be in the wrong neighborhood really quick. I wasn't raised in an area like that. I was raised in an area, you know, with roads winding, and country, and a lot of trees, and everything was green. It's just different. But I'm established; my business is here; my kids grew up here. The thought of moving to rural Pennsylvania — they'd just as soon die as do that. So that being said, there's no finer place to raise your kids than in Shadow Hills. If it wasn't for the L.A. city schools, it would be the greatest place in the world.[6]

For McCullough and others, urban landscapes are thus subtly associated with gangs and criminality. As we shall see shortly, the effort to shape children's moral development, as well as their educational and occupational futures, is critically important to adults' interpretations of rural landscapes.

While rural residents' feelings about urban landscapes are pronounced, Shadow Hills residents understand that their neighborhood is more likely to evolve into a typical suburban landscape than a dense urban landscape. Thus, interviewees were more likely to contrast rural Shadow Hills with suburbs elsewhere in the San Fernando Valley than with central city areas, from which they are geographically and socially removed. Rural dwellers believe that typical suburban neighborhoods are marked by monotony, boredom, and social dysfunction. Leslie Forster, a white woman who works as an assistant to a real-estate developer, grew up in Shadow Hills in the 1970s. As a child, she was involved with a 4-H club and learned to work with animals. Shortly after she and her husband married, they bought a new tract home in Saugus, an "exurban" community on the far northern fringe of Los Angeles. Forster described that home as "cookie cutter," and she and her husband moved back to Shadow Hills after just a few years. She explained, "We didn't like the commute, and we missed being close. I was always walking distance to my family, and then you know we liked animals, having animals and everything, and we just didn't like having everybody on top of us."[7] Thus, from her perspective, traditional suburbs are also considered to be too dense. Rural residents also dislike typical suburbs because they associate them with monotony of architecture as well as lifestyle, which they believe leads to anonymity and lack of a sense of community among neighbors. Linda Ellison told me, "I love that you never know what you're gonna find [in Shadow Hills] and it's all different. My nightmare is a tract home."[8]

The original stated purpose for instituting legislation to protect the rural landscape in Shadow Hills during the 1960s was to create a place where horse-keeping could be practiced. Yet most residents understand that, in a broader sense, horse-keeping is a strategic way to protect a whole rural way of life, particularly since up to 50 percent of residents in Shadow Hills do not and have never owned horses, but simply enjoy the large lots and rural aesthetic. As Ellison (a non–horse owner) explained to me, echoing the perspective of many, "You know, I don't think it's all about horses. I think it's about, what do you want done in your neighborhood, and do you want apartments, and do you want people crowded on each other, and do you want all your houses to look alike." She elaborated by contrasting what she liked about living in Shadow Hills with more typical suburbs. "We like that the properties are large. We love our neighbors, we have amazing neighbors. . . . I don't want to live in a place that's gross; on the other hand I don't want to live in a place that looks like Stepford, you know."[9] Her analysis associated the rural landscape, in large part because of its large lots, with a stronger sense of community. By contrast, urban areas were described as "gross" and suburban areas as "Stepford," referring to the popular television series that focuses on suburban dysfunction.

Suburban areas were also associated with a sense of elitism, unfriendliness, and a lack of concern for others. Eric Franco, who also does not own horses, contrasted Reseda, a postwar suburb with much smaller lots and more typical suburban landscape features such as strip malls, with the rural parts of the north San Fernando Valley. He told me,

> My parents live in Reseda. You can't do anything; everything is watched. People are very, very . . . uh, stuck-up. They stick to themselves. At my house, I'll be in the front yard, watering the lawn, and someone will ride by on their horse, and they'll say hello, or I'll say hello. I'll be at my parents' house, and I go out to my truck to get something, and someone will be walking by on the sidewalk, and I'll say "good evening," and she'll look at me like I'm going to rape her. I mean, they're so afraid, because there's so much chaos. This rural living brings out the best in people.[10]

In Franco's interpretation, suburbs create chaos, fear, and anonymity, while rural landscapes generate friendliness, trust, and an open mind. Evan Jones, a retired landscape gardener who has lived in Shadow Hills for more than fifty years and has never owned horses, echoed this sentiment: "[It is] a very friendly neighborhood. You can almost draw a line between this neighborhood and the other communities because I don't think anyone else has it. [Other communities have] more of a selfish attitude."[11]

One of the strongest beliefs that many interviewees attached to the rural landscape was the idea that rural living generates a strong sense of community that is missing in both urban and suburban neighborhoods. This notion is firmly linked in their minds to the possibility of outdoor living and a greater connection to animals and the environment. Lisa Burkett, who had lived in Shadow Hills since 1969, remembered with fondness her first impression of the neighborhood, telling me, "The first thing that I loved about Shadow Hills when we moved into that little house . . . we woke up Saturday morning and heard the clip-clop of horses. . . . We opened the window, and these people had come to get their friends, to ride. I mean, where do you hear that, any place?"[12] Michael Castalucci, a public relations consultant, explained these dynamics in similar terms, saying, "I think L.A. is very much a town where people stay in their houses. They go to work; they come home; they stay in their houses. What's cool about Shadow Hills is it's outdoor living too. It's barbecues; it's trail riding; it's jogging; it's riding your horse, walking your dog, riding your mountain bike. It really is a good California lifestyle in Shadow Hills."[13] Linda Ellison explained her love for the rural landscape through reference to its "wild" nature and the proximity of animals. "I like that it's kind of wild here. . . . And I love that any day of the week when your windows are open you hear the horses going by, I love that. And the coyotes, we still have so many, and it seems that we can kind of avoid them better than other areas, and I don't ever hear anybody complaining about them; people know what they're in for here — not city folk, although that's changing. I like the country kind of people that are here that are a little bit more in tune with their environment than, you know."[14] For her and others, being "in tune" with the environment appears to be closely related to having better relationships with one's neighbors and a stronger commitment to place. When asked why the rural community is worth protecting, Leslie Forster told me:

> Because, I mean it's a peaceful way to grow up, you come home and it's just wonderful to be able to see nature. The thing is, I mean, you have nature in other neighborhoods, but we're just more open and . . . it's not just the nature and it's not just the open space but it's just the community in itself. Sometimes I call it Mayberry, you know, like Andy Griffith, where people get to know their neigh-

bors. In a lot of other places people don't know their neighbors. . . . We have a lot of activities like barbecues and pancake breakfasts and . . . people sit out on their porches, and we watch the horses go by and the people go by.[15]

Jim Huck, a lawyer, made the relationship between the rural landscape and a strong sense of community explicit. He told me that there is a strong sense of cohesion in Shadow Hills "because you actually have a community. Because you're not separated by the corner of Walk and Don't Walk. You actually have geographic boundaries. This is it. Sameness — you're in the community."[16]

Rural residents are particularly enthusiastic about how they think rural landscapes shape the development of children's morals and character. Their understandings contrast sharply with beliefs about how growing up in an urban area, especially in apartment buildings, affects children. Eric Franco, who had offered the story about the gang member in the apartment building, explained that a concern for his children's safety was a major reason for his decision to buy a home in Shadow Hills in the early 1970s. He said, "I knew that I was going to have kids someday, and I didn't want to sit up at night and wait to see if they came home safely, or drive-by shootings. So I bought this house." He elaborated by describing how he believes the rural lifestyle affects the development of children: "They come home from school, they do their homework, then they go out and take care of the pigs and the horses and the cows and the chickens. They cannot leave the house until they do their chores. And that gives the child responsibility and makes a stricter environment."[17] This was the same person who told me he believes apartment buildings create chaos and are home to parents who have "millions of kids" and don't supervise them; thus, he has constructed an implicit contrast between the moralities, values, and behaviors of children who grow up in rural versus urban environments.

Similar, though more subtle, perceptions were common among the parents and teachers with whom I spoke. Donna Reese, a teacher who works in the Glendale public school system but lives in Shadow Hills, contrasted the experience of her students, who live in a relatively dense suburb, with those who grow up in a rural area. She explained that she works primarily with Armenian and Korean children, and that they all live in cramped apartment buildings, with nowhere to play. While sympathetic to them, she also implicitly contrasted their moral development with children who group up in rural areas, noting that riding and caring for horses teaches children responsibility. She commented that even six year olds will learn that they can control a one-thousand-pound animal if they treat it with respect. Ellison, who had also been a teacher before choosing to stay home with her young son, agreed that living in a rural community gives children a greater connection with the environment as well as sensitivity toward animals. She stated that the sheer fact of having to maintain a larger property teaches children responsibility: "Having chores, you know? I have to mow my lawn, or I have to go clean up horse poop in the yard, or I have to bring the bins out. There's a lot more work involved in having bigger properties, and I think, I see that a lot of parents are good about involving their children in that, and I think that's as good as a lot of what you get out of books, experiential learning. You know, they're not—I'm sure a lot of them are still in front of the TV, but there are just a lot of things going on outside."[18] Similarly, Leslie Forster, who had grown up in Shadow Hills among animals, shared her opinion that living in a rural community instills strong values in children. "It teaches you responsibility because you have animals to take care of; it teaches you bonding; I think that it teaches you tons of values, good values that are important today . . . honesty, a work ethic because you're used to doing things, and sharing."[19] Finally, according to Michael Castalucci,

> Within our equestrian community we have people whose passion and whose life-style is horses. And it's just unique. I like exposing myself to it; I like exposing my kids to it. I really despise pop culture. I despise it, and I do battle with my children over it all the time. So I'm constantly kicking them out of the house and telling them go check the animals out and find something in the real world. To the degree we can provide a decent environment where our kids can go outside and be unafraid . . . I certainly worry when my younger boy goes out, that he stays close to the house, but at the same time, when his friends come over, they have plenty to do outside. They can do it on our property; they can do it on the empty lots next door; they can do it on the street.[20]

Rural residents' projections about how landscapes shape children's development, and their efforts to control their own kids' future, are important because they tell us something about how rural white folks see themselves in relationship to others who inhabit, or are associated with, urban and suburban landscapes.

In similar ways, rural landscapes and communities are believed to powerfully shape adult behaviors and interactions. While urban and suburban landscapes are interpreted as producing undesirable human behavior (albeit in different ways), rural landscapes are imagined to create moral, disciplined, and caring citizens who are politically and economically independent and not concerned with money. Elaine Hillsboro, a real-estate agent who has worked in the northeast San Fernando Valley for nearly thirty years, told me that one of the reasons people like to buy homes in the area is because "people like a small town feeling." She seemed to believe that a particular kind of person—one who does not care about, and cannot be corrupted by, political and economic forces—is drawn to the rural lifestyle, and that the rural lifestyle itself cultivates such a personal philosophy. She elaborated by referencing the film *Sweet Home Alabama*: "I had a customer once come in with no shoes on and told me not to tell anybody they won the lottery. [*laughs*] But they wanted to remain country folks. Like that movie, what's it called, something *Sweet Home Alabama*? And the actress, you know, goes to the big city, and she really found out her happiness was right there in her hometown. Yeah, but uh . . . that's really what's good about this area, I think. I guess you can tell I like it here, huh? [*laughs*]"[21] Interviewees associated rural landscapes with humility and lack of materialism. These beliefs obscure the real material investments that property owners have in the rural landscape as a source of wealth and social status and instead construct rural residents as immune from, and thereby nonparticipants in, larger structural forces through which relationships of power and inequality are created and sustained in Los Angeles.

Rural dwellers' efforts to construct themselves as innocents derive partly from their ideological understandings of rural landscapes and the western frontier myth. For example, lawyer Jim Huck contrasted Shadow Hills with other suburban communities, especially gated communities or common-interest developments (CIDs). He explained, "Those communities have rules and restrictions, and your house has to be painted this color or this color or that color, and your roof has to be that color, and the trail rails have to be this color. We don't have those rules." He then contrasted his perceptions of CIDs with Shadow Hills, intending to offer evidence of the independence of Shadow Hills residents. He said, "I think the people who currently live in Shadow Hills would not be happy. . . . They're not rule breakers, but they live within the law, but they don't like to be told what to do. And those other people, they pay to have someone tell them what to do."[22] In Huck's analysis, Shadow Hills' extensive zoning requirements and community plan—which he plays a central role in upholding, through his work as the land-use chairman of the Shadow Hills Property Owners Association—apparently do not perform the same function as the CC&Rs (covenants, conditions, and restrictions) applied to many contemporary real-estate developments. Two distinctions appear to be important to him. First, horse-oriented zoning is enforced by the city and thus paid for by *all* taxpayers, while CC&Rs are enforced by privately run property owners associations, which are supported financially by homeowners. In the San Fernando Valley's legally designated rural communities, the urban state's role in protecting and subsidizing the rural horse-keeping lifestyle is made invisible by the aesthetic of the "wild" rural landscape and open space. The urban state's

subsidies and protections have become naturalized in the rural landscape itself, which is imagined to be unmediated by land-use policies in the same way
that urban and suburban communities, especially common-interest developments, are. As a result, Huck and others can imagine that their community is
less regulated and that, therefore, they as individuals are more independent.
Second, the Shadow Hills zoning requirements are designed to support a low-
density, rural horse-keeping area on the basis of preserving heritage, while
CC&Rs in common-interest developments are explicitly designed to support
the preservation of property values. Concerns with property values are just as
pronounced in the San Fernando Valley's rural neighborhoods, but the focus on
rural western heritage obscures such economic investments; as we have seen,
rural dwellers imagine themselves to be exempt from such concerns. James
Duncan and Nancy Duncan observed a similar dynamic among rural residents of the elite community of Bedford, New York. They explain that residents
"know that their landscapes depend upon a politics of anti-development. But
while at a certain level being aware of this, for the most part they tend to naturalize their privilege, having no reason to trace the far-reaching, unintended
consequences and unacknowledged conditions of that privilege."[23] The rural
landscape in Los Angeles similarly naturalizes residents' social and economic
investments in property and exclusion, as well as the urban state's role in creating the rural landscape, through reference to mythologies of rural land and
western heritage.

Most rural residents state that they love Los Angeles's rural neighborhoods
because they offer a small-town sense of community, replete with all the moral
and ethical characteristics thought to flow naturally from rurality, within an expansive metropolitan region. In this respect, Shadow Hills residents distinguish
between their neighborhood and other kinds of rural landscapes in the Midwest
and the U.S. South. What becomes apparent is that Shadow Hills residents are
not so much interested in the protection of rurality per se as they are invested
in a particular set of geographic and social relationships between the rural and
the urban landscape in Los Angeles, which allow them to enjoy rural amenities
within close proximity to urban capital, employment, and cultural offerings.
Much like the gentleman farmers of a previous generation, they are invested in
the preservation of their abilities to enjoy the strategic combination of urban
and rural life in suburban Los Angeles. This sentiment becomes clear in the
way that rural residents talk about the values of their neighborhood. During
a monthly meeting of the Shadow Hills Property Owners Association, one of
the board members introduced herself to new members by explaining why she
liked the community. She said, "Most of us moved here because we liked the ru-

ral atmosphere," but went on to note the advantages of living near more-urban areas of Los Angeles. "It feels like you're away from the city and yet you're really not, and you still have the convenience."[24] A commercial real-estate developer offered a similar sentiment. "I just love the rural atmosphere. . . . If you weren't raised in this city, it kind of gives you the feeling that you're not in the city when you really are."[25]

When pressed to be more specific, interviewees typically offered a combination of practical and emotional reasons why the rural neighborhood in the global city is so special to them. Freeways were often central to their explanations. As a board member of the Shadow Hills Property Owners Association expressed, "It's near the freeways, it's near the big city, but you can come over here and feel this peacefulness."[26] Leslie Forster, who works for a real-estate developer and is a block captain for the police advisory board, told me, "[People are drawn to live in Shadow Hills] because logistically we're close to the 5 and the 210 freeway, so we're good that way, and we're also close to the Hollywood Freeway, but the thing is I think that people choose this because they see, you know, they like the country atmosphere. They like the feeling here, and I've found that even if they're not going to have horses, they like seeing the horses on the street; they like being around this country atmosphere."[27] Castalucci, a public relations consultant who travels frequently, explained to me the multiple reasons why his family chose to buy a home in Shadow Hills, again merging practical considerations about access to urban employment opportunities with symbolic interests in the aesthetics and lifestyle associated with a rural landscape.

> We really just liked the size of our lot and we definitely liked the rural atmosphere. At the time there were no streetlights in the area where we lived. There were still some dirt streets. . . . And we were kind of intrigued by the chickens and a lot of the farm animals we saw around town and decided to just give it a go. . . . And the other benefit we enjoyed was just not having very many neighbors or traffic. . . . [But] I also think Shadow Hills is very well located for people who could work downtown; they could work in Pasadena; they could work in the San Fernando Valley; they could work on the Westside; they could work up in Valencia, Santa Clarita. So it's got a good unique location; we're close to a lot of freeways.[28]

Castalucci was acutely aware of the benefits of living in Shadow Hills, a rural community in an urban setting. He understood that to live in a semirural community with horse-keeping rights, while still in close proximity to abundant employment opportunities, is a rarity — something to be protected, but also something that makes for a sound real-estate investment.

The rural northeast Valley's close proximity to cultural amenities and urban economic opportunities distinguishes it from rural areas elsewhere in the country. Edward Burkett, a retired construction worker, told me,

> When I was working, and I'd come home, driving over that hill from Sun Valley, through Shadow Hills, it was like I was driving into another world. It was quieter, peaceful. We love theater; we like to go to the theater a lot. There's hundreds of live staged theaters in the Los Angeles area. And if we were to move out into one of those small towns, you don't have that. And we like to ballroom dance, and there's lot of places to ballroom dance. So we're close enough to L.A. to have all the advantages, yet we're far enough away that we get to have these advantages.[29]

Similarly, Eric Franco told me of what had happened to one of his friends who moved away from Los Angeles. He said, "A lot of guys want to go and move to Kansas, you know, because it's peaceful, it's quiet. My buddy moved to Springfield, Illinois. He's got the lake across the street, and he says 'I'm as bored as heck.'"[30] In this regard, residents understood the value of their rural neighborhood in the northeast San Fernando Valley in relationship to "truly" rural areas, such as small towns in more remote areas of the state or country, which lack the cultural amenities and economic opportunities of a major metropolitan region.

Clearly, historical visions of rural urbanism persist in contemporary Los Angeles, and they are informed — as they have always been — by ideological interpretations of the relative values of urban, suburban, and rural landscapes. Residents' reasons for living in rural neighborhoods, and their perceptions of why rural landscapes and lifestyles are so special, vary little from the gentleman farmers of a century ago. For most, it is not just Shadow Hills' location close to downtown and other urban centers that makes the neighborhood valuable. Rather, it is the possibility of having a small-town sense of community, horse and animal ownership, and a rural landscape *in such close proximity to the city* — the ability to truly have "the best of both worlds," of rural and urban living — that is special. This distinction sets Shadow Hills apart from denser areas, which are perceived as being dangerous, chaotic, and immoral; as well as from more typical suburban neighborhoods, which are perceived as lacking both a sense of place and a sense of community; and from rural areas in the interior of the country, which are perceived as lacking the cultural and economic opportunities of metropolitan life in Los Angeles.

This sense of distinctiveness rests on a historically specific set of interdependencies among the urban state, the rural community, capitalists and laborers, and cultural producers in Los Angeles through which the privileges of whiteness have been and continue to be produced. Yet the ambitions of real-estate developers, the changing political interests of city and county representatives, the shifting demographic makeup of the metropolitan region, and the growing poverty of the region and the widening gap between rich and poor make these historic relationships increasingly fragile. The same economic and political forces that have transformed Los Angeles in the past half century have put tremendous pressures on the city's rural districts, particularly in the area of new residential construction. Rural residents feel inundated by the sheer number of residential projects proposed for the few remaining undeveloped land parcels in their neighborhoods and frustrated by what they perceive to be a declining commitment from the city and county government to protect the rural landscape. During the time I conducted my fieldwork in the northeast Valley, virtually every community meeting was devoted to the analysis of at least one, and usually more than one, new residential development. Proposed residential projects in Shadow Hills included an infill development of eight or ten homes, nestled within a corner of the neighborhood on an old flower ranch once owned by or leased to a Japanese American family, that was relatively acceptable to current residents; a 21-home project on an old horse ranch, which has been consistently delayed for many years through lawsuits brought by Shadow Hills residents, who protest its negative environmental impacts; and a 270-home project called the Whitebird/Canyon Hills subdivision, proposed in 2004 and universally loathed by residents, that would be located in the foothills surrounding the 210 Interstate Freeway but that has not, as of this writing, been approved.

Real-estate developers frequently target rural communities for new residential developments because they are some of the very few areas remaining in Los Angeles County that have significant open space. However, much of the "open space" in the San Fernando Valley's rural neighborhoods actually consists of privately owned lots that are zoned for residential development but have not yet been built upon. Typically, these lots are owned and being held by real-estate developers who are at various stages in the proposal process, trying to get a development approved. They remain "open" in part because of decades of homeowner activism to resist or exclude unwanted developments. In the meantime, children play in and people ride their horses through these "open spaces," and they are deeply reluctant to give those spaces up without a fight.

Even within these contested open spaces, however, real-estate developers do not typically propose residential projects that would help to ameliorate the city's chronic affordable housing crisis. Instead, the developments they put forward tend to fall into one of two types, both of which are aimed at Los Angeles's upper middle class. Proposed developments may be very large "equestrian estates" with hacienda-style homes on five acres of land or more, or they may be tracts of suburban ranch-style homes on comparatively small lots that would none-theless command high prices in Southern California's bloated real-estate mar-ket. Existing rural residents generally oppose both such kinds of developments. They believe that suburban tract-home developments are not appropriate for the area because they represent the incursions of monotonous suburbia, which, as we have seen, they associate with an unwanted set of values, morals, and behaviors. But neither do they believe that the architectural aesthetic of large country estates, with the social class connotations of a landed and moneyed elite, properly reflects who they are and what they hold to be important. Thus, rural dwellers are negotiating a complex set of desires and commitments that are embedded within the historical and contemporary practice of rural urban-ism — contradictions that are inherent within the struggle to maintain a rural lifestyle and landscape in Los Angeles, but also within the shifting racialized class dynamics of the region.

Rural residents have to balance their desires for urban services, conve-niences, and opportunities with their equally strong desires to cultivate what they believe to be the moral and cultural characteristics of a rural lifestyle. At the same time, rural dwellers balance their abstract commitment to private-property rights with their desire to shape, control, and exclude unwanted de-velopments. These competing interests and motivations create a diversity of opinion within and among rural residents that manifests itself continuously in organizational and neighborhood meetings as residents struggle with how to respond to change. Some residents oppose virtually all proposed developments. Others articulate their commitment to private-property rights and state that they oppose only "nonconforming development" — that is, development that does not conform to the existing land-use policies. What brings these diverse people together are their commitments to rural land-use policy as a bulwark against unwanted landscape change and its associated social transformations. The focus on rural land-use policies allows these tensions and contradictions among neighbors, and between rural residents and the urban state, to be tem-porarily though incompletely resolved.

Some rural residents clearly and unequivocally oppose all new develop-ment. Linda Ellison expressed this perspective most passionately. When I asked her what she considered to be the greatest threat facing the community, she replied:

> Oh, the developers. Hands down. It makes me sick. You know, I'm a newer resi-dent, but I feel like my philosophy is very old school; I like it for what it is. And

in the few years that we have been here, we have seen a tremendous amount of change. . . . I'm ultra-sensitive, I realize that, but just watching all these properties that used to be wild being razed and paved, you know, it hurts my soul. And we talk about, if we move, we would look for another area that's like this somewhere, but I would almost rather go to another place that's already done, because watching it happen just hurts, you know? It just really bothers me; it really gets to me. And also when you hear the stories — which are true — like developers agree to one thing, like put in a horse trail, and then not do it, or [to] put in the horse trail and trees and do something that's good for the whole community and then not do it because that's not lucrative for them — I just don't have any patience for that.[31]

Referring to people like Ellison, Richard Eagan suggested that individuals who inhabit a rural landscape are especially passionate about resisting change. He said, "If people move into the neighborhood, they don't want it to change from the way they moved in; that's why they bought their house . . . [and] I think that the rural, animal nature of this area intensifies that desire to keep it rural. Rural basically means open space. Trees, bushes, whatever. It doesn't mean three-story mansions that are built within five feet of the property [line]."[32] Thus, interviewees' beliefs that rural landscapes inculcate a stronger sense of community and independence of thought also firmly ground their resistance to change.

Other rural dwellers did not share such strong fears of new development. When I asked them about their neighborhood's reputation for being "antidevelopment," some interviewees agreed that many local people are, but they wanted to distinguish themselves from that stereotype. They stated that they personally understand that new development will occur, and that they support the exercise of private-property rights. Eric Franco noted: "A lot of them don't want to be — a lot of them can't accept change. They don't want change. And in order to live in this world, there's always going to be change. And Shadow Hills is one of the few places left with land. I don't want to see it be developed either, but you've got to get with the times."[33] Similarly, when I asked Leslie Forster, who works as the assistant to a real-estate developer, if she thought that the existing rural land-use policies were endangered by proposals for new development, she replied: "Yes, because . . . development is money and obviously the more houses you get the more money you make. So I know the community plans, obviously, they're always under siege." She continued, "But I also am a fair person and a reasonable person, and I feel that everybody has property rights, and what I like — even though I wish everybody was real country and horses and everything, that's not everybody's ideal to have. So I have to respect what they like."[34]

Opposition to "nonconforming development" became a way for rural residents to balance their competing commitments to the principle of private-property rights, on the one hand, and their practical desire to shape, control, and exclude unwanted development, on the other. Many rural residents told me that they do not oppose all development but rather are against only those development proposals that do not conform to the existing land-use policies. As interviewees described the concept to me, "nonconforming development" would include all industrial and most commercial development, multifamily homes, and lots smaller than twenty thousand square feet or those that do not have a guaranteed, permanently secured place for horse-keeping. Michael Castalucci told me, "I would say that there's a very strong curiosity about what type of development is going to happen, and making sure that development conforms with the character here. I could be wrong in my read about that. I think there are a lot of people that don't want anything to change. But the majority of what I see — I feel that the SHPOA [Shadow Hills Property Owners Association] group is reasonable."[35] Similarly, Gary McCullough, a real-estate developer, explained, "I live here, I don't want development either, but I understand it's going to happen. Now, I think they should make everybody develop right to what the guidelines say."[36] Jim Huck explained that activists in the north Valley are actually in favor of new projects, as long as they are consistent with existing zoning and land-use policies. He elaborated, "We are actually pro-horse development, development of horse-keeping properties. We are in favor of complying with the current zoning laws and the current community plan. We are against people who try and change the community plan that we've fought for for the last thirty years and people who think they can just waltz into the community and start putting up things that are inconsistent with the community plan. So actually we are very pro-development of projects that are consistent with the community plan, consistent with the zoning."[37] For each of these people, activism to ensure that new development conforms to the existing character, enshrined in the zoning, community plan, and other policies, is a means of maintaining the social status and lifestyle now associated with the neighborhood.

Within these narratives, of course, the existence and maintenance of those rural land-use policies first crafted and implemented in the 1960s is crucial. These policies enable existing homeowners to control the kinds of developments that are proposed and constructed in their neighborhood and, in doing so, to exert some control over their own social status. Opposition to "nonconforming development" becomes a legitimate way to exclude unwanted land uses and people *and* to sustain their property values, social status, and way of life, all the while maintaining an abstract commitment to private property rights and rural western heritage. Opposition to "nonconforming development" also enables rural residents to avoid appearing as if they are simply engaged in standard suburban NIMBY politics and to reframe their demands as concerning something larger than individual self-interest or social-class privilege. In this respect, focus on the rural landscape is a way of affirming and reinforcing one's identity and status in the face of potential social change, but in ways that are socially acceptable and politically compelling.

Residents clearly associate landscape change with demographic change, though they have diverse opinions about the degree of threat that new residents pose to the future of the rural neighborhood. Their interpretations hinge on the questions of whether new residents will choose to own horses and whether they will uphold the long-standing tradition of land-use activism for which current Shadow Hills residents are renowned among real-estate developers in the city. Virtually all current residents believe that most new residents will not be horse owners. Richard Eagan, a contractor, told me, "I think most of the people moving in are going to be non–horse people. Because you can maximize the size of these houses on these lots by not putting horses in . . . so just monetarily these developers putting in the smallest lot they can possibly put in with the largest house on it."[38] For Eagan, the demographic threat is exacerbated by the nature of inflated property values and a citywide housing shortage, as well as the power of the real-estate industry as a vested economic interest in Los Angeles.

A minority of current rural residents believe that new residents are a major threat to the future of the rural community, especially if they do not choose to own horses. Their fears appear to bear no relationship to whether they personally own horses. Eric Franco, a non–horse owner, told me, "All of the people in my neighborhood have horses. But these new homes that are coming in, they're trying to get rid of them. And I say, 'You moved here, we didn't move into your neighborhood.'" Later in the interview, when I asked him what he perceived to be the greatest threat facing the neighborhood, he answered, "People that came from other parts of California or other parts of the Valley or Los Angeles that thought, by living in a horse area . . . they come here thinking that rural living, equestrian living, would be great. And they find out that they don't like the smell of horse manure, they don't like hearing roosters crow at 5:00 in the morning, or goats and lambs making all that noise . . . so they work with each other to get rid of what they moved into."[39] Linda Ellison offered a more detailed explanation of how this process might work: "When it comes to people voting about horse measures or the zoning or certain things, they're not going to care, so they're not going to vote that way, that's what I see happening." But for Ellison, the distinction seemed to be less about interest in owning horses personally than about whether a new resident was committed to the rural lifestyle and landscape in principle and in practice. She elaborated: "I don't think it really matters whether you own horses or not; I don't think that's the issue. Because we don't own horses. But every time there's a horse issue, I'm going to stand up for it. I would pay more taxes if I had to; I fully support it. So I hope that it doesn't ever become an issue of those who have horses and those who don't, because I think that it's more mindset."[40] For many rural residents, then, the conflict comes down to different cultural commitments to rurality among diverse populations. These different cultural commitments are explained through reference to past residential patterns, and specifically to the kinds of landscapes that newcomers have inhabited in the past, rather than to racial, ethnic, or national origin differences. Because rural residents believe that urban and suburban landscapes inculcate different kinds of values, they fear that newcomers to the neighborhood who are migrating from urban and suburban areas will have different value systems and will quickly destroy the existing rural landscape and lifestyle because they don't understand or don't value it.

Some of those who were most worried about the influx of non–horse owners had been influenced by their personal experiences elsewhere in Southern California. They pointed to changes that have occurred in other, formerly rural neighborhoods in the San Fernando Valley, where landscape transformation has gone hand in hand with demographic transformation in the past half century. Many San Fernando Valley neighborhoods that were once rural, semiagricultural, and almost exclusively white have become far more dense in the last twenty to twenty-five years, with significant clusters of industry, strip malls, and apartment complexes. At precisely the same time, they have lost virtually all their white populations, who appear to have been more politically invested in the preservation of rurality than newcomers and to have had the social and political capital to make their organizing efforts successful; as these residents have left Los Angeles, they have taken their social capital with them. Rural residents of contemporary Shadow Hills narrated these changes by emphasizing the urbanization of the rural landscape and the failure of the urban state to protect rurality. They interpreted these changes as the outcome of unequal cultural commitments to rurality among diverse populations, and as evidence of what they fear will happen in their neighborhood if they are not successful in upholding the rural land-use policy amid the influx of newcomers.

Given the demographic and economic changes in Los Angeles over the last forty years, their narratives are unavoidably tinged with racial, class, and national overtones. Patricia Wheat was explicit about the relationship she perceived between demographic change and landscape change. Prior to moving to Shadow Hills in 1989, Wheat had owned horse property in La Cañada, a suburban community that had been almost exclusively white but began to attract a large Korean American population beginning in the 1980s. Demographic change, along with real-estate development pressures within the Los Angeles region as a whole, had eroded many of the neighborhood's horse-keeping properties. Wheat offered her interpretation of how the growing Korean demographic had changed the community:

> The Korean people tend not to be horse owners. When we lived in La Cañada, a large contingent of Korean people moved in because of the quality of education there. . . . And as they moved in, in greater and greater numbers, we began to hear little complaints about the flies and smells. . . . And horse people started flying out like mad and moving in this direction. Immediately, many of those Korean families started buying those acre-size lots and larger, split them in half, made them into flag lots, and now La Cañada is a community at war. And unfortunately, it's almost become a race war, between Korean people who want to live their lifestyle in La Cañada and people who have lived there for a hundred years, already have their own culture, thank you very much, and wish to continue living that way.[41]

Wheat perceived the demographic change in La Cañada as a result of different commitments to a horse-keeping lifestyle among Koreans and among racially unmarked, presumably white "horse people." Those perceptions of irreconcilable cultural difference led her and many of her La Cañada neighbors to move to neighborhoods where the rural landscape was still protected, such as Shadow Hills, in a clear case of white flight that was linked to interpretations of landscape and culture. She explained, "Actually, boarding horses for me started as an accident. You know, too many of my friends in La Cañada were in the same boat that we were in." These experiences had informed Wheat's beliefs about the dangers that significant demographic and social-class change posed to rural areas in Los Angeles. She told me, "Trying to keep areas the way they are, whether it's a horse area, an ethnic area, or whatever it is — it's really the only salvation, I think. Because you start pushing non–horse people with horse people, non–bird people with bird people, people who don't speak English with people who do speak English, and you get chaos."[42] For Wheat, the fear of large numbers of newcomers was directly rooted in her own past experiences within a transitioning neighborhood, leading her to believe that different ethnic groups have different cultural commitments to the rural and suburban lifestyles that are basically irreconcilable.

Similarly, Evan Jones told me why, from his perspective, horse-keeping had deteriorated in nearby Sylmar. He said, "You see, with Sylmar, the wrong people have been moving in there." When I asked him what he meant by the "wrong people," he elaborated:

> People who . . . they feel they shouldn't have a horse community where they want to build their home. . . . There were some nice properties there, nicely built homes, not oversized, with lots of land around them. That was a very verdant area right around there, originally. And the horse people were doing fine until people who would come in and buy properties, and they'd have a ruling that you had to have horses or buy a horse to keep on their property. They just came in and bought land to build on, period. And they took the bull by the horns, and most of the horse people have moved out. We had one family who moved over to Quartz Hill, out near Palmdale, Lancaster. . . . So these people were moving in in great numbers, actually pushing the horse people out to the edge. One upset the other, and the balance wasn't there, and horse-keeping's out the door.[43]

Although Jones's narrative is more subtle than Wheat's, his explanation, when placed within its historical context, is inflected with racial, class, and national references. During the period he described, Sylmar changed from a middle-class white community to a predominantly working-class Latino community. Together, these two stories point to the primary demographic shifts that face white middle-class residents of the rural San Fernando Valley, embodied by working-class Latinos and middle-class and wealthy Korean immigrants. As rural residents of the northeast Valley have observed and participated in these changes, they have concluded that landscape change and unwanted social change go hand in hand.

The trends that both Wheat and Jones describe in La Cañada and Sylmar fall squarely within historical and contemporary patterns of white flight from the San Fernando Valley. Beginning in the late 1970s, many working-class and middle-class whites fled the suburbs of the San Fernando Valley, which were perceived as becoming "too urban." Those who left the Valley during this period were frustrated by the city's high housing costs and taxes, as well as what they perceived to be the corruption and inadequacy of local government, especially the Los Angeles public school system. Their frustrations and resentment manifested themselves in political struggles over rising property taxes and against school desegregation and in recurrent attempts at Valley secession. As secession has repeatedly failed, many working-class and middle-class whites have simply chosen to leave the city, armed with a disenchantment toward "big city" life and what they perceived to be its programs of social engineering and political corruption. They typically purchased properties on the outskirts of Los Angeles County, in neighborhoods such as Acton, Santa Clarita, and Palmdale, where they felt that a small-town quality of life and commitment to the values of rural America still held sway. Real-estate agent Elaine Hillsboro offered her interpretation of these patterns. She explained the outward migration of former San Fernando Valley residents to the exurbs of Los Angles County as a desire for more space among "country folks." "Most people, country folks, they like to have some space. . . . If they're country folks, you get crowded real quick. That's why it's interesting that people think, wow, five acres is a lot now. But you can't get anything, five acres, unless you go to Tehachapi or Acton, or somewhere out there."[44] Thus, ideological investments in the cultural values attributed to rural life and attendant fears of urbanization have contributed substantially to demographic change in Los Angeles in recent decades, and similar ideologies and anxieties may continue to propel waves of white middle-class flight away from the San Fernando Valley in the years to come.

Residents of Shadow Hills frequently point to their neighborhood's most recent residential development, the Rancho Verdugo Estates, which was completed in 2003, as evidence of the linked demographic and lifestyle tensions they perceive facing their community. For years, a group of resident activists, especially the Shadow Hills Property Owners Association, had worked closely with the developer of the Rancho Verdugo Estates in an effort to make the development conform to existing land-use policies. They collaborated to produce a subdivision of tract-style houses — all much larger and more expensive than existing homes — that satisfied the twenty thousand square feet minimum lot size, defined explicit areas for horses, and were linked into the larger neighborhood by a bridle-trail system. They also developed a plan for McBroom Street, the dirt road that would become the primary access street into the subdivision. Three-quarters of the street have been paved, a fenced bridle trail has been added on one side, and an unfenced eight-foot dirt and gravel trail has been left on the other side for horseback riders (see figure 15). These compromises were intended to satisfy the multiple and competing desires of new and existing residents — for a smoothly paved street combined with the aesthetic and softer footing of a dirt road. Despite residents' efforts, however, the project that was actually built and marketed did not satisfy all their initial hopes and demands. Some of the lots ended up being smaller than the twenty thousand square feet minimum lot size because of the area's hilly topography, which reduced the overall usable space and precluded horse ownership. Most new residents — who are a diverse ethnic lot of native-born white Americans, European immigrants (especially Armenians), and Asian immigrants (particularly Koreans) — are not horse owners. At the time of my fieldwork, only two new residents of the Rancho Verdugo Estates had constructed horse facilities in their yards, and one of these was Gary McCullough, who had moved from another home in Shadow Hills. Indeed, some have used the dedicated horse space for other purposes such as a swimming pool, a batting cage, or a golf putting range, although the construction of permanent structures in these areas is prohibited. Furthermore, because the new development has its own homeowners group, new residents have shown little interest in becoming part of the Shadow Hills Property Owners Association.

In my interviews and in community meetings, residents expressed their disappointment and frustration with this experience, for which they had high hopes, and took it as proof of the decline of their cherished lifestyle and their growing social isolation within a rapidly changing city. Residents' experience with the Rancho Verdugo Estates has made some of them distrustful of even the most cooperative real-estate developers, wary of newcomers, and pessimistic about the semirural neighborhood's future. Patricia Wheat recalled her experience working with the developers of the Ranch Verdugo Estates: "They wanted to make it an absolutely exclusive gated community and cut out the entire, you know, horse community of Shadow Hills, and although we couldn't very well

FIGURE 15 McBroom Street in Shadow Hills, with the Rancho Verdugo Estates in the background. Prior to 2003, this street was a dirt road. Residents worked with the developer to pave part of the street, leaving an eight-foot dirt/gravel path for horseback riders on one side, and to construct a fenced dirt horse trail at the developer's expense on the other side. Photo by author, 2006.

stop them from doing the subdivision, unfortunately, we did make damn sure that we had access to the trails."[45] Wheat's narrative captures clearly the sense, shared by many rural dwellers, of being marginalized by the dynamics of real-estate development and the trend toward gated communities within Southern California, as well as their desire to shape and control the developing landscape to ensure it conforms to the existing rural character. To some rural residents, the Rancho Verdugo Estates also symbolizes the linkage between the potential impacts of nonconforming development and newcomers who are not committed to maintaining the rural lifestyle. According to Linda Ellison,

> We've got a whole other brand new subdivision over here, Rancho Verdugo; I will mention it by name and I'm not ashamed. Those people — because I've met some of them; I've talked to them at different things — they moved here because Glendale doesn't have enough property for them. They don't ever plan on owning a horse; they don't care that there are horses here; they could care less about that. You know what they miss? They miss having a strip mall closer. They want to have strip malls. And you know, that is a threat to the neighborhood because I moved here to get away from strip malls. If I wanted strip malls, I'd be back where I was, in the middle of Los Angeles.[46]

Both Wheat's and Ellison's sentiments express clearly the connections that rural residents make between rural and urban landscapes and different value systems, and the sense of anxiety that develops when they perceive the rural landscape to be changing.

However, other contemporary rural residents are confident about the ability of the rural community to absorb newcomers, even those who are not interested in horses, as long as the existing rural land-use policies are upheld and defended. Lawyer Jim Huck stated,

> I think the future of the neighborhood is going in exactly the right direction. We have basically surrounded ourselves with open space or some geographic boundary. We have what we need in place to continue to develop the neighborhood with the existing community plan and zoning requirements, and if people comply with that it should be fine. And whether people actually end up owning horses or don't own horses, that's an individual matter up to them, but at least there will be availability to own horses and a place to put them and a place to ride them, without having a trailer to go someplace.[47]

Others believed that the rural culture of the community was strong and cohesive enough to absorb and socialize newcomers. Leslie Forster told me, "I think that people choose this [neighborhood] because they see, you know, they like the country atmosphere; they like the feeling here. I've found that even if they're not going to have horses, they like seeing the horses on the street, they like being around this country atmosphere, so it's not like they're like a threat. . . . I don't have that fear. But I know a lot of people do, and I feel bad about that . . . because I don't think that it's well founded."[48] Still others told me that the political power of existing activists was strong enough to offset the passivity of newcomers who could not be counted on to protect the rural land-use policies. When I asked Richard Eagan if he agreed with some residents that non–horse owners posed a threat to the neighborhood's future, he responded, "[It] definitely is a threat. Yeah, but I think that they're going to be in the minority. I think that the horse people, the horse people are real strong here, and as long as they stick together they'll win in the end."[49] Similarly, Gary McCullough responded to my query about the impact of newcomers by saying, "That's a big concern. I don't disagree. In my own neighborhood it's that way. [But] I think as long as you have a core group that always protects the rights for horse owners, there's always going to be a segment of the population that wants horses. It's such a unique area; it's so close to the city to be able to have them, and to be so close to the national forest too. I mean it's a great area."[50] Therefore, substantial disagreement exists among current rural residents about the degree of threat that the forces of urbanization and demographic change pose to the rural landscape, and specifically about the potential impact of new residents who do not plan to own horses.

However, despite their differences of opinion about potential change, new-comers, and new developments, *all* rural residents agree that protection of the existing rural, horse-oriented land-use policies is paramount. In this respect, the continued support of the urban state is crucial. The ability of contemporary semirural residents to continue to enjoy their lifestyle and landscape rests on the urban state's continued commitment to maintain rural land-use policies amid the city's changing needs and priorities — a commitment that is, in many rural dwellers' eyes, declining rapidly. Many rural residents perceive that political representatives are simply unfamiliar with rural life as practiced in a global city, and they argue that this lack of familiarity is dangerous. According to Jim Huck, "To a large extent the city council would never know Shadow Hills existed. Because they never get out here, and if they did, they would be surprised at what was or wasn't here."[51] Richard Eagan concurred, telling me, "They don't understand this area. They really don't get it." Eagan went on to argue that neglect and unfamiliarity by the city contributes to an "anything goes" attitude among residents and real-estate developers who think they can get away with illegal or dubious activities because they are not likely to be noticed. He said,

"People come up, and they think they can do whatever they want. They think this is their opportunity to, let's say, do things that they couldn't do on Ventura Boulevard, or over on Laurel Canyon. They think this is out of the way and people don't care about it. What they don't realize is that we've been here a long time, and it's not just me; we know what's supposed to be happening, and it gets watched closer than a lot of other places."[52] Later, Eagan walked with me into his backyard, perched high in the hills of Shadow Hills, from where we could see the vast stretch of the Hansen Dam recreation area and the foothills of the northeast Valley below. He pointed to several buildings and projects, scattered throughout the hillsides before us, that violated the community plan and zoning ordinances but which had been granted variances and permits. He explained, "I think the planning department is terrible in Los Angeles. I could show you stuff that they let happen in my house. Just terrible . . . [in terms of letting people] do pretty much whatever they want. . . . That building should not be here, OK. . . . Now see those houses over there; they're a monstrosity. They allowed that to go there, and it, it's a scar on the mountain. Yeah, the neighborhood fought that and the neighborhood lost, and city planning thought that was okay. And it's just one thing after another. Just one thing after another."[53]

For Eagan, the landscape of nonconforming development is proof of the ineptitude of both the city planning department and the Los Angeles City Council and their willingness to overlook zoning codes and legalities of the local planning process. These experiences confirmed to Eagan and others that the northeast Valley's rural lifestyle was no longer a priority for protection by the urban state. As Patricia Wheat told me, "I just have absolutely no trust for anybody in bureaucracy." When I remarked that her sentiment seemed to be a common one, she replied, "Well, it's not because we have native, innate biases; it's because we've all been burned so badly so many times."[54]

These sentiments inform rural dwellers' complex relationship with the urban state, which is marked by both dependency and antagonism. Contemporary rural residents remain dependent on the urban state, through its commitments to rural land-use policy, to ward off unwanted changes that would endanger their ability to continue enjoying the rural lifestyle in Los Angeles. When the urban state does so, rural residents feel temporarily protected from the monumental political, economic, and social changes affecting the city as a whole. But most of the time, rural dwellers are wary and distrustful of the shifting and unreliable commitments of the urban state and its representatives. Those who become "fed up" with life in Los Angeles and the urban state's perceived shift away from protection of the rural lifestyle have left the San Fernando Valley in recent years. Those who stay engage in everyday social practices and build political movements intent on affirming the centrality of the rural frontier myth to the American experience and defending against unwanted change. These social practices and intentional social movement activity are the subject of the next chapter, which examines how rural residents of the San Fernando Valley strategically construct and position "rural culture" within an urban political scene that emphasizes both multicultural identity politics and a normative discourse of color blindness.

CHAPTER EIGHT

"Rural Culture" and the Politics of Multiculturalism

Whiteness in the northeast San Fernando Valley at the beginning of the twenty-first century remains persistently but tenuously linked to the rural landscape, within a city where whites are now a numerically declining but structurally privileged minority. Within this context, the historic relationships between the rural landscape, the urban state, real-estate developers, and capital are being reworked and redefined, and so too are the meanings and articulations of whiteness. Contemporary rural inhabitants of the northeast San Fernando Valley struggle to position their lifestyle as valid and valuable amid the shifting needs of the metropolitan region. In response to the perceived gains of immigrants and nonwhites (especially Latinos) in the northeast Valley, and the perceived and actual retreat of the urban state from its historic commitment to rurality, contemporary rural residents try to situate the rural lifestyle as just one culture out of many in Los Angeles. Drawing on both well-established myths of the rugged, individual frontiersman and woman *and* ideas of white victimization by identity politics that are central to neoconservatism and the New Right, rural residents argue that "rural culture" is disenfranchised and victimized and thus equally or more worthy of state protection and resources than are racial minority groups. Through this process, they construct the rural landscape and lifestyle within the discursive mandates of both multicultural identity politics and color blindness, racial ideologies that would otherwise appear to be contradictory.

The frontier myth and narratives of rural western heritage are useful in this context because they invoke multiple contradictory meanings at once. From the conventional and hegemonic perspective, the frontier myth is the nation's origin story, a presumably color-blind history with which all can identify. In this regard, contemporary rural communities in Los Angeles symbolize a valuable history of western heritage that is worth protecting, at least in part because that history/mythology is constructed to be exempt from the messiness of racial and class politics. By contrast, from the perspective of critical social theory, environmental studies, and the "new" western history, myths of the frontier and western heritage are narratives of Anglo-American supremacy that justify histories of American imperialism and conquest. From this perspective, the semirural communities in Los Angeles celebrate such histories while reproducing whites' historical racial, class, and environmental privileges.

Rural activists in the northeast San Fernando Valley must navigate these tensions and contradictions in their land-use activism, engagements with the state, and everyday social practice. Their actions are both affirmative, celebrating the history and value of the rural lifestyle and western heritage, and defensive, consisting of exclusionary reactions to the linked forces of landscape change and social change, both actual and feared, in the northeast San Fernando Valley and Los Angeles more broadly. Through these diverse practices, in a cyclical manner, rural residents share, test, modify, and affirm their beliefs about rurality and urbanity, the proper role of the urban state, race, class, and the state of the nation. In this chapter, I examine how these tensions and dialectics played out during my fieldwork in the northeast San Fernando Valley. I focus on the process of political redistricting in spring 2002; a series of altercations among Latinos and whites in the Hansen Dam public recreation area during the summer of 2002; the annual celebration of the Day of the Horse Festival, beginning in 2003; a negative critique and unflattering portrait of horse-keeping communities that appeared in the local press; and residents' responses to my interview questions about perceived social-class and racial disparities between the northeast Valley's rural districts and the city as a whole.

In 2002, Los Angeles began the process of redrawing its city council district boundaries, in accordance with the population data collected by the 2000 census and with fair and equal representation mandates of the 1965 Voting Rights Act. This redistricting process occurs every ten years after the federal census, but in this redistricting cycle and for the first time in Los Angeles, the city council appointed a redistricting commission to provide recommendations on district boundaries. The commission was created as part of the new city charter approved by voters in 1999, which was intended to connect citizens more closely with their local government and to enable their more active participation in the redistricting process. The commission consisted of twenty-one leaders from the business community and nonprofit sector appointed by city council members, the city attorney, the city controller, and the mayor.[1]

Under the district map created in 1992, Shadow Hills was included in City Council District 2. District 2 was one of the most convoluted and geographically noncontiguous districts in the city, reaching from the San Gabriel Mountains on the northeast side of the Valley to the Santa Monica Mountains on the southwest. The new District 2 proposed by the redistricting commission continued this pattern and joined Shadow Hills with suburban communities of the distant west Valley, but with two key differences. First, the proposed district split off a portion of Lakeview Terrace from the other semirural communities in the northeast Valley, instead joining Lakeview Terrace with the adjacent District 7; and second, it proposed to make District 2 one of five "Latino-electable" districts in the city due to the northeast Valley's sizable Latino population concentrated in Pacoima, Sylmar, Sun Valley, and Arleta.

The proposed relocation of Lakeview Terrace from District 2 to District 7 was a hot-button issue because it symbolized to rural residents the major changes under way in the Valley in the last several decades, particularly the transformation of rural areas. Since 1968, Lakeview Terrace has been included in the community plan that covers Shadow Hills, La Tuna Canyon, and Sunland-Tujunga, which protects the "rural atmosphere" of those neighborhoods. However, Lakeview Terrace has become more diverse than these other areas in terms of its racial and ethnic composition as well as its patterns of land use. Some areas within Lakeview Terrace have numerous apartment buildings and commercial centers, mostly strip malls. Yet Lakeview Terrace also retains some horse-keeping properties, including several large ranches; access to Hansen Dam; and many equestrian trails. Thus, the physical territory of Lakeview Terrace during the redistricting process was literally caught in between two competing constituencies — rural, mostly white equestrians, and a growing Latino electorate — and fully symbolized the scope of change in the northeast San Fernando Valley. From the perspective of rural residents in Shadow Hills and La Tuna Canyon, the idea of moving all of Lakeview Terrace into District 7 would seem to seal the neighborhood's fate in its transition from mostly white, rural, and horse-keeping to majority Latino, urbanized, and nonrural. At the time of redistricting, District 7 included Pacoima (the Valley's historically nonwhite neighborhood) as well as Arleta and Sylmar, formerly all-white neighborhoods that have transitioned to majority Latino in the last few decades. District 7 was then represented by Democrat Alex Padilla, a Mexican American who had grown up in the northeast Valley and was, at the time, president-elect of the Los Angeles City Council.

Residents of the rural northeast San Fernando Valley had long been discontent with the district created in 1992, which forced them to share a council representative with distant suburban communities perceived as having completely dissimilar interests and cultures. However, the proposed council district created by the redistricting commission was unacceptable to them because it would continue this pattern, but with the added offense of dividing three of the northeast Valley's legally protected rural communities — Shadow Hills, La Tuna Canyon, and Sunland-Tujunga — from a section of Lakeview Terrace. They argued that by splitting "rural communities of interest" into two council districts, their power as a voting bloc would thereby be reduced. As they engaged in the redistricting process, middle-class white rural residents constructed "rurality" as a political identity that was now more endangered than the voting rights of racial minorities, and which therefore should be considered more important than race in the drawing of district lines.

In February 2002, members of the Northeast Valley rural communities formed their own committee to protest the official commission's map and to create an alternative set of district boundaries. This group, called the Northeast Valley Rural Foothills Redistricting Map Committee (hereafter the Northeast Valley Committee), was organized by residents from the communities of Shadow Hills, Sunland-Tujunga, La Tuna Canyon, and the affected area of Lakeview Terrace. Their goal was to create a rural foothill district that would include these four primary communities, along with the Valley neighborhoods of Sylmar, Pacoima, and "rural Sun Valley," in the interests of maintaining rural "communities of interest" together in one council district.[2] The inclusion of only rural Sun Valley is important, for the inclusion of Sun Valley as a whole would mean the incorporation of an area that is highly industrial, with numerous junkyards and automobile repair facilities, and densely populated by low-income and middle-income Latinos. Rural Sun Valley, by contrast, lies immediately to the southwest of Shadow Hills and consists primarily of large lots, single-family homes (including some stone houses that have recently been targeted for the formation of a historic district), and a population that is more racially mixed. Sylmar and Pacoima, for their part, would also contribute significant numbers of Latinos, to make the second council district a "Latino-electable" district. Although most equestrians had left Sylmar in the 1980s, the presence of a few remaining stables and horse-related businesses made the neighborhood acceptable for inclusion. The Northeast Valley Committee created an alternative district that was 39.6 percent Latino, although no numbers were made available about how many of these Latinos were actually registered voters. The committee explained that its proposed district was a "dream district" because it kept rural communities of interest together while meeting the mandate to create a Latino-electable district.[3]

The Northeast Valley Committee distributed and posted flyers urging residents of the northeast Valley's rural neighborhoods to attend the redistricting commission's hearings. One flyer said,

> It's time for a change. The people of Sunland/Tujunga, Lake View Terrace, La Tuna Canyon, Sylmar, Sun Valley, Hansen Dam, and Shadow Hills deserve to have the district that was seized from them in the '80s by the L.A. City Council, returned to the rightful owners, the rural Northeast Valley residents. Our District 2, which now reaches from Tujunga to Mulholland, shows what happens behind closed doors at City Hall when politicians gerrymander the communities of the city in order to preserve their power. Join with your neighbors and let City Hall know that you care.[4]

Similarly, Nancy Snider, president of the Lake View Terrace Home Owners Association, wrote to the Listserv of the local chapter of Equestrian Trails, Inc. (ETI), to encourage subscribers to express their opinions in writing to the redistricting commission. Snider offered a sample letter that others could copy or emulate, which said: "The tentative redistricting plan shows the communities of Lake View Terrace, La Tuna Canyon, Shadow Hills, and Sunland/Tujunga as no longer part of the same district. These rural foothills communities should stay together since we all share a common goal and interest which are not the same as the rest of the valley. All these communities share a rural and equestrian lifestyle which we must preserve and protect. . . . The voices of the people in Lake View Terrace, Shadow Hills, La Tuna Canyon, and Sunland/Tujunga should not be ignored."[5] In each of these calls to action, the rural and equestrian lifestyle was affirmed and constructed as a special, endangered culture that is just as worthy of protection as the voting rights of Latinos and other historically disenfranchised racial groups. Similarly, Tim Borquez, a member of the alternative map committee, urged his neighbors and fellow community members to attend a special meeting of the Los Angeles City Council Redistricting Commission. He wrote, "This city refuses to listen to what our community wants and must understand the cost of their willingness to heed to our wishes. This is a major land grab by District #7 in order to split the voting power base of our rural communities, without the consequences of having to answer to our whole community on election day! The time to respond is now!"[6] Borquez's language of a "land grab" by District 7 subtly harkens to the language of westward movement and the skirmishes around homesteading in conquered territories as a way to combat the perceived incursions of a ruthless urban state, as well as Latino voters, into rural territory.

The Northeast Valley Committee convened several meetings intended to cultivate support for their alternative map among newcomers to the redistricting process. At each meeting, leaders introduced the Voting Rights Act. Amid the complexities of the process, the act's racial requirements nearly always occupied much of the public's attention. The requirement that the northeast Valley area be a Latino-electable council district caused particular consternation. Many white attendees said that they could not understand why this sort of requirement was still necessary or why it should apply to their community. They repeatedly exclaimed, "We don't care about race!" and numerous people asked aloud, rhetorically, "What happened to our color-blind society?" The general sentiment seemed to be that racial integration and equality had been achieved, whereas the rural lifestyle was now what needed to be protected. As one white attendee at a meeting argued, "You would certainly find a reasonable amount of integration here [in the communities of Lakeview Terrace and Sunland-Tujunga]." Another white woman stated, "We have plenty of Latino horse people in this area, and we have more in common with them than with white people who want to live in a condo." Yet only two identifiable Latinos were in attendance at this particular meeting of over one hundred people. Later in the meeting, both stood and identified themselves, then echoed their support for keeping rural communities of interest together.[7] By offering themselves as examples, they legitimated and validated the claims of the white people in the room who claimed that the United States was beyond race and should now emphasize universal, common values. Indeed, rural residents often appealed to a rhetoric of "common interests" that appeared to be based on demonstrated commitments to a rural landscape and lifestyle but elided the ways in which access to that lifestyle has been and continues to be structured by patterns of economic inequality and social practices of exclusion. At one meeting, someone asked, "Why are we doing this on the basis of race and not common interests?"[8] By this logic, race was not a justifiable common interest, but rurality and horse-keeping were. The opposition constructed between (racially unmarked) rural "common interests" and (nonwhite) racial identity normalized the concerns of rural dwellers as nonracial and prevented rural residents from seeing how racial identity could actually function as a common interest for communities of color based on historic patterns of exclusion, segregation, discrimination, and political disenfranchisement.

White residents clearly perceived themselves to be victims of the redistricting process's emphasis on creating a Latino-electable district. At one meeting of the Northeast Valley Committee, when the topic of the Voting Rights Act was broached, the white woman sitting next to me asked her companion, "What happened to *our* rights?" to which the other woman responded, "We don't have any. We're the minority now." Later in the meeting, one of the leadership sarcastically asked, "What happened to the melting pot?" and many people in the audience nodded their heads vigorously.[9] These two questions exhibited the conflicting desire of local residents to believe that racial equality had been achieved in American society, while simultaneously seeing themselves as victims of a multiculturalism that caters to "special interests" (race) rather than "common interests" (rural lifestyle). Yet local residents' preoccupation with race slipped out at other moments during these meetings. At one meeting, attendees complained about the possibility of sharing a district with nearby low-income communities, and one woman remarked, "Soon we're going to look like Watts up here."[10] Her remark echoed the belief among rural dwellers that low-income and high-density housing (and the racialized groups associated with such housing) would lower property values and introduce crime into the area. Even though redistricting itself does nothing to change land-use policy within individual neighborhoods, her comment reflected the assumption that simply sharing a district with communities of color would attract denser housing and urban landscapes and would lead to the election of a city council representative supportive of these types of changes, thus repeating the cycle of perceived white rural victimization at the hands of urban agencies considered to be unresponsive and unsympathetic.

The Northeast Valley Rural Foothills Redistricting Map Committee presented its alternative map at the redistricting commission's final public meeting on March 26, 2002. However, the redistricting commission's final map disregarded most of the committee's suggestions. The final district actually differs little from that originally proposed by the redistricting commission, despite numerous meetings with residents throughout the northeast San Fernando Valley, with one critically important exception — the new District 2 keeps Lakeview Terrace in the district along with the northeast Valley's other rural neighborhoods. Thus, rural activists won the most important dimension of their struggle: maintaining the voting power of rural communities of interest. The current District 2 represents 7 percent of the city's residents. The district is 51.5 percent non-Hispanic white, 33.9 percent Latino, 6.4 percent Asian and Asian American, and 3.8 percent African American (information about how many of these Latinos were registered voters was not available). Approximately 15 percent of individuals in the district live below the poverty line, though poverty within the district is disproportionately concentrated in its Latino neighborhoods.[11] The new council district's boundaries went into effect with the first city election in November 2002, in which Democrat Wendy Greuel, a white woman who has repeatedly affirmed her commitment to the rural lifestyle, was reelected.

Rural activists in the northeast San Fernando Valley came away from the redistricting process confirmed in their belief that the urban state unduly privileges an artificial construct of "race" over the naturalized "common interests" of the rural lifestyle. Because the local redistricting committee encouraged these discourses and provided a rare forum for residents to engage racial issues and demographic change explicitly, these meetings served an important purpose beyond the mere drawing of boundaries. By collecting large groups of predominantly white people and enabling them to share their feelings of victimization by the urban state, their frustration over racial politics, and their fears of a changing way of life, these meetings facilitated the construction of a collective identity as color-blind, middle-class white people. They also provided a forum for the cultivation of a growing sentiment that a "nonracial" rural culture is increasingly threatened by the city's shifting demographics, economy, and political structures.

Throughout the redistricting process, many residents of the semirural San Fernando Valley maintained that their neighborhoods harbor a climate of peaceful coexistence among diverse ethnic and racial groups, especially among whites and Latinos. They suggested in these meetings and in community forums convened for other purposes that rural horse culture allows and embraces difference. They contended that, in a rural community, ethnic and racial differences are less important than a shared love for horses, other animals, and the rural lifestyle. Yet this perspective minimizes the structural inequalities that persist in this corner of the San Fernando Valley, as well as the real tensions that manifest themselves in everyday struggles over public and private space. Just a few months after the redistricting meetings concluded, tensions among Latinos and whites in Hansen Dam erupted, unsettling the claims that rural white residents had articulated about color blindness, rural cultural unity, and peaceful integration in the northeast San Fernando Valley.

During the summer of 2002, several altercations between horseback riders and pedestrians occurred at Hansen Dam, a 1,300-acre flood control channel in the northeast San Fernando Valley that also functions as a major public park and environmental preserve. Hansen Dam is surrounded by residential communities with distinctly different ethnic, racial, and social-class compositions (see figure 16). It is bordered by majority-white Shadow Hills on the southeast end and by predominantly Latino neighborhoods, including Sylmar, Arleta, and Pacoima, on its northern and western borders. Politically, Hansen Dam falls within Council District 7 (represented by Alex Padilla), but it is also bordered by District 2 (governed by Wendy Greuel). These competing constituencies use the dam in different ways, and their recreational patterns have led to conflict among users.

On any given day but especially on weekends, numerous Latino youth and families from surrounding neighborhoods come to use the dam's recreational

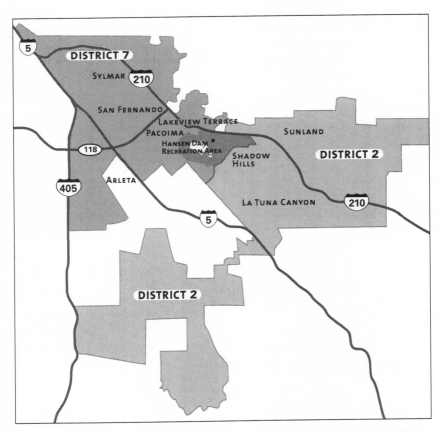

FIGURE 16 Neighborhoods in the northeast San Fernando Valley, centered on Hansen Dam. The northeast Valley is divided between Los Angeles City Council Districts 2 and 7; district boundaries are indicated. Map by Jacky Woolsey.

facilities. Often they swim in the streams and have picnics on the sandy banks. Equestrians from the surrounding neighborhoods ride their horses through these same areas, and on a few occasions the families' music, plastic bags, or noise have scared the horses. Informal grumbling about these experiences was common at local organization meetings and over e-mail Listservs during the time I conducted my fieldwork. The issue seemed to have a much longer aegis. As a youth growing up in the neighborhood, I can recall that, in the mid-1980s, Latino families parked their cars on the residential streets within Shadow Hills and walked down into the dam from that entrance. By the early 1990s, "No Parking" signs had been posted on these residential streets, effectively eliminating use of the Shadow Hills access point by nonresidents and forcing them to enter the park from the Pacoima entrance, several miles away, in the majority-Latino-and-black neighborhood.

In June 2002, simmering tensions between Latino pedestrians and white equestrians in the dam boiled over. One incident in particular was publicized through e-mail and discussed at community meetings. The woman involved, Sharon Gibson, sent a lengthy e-mail describing the incident to the Listserv of ETI. Captioned with the subject line "Rough Ride," the e-mail opened as follows:

> Hans and I had the ride from Hell this afternoon! Since Gabriello [sic] Park re-opened, a lot of people are drifting down from the park and into the streambeds . . . where we've been riding for the last several years. Anyway, these people bring picnics, fishing poles, bathing suits, and millions of kids, including some in strollers! They leave their trash and disposable diapers littered about and lately I've seen beer bottles just under the surface of the waterways where your horse could step on them. They completely ignore the signs that say "no fishing, no swimming, no bicycles, no camping," etc.[12]

Gibson described how she and her riding partner, Hans, were riding through one area and had to take a detour because of a large group of people in the waterway. They chose a smaller stream, mostly overgrown with reeds, and as they emerged from a dense and narrow section,

> all of a sudden there are about 17 women and children swarming around saying that they're building a dam so the kids can swim and we can't pass through. Hans tells them it is not a swimming hole, it's a horse trail and it's illegal to dam the stream. There is a big opening so he rides through. As I come to the opening, it closes, blocked by the women who've started screaming at us. Now our horses are separated — I can't go forward and Hans can't come back. They start splashing

water at Nick (Hans' horse). . . . Nick does pretty well until they start throwing ROCKS at him, which HIT him! I'm trying to tell them to SHUT UP and just let us pass before one of the kids gets hurt.[13]

One can imagine the confusion and near chaos at this scene, where the different groups involved clearly had very different and contentious ideas about how the stream could or should be used: for swimming or for horseback riding. In fact, there is no officially established use for the waterway; it is used for both purposes. Hans then got off his horse and tried to talk to "the main offender, who [was] brandishing a big rock at him." After loud verbal disagreements, according to Gibson's narrative, a Latino man punched Hans in the eye twice, and Hans was not able to defend himself because he was still trying to control his horse. Ultimately, several other people on horseback came along and the Latino park users began to disperse. Gibson said, "I don't know if they finally figured out it really was a horse trail, or thought the other riders were our reinforcements."[14]

Throughout the narrative, the ethnic or racial identities of the people in the stream had not been mentioned, but for those subscribers to the Listserv who were familiar with the history of these kinds of tensions at Hansen Dam, it would have been obvious that they were Latinos. Gibson briefly alluded to, but then dismissed, the racial tensions at work. During the skirmish, she explained, "One of the women is screaming at Hans that we just don't want them there because they're Mexican and not Americans, which of course, is highly entertaining since Hans isn't an American either!" On the basis that her riding partner and husband, Hans — presumably a European immigrant — was not an American citizen, she thus dismissed the charge of racism as preposterous. But she concluded the story by saying, "Needless to say, I'm pissed. REALLY pissed! Lots of people are going to hear about this! It's a third world country we live in! Boy, do I miss my quiet rides in Sylmar! Okay, that's my rant — now I have to go become an activist again."[15]

Gibson's concluding thoughts bring together many of the fears and anxieties that rural activists have about landscape change and demographic change. The woman's narrative conflates the entire incident — the ethnic Mexicans' presence in the streams, their purported disregard of signs, and their attempts to keep horseback riders out of the places where their children are swimming — with life in a "third world country," a racialized marker of social decline and perceived abandonment of Anglo-American standards of civilization. It then becomes clear that Gibson had, at one time, lived in Sylmar, presumably before the neighborhood changed from predominantly white and horse-keeping to predominantly Latino. In a manner reminiscent of Evan Jones's narrative of how and why Sylmar had been transformed (examined in the previous chapter), she subtly blames ethnic and racial change for her inability to enjoy "quiet rides" in Sylmar and now in Shadow Hills. Moreover, her fury over the incident renewed her commitment to rural land-use activism, confirming the way in which beliefs about the linking of landscape change and social change (especially with regard to race, ethnicity, and social class) propel patterns of political mobilization in the northeast San Fernando Valley.[16]

This incident brought to the surface many of the long-standing tensions that had simmered in the northeast San Fernando Valley for years. White rural residents deconstructed and interpreted the incident, as well as the broader subject of tensions among users of Hansen Dam, on e-mail lists and in community meetings. Throughout these discussions, Latinos were constructed as outsiders and criminals. Gillian Black (pseudonym), then the president of ETI, wrote to that organization's Listserv a week after the altercation. Her e-mail began with the reminder, "Many of you know that Hans and Sharon were assaulted and battered in the dam area." Her language thus elevated the incident to a case of aggressive physical assault in which Hans and Sharon were constructed as innocent victims, rather than as people who, from the perspective of the Latinos involved in the incident, could have hurt their children by riding too close to an area where children were swimming. Black then shared information she had been collecting about other incidents at Hansen Dam involving whites and Latinos, including allegations of a dog attack, attempted child abductions and sexual assaults, public exposure and indecency, and the firing of illegal weapons. She warned readers of the Listserv that "Hansen Dam [was] in danger of being lost to equestrians." As a countermeasure, Black suggested, "[We should] form a coalition of several organizations, receive the appropriate training and start patrolling our park even if we are only the eyes and ears and educators."[17] In the meantime, she and other organizational leadership pursued their goal of bringing a mounted patrol unit to police Hansen Dam and to mediate between conflicting users.

During this period, an anonymous group of people began to put together *The Hansen Dam Papers*, a series of pamphlets explicitly modeled on the *Federalist Papers* written in New York in the aftermath of the American Revolution. The pamphlets were made available at meetings of the Shadow Hills Property Owners Association, the Foothill Trails District Neighborhood Council, and other groups. They generally focused on environmental issues within Hansen Dam and specifically the discovery in 2002 of the U.S. Army Corps of Engineers' practice of dumping waste into Hansen Dam's protected habitat areas. However, those activists who exposed, monitored, and protested this environmental issue also became engaged in the social and ethnic tensions in the dam, joining with equestrian organizations to promote the goal of a mounted patrol that would monitor Latino users and other "outsiders." In the third issue of *The Hansen Dam Papers*, released September 10, 2002, the authors republished the testimony of a "concerned citizen" who had written the following to the Army Corps of Engineers:

> Along the stream in the Big Tujunga Wash, equestrians have been reporting big groups of people going into the bushes to picnic with open fires also leaving trash. This last weekend it was reported to me that there were guns and pellet guns present and the riders came across a shot-down dead egret. Several weeks ago myself and two other riders stopped about 50 people who were going down to the stream. They told me that they always go down there and they were parking in [a] residential area. . . . This has been an ongoing problem and getting worse. We need patrols here in Hansen Dam, especially in the Big Tujunga Wash stream areas. These areas can only be patrolled by horseback or by foot. . . . It is alarming to know that recently in the past months attacks were made on equestrians and now our wildlife are targets. This is not going to go away, it will only get worse.[18]

Noting that patrols would not occur unless substantial evidence could be collected to show that they were needed, the editors of *The Hansen Dam Papers* urged readers to report all "criminally or environmentally abusive behaviors" they observed while riding or hiking at the dam to their citizen activist group and local officials. They encouraged readers to carry cell phones and cameras to document abuses such as "soiled diapers tossed into the river, dead egrets, blackened campfire pits, torn up fencing, safety hazards, etc" but warned, "Don't endanger your life by blatantly taking photos of criminals in action! *Be smart and safe.*" In this invocation, soiled diapers, used campfire pits, and dead birds were constructed as the acts of dangerous, deadly criminals; these acts were subtly associated with the working-class and middle-class Latinos from adjacent neighborhoods.

In their collective processing of these incidents, rural white residents portrayed Latino users as, at best, irresponsible park users and "breeder" parents who have too many children and then put them at risk, and, at worst, as dangerous criminals who must be controlled and monitored. Such characterizations are central elements of what anthropologist Leo Chavez calls the Latino Threat narrative. The Latino Threat narrative posits that "Latinos are unwilling or incapable of integrating, of becoming part of the national community. Rather, they are part of an invading force from south of the border that is bent on reconquering land that was formerly theirs (the U.S. Southwest) and destroying the American way of life."[19] In the northeast San Fernando Valley, these fears of and anxieties about the Latino Threat are negotiated through struggles over the future of the rural landscape and in conflicts over public space that is shared between "holdouts" of white, rural neighborhoods and communities that have changed from rural to urban, and white to Latino, in recent years. Rural white dwellers' fears of the Latino Threat were apparent in the struggles over the redistricting commission's mandate to create a Latino-electable district; they also came to the fore in the way that rural equestrians responded to the physical altercations at the dam, and in particular in their language of being victimized by Latino criminals in what had once been spaces enjoyed peacefully by white equestrians and rural dwellers.

The tension between competing visions of the ideal relationship between humans and the environment emerged frequently in these debates and was implicitly racialized. Equestrian leaders situated themselves, as people on horses, as the most logical and appropriate caretakers of the area, based on their proposition that, as horse people and rural dwellers, they are more in tune with the environment. Throughout their discussions of these incidents, local equestrian residents consistently referred to the dam as "*our* pretty park," "*our* wildlife," and "*our* beautiful riding area" (my emphasis). Latino pedestrian families, by contrast, were defined as outsiders who engage in inappropriate uses of natural areas based on ignorance or disrespect. In response to a survey conducted by the Los Angeles Department of Recreation and Parks concerning equestrian usage of the dam, one Shadow Hills resident recommended, "We need some sort of oversight for the 'weekenders' that frequently heckle or threaten the equestrians."[20] The "weekenders" to which she refers are overwhelmingly Latinos who live in nearby neighborhoods adjacent to Hansen Dam, yet she implies that they are outsiders who must be monitored in public space because of their tendencies toward criminality.

One weekend soon after, in the summer of 2002, the Los Angeles Police Department assigned a mounted posse to patrol the dam. An informal group of Shadow Hills residents rode through as well, talking to the Latino families, suggesting alternate play areas for the children, and distributing trash bags. Gillian Black, the organizer of this informal group, commented later at the Shadow Hills Property Owners Association meeting that it was far better to handle the situation with Los Angeles law enforcement than to let vigilante groups begin to form on their own. Her comments, and indeed the entire movement to secure a mounted patrol at Hansen Dam, reflect a particular relationship with the police that is inflected by racial and class biases. While whites often see the police as sources of protection, Latinos and other nonwhites have often experienced the police as sources of harassment, profiling, violence, and, for undocumented immigrants, the threat of deportation.[21] Furthermore, although the choice of a mounted patrol resulted primarily from the lack of vehicle access to the area, the position of the police as fellow equestrians — and the fact that several members of the posse actually live or keep their horses in Shadow Hills — creates a shared interest between law enforcement and the equestrian users of the area. Los Angeles police only patrolled the area on one occasion during my fieldwork, and tensions between the two user groups had died down by the end of the year. Nonetheless, a coalition of resident activists continues to occasionally lobby the Los Angeles Police Department for regular mounted patrols through the area and the establishment of emergency phone booths.

These incidents at Hansen Dam and the way in which they were resolved are an important window into the complex forces of environmental racism in contemporary Los Angeles. As we saw in chapter 5, unequal access to parks and recreational facilities is a major problem in Los Angeles, and majority-white communities have far greater access to open spaces such as Hansen Dam. Yet patterns of racially distinct usage persist even when natural areas are relatively accessible and free or low cost, as is Hansen Dam. A key factor turns out to be the perception of discrimination en route to and within natural areas. In their telephone survey of nearly nine hundred people conducted during the summer of 1994, Tierney, Dahl, and Chavez found that perceptions of discrimination were a significant factor affecting whether people of color chose to visit natural areas in Los Angeles, even after controlling for respondent income and education. They concluded that "the decision to visit an undeveloped natural area is more than just a transportation and income issue," and that the perception of hostility in local neighborhoods was a key deterrent.[22] Certainly, the events that took place at Hansen Dam during the summer and fall of 2002 confirm this finding.

But these incidents also confound the claims that rural residents made during the redistricting process, just a few months before, that Latinos and whites could come together in the rural community through a shared love for the rural landscape and the equestrian lifestyle. Rather, what became apparent in the redistricting process and in the collective response to altercations at Hansen Dam is that white rural residents of the northeast San Fernando Valley believe their lifestyle is under attack, both by the urban state and by the growing population of Latinos in nearby neighborhoods and throughout Los Angeles. Rural residents believe that the urban state is no longer willing or able to protect the rural lifestyle, and that Latinos and other nonwhites have benefited at their expense. In response, rural residents engage in a wide range of social practices through which they struggle to affirm the centrality of the rural frontier myth to the American experience and to construct "rural culture" as a valid political claim in the arena of multicultural identity politics. Such practices are intended to celebrate the frontier myth and to keep it at the forefront of the local imagination, reminding representatives of the urban state and other urban residents about the value of a hegemonic version of regional and national heritage.

On an everyday level, the affirmation of the rural past happens through the everyday, mundane choices that semirural residents make about personal dress, home decoration, and yard design. Despite their positions as urban professionals, many rural dwellers regularly wear clothing and accessories that represent the "Wild West" experience, such as cowboy hats and boots, large silver belt buckles, and western-style button-up collared shirts. Homeowners in the northeast San Fernando Valley's rural neighborhoods also decorate their homes, barns, and yards with iconographic representations of the "Old West" such as wagon wheels, cowboy figurines, and paintings of wild stallions. Businesses, of which there are few, use similar symbols in their signage, such as the Stallion Market, which features a large painting of a black stallion on its exterior wall, and a hair salon that features a wagon wheel on its facade (see figure 17).

Rural residents and business owners work to shape the landscape in this way partly because they want to express their identities as "cowboys" and "country folks," and partly because they interpret the rural landscape's aesthetic as a sort of moral compass guiding their land-use activism. During the time I conducted fieldwork in the northeast Valley, members of local organizations would periodically send messages to their organizations' Listservs with poetry and short stories celebrating the rural landscape as a symbol of appropriate morals, values, and actions. For example, in April 2002, Kathy McHugh, a member of ETI, forwarded a short essay titled "Dirt Roads," by author Paul Harvey, to ETI's Listserv. Harvey's short essay begins: "What's mainly wrong with society today is that too many dirt roads have been paved. There's not a problem in America today, crime, drugs, education, divorce, delinquency that wouldn't be remedied, if we just had more Dirt Roads, because Dirt Roads give character. . . . Our values were better when our roads were worse!" Taking dirt roads as a symbol of a purportedly simpler time, Harvey's essay claims that there is better education, less crime, and "no drive by shootings" in places where there are dirt roads. He makes references to "city dudes," who, he suggests, "worship their cars more than their kids," lack patience, and do not value the environment—associa-

FIGURE 17 Exterior of the Stallion Market in Shadow Hills. According to the terms of the community plan and zoning, commercial properties are allowed in only three places; those few business that do exist use symbols of the rural, frontier experience. Photo by author, 2006.

tions that are fully shared by the Valley's rural dwellers. For Harvey, the contrast between rural and urban life is wholly symbolized by the contrast between dirt and paved roads, as when he writes, "Most paved roads lead to trouble, Dirt Roads more likely lead to a fishing creek or a swimming hole." Harvey's essay presents a romanticized and idealized portrait of rural life that is distinctively and purposefully opposed to the symbols of urban life. As residents of one of the largest and most complex cities in the world, rural residents of the northeast San Fernando Valley nonetheless embrace these literary forms as a guide for their action. McHugh, who forwarded Harvey's essay, prefaced it with her own comments: "With all of the trouble we rural cowboys have in L.A., this tells a good story! Keep this for every meeting with the city or developer that you meet! Put it in every newsletter that you can . . . spread the word about the importance of our lifestyle in the country!"[23]

And they do. Residents devote countless hours to meetings in which they debate the merits and flaws of proposed developments and strategize about how to resist the plans or tailor them to their liking. When necessary, residents file appeals and work through the legal process to ensure that the rural landscape is preserved, and they work with developers to include features such as equestrian trails and dirt roads that will enhance and reproduce the aesthetics of rurality. Throughout these engagements with the urban state and capital, residents of the Valley's rural neighborhoods construct and perform identities as "country folks" and mobilize the symbols of rural western heritage to secure protections from the urban state and concessions from developers.

They use festivals for similar purposes. In July 2002, the California State Legislature adopted a resolution marking December 14 as the Day of the Horse. Since then, the Foothill Trails District Neighborhood Council (FTDNC), which represents Shadow Hills, Lakeview Terrace, and La Tuna Canyon, has planned and hosted the San Fernando Valley's annual Day of the Horse Festival. The festival is cosponsored by Los Angeles City Council Districts 2 (represented by Greuel) and 7 (represented by Padilla) and is held in a riding ring at Hansen Dam. The festival's program booklet proclaims: "Nowhere within the state of California is there a stronger 'horse culture' than here in the Northeast San Fernando Valley. Therefore it was natural for the FTDNC to use 'Day of the Horse' as its signature outreach. . . . This is more than just a celebration of the Horse — it is a celebration of the foothill community."[24] The Day of the Horse has been held annually since 2002, and although the format varies slightly from year to year, it typically includes a historical pageant or parade, performances by equestrian organizations, informational tables staffed by those organizations and relevant city agencies, food, country-western and mariachi music, and socializing. Above all, the event is explicitly intended as an opportunity to build support among political representatives of the urban state for the protection of the rural lifestyle in Los Angeles.

The Day of the Horse Festival is intentionally multicultural and multilingual, presenting the rural, horse-keeping culture as a distinctive culture that is capable of bridging cultural, ethnic, and linguistic differences and is therefore both "color blind" and worthy of state protection as an endangered social group. At the same time, and without apparent contradiction, the narrative tropes of the frontier used in the event celebrate the Anglo-American conquest of the West. The 2003 festival opened with a so-called historical pageant featuring, in order, the First Vaquero, the Mexican Charro, the Buckaroo, and the American Cowgirl. Four riders carried the flags of Spain, Mexico, California, and the United States in sequence. There was no representation of California's indigenous equestrian traditions. With the members of the historical pageant standing behind them, council members Greuel and Padilla, along with California

State Assembly member Cindy Montañez, entered on horseback, dismounted, and gave speeches recognizing the importance of the San Fernando Valley's many horse traditions and of the Day of the Horse celebration. Greeted by exuberant applause from her constituents, Greuel said, "I am proud to be celebrating Day of the Horse with the greater Foothill communities. Horse-keeping is a tradition that contributes to the Valley's rich diversity and one that we should passionately protect for future generations." Padilla echoed these sentiments, remarking, "This event is an excellent example of the community's commitment to preserving and celebrating the rural, horse-keeping lifestyle. I commend you for the multicultural approach to the event ensuring that the outstanding pageant and diverse presentations will be enjoyed by all." Afterward, riders presented demonstrations of various equestrian traditions, such as rodeo, vaulting, drill teams, and *charreria*, and some organizations performed historical reenactments of western American experiences. Among these reenactments was a performance by the New Buffalo Soldiers, a group of about eight African American men (most of whom are residents of Shadow Hills or Lakeview Terrace) who reenacted a "typical" scene from the historic black cavalry in which African Americans suppressed unnamed (presumably indigenous or Mexican) bandits in the West.[25]

Thus, in the organization of the Day of the Horse Festival, the historic settlement of the West becomes a universal experience in which diverse ethnic and racial groups participate as equals, and in which nation-states and racial formations pass progressively and peacefully from one era to another. The ugly content of that history — conquest, genocide, dispossession, and exploitation — is erased from the story. Instead, the version of multiculturalism celebrated at this festival is a benign multiculturalism that incorporates cultural difference without regard to power and structural inequality, past and present, and in stunning contrast to the real ethnic tensions that exist among Latinos and whites in the northeast San Fernando Valley — including the physical skirmishes that had taken place a year before, not more than a half mile from the site of the festival. In his analysis of the enormously popular Los Angeles Fiesta, coordinated by the Merchants and Manufacturers Association beginning in 1894, historian William Deverell has observed that such romanticized portraits of history explain and justify the conquest as a peaceful and righteous occurrence. By situating American Indians, Mexican Americans, and Anglo-Americans as peaceful cohabitants of the West who now come together to celebrate their shared history, such performances gloss over the bloody and violent historical struggles among these groups and their persistently unequal structural outcomes, especially the resolution of competing claims on land ownership and the racialization of local labor markets. Deverell concludes that, at the turn of the twentieth century, "La Fiesta offered elite Anglos in Los Angeles the ideal vehicle by which to forget — whitewash — both the unpleasantness of recent decades as well as the entire bloody history of the Southwest throughout the eighteenth and nineteenth century."[26]

A century later, at the turn of the twenty-first century, the Day of the Horse Festival and the multifaceted affirmations of "rural culture" in the northeast San Fernando Valley perform a similar function. Amid the context of identity politics in Los Angeles centered on race, immigration status, and social class, symbols and narratives of the western frontier affirm narratives of American imperialism in the name of white supremacy, while also presenting the rural lifestyle as just one culture among many — a politically useful claim in contemporary Los Angeles. This duality was confirmed by the support of elected Latino representatives such as Padilla and Montañez, as well as the participation of Latino and black horseback riders, in the Day of the Horse Festival — people who were seldom or never present at the land-use meetings I observed, and whose presence in other contexts would be considered a threat to the rural landscape and lifestyle.

Through their involvement in urban political processes such as redistricting and real-estate development, their everyday social interactions in public spaces and parks, and the staging of ceremonies and festivals such as the Day of the Horse, rural activists in the northeast San Fernando Valley contribute to a culture of rural whiteness that is exclusionary, in a low-intensity way, and maintains the material privileges of the area. And yet Shadow Hills' rural residents do not perceive themselves as privileged, nor do they believe that their activism to preserve the rural landscape and lifestyle contributes to a culture of exclusion in the northeast San Fernando Valley. Although the majority are well-paid urban professionals who own large suburban lots with high real-estate values, residents genuinely understand themselves to be ordinary, working-class or middle-class people who have simply worked hard to achieve the American dream. Even when asked directly about their neighborhood's (and by extension, their own) privilege relative to the larger metropolitan region, rural residents narrate these patterns in ways that legitimate and justify inequality. Overwhelmingly, they do so by appealing to narratives of rural America and western heritage. For the most part, this ideological work occurs in the everyday dynamics of informal conversations among neighbors and in property owners association and neighborhood council meetings. However, an explosive incident in late October 2002, during the height of my ethnographic research, brought these issues to the surface and laid bare the dynamics through which rural whites in Los Angeles understand and narrate their racial and class subjectivity.

The incident was precipitated by increased attention to the northeast San Fernando Valley's rural lifestyle from Wendy Greuel, who was elected to represent the area to the Los Angeles City Council in 2002 in the aftermath of the redistricting process described earlier. Greuel ran her election campaign on a commitment to preserving the Valley's unique horse-keeping lifestyle, rural landscapes, and open space. In late July 2002, just a few months after her election, Greuel and fellow council member Ed Reyes, both of whom sit on the City Council's Planning and Land Use Management (PLUM) Committee, introduced a motion for a study of city horse-keeping regulations. It stated:

> The horsekeeping tradition of Los Angeles is as old as the city itself. However, that tradition has been *under attack* in recent decades from a variety of forces. The city's need for housing has resulted in the subdivision of hundreds of horsekeeping properties into smaller suburban lots and the concentration of horse ownership in the San Fernando Valley in a few areas in Shadow Hills, Lakeview Terrace, La Tuna Canyon, and Chatsworth. The ongoing loss of horsekeeping property is *exacerbated* by a regulatory structure that is complex, overlapping, and potentially inconsistent. . . . Accordingly, there is a serious need for comprehensive review of the horsekeeping regulations that affect Los Angeles residents and for action by the City Council to protect and strengthen horsekeeping rights.[27]

The language of the motion is notable for its assertions of horse owners' victimization by urban government and declaration of their rights to continue their horse-keeping lifestyle in the San Fernando Valley. Such sentiments of victimization and rights are a driving force in contemporary rural land-use activism, enabling "rural culture" to be strategically positioned as a viable and valuable but threatened force within urban multicultural politics.

Greuel and Reyes then moved that an evening meeting of the PLUM Committee be held in the equestrian areas of the city and attended by representatives from the Department of City Planning and Department of Animal Services, as well as the city attorney. The special evening meeting was held in October 2002, during which Greuel and Reyes listened to a presentation coordinated by equestrian residents of Shadow Hills, Lakeview Terrace, La Tuna Canyon, and Chatsworth. The third member of the PLUM committee, Hal Bernson, who represented equestrian constituents in Chatsworth, was noticeably absent, taken as proof of his disregard for — and, according to some, outright hostility to — the horse-keeping lifestyle and rural landscape there.

Approximately 250 people, overwhelmingly white and middle-aged or elderly, crowded Greuel's field office in Tujunga. Many wore their characteristic cowboy boots, jeans, and hats. One by one, local leaders stood at the microphone to offer their perspectives on the value of rural horse-keeping and the inadequacies of existing land-use regulations. The president of a local social equestrian organization appealed to Greuel and Reyes, arguing that "horse-keeping *was* the San Fernando Valley," while another activist claimed, "We are the most rural agricultural areas left in the city." The land-use chairman of the local property owners association argued, "Most of our urban centers began as ranchos," adding that one could still feel old Los Angeles as "the *caballeros* kick up dust along the trails." Other speakers stressed that horse-keeping neighborhoods have lower levels of crime and that horses teach children responsibility, empathy, and self-respect. One resident then stated, "Horse-keeping is only viable in this area if it is tied to land use," thereby paving the way for requests for favorable zoning, improved equine licensing procedures, and city subsidization of trail construction and maintenance. At the end of the hearing, both Greuel and Reyes reiterated their commitments to preserving the unique equestrian areas in the city.

Shortly thereafter, residents planned a community trail ride with Greuel and the local news media to cement their ideas and call broader public attention to their concerns. On a Sunday morning in late October 2002, Greuel, her land-use planning deputy, fellow city council member Janice Hahn, and a reporter from the *Los Angeles Daily News* went on a two-hour horseback ride (on borrowed horses) with over sixty-five residents from Shadow Hills, Lakeview Terrace, and La Tuna Canyon. The ride ended with a community barbecue at the Hansen Dam Recreation Center. Greuel proclaimed, "We want to preserve the horse-keeping tradition here in the San Fernando Valley. Today's ride is a celebration of that tradition with my constituents. We want to ensure that people with horses have *equal rights* when it comes to planning and land use in the city of Los Angeles."[28] Again, Greuel drew on the language of equal rights associated with nondiscrimination legislation but twisted its intentions to argue for protecting the "rights" of a historically privileged equestrian community that is mostly white; such co-opted language is a key feature of color blindness. Since this ride, Greuel has proven herself a consistent and reliable advocate of her constituents' claims to represent rural heritage.

A week after Greuel's October 2002 PLUM meeting with her constituents, Joseph Staub, a teacher from the nearby Valley community of Van Nuys, wrote an editorial to the *Daily News* challenging Greuel's focus on protecting horse-keeping and critiquing her language of victimization and horse-keeping rights. He observed,

> In light of the challenges facing the city of Los Angeles, especially the Valley, these days — and without mentioning those facing our country on the brink of war — it seems a gross overstatement to declare that the loss of a few horses would be a "tragedy for this city." A real tragedy for Los Angeles would by definition be something that affects the city as a whole: the struggling economy, for instance, or the effect of terrorism. There are more such things, including some now ongoing: the rising crime rate, the lack of affordable housing, the failing schools, the questionable quality of the air and water. These things are tragic. . . . The horse-keeping question is probably ignored by the vast majority of Angelenos, who have better things to do — such as make ends meet — than to worry about those whose lives would be just ravaged by not being able to keep a horse in the backyard.[29]

Staub went on to question the very idea of horse-keeping as a "rich tradition," instead asking why the San Fernando Valley's other histories were not subject to such nostalgia and protection.

> What exactly is a rich tradition? Is it a tradition that has a varied and interesting history? Or is a tradition deeply woven into the fabric of a community in which it exists? In neither case does horse-keeping qualify, except perhaps in a few blocks of Greuel's contributor base, and that's using a fairly open definition of "community." Why would Greuel worry about such a trifling issue when so many other "rich traditions" in the Valley are dying as well? The Valley used to have a tradition of being a suburban paradise. It was the place to which people moved to build a new life for themselves and their families — far from the ills of the city, but close enough to be a part of it. . . . Actually, the Valley used to have a tradition of being all ranch land and pasture — or even wilderness, if one goes back far enough. But we never hear of returning to that "rich tradition," probably because doing so would reduce both the tax base and the contributor pool for politicians.[30]

Staub's editorial pointed to the larger structural issues involved in the protection of rurality and the relational production of inequality. He also noted the biases involved with using rural heritage to secure exclusionary land-use protections for a privileged few. In this way, he struck directly at the contradictions of rural urbanism that had been at work in the San Fernando Valley for more than a century, as well as the more recent contradictions in residents' efforts to construct rurality as a simultaneously inclusive, color-blind, and besieged culture.

Not surprisingly, the response to Staub's letter among Shadow Hills residents was heated and emotional. Numerous residents wrote responses to the *Daily News*. Most were not published, but writers copied their letters to e-mail Listservs and shared them in neighborhood meetings. Also, during my interviews in the summer of 2005, three years later, I used Staub's editorial to initiate a conversation about residents' perceptions of their social status. Their responses offer a unique window through which to examine the negotiation of identity among contemporary, middle-class, semirural whites in Los Angeles and the urban U.S. West.

Interviewees focused almost exclusively on Staub's suggestion that they were wealthy, politically powerful elites. They virtually ignored the rest of his editorial including his commentary about issues of affordable housing, crime, poverty, and the public school district, as well as his query about the relative lack of protection afforded the San Fernando Valley's other traditions. The most common reaction was to deny Staub's charge that they, as individuals, were wealthy or politically powerful. One person wrote to the e-mail Listserv of the neighborhood council: "I am a horseowner, but I ain't wealthy. I don't go to movies or eat at restaurants, because there's no cash for such frivolities in our horse household."[31] Richard Eagan, a white male contractor, agreed, using himself as an example, "Well, I'm not wealthy. And I think it's actually cheaper to keep a horse on your property than to board it anywhere else."[32] Gary McCullough, a white male real-estate developer, argued, "I mean, I'm not elitist; my wife's not elitist; we don't have that much"; this was the same gentleman who had just told me he spent over $700,000 on a new home in the Rancho Verdugo Estates.[33] Finally, a longtime resident of nearby Sunland-Tujunga, which shares a community plan with Shadow Hills, pointed to her childhood experiences as proof of the nonelite class status of local horse owners. She wrote to the neighborhood council e-mail Listserv: "My sister, two brothers, and I were raised in a two parent home on a single income, (L.A. Unified [School District]) teacher's salary. Far from the rich or eletists [sic] that many people picture horseowners to be. My wardrobe generally consisted of hand-me-down jeans from my brothers and if I was really lucky, maybe a pair of Jordache. Our horses got the basics and lots of love. I couldn't imagine raising my child without horses. We live on the very same street that my husband and I grew up on and couldn't imagine living anywhere else."[34] This person minimized the economic dimension of horse-keeping (especially a large lot) and instead focused on the aesthetics and emotions involved with the horse-keeping lifestyle. Indeed, while she meant for her experience to serve as evidence of the neighborhood's nonelite status, in fact her ability to buy property as an adult in the same area where she grew up, despite dramatic increases in housing prices there and overall downturns in the regional economy, confirms that a significant way in which social-class status is reproduced among white Americans is through intergenerational transfers of wealth and social capital.

Rural residents understood class as an individualized matter of attitudes, consumption, and aesthetics. They often pointed to the consumption choices that rural dwellers and horse owners make as evidence of their working-class and nonprivileged status. The message seemed to be that they were not economically privileged because, unlike *truly* wealthy people, they choose to spend their money on horses, rather than luxury cars, expensive restaurants, or designer clothes. Patricia Wheat, the owner-operator of a large ranch and horse-boarding facility, argued in her unpublished letter to the *Daily News*, which she shared with me during our interview, that "disposable income, if any, too often finds its way into the pockets of Veterinarians, Farriers, and the local feed and tack store owner."[35] McCullough offered a similar assessment, telling me, "Here in Shadow Hills you have a bunch of cowboys, a bunch of women, mostly women, that just love horses. It's not about, do I have the prettiest horse or the best saddle. In Shadow Hills it's about anything but that. It's about the poker rides, the getting together, the whole rural atmosphere."[36] He conceived of class as a matter of aesthetic tastes rather than as the ability to mobilize power and resources. By his conception, elites are preoccupied with showing off their wealth through flashy displays of consumption such as pretty horses and expensive equipment; Shadow Hills residents, by contrast, are more concerned with developing authentic community, which he associates with the rural western lifestyle.

Crucially, each person directly invoked ideologies and symbols of western heritage to deflect charges of elitism and to construct a working-class, nonprivileged identity. For example, residents frequently described themselves and their neighbors as "country folks" and "cowboys." They pointed to the fact that they care for their horses themselves, rather than hiring laborers to feed, groom, water, and clean up after them. One resident wrote to the neighborhood council Listserv, "If [Staub] thinks horsekeeping is an elitist's pastime, he should try mucking manure twice a day, which most of us do ourselves."[37] Another wrote, "I submit that man's relationship with the horse is, indeed, rich with tradition, not to be confused with a tradition of the rich. Aside from earning a living and delighting in creatures large and small, horse people, large and small, are generally occupied working with, riding, feeding, cleaning, or grooming their horses. They are, happily, too broke and/or too busy to participate in urban pursuits like mall crawling, practicing Mr. Clinton's new age non sex or experimenting with drugs."[38] In this respect, rural dwellers likened themselves and their neighbors to working ranch hands, thereby eliding many local residents' day jobs as lawyers, engineers, consultants, and contractors.

Residents also positioned themselves as working-class and nonelite by referencing the materiality of a horse-keeping lifestyle — specifically, dirt, manure, and animal flesh. For example, Michael Castalucci, a white male public relations consultant, told me, "These are not nouveau riche horse owners. These are people who take better care of their horse's environment than their own."[39] Similarly, Richard Eagan referred to rural residents as "down to earth dirty cowboys" and asked me rhetorically, "What [sic] are elite? I don't think so. There's [sic] more down to earth people out here. People get up in the morning and clean horse manure."[40] As sociologist Steve Garner has argued, whiteness has historically been predicated on assumptions of cleanliness and purity; he theorizes that whites' efforts at exclusion are intended to expel "dirt from clean places."[41] Thus, Eagan's and Castalucci's comments can be read in several ways. On the one hand, by claiming that their lifestyle is associated with dirt and horse manure, the statements of Shadow Hills' residents can be interpreted as claiming a working-class identity associated with blue-collar labor as well as, in subtle ways, a not-quite-white status that is politically useful in multicultural Los Angeles. On the other hand, because they point out that rural whites are *cleaning* these dirty environments, Eagan's and Castalucci's explanations can also be interpreted as efforts to reinforce their whiteness. That is, in implicit opposition to their comments and complaints about the soiled diapers left behind by Latinos in Hansen Dam's recreational areas, by arguing that rural whites ensure that even horses live in clean, well-maintained environments, they construct a subtle sense of cultural superiority and purity in relationship to the natural environment.[42] Either way, reference to the materiality of horse-keeping allowed discursive positioning as white but distinctly not elite.

Another way in which rural residents constructed a nonprivileged identity was by contrasting symbols of western frontier heritage with East Coast equestrian traditions. As Eagan explained, "They [critics such as Staub] associate fancy English horses with being elite, maybe chasing foxes on Sunday afternoon or something, but. . . . Yeah, that's not, this is really down to earth dirty cowboys on their horse who they've had since it was a baby."[43] Interviewees made similar distinctions through reference to different breeds of horses. According to McCullough, "We don't have Thoroughbred horses that do this or that. We just have mutts. Most of the horses in Shadow Hills are rescued mustangs, or things like that. There's not a lot of horses whose owners have spent twenty thousand dollars on them. It's more like, look what I got for three grand, look what he does. . . . Yeah, you go to Flintridge, somewhere like that, eight out of ten horses are Thoroughbreds, some hugely expensive kind of horse that does all this jumping and everything else. Here they're worried about whether it can do barrel racing, not jumping — you know, how is he around cows."[44] Here, different breeds of horses were used to explain the social-class differences between people, and more specifically between elites and "country folks." In particular, ranch horses that are used to herd cattle are *working* horses, while Thoroughbreds are used in competitive sports as financial investments and to generate social distinction for their owners.[45]

Finally, interviewees differentiated their neighborhood, which they identified as working class and western, from other neighborhoods in Los Angeles County that allow horse-keeping but are perceived to be wealthier and "truly" elite (but are equally white or more so). One person responded vehemently: "There's not that dressage, equitation group that you have in Flintridge with the riding academy. Or even Burbank. . . . It's more of a cowboy, as opposed to Flintridge is more of a dressage group. You've got cowboys out here, there's no elitists out here. . . . It's not true. He [Staub] didn't know the Shadow Hills group. He's thinking horse owners who were — yeah, you go to Malibu Riding Club, even Burbank Equestrian Center. Those people are paying six hundred dollars a month to keep a horse. To classify Shadow Hills in there, I'd say it's the exact opposite."[46] Another explained to me, "Even La Cañada is different. . . . People who have these fancy horses don't even ride them in the wash because there's too many rocks." He continued, "You know some of the English stables, like the one up on Little Tujunga Canyon, Middle Ranch. That's elite. . . . But it ain't people from this neighborhood."[47]

Each of these responses brings together a complex web of associations between regional narratives of heritage and associated equestrian traditions, animal breeds, and distinct neighborhoods in Los Angeles in order to construct a nonprivileged subjectivity. Rural dwellers overwhelmingly disassociated themselves from an English horseback-riding tradition that is culturally associated with the elite as well as the perceived immobility and aristocracy of British society. Instead, they embraced symbols and narratives of rural western heritage associated with working-class ranch life, meritocracy, and ideals of rugged individualism and democracy. The San Fernando Valley's rural residents conceive of themselves and their neighbors as cowboys and country folks. And they labor to map these working-class narratives and ideologies onto their neighborhood as a form of social distinction from other places perceived to be fundamentally different. Their responses both draw from and extend existing discourses about social-class inequality in the United States as something that is individualized rather than structural, and as a matter of consumption and aesthetics rather than a key determinant of life chances. The western frontier myth and ideologies about rural land conform neatly to these ideas.

Rural residents offered similar narratives of individualism, consumer choice, and benign cultural difference to explain the whiteness of their neighborhoods relative to the larger metropolitan region. During my interviews, I contrasted the demographic makeup of Shadow Hills with that of Los Angeles County as a whole and asked interviewees to offer their interpretations. Some offered stories of the continuing influence of "rednecks" and white supremacist groups in the community as a reason for its disproportionate whiteness, while making it a point to differentiate themselves from explicit racists, usually by naming non-white individuals with whom they have relationships. Others speculated that cultural differences among ethnic and racial groups — specifically, different levels of interest in horse-keeping and a rural lifestyle — were accountable for the discrepancy. Still others argued that love for horses acts as an equalizer, bringing together individuals without regard for class, ethnic, or racial differences. Their responses are consistent with contemporary racial discourses of color blindness that obscure the power of race as an organizing principle in American society, instead imagining the persistence of inequality to be the work of conscious, deliberate acts of discrimination among individual racists or as a reflection of benign cultural difference and voluntary separation. In fact, some interviewees explicitly identified themselves as "color blind."

Several interviewees told me about the entrenched history of white supremacist groups in the area as a way to explain its disproportionate whiteness relative to the greater metropolitan region. Richard Eagan told me, "Well, I'll tell you, there's a lot of rednecks up here. A lot of really prejudiced people. The headquarters of the Ku Klux Klan is right over here in Lakeview Terrace . . . [and] Sunland-Tujunga is known for being racist."[48] Eagan is correct that the Sunland area, just east of Shadow Hills, has a long history of white supremacist motorcycle gangs, such as the Hell's Angels, who have historically created a climate of racialized fear and intimidation throughout the surrounding neighborhoods. Michael Castalucci told me that when he first moved to Shadow Hills in the mid-1980s, he had heard about motorcycle gangs who were active in the area. "The motorcycle places in Tujunga, a lot of which have closed down now, a lot of people felt the Hell's Angels and others were very active in this area and that they have a very high degree of prejudice." He had never seen the gangs himself until immediately after the Rodney King incident in 1992, when a police officer patrolling the streets of Shadow Hills told him not to worry, because he lived in one of the safest parts of the city. When the consultant asked why Shadow

Hills was so safe, the police officer told him, "'You go up to Foothill Boulevard right now, the Hell's Angels are patrolling back and forth with shotguns and if they see anybody they don't like they're going to shoot them themselves.' This came from a police officer. . . . So I got in my car and I drove right up to Foothill Boulevard and they [*sic*] were right. . . . So I think there was some prejudice, a bit of a redneck community, and people of color don't live up in this area because the Hell's Angels don't want them to."[49]

In the same way that Shadow Hills residents distinguish themselves from horse-keeping neighborhoods elsewhere in Los Angeles that are perceived to be wealthier and more elite in order to minimize their social-class privileges, they are also keen to distinguish themselves from Sunland-Tujunga, a more working-class neighborhood, in order to deflect charges of racism and segregation and locate blame for the disproportionate whiteness of Shadow Hills. They do so through complex and sometimes contradictory use of the terms "rednecks," "cowboys," and "country folks." Elaine Hillsboro, a real-estate agent, made the duality of such labels extraordinarily clear. When I asked her about the disproportionate whiteness of Shadow Hills, she told me that a resident leaving the area appealed to her to keep the neighborhood white: "Well there's a lot of rednecks still in Shadow Hills. . . . Professional and rednecks both. Country folks. I had one client call me a few months ago and said, 'I got a deal for you, cause you got to keep this redneck community alive.' Yeah, they're just hardworking, ordinary, regular old people."[50] Sociologists and anthropologists have observed that poor and working-class whites, captured under the referent of "rednecks," are politically useful to the perpetuation of white privilege. In a society that imagines itself to be color blind, poor and working-class whites are disproportionately blamed for the persistence of inequality because they absorb blame for white racism through a thoroughly unfounded assumption that poor and working-class whites are likely to be more racist and more likely to act on their racism than middle-class whites.[51] However, it is also true that whites of all class backgrounds sometimes embrace a "white trash" or "redneck" identity." Annalee Newitz and Matthew Wray argue that these performances became especially popular in the 1990s because they allowed whites to assimilate the language of multiculturalism, creating an ethnic identity with its own version of victimization that allows them to participate in a multicultural society as equals rather than as oppressors.[52] This set of possibilities allows middle-class whites in places like Shadow Hills to put on and take off a "redneck" or "country folk" identity when it is politically expedient for them to do so. This process also works through processes of socio-spatial distinction, as rural residents of Shadow Hills construct themselves as working-class "country folks" to deflect charges of social-class privilege but then disassociate themselves from working-class neighborhoods, which they blame for explicit racism, when asked about the disproportionate whiteness of their community.

Most interviewees constructed themselves as color-blind people who accept and embrace diversity, and who are more concerned with maintaining a (presumably color-blind) rural culture in which all can participate than with racial or ethnic differences. One way they did so was by telling me of their friendships and relationships with people of color, though I never asked them to do so. A common response among interviewees, when I asked them to explain the disproportionate whiteness of their rural community relative to the Los Angeles metropolitan area, was to instead name nonwhite individuals or families living in the neighborhood. They often made a point of naming one individual or family from each racial category. For example, Castalucci explained, "I know a Latino family that lives in Sunland, the Rodriguez family. I know an African American kid who lives here, but to be honest I don't see a lot of ethnic diversity here."[53] Similarly, Jim Huck gave me examples of Hispanic and African American people who live in Shadow Hills.

> Hmm, Hispanics, the guy across the street is Hispanic; he runs a company and he has lots of horses. OK? And there are some other people, some of my clients, who are Hispanic who live in Shadow Hills and own probably one of the most expensive houses in Shadow Hills. And um, oh! There's a lady, she's really delightful. . . . Well yeah, [name] is Hispanic. And she is really, really aggressive. She's really nice, but she is really aggressive about protecting her property . . . and uh, African Americans. Actually this guy I mentioned. . . . He's one of our best friends. He lives in Lakeview Terrace . . . and [he] is the best horse person you would ever meet . . . but there are a lot of people in his area where he lives who own horses and are African American.[54]

Huck struggled, in this instance, to name an African American resident of Shadow Hills, and ultimately resorted to an unnamed best friend who lived in adjacent Lakeview Terrace. Eric Franco, a small business owner, offered a similar response: "Down the street I've got a Spanish [sic] family; they ride up and down the street all day and all night. . . . But then [another Latino person], he lives around the corner from us, he doesn't even want to smell a horse, but he likes being in that area because it's a rural area. So we have two African American families who live in our neighborhood, one of them is equestrian; the other one's a football player."[55] Thus, naming nonwhite individuals was a common response, probably intended to show that the interviewee was not personally racist, since he or she had nonwhite friends, acquaintances, or neighbors. However, sociologist Eduardo Bonilla-Silva has demonstrated that many whites tend to inflate the intimacy of their relationships with nonwhites as a way to minimize their participation in maintaining a segregated society, and the unnamed neighbors and "best friends" suggest that similar dynamics are at work in the rural northeast San Fernando Valley.[56] And although several Shadow Hills residents named Latino or African American friends and neighbors, not one interviewee named an Asian American individual or family they knew personally, even though Asian Americans (particularly Koreans) are the fastest growing ethnic group in Shadow Hills.

Thus, most people identified themselves as "color blind" and explained the relative whiteness of Shadow Hills, compared with the larger metropolitan region, as the work of individual racists. They often took great care to show me, through references to their friendships and relationships with neighbors, that they personally were not responsible for such patterns. Indeed, several interviewees expressed their dismay that the neighborhood was relatively homogeneous. But many also pointed to divergent levels of interest in horseback riding and the rural lifestyle, which they understood to be an outcome of inherent cultural differences among ethnic and racial groups, as a possible explanation for Shadow Hills' disproportionate whiteness. Linda Ellison, a stay-at-home mother and former teacher who had once served as a Peace Corps volunteer in West Africa, lamented the lack of diversity in Shadow Hills, saying, "That is one of the things that makes me sad about living here is because it is too white. I would prefer a more diverse neighborhood." When I asked her if she had any possible explanations about the relative lack of diversity in the neighborhood, she said, "I don't know. It's a tough one. I would say Asian and African American people are not traditionally horse people. I would say that's it right there for those people."[57] Similarly, Jim Huck told me, "Owning and riding horses, I've actually not seen a bunch of people who are Asian do that. I don't know whether it's a cultural thing. It's not that they don't have the financial resources to do that. I mean, substantial portions of San Marino, La Cañada, they have financial resources with which to own and ride horses, so I kind of think there's just not an interest in that."[58]

Although they speculated that not all ethnic and racial groups are equally interested in horseback riding and the rural lifestyle, many interviewees nonetheless believed that horseback riding, as a lifestyle choice, could easily incorporate difference and operate above the specter of economic and racial inequality; in this way they believed that horseback riding and rural culture more broadly were inclusive equalizers. For example, in response to Joseph Staub's charge that Shadow Hills horse owners were politically powerful and economically privileged, some members of the ETI Listserv began to discuss putting together a public relations campaign. They wanted to dispel what they perceived to be the myths of equestrian wealth and power and to show instead that horseback riding is a universal, morally elevating practice in which people of different social classes and ethnic backgrounds can participate. One woman suggested that neighborhood residents submit articles and opinion pieces to the local press at regular intervals highlighting the universality of rural culture and horse-keeping in bringing people together across difference. In particular, she asked, "What about a piece on the free riding lessons going on for the neighborhood kids at Stonehurst [Park]? — you know, maybe a photo of a 'diverse' group and what the riding means to them or what they would be doing otherwise."[59] Her remark, and especially her decision to put the word "diverse" in quotes, suggests that she understands the necessity of appearing to be multicultural and inclusive in the press, though for her it appears to be a concession to "political correctness" rather than a genuine sentiment. Her comments about finding out what the children "would be doing otherwise" echoes the belief that urban children are susceptible to gang activity and criminality, and that horseback riding and rural culture more generally teaches children proper morals and values that they would not otherwise develop.

Rural residents commonly expressed their belief that a shared love for horses overcomes racial prejudices and attitudes, as well as social-class inequalities and cultural differences. As Huck explained, "People who have horses are friends with each other. Regardless of where they live. So you know, OK, we kind of all meet out at the end of the day. And riding horses is really a great equalizer. It's not, I mean, I'm better educated so I'm a better horse rider. That doesn't matter at all. You know, I don't know that that's an issue. It's certainly not an issue for me and I don't know anybody for whom it's an issue."[60] Patricia Wheat agreed with his ideas. As someone who boards other people's horses on her own property, Wheat is more likely than other rural residents of the northeast Valley to come into contact with horse owners who do not live in their own neighborhood. She told me that horse culture enables the bridging of other kinds of difference, which fade in importance among people who love and care for horses. She explained, "There are many different types of people in the horse communities, but because of the homogeneity of horses we all adapt to the same culture. Therefore, it is an acceptable culture in a diverse community. In a, in a racially diverse community. Because they have something else to worry about . . . we just fight over horses, we don't have to fight over language, race, lifestyle, et cetera. And we do, even with . . . some of the Mexicans, we feel, are too rough with their horses, and they feel that we're a bunch of wienies, and that's okay. But at least it's not racist; we're fighting over horses."[61] In her mind, ethnic tensions between Mexicans and whites in Shadow Hills are solely the result of cultural differences about how to treat horses. Like others, she regards these cultural differences as harmless.

Yet, as we have seen in this chapter, tensions between whites and people of color, especially Latinos, are alive and well in the northeast San Fernando Valley. Notions of inherent and irreconcilable cultural difference consistently come to the fore in negotiations over real-estate development, use of parks, and redistricting, among other issues. Moreover, beliefs about cultural difference are not benign or divorced from structural patterns of inequality. Rather, perceived cultural differences lead to fear and anxiety about change and influence the material decisions that semirural whites (as well as all people) make about neighborhoods, schools, and employment. These individual and personal decisions, in turn, inform the structural inequalities upon which perceptions of essential cultural difference are based. Within a purportedly color-blind society in which inequalities clearly persist but can no longer be mentioned in the dominant racial discourse, landscapes and culture thus stand in for unspeakable forms of racial, class, and national difference.

In twenty-first-century Los Angeles, the rural landscape and narratives of rural western heritage remain a critical locus for the negotiation of white identity. Focusing on the rural landscape as a way to resist social change allows rural residents of contemporary Los Angeles to sustain their lifestyle and its associated material and symbolic privileges in politically acceptable and strategic ways, while obscuring the effects of their activism on patterns of racial and class isolation and separation in the city. Simultaneously, their activism and discursive practices reinforce a white American connection to the frontier thesis as the nation's origin story, persistently fusing whiteness, material privilege, and nationhood through reference to the rural landscape. These practices and processes — drawn with equal measure from long-established rural western mythology as well as the relatively recent innovations of the "white backlash" and "color-blind racism" — are among the key contours of whiteness in the U.S. West at the turn of the twenty-first century.

CONCLUSION

The processes that I have analyzed in this book are far from obsolete. Nor are they limited to a few neighborhoods on the fringes of the San Fernando Valley. Rather, the central practices of rural urbanism persist in shaping the linked development of metropolitan regions and racial formations in the contemporary American West. In this brief concluding chapter, I apply the book's key findings and insights to understand how urban interests at the turn of the twenty-first century continue to produce rural places as a project of American empire and whiteness throughout the U.S. West; similar processes are under way in many former European imperial nations.

In 1997, the *New York Times* reported that, after nearly a century of urbanization, the national trend of rural to urban migration had been reversed. At the turn of the twentieth century, people from rural areas of the country had flocked to booming U.S. industrial cities seeking opportunities in employment, recreation, and culture. By the turn of the twenty-first century, however, a new generation of migrants abandoned city life and sought sprawling ranches and country homesteads in places such as New Mexico, Illinois, Oregon, and Wyoming.[1] During the 1990s, 75 percent of the nation's rural counties experienced rapid growth.[2] And by the close of the millennium, nearly two million people had moved from metropolitan areas in California and on the East Coast to the mountain West, the Upper Great Lakes, the Ozarks, and the Appalachian foothills.[3]

Urban-to-rural migration is propelled, in large part, by the changing geography of investment and employment among the nation's top firms. In the past two decades, high technology and professional service firms have increasingly relocated to rural areas to take advantage of lower land and energy costs and to capitalize on technological innovations such as high-speed Internet access and affordable overnight shipping. In doing so, they are remaking the metropolitan West and redrawing the boundaries of urbanity. In 1999, for example, *Forbes* highlighted the town of Fairfield, Iowa (dubbed "Silicorn Valley"), which has been dramatically transformed by the Internet economy and Airborne Express's decision to locate its national headquarters there; numerous high-tech firms now cluster in what was once a small rural town. Economically struggling rural towns and small cities compete for capital investment by offering a wide range of incentives, including subsidized infrastructure development and tax breaks, and by promoting the virtues of their communities that are likely to appeal to migrating workers and investors. In this respect, the collaborations between growth-machine interests in the twenty-first-century West mirror those that transformed Los Angeles into a major urban industrial center a century ago. In the decades before World War II, city boosters in Los Angeles sponsored agricultural lectures and financed irrigation systems, while also promising that urban amenities such as opera, symphonies, and well-stocked libraries were just a short ride away, in order to lure gentleman farmers to buy property in the San Fernando Valley. They contrasted the Valley's semirural landscapes with the dense, crowded, older cities of the East Coast and the Midwest. Now, in the first decades of the twenty-first century, city boosters in rural areas such as Fairfield promote their excellent schools, plentiful open space, and all-American values, which they contrast both explicitly and implicitly with older urban areas like Los Angeles.

As in decades past, real-estate developers, planners, boosters, the media, and cultural producers are collaborating to produce rural places that appeal to the romantic longings and frustrations of urbanites and suburbanites. Some contemporary urban-to-rural migrants are moving to small towns and hamlets, where they purchase and renovate inexpensive older homes, but others are moving to mass-produced subdivisions, seemingly in the middle of nowhere, built by established development corporations, financed by global capital, and easily accessible by interstate highways and regional airports. Urban growth-machine interests continue to incorporate and mobilize ideas about rural land and the frontier West into their real-estate development plans. Sprawling master-planned communities, many of them gated, dot the edges of cities throughout the desert and mountain West. They feature names such as The New Frontier, Saddle Creek Ranch, Huntsman Springs, Frontier Trace, and The Ranch Club. Like the Weeks Poultry Colony in the west San Fernando Valley in the 1920s, or the Porter Ranch subdivision completed in the mid-1970s, these residential communities promise that home buyers will be able to capitalize on all the latest luxuries (promoted as necessities) — such as golf courses, spas, and fully equipped business centers — while enjoying the aesthetics and values of a rural western retreat as part of their everyday life. According to Joel Kotkin, author of the *Forbes* article, urban sophisticates are increasingly willing to relocate — taking with them their wealth, networks, and social capital — both because of the lower cost of living in rural areas and because new technologies allow them to pursue their idyllic rural dreams while holding on to big-city paychecks.[4] As planners and boosters in Los Angeles would have said a century ago, the new

migrants still very much want to have the "best of both worlds." And by all accounts, they are getting it.

But the newest articulations of rural urbanism are also, as in their earlier
incarnations, very much a racialized phenomenon. Urban-to-rural migration
is occurring almost exclusively among middle-class and working-class whites,
who are leaving cities on the Pacific Rim and the East Coast that have experienced both substantial Latino and Asian immigration and economic restructuring in recent years. When high-tech firms move to rural areas, they typically
bring their middle-class managerial employees (but not their janitors, who are
in any case mostly subcontracted) with them. Working-class whites, for their
part, have also been seeking out rural locales because of increased competition
from immigrants for rapidly disappearing low-skill manufacturing and service
jobs that were once plentiful in established urban areas. As industry and immigrants have moved into the suburbs of older cities such as Los Angeles, many
working-class and middle-class whites have decided to leave, in what demographer William Frey speculates may be an instance of "new white flight." In a
series of important articles on the subject, Frey demonstrates that in states with
high rates of international migration low- and middle-income whites appear to
be most likely to move away because of increased competition for low-skilled
jobs, the indirect social costs of a growing population of immigrants (rising
taxes, overcrowded schools, and language barriers), and simple fear of unfamiliar people.[5] And while important social-class distinctions exist among the new
urban-to-rural migrants, they nonetheless have three things in common: they
are pursuing the changing geography of employment opportunity in the United
States; the places they are leaving behind are suburbs rather than central cities;
and their decisions to move rest on both their frustrations with (sub)urban
life and their romantic, almost mythic ideas about rural communities. Indeed,
many whites who have migrated to rural areas cite the poor quality of urban
school districts, rising property taxes, poverty, gang violence, and fear of crime
as factors leading to their relocation decisions. These are all racialized con-
structs that link perceptions of racial identity and changing social status with
threatened suburban and semirural landscapes. For example, Paul Tarnoff left
a successful career in mergers and acquisitions in Washington, D.C., to move
to rural Fairfield, Iowa. He explained, "I wanted a better quality of life. Two
kids were kidnapped in our neighborhood back home. Now my daughters ride
horses . . . and you don't worry about what's going to happen to them."[6] Many of
the people we met in the previous chapters share such sentiments. Like Tarnoff,
many residents of Los Angeles's semirural suburbs believe strongly that urban
life brings out the worst in the human character and destroys a sense of place

and a sense of community. They fear the urbanization of the rural landscapes they inhabit and occupy, because they associate urbanization with demographic change and a general decline in their quality of life. Some have moved out of the San Fernando Valley in recent years and are surely represented among the urban-to-rural migration stream; others whom I interviewed have stuck it out so far but say they are at their "wit's end" and on the verge of leaving at any time.

These patterns of urban-to-rural migration testify to the ways in which working-class and middle-class whites are reworking their lives in an effort to consolidate their material privileges, escape what they perceive to be the unbearable social costs of urban life, and reclaim their central position within narratives of American history and culture. For these people, rurality offers a way to restore much of what they feel is missing or threatened in their lives. White migrants contrast their frustrations with urban and suburban life with what they perceive to be the simplicity, strong sense of community, and authentic American character they associate with rural areas. These are very old ideas, and they clearly persist into the twenty-first century. For instance, Kathy and Jim Wiley moved from Burbank, California, to Wilmington, Ohio, in 1997. Both had worked for Warner Brothers — Jim as a manager, Kathy as an executive secretary. They referred to the corrupting influences and emptiness of urban life to explain their decision to move. According to Jim, "Living in L.A., my vision became blurred and twisted. I was spoiled. I had secretaries doing everything for me. All I did was talk on the phone and sit in traffic."[7] He quit his job at Warner Brothers and took a job at Technicolor, which had recently relocated to Wilmington; his dissatisfaction, then, was not with the nature of his job but rather with where it was located. In Wilmington, Jim nurtured a fascination with tractors and basked in the area's four distinct seasons. However, both he and Kathy — like virtually all the other migrants documented in the proliferating media on the topic — admitted that achieving a strong sense of community and "authentic" rural life was much harder than they had imagined, both because crime still occurred with surprising regularity in their new semirural neighborhoods and because longtime rural dwellers showed some reluctance to accept them. No doubt the established residents of rural Fairfield and Wilmington, among many other places, just like the residents of the rural northeast San Fernando Valley whom we met in the previous two chapters, are fearful of what the migration of urban dwellers from Southern California and other big cities means for their rural quality of life. Meanwhile, if one reason for whites' urban-to-rural migration is a desire to escape the perceived and real social costs of immigration from Asia and Latin America, then they may be in for a rude awakening, as those same immigrants (especially Latin American immigrants) are also heading to the rural interior and smaller cities in the U.S. West, seeking out job opportunities in the factories and fields of the new low-wage manufacturing economy — the underbelly of the high-tech, high-skill economy — that is simultaneously and just as profoundly remaking the region.

What are likely to be the political implications of these linked demographic and geographic trends? My ethnographic research in the northeast San Fernando Valley suggests that as white migrants' expectations about rural life collide with a more complex rural reality, and as the changing metropolitan West comes to look a lot more like the older cities on the coasts that they left behind, political movements will develop among white rural dwellers who are ideologically and economically invested in the preservation of rural landscapes and western heritage. As in the San Fernando Valley, participants will mobilize skills and personal connections developed through generations of accumulated wealth and social capital and through their privileged positions at the upper end of the contemporary economy within networks of global capital. Working collectively, their desires to preserve a rural life and the skill sets they have at hand to do so are likely to consolidate whites' historic material privileges while cultivating a nonprivileged, perhaps defensive and reactionary white identity rooted in protection of rural landscapes and the values believed to cohere within them. There is some evidence that this is already happening. Emerging rural social movements articulate a sense of white victimization by multicultural identity politics. For example, James McCarthy and Euan Hague observed that Wise Use activists in rural New Mexico mobilize a besieged "Celtic" identity as part of their strategy to protect rural primary-commodity producers' privileged, subsidized access to federally owned lands. McCarthy and Hague concluded that "a particular utility of Celtic identity is that it allows adherents to have it both ways: to claim membership in an oppressed, marginalized group within Western countries, entitled to whatever political benefits might follow, while still asserting and reaping all of the benefits of white privilege."[8] The activities of such groups not only seek to protect whites' historic privileges but also contribute to a generalized rural environment that is often unwelcoming or outright hostile to nonwhite immigrants and native-born people of color.[9]

Equally fascinating is that the trend of urban-to-rural migration is not unique to the U.S. West but rather is occurring throughout much of Europe's former imperial powerhouses, where rural landscapes, because of their historic centrality to the imperial project, have become key sites for the reworking of whiteness in the postcolonial era.[10] As Sarah Neal has argued, "during colonialism it was English rurality that represented what was particularly civilized and culturally superior about Britain"; constructions of civilization and cultural superiority were likewise constructions of whiteness.[11] For Caroline Knowles, "the countryside stands in for more than it is: it produces, embodies, and sustains whiteness on behalf of the nation."[12] She notes that the English countryside has been a preferred location for returning imperial authorities who associate rurality with an authentic, timeless (white) English heritage. In other national contexts, too, observers have noted a major demographic trend of urban-to-rural migration (which they call "counterurbanization") among middle-class whites, for whom the countryside is imagined to be a safe and stable retreat from urban violence and crime, immigrants, and the demands of multicultural identity politics. Such fantasies express a desire for a purportedly lost world in which the associations between white supremacy, imperialism, and nationhood were unproblematic and indeed deliberately cultivated. As Knowles observes in her study of rural South Devon, "Empire hangs around in an air of arrogance, in the substance of accumulated privilege, and in a nostalgic longing for a past of international prominence, imagined secure borders, and racial homogeneity."[13] Such anxious fantasies and longings — not unlike those that Frederick Jackson Turner articulated about the U.S. West more than a century ago — structure the contemporary social relations of rural areas, generating low-intensity hostility and occasionally aggressive and explicit terrorism directed toward racial and ethnic minorities. Exclusion takes the form of organized resistance to policies that would locate asylum seekers in rural areas; fascist and white supremacist organizations have also targeted rural areas in the United States and Britain as key recruiting grounds for new members.[14]

However, the racial motivations and anxieties underlying such acts of rural exclusion are typically elided by the belief among rural white dwellers and policy makers in Europe that racism is inconsequential in rural places because of their overwhelming whiteness. This belief reflects the commonplace perception that race is something only nonwhites "have," thus normalizing whiteness as the experience against which all others are measured.[15] As Jon Garland and Neil Chakraborti note, "If there are low numbers of minority ethnic people, then, so the logic goes, there must be little or no racist harassment."[16] By this logic, rural whites are innocent nonparticipants in the structuring of racialized social relations that only occur in *other* kinds of places — specifically, urban settings that are more racially diverse. This active dismissal of the complicity of white people and places in the persistence of structural racism is a key dimension of the postcolonial, color-blind world. It is also testifies to the power of rural landscapes, and of transition narratives of the frontier West that pass as stories of regional and national heritage, to construct whiteness in covert, invisible, and naturalized ways.

At bottom, then, the latest articulations of rural urbanism throughout the expanding metropolitan regions of the U.S. West constitute a fundamental re-investment in imperial transition narratives of the frontier and in closely related ideas about rural land that justify and celebrate American expansion, dispos-session, and conquest, as well as the deeply unequal social structures estab-lished through these processes. Through the mundane workings of urban policy making and urban political struggle, the dynamics of twenty-first-century rural urbanism reinscribe the central elements of the frontier narrative in physical landscapes throughout the twenty-first-century American West. Such rural landscapes, in turn, affirm and extend the validity of imperial transition nar-ratives as meaningful representations of American history, propel the develop-ment of new race-based social movements that seek to protect historical white privileges through the preservation and protection of rural land, *and* generate continued wealth, prestige, and power for their occupants and investors. In all these ways, rural landscapes are flexibly adapted to the changing discourses and practices of racial politics — in recent years, the emergence of multiculturalism and color blindness, and, in the years to come, new forms of hegemonic white-ness about which we can only speculate.

NOTES

INTRODUCTION

1. Lifetime Savings and Loan Association, Brochure for Porter Ranch Master Plan, July 1965, San Fernando Valley Historical Society City Box Collection, repository L77.17, San Fernando Valley Issues Digital Library, California State University Northridge.

2. Ibid.

3. Cronon, *Nature's Metropolis*; Williams, *Country and the City*.

4. Roderick, *San Fernando Valley*, i.

5. Ibid., v.

6. Abbott, *Metropolitan Frontier*; Nash, *American West in the Twentieth Century*; Nash, *American West Transformed*.

7. In Sacramento, California, for example, landowners hired Morton McCarver, an experienced town-site developer from Iowa, to design the urban plans; Portland and Seattle are also well-known examples of this trend. See Reps, *Forgotten Frontier*. And in New Mexico, as Maria Montoya observes, a former Dutch colonial administrator was brought in to manage and implement the Maxwell land grant because of the widespread reputation among Americans that the Dutch were excellent colonial administrators. Montoya, *Translating Property*, 126–31.

8. Reps, *Forgotten Frontier*, 61.

9. Abbott, *Metropolitan Frontier*.

10. Ibid.; Nash, *American West Transformed*.

11. Winant, *World Is a Ghetto*, 21.

12. Ibid., 1, 21, emphasis in original.

13. Shaw, *Cities of Whiteness*, 31–32.

14. Montoya, *Translating Property*, 8.

15. Ibid., 8–9.

16. Ibid., 8.

17. For the impact of the U.S. Land Commission in California, see Almaguer, *Racial Fault Lines*, esp. chap. 1; Pitt, *Decline of the Californios*. For the Homestead Act, see White, *It's Your Misfortune*, esp. 143–48.

18. For the history of alien land laws, see R. Daniels, *Asian America*, 138–45; for restrictive covenants, see Massey and Denton, *American Apartheid*, 17–59.

19. Harris, "Whiteness as Property."

20. Brace, *Politics of Property*, 210.

21. Razack, *Race, Space, and the Law*, 2–3; see also Blomley, "Law, Property, and the Geography of Violence"; Limerick, *Legacy of Conquest*.

22. Knobloch, *Culture of Wilderness*, 2.

23. The legacy of such ideologies throughout the nineteenth and twentieth centuries was a primary concern for the emergent field of American studies in the mid-twentieth century; for a review and analysis of the treatment of rural and pastoral themes in American literature, see Smith, *Virgin Land*, and Marx, *Machine in the Garden*. For more recent studies of the endurance of the frontier myth in American popular culture, see Mann, "Why Does Country Music Sound White?"

24. Blomley, "Law, Property, and the Geography of Violence."

25. Turner, *Frontier in American History*, 2.

26. Knobloch, *Culture of Wilderness*, 149.

27. McWilliams, *Southern California*, 70.

28. For critical historical perspectives on the indigenous experience of the Spanish missions, see Haas, *Conquests and Historical Identities*; Hurtado, *Intimate Frontiers*. For a discussion of how these processes affected California Indians in the Mission San Fernando, see Jorgensen, "Chiniginich Is Very Angry," 30–36.

29. The literature on the Spanish fantasy past is rich and extensive. See Deverell, *Whitewashed Adobe*; DeLyser, *Ramona Memories*; Kropp, *California Vieja*; Rawls, "California Mission."

30. De Oliver, "Historical Preservation and Identity"; Montgomery, "Trap of Race and Memory"; Wilson, *Myth of Santa Fe*.

31. McWilliams, *Southern California*, 71.

32. Delaney, "Space That Race Makes," 7.

33. Anderson, "Idea of Chinatown"; Delaney, "Space That Race Makes"; Gilmore, "Fatal Couplings"; Schein, *Landscape and Race*.

34. Omi and Winant, *Racial Formation*, 84.

35. Ibid., 83.

36. Schein, "Place of Landscape"; Saito, *Politics of Exclusion*, esp. 8–9.

37. Cosgrove, *Social Formation and Symbolic Landscape*, 13, 14.

38. Massey, "Geographies of Responsibility"; Barraclough, "South Central Farmers."

39. Delaney, "Space That Race Makes," 13.

40. Morrison, *Playing in the Dark*; Duncan and Duncan, "Aestheticization"; Duncan and Duncan, *Landscapes of Privilege*; Hoelscher, "White-Pillared Past"; Kobayashi and Peake, "Racism Out of Place"; Schein, *Landscape and Race*.

41. Duncan and Duncan, *Landscapes of Privilege*, 3.

42. Ibid., 25; see also Cosgrove, *Social Formation and Symbolic Landscape*; S. Daniels, *Fields of Vision*.

43. Mitchell, *Cultural Geography*, chap. 4.

44. Anderson, "Idea of Chinatown"; Mitchell, *Lie of the Land*; Samuels, "Biography of Landscape."

45. Baker and Biger, *Ideology and Landscape*.

46. Howard Winant, "Behind Blue Eyes," 75.

47. Crenshaw, "Color-Blindness, History, and the Law"; Lipsitz, *Possessive Investment in Whiteness*, chap. 2.

CHAPTER ONE *Creating Whiteness through Gentleman Farming*

1. Knobloch, *Culture of Wilderness*, 3.

2. Ibid., 5.

3. See esp. Hurtado, "Customs of the Country: Mixed Marriage in Mexican California," in his book *Intimate Frontiers*, 21–44; Camarillo, *Chicanos in a Changing Society*; Haas, *Conquests and Historical Identities*.

4. Camarillo, *Chicanos in a Changing Society*, 114; Pitt, *Decline of the Californios*, esp. chaps. 5 and 6.

5. Mayers, *San Fernando Valley*; Roderick, *San Fernando Valley*.

6. Deverell, *Whitewashed Adobe*, 4.

7. Starr, *Inventing the Dream*, 89.

8. Wild, *Street Meeting*, 38.

9. Ibid., 42.

10. Hise, *Magnetic Los Angeles*. For theoretical arguments about Los Angeles's unique form of polynucleated (sub)urban development, see Dear, *Postmodern Urban Condition*, especially chaps. 1 and 7; Dear, *From Chicago to L.A.*

11. Quoted in Hise, *Magnetic Los Angeles*, 10.

12. Nicolaides, *My Blue Heaven*.

13. Wild, *Street Meeting*.

14. Quoted in Garcia, *World of Its Own*, 20.

15. Ibid., 31.

16. Ibid., 21.

17. Fogelson, *Fragmented Metropolis*, 68–73.

18. Quoted in Garcia, *World of Its Own*, 34.

19. Starr, *Inventing the Dream*, 45.

20. Garcia, *World of Its Own*, 35.

21. *Southern California Paradise*, 67.

22. Quoted in Garcia, *World of Its Own*, 25.

23. Elizabeth Boswell, "Real Living," *Los Angeles Times*, September 20, 1931, J2.

24. Los Angeles County Chamber of Commerce, *Los Angeles County, California*, 37.

25. Ibid., 51.

26. Russell Richardson, "The Drama of the Soil," *Los Angeles Times*, January 2, 1929, G3.

27. Ibid.

28. "The 'Little Farmer,'" *Los Angeles Times*, April 19, 1925, J4.

29. Ross H. Gast, "The Southland Garden and Small Farm Home," *Los Angeles Times*, July 15, 1928, J5.

30. Fogelson, *Fragmented Metropolis*, esp. chap. 9.

31. United States Bureau of the Census, *Fourteenth Census of the United States, 1920*, Enumeration District 128, sheets 4B–8A.

32. "A Diversified Farm," *Los Angeles Times*, April 27, 1930, 114.

33. "Found Their Brook: Oregon Couple Realize Desire to Be Near a Stream," *Los Angeles Times*, March 27, 1932, J10.

34. Keffer, *History of San Fernando Valley*, 73.

35. The film *Chinatown* is best known for this perspective, but see also Fulton, "Redefining Chinatown," in *Reluctant Metropolis*, 101–24.

36. George P. Clements, "The Time to Look Is before the Leap," *Los Angeles Times*, December 25, 1927, K3.

37. A Ranch Woman, "Summer Work? Sure! Cull Out Bad Hens!" *Los Angeles Times*, July 1, 1928, J13; Gast, "Southland Garden"; Marston Kimball, "You Don't Prune for the Fun of It, but to Get More Fruit," *Los Angeles Times*, February 10, 1929, K3.

38. "Vaile Heads Farm Bureau," *Los Angeles Times*, November 6, 1919, II13; "To Show Methods of Saving Girdled Tree," *Los Angeles Times*, June 5, 1921, IX11; "To Discuss Trunk and Root Trouble," *Los Angeles Times*, April 16, 1922, FT5; "Hodgson to Lecture," *Los Angeles Times*, March 25, 1923; "Expert to Demonstrate Culling of Hens," *Los Angeles Times*, June 21, 1925, K13; "An Interesting Series for Poultrymen," *Los Angeles Times*, June 20, 1926, K13; "Dates and Places for Poultry Talks Listed," *Los Angeles Times*, January 30, 1927, 10; "Poultry Breeding Will Be Discussed," *Los Angeles Times*, February 19, 1928, J16.

39. Los Angeles County Fairplex, "About Fairplex—History 1921 to 1929," http://www.fairplex.com/fp/AboutUs/History/1920s.asp.

40. "Trapnesting for Eggs of Standard Size," *Los Angeles Times*, July 20, 1924, H15; "Junior Egg Production Contest Ends," *Los Angeles Times*, October 5, 1924, J13; "Some Phases of 'Ag Club' Work in Los Angeles County," *Los Angeles Times*, December 19, 1926, J8.

41. Ingeborg Dahl, "'Break' for Someone: This School Course Pays for Itself," *Los Angeles Times*, November 5, 1933.

42. "Club Poultry Contest Results Told," *Los Angeles Times*, October 12, 1924, 114.

43. Ross H. Gast, "They Want to Help," *Los Angeles Times*, October 27, 1929, G11.

44. Ross H. Gast, "Little Farm Homes," *Los Angeles Times*, July 20, 1930, J17.

45. Starr, *Inventing the Dream*, 160–65.

46. Ibid., 173.

47. Robert Lyans, "Old Mission Center of Citrus Industry," *Los Angeles Times*, September 2, 1928, K11.

48. Gonzalez, *Labor and Community*, 23–24.

49. Ibid., 25.

50. Starr, *Inventing the Dream*, 165.

51. Ibid.

52. Clements, "Time to Look."

53. Garcia, *World of Its Own*, 31.

54. Bokovoy, "Inventing Agriculture in Southern California."

55. Roderick, *San Fernando Valley*, 72–74; "Reclamation Leader Dead," *Los Angeles Times*, October 8, 1922, IV13.

56. "Little Lands Wall Plaque," courtesy of Little Landers Historical Society, San Fernando Valley Digital Archive, http://digital-library.csun.edu/u?/SFVH,3281.

57. "The Chosen Valley of the Little Landers," *Los Angeles Tribune*, April 20, 1913, San Fernando Valley Digital Archive, http://digital-library.csun.edu/u?/SFVH,955, bold in original.

58. Ibid.

59. William Elsworth Smythe, "The Social Revolution of the Soil: The New Life of the Land," *Little Lands of America*, July 1916, 19, quoted in Bokovoy, "Inventing Agriculture in Southern California."

60. "Chosen Valley."

61. Hitt, *After Pearl Harbor*.

62. "File Complaint," *Los Angeles Times*, April 16, 1917, I12.

63. Weeks, *One Acre and Independence*, 12.

64. Ibid., 6.

65. San Diego Historical Society, "William Elsworth Smythe," http://www.sandiego-history.org.

66. Quoted in Roderick, *San Fernando Valley*, 75.

67. Weeks, *One Acre and Independence*, 102.

68. "Weeks Colony Elects Heads," *Los Angeles Times*, December 19, 1925, 5.

69. Ibid.

70. "Weeks Colony Egg Plant Is Burned," *Los Angeles Times*, May 6, 1925, A11.

71. "Will Ask for Water Extensions," *Los Angeles Times*, March 16, 1924, D7.

72. Weeks, *One Acre and Independence*, 133.

73. Ibid., 9.

74. Celeste Dameron, interview by Michael Nesbit, Northridge, California, October 28, 1989, Special Collections and Archives, California State University Northridge.

75. Ibid.

76. Wild, *Street Meeting*, 13.

77. Garcia, *World of Its Own*, 29–46.

78. Kim, "Racial Triangulation of Asian Americans," 108–9.

79. Ibid.; Lee, *At America's Gates*.

80. Roderick, *San Fernando Valley*, 139.

81. Starr, *Inventing the Dream*, 172–73.

82. Ibid., 172, 173.

83. Ross H. Gast, "Preparing 'Bunch Stuff' for the Local Markets," *Los Angeles Times*, June 22, 1924, H9.

84. Ibid.

85. "The 'Little Farmer,'" *Los Angeles Times*, April 19, 1925, J4.

86. Ibid.

87. Roderick, *San Fernando Valley*, 110–12.

88. Gonzalez, *Labor and Community*, 7.

89. Roderick, *San Fernando Valley*, 111.

90. Gonzalez, *Labor and Community*, 9.

91. McWilliams, *Southern California*, 218.

92. "Modern Houses for Mexican Workmen," *Los Angeles Times*, January 1, 1918, 119; on the role of the California Commission on Immigration and Housing in encouraging improved housing for migrant workers, see Mitchell, *Lie of the Land*.

93. Roderick, *San Fernando Valley*, 139.

94. Ponce, *Hoyt Street*.

95. "Thieves Are Caught at San Fernando," *Los Angeles Times*, January 31, 1917, 112.

96. "Romance of Bandit and Maid Told," *Los Angeles Times*, June 8, 1930, C8.

97. "San Fernando Soon Offering Two-Day Fiesta," *Los Angeles Times*, May 31, 1931, A6.

98. Quoted in Roderick, *San Fernando Valley*, 139.

99. "Study Made of Valley's Mexican Relief Recipients," *Los Angeles Times*, July 29, 1938, A3.

100. Quoted in Gonzalez, *Labor and Community*, 12.

101. "Foiled 'Reds' Out in Open," *Los Angeles Times*, February 1, 1919, 111.

102. Ibid.

103. The Depression era witnessed the emergence and empowerment of the Associated Farmers. Essentially a conglomerate of vigilante groups, the Associated Farmers terrorized and intimidated striking workers throughout the fields of California. Yet the members of the AF were some of the state's highest political officers and social elites, including members of the Los Angeles Chamber of Commerce, many of whom served on the AF's board of directors and made financial contributions. See Pichardo, "Power Elite."

104. "San Fernando Lemon Packing House Closed," *Los Angeles Times*, August 27, 1938, 2.

105. "Lemon Pickers' Strike Ended," *Los Angeles Times*, September 2, 1938, 4.

106. "Strike Imperils Huge Poultry Farm," *Los Angeles Times*, October 12, 1939, 18.

107. "State Offices for CIO Farm Workers Moved Here," *Los Angeles Times*, October 13, 1939, A12; "Court Rules Nonunion Goods May Be Picketed at Stores," *Los Angeles Times*, November 16, 1939, 8.

108. "Pickets Arrested for Disturbing Peace," *Los Angeles Times*, December 22, 1939, 17.

109. Garcia, *World of Its Own*, 21.

110. Critical whiteness scholars have argued that whiteness as a racial category achieves meaning through constant reference to an external Other, that is, through disavowal of what it is not; at the same time, white identity and white material supremacy are deeply dependent on the labor, exploitation, and oppression of those who are ex-

cluded. See Lopez, *White by Law*; Jacobson, *Whiteness of a Different Color*; Roediger, *Wages of Whiteness*.

CHAPTER TWO *Narrating Conquest in Local History*

1. Roderick, *San Fernando Valley*; Davis, *City of Quartz*; Scott, *Technopolis*.

2. "Valley Population Near Million; Growth Slows," *Los Angeles Times*, April 29, 1971, SF1; Preston, *Changing Landscape*.

3. Meeker, *San Fernando Valley Profile*.

4. Massey and Denton, *American Apartheid*.

5. Davis, *City of Quartz*, 168.

6. Ibid.; Meeker, *San Fernando Valley Profile*.

7. Katznelson, *When Affirmative Action Was White*.

8. Meeker, *San Fernando Valley Profile*, 31.

9. Lankershim Branch Publicity Department, *Daughter of the Snows*, 53.

10. Jimmie Hicks, "Typescript biography of William Wilcox Robinson," p. 52, box 3, folder 13, W. W. Robinson Papers, Charles E. Young Research Library Special Collections, UCLA.

11. Ibid.

12. Ibid.

13. Quoted in Hicks, "Typescript biography," 53.

14. Ibid.

15. Richard Lillard, "Review of *Land in California*," *Pacific Spectator* 4 (1950): 181, quoted in Hicks, "Typescript Biography."

16. Robert Kirsch, *Los Angeles Times*, February 21, 1960, V6.

17. Blomley, *Unsettling the City*; Lopez, *White by Law*; Harris, "Whiteness as Property."

18. Robinson, *Story of San Fernando Valley*, inside cover.

19. Hicks, "Typescript biography."

20. San Fernando Valley chapter of the Daughters of the American Revolution [hereafter DAR], *Valley of San Fernando*, 15.

21. Ibid.

22. Ibid., 10.

23. Ibid.

24. Ibid., 18.

25. Los Angeles Valley College Historical Museum Association, *Valley History*, 3.

26. Costo and Costo, *Missions of California*; Haas, *Conquests and Historical Identities*.

27. Warner, Hayes, and Widney, *Historical Sketch*, 15.

28. "Bienvenidos, Amigos!" undated brochure for the Mission San Fernando Rey de España, box 13, folder 29, W. W. Robinson Papers, Charles E. Young Research Library Special Collections, UCLA.

29. Rawls, "California Mission," 345.

30. Deverell, *Whitewashed Adobe*, 9.

31. Lankershim Branch Publicity Department, *Daughter of the Snows*, 14.

32. DAR, *Valley of San Fernando*, 23, 25.

33. "Bienvenidos, Amigos!"

34. Conner, *Romance of the Ranchos*, 28.

35. Camarillo, *Chicanos in a Changing Society*; Pitt, *Decline of the Californios*.

36. DAR, *Valley of San Fernando*, 11.

37. Howard Kegley, "Days of Land Baron Passing," *Los Angeles Times*, June 25, 1922, III.

38. Conner, *Romance of the Ranchos*, 29.

39. Ibid., 2.

40. Blomley, "Law, Property, and the Geography of Violence."

41. DAR, *Valley of San Fernando*, 27.

42. Robinson, *Story of San Fernando Valley*, 7.

43. DAR, *Valley of San Fernando*, 29.

44. Ibid., 41, 43.

45. Robinson, *Story of San Fernando Valley*, 21, emphasis added.

46. Conner, *Romance of the Ranchos*, 2.

47. DAR, *Valley of San Fernando*, 40.

48. Ibid., 40–41.

49. Lankershim Branch Publicity Department, *Daughter of the Snows*, 21.

50. Ibid., 15.

51. DAR, *Valley of San Fernando*, 57.

52. See Magliari, "Free Soil, Unfree Labor."

53. DAR, *Valley of San Fernando*, 117, emphasis added.

54. Conner, *Romance of the Ranchos*, 2.

55. Sackman, *Orange Empire*, 26.

56. Lankershim Branch Publicity Department, *Daughter of the Snows*, 43.

57. Ibid., 45–47, emphasis added.

58. Ibid., 119, emphasis added.

59. Ibid., 11, 9–10.

60. Ibid., 11, 13.

61. Watts, "Photography in the Land of Sunshine," 360.

62. Lankershim Branch Publicity Department, *Daughter of the Snows*, 47, 41, 52, 47.

63. DAR, *Valley of San Fernando*, 8.

64. Ibid.

65. Ibid., 117.

66. Don Mitchell found similar dynamics at work in his study of migrant workers in Central California's agribusiness industry in the early twentieth century. See Mitchell, *Lie of the Land*.

67. See Johnson, *Soul by Soul*.

68. Lankershim Branch Publicity Department, *Daughter of the Snows*, 30.
69. Ibid., 32.
70. DAR, *Valley of San Fernando*, 99.
71. Ibid., 63.

CHAPTER THREE *Producing Western Heritage in the Postwar Suburb*

1. Yarbrough, *Those Great B-Western Locations*, vol. 1.
2. Corkin, "Cowboys and Free Markets."
3. Ibid., 72.
4. Mitchell, "Writing the Western," 12.
5. Simmon, *Invention of the Western Film*, 130.
6. Lukinbeal, "Cinematic Landscapes."
7. Avila, "Popular Culture; Avila, *Popular Culture*.
8. Rand, *Wide Open Spaces*; see also Corkin, "Cowboys and Free Markets."
9. Shively, "Cowboys and Indians."
10. Ritter, *Tex Ritter*, 44.
11. Jenkins, *San Fernando Valley*.
12. Quoted in Roderick, *San Fernando Valley*, 114.
13. Robinson, *Story of San Fernando Valley*, 42.
14. Quoted at Kevin Roderick, "The Valley Observed: San Fernando Valley History and Sense of Place," http://www.americassuburb.com/wood.html (accessed March 10, 2008).
15. Lukinbeal, "Cinematic Landscapes," 17.
16. Mitchell, "Writing the Western," 15.
17. Fogelson, *Fragmented Metropolis*.
18. Magers, *So You Wanna See Cowboy Stuff?*; Yarbrough, "Those Great B-Western Locations."
19. Robinson, *Story of San Fernando Valley*, 42.
20. Ronald Davis, "John Ford: Western Mythmaker," in Etulain and Riley, *Hollywood West*, 66.
21. Richard Etulain, "Bronco Billy, William S. Hart, and Tim Mix," in Etulain and Riley, *Hollywood West*, 9.
22. Roderick, *San Fernando Valley*, 83–100.
23. Glenda Riley, "Barbara Stanwyck: Feminizing the Western Film," in Etulain and Riley, *Hollywood West*.
24. Rothel, *Those Great Cowboy Sidekicks*.
25. John Lenihan, "John Wayne: An American Icon," in Etulain and Riley, *Hollywood West*.
26. Magers, *So You Wanna See Cowboy Stuff?*; Rothel, *Those Great Cowboy Sidekicks*.
27. Hintz, *Horses in the Movies*, 80–87; Amaral, *Movie Horses*, 141–52.
28. Roderick, *San Fernando Valley*, 124.

29. Professional Rodeo Stock Contractors Association [hereafter PRSCA], *100 Years*, 94–95.

30. Ibid., 121.

31. See "L.A. Riding School Planned," *Los Angeles Examiner*, December 23, 1959; also see PRSCA, *100 Years*, 170–71.

32. Quoted in Rothel, *Ambush of Ghosts*, 198.

33. Yarbrough, *Those Great B-Western Locations*, 2.

34. Ibid.

35. Sherman, *Quiet on the Set!* 59.

36. Jurca, "Tarzan, Lord of the Suburbs."

37. Ehrheart, "World's Most Famous Movie Ranch," 4.

38. Ibid., 14.

39. Ibid., 11, 12, 15.

40. Quoted in Rothel, *Ambush of Ghosts*, 213.

41. Ehrheart, "World's Most Famous Movie Ranch," 16.

42. Yarbrough, *Those Great B-Western Locations*.

43. Yarbrough, "Those Great B-Western Locations," 14, 16.

44. See White, *It's Your Misfortune*; Rothman, *Devil's Bargains*.

45. Anna "Queenie" Billings, interview by Ava Kahn, Chatsworth, California, December 13–14, 1978, Special Collections and Archives, California State University Northridge.

46. Jess Graves, interview by Ava Kahn, Chatsworth, California, December 14, 1978, Special Collections and Archives, California State University Northridge.

47. "Ralphs Will Open Store in Canoga Park," *Los Angeles Times*, March 19, 1959, B2.

48. Gustafson, "Simi Valley Freeway," *California Highways and Public Works Magazine* 45 (September–October 1966): 32, quoted in Biolchino, "From Rural Village to Metropolitan Suburb," 99.

49. Ehrheart, "World's Most Famous Movie Ranch," 23.

50. Ibid., 23, 27.

51. Ibid., 25, 23.

52. *Corriganville Movie Ranch Pictorial Souvenir Book*, 8.

53. Ehrheart, "World's Most Famous Movie Ranch," 24.

54. *Corriganville Gazette* 1, no. 3:2, Autry Research Library of the Autry National Center, Griffith Park, California.

55. *Corriganville Movie Ranch Pictorial Souvenir Book*, 5.

56. Lynn Rogers, "Varied Attractions Seen on Auto Tour," *Los Angeles Times*, April 15, 1951, E10.

57. "Eye-Popping Sights Thrill Children at Film Ranch," *Los Angeles Times*, September 24, 1951, sec. SF, p. A1.

58. "Compton Girls Will Go West on Annual Trip," *Los Angeles Times*, November 8, 1953, G12.

59. "YMCA Offers Youth Trips," *Los Angeles Times*, May 29, 1960, GB3; "Outings Planned for Retarded Children," *Los Angeles Times*, July 7, 1963, sec. OC, p. B19; "Playground Will Sponsor Trip to Corriganville," *Los Angeles Times*, August 11, 1963, sec. SG, p. B11.

60. "Shows Slated as Feature of Scout Week," *Los Angeles Times*, February 4, 1957, 4; "Scout Birthday Party Featured at Jamboree," *Los Angeles Times*, February 10, 1957, 3.

61. Cecilia Rasmussen, "In Prejudiced Era, Ranch Welcomed Dudes of All Colors," *Los Angeles Times*, February 22, 2004, B4.

62. Raymond White, "Roy Rogers and Dale Evans," in Etulain and Riley, *Hollywood West*, 37.

63. Ray Merlock and Jack Nachbar, "Gene Autry: Songs, Sidekicks, and Machines," in Etulain and Riley, *Hollywood West*; La Chappelle, *Proud to Be an Okie*, 138.

64. Winant, "Behind Blue Eyes."

65. Autry National Center, *Cowboys and Presidents*; Wills, *Reagan's America*.

66. Quoted in "Cowboy Talk," from Autry National Center, *Cowboys and Presidents*.

67. McGirr, *Suburban Warriors*.

68. La Chappelle, *Proud to Be an Okie*, 140, 141.

69. Ibid., 148.

70. Quotations in La Chappelle, *Proud to Be an Okie*, 142 (Autry on Dornan), 142 (Ritter on Wallace), 146 (Ritter on "minority voice").

71. See "S-T Honorary Mayor Keeps Old West Alive," *Los Angeles Times*, April 26, 1959, GV2; Pozzo, *Hollywood Comes to Sunland-Tujunga*.

72. Pozzo, *Hollywood Comes to Sunland-Tujunga*; Roderick, *San Fernando Valley*, 119.

73. Robinson, *Story of San Fernando Valley*, 42.

CHAPTER FOUR *Protecting Rurality through Horse-Keeping in the Northeast Valley*

1. Ken Fanucchi, "Shadow Hills: Good Life Arrives on Horseback," *Los Angeles Times*, December 18, 1966, sec. SF, p. A1.

2. "Valley Man Named Equestrian President," *Los Angeles Daily News*, July 1, 1975, B1.

3. Davis, *City of Quartz*, chap. 3; DeFronzo-Haselhoff, "Motivations for the San Fernando Valley Secession Movement"; HoSang, "Racial Propositions"; Sonenshein, *City at Stake*.

4. Omi and Winant, *Racial Formation*, chap. 4.

5. Kruse, *White Flight*; Lassiter, *Silent Majority*; McGirr, *Suburban Warriors*; Nicolaides, *My Blue Heaven*; Sugrue, *Origins of the Urban Crisis*.

6. Sugrue, *Origins of the Urban Crisis*.

7. Lassiter, *Silent Majority*, 2.

8. Kruse, *White Flight*, 15.

9. Lassiter, *Silent Majority*, 3.

10. Lawrence, *Hoofbeats and Society*, 63.

11. See also Denhardt, *Horse of the Americas*, 110–14; Stong, *Horses and Americans*, chap. 10.

12. Hintz, *Horses in the Movies*, 11.

13. DeMarco, *Horse Bits*.

14. Amaral, *Movie Horses*, 141–52; Hintz, *Horses in the Movies*, 80–87; Professional Rodeo Stock Contractors Association [hereafter PRSCA], *100 Years*, 94–95, 121, and 170–71.

15. Budiansky, *Nature of Horses*, 71.

16. Quoted in Budiansky, *Nature of Horses*, 72.

17. Cassidy, "Social Practice of Racehorse Breeding."

18. "Horse Sales Offer Chance to Strut in Western Duds," *Los Angeles Examiner*, June 4, 1950.

19. *Equestrian: Magazine of the Horse World* 9 (1947): 44.

20. "New Kellogg Horse Show Opens Jan. 6," *Los Angeles Examiner*, December 12, 1958.

21. PRSCA, *100 Years*, 12, 29, 16.

22. "Huge Horse Show Slated at Sports Arena in June," *Los Angeles Examiner*, December 21, 1960.

23. "Northridge Hosts Big Horse Show," *Los Angeles Examiner*, May 24, 1959; "Top Horses Jump for $7000," *Los Angeles Examiner*, September 17, 1960.

24. *Equestrian: Magazine of the Horse World* 9 (1947): 7.

25. "Devonshire Horse Show Set June 3–6," *Los Angeles Examiner*, May 14, 1961.

26. "John Wayne to Present Riding Prize," *Los Angeles Examiner*, August 28, 1961.

27. "Horses Riding High Again; Booming Industry Here," *Los Angeles Examiner*, May 16, 1960.

28. For example, thirty horses ran away from a stable in Glendale: "Traffic Snarled as Horses Hold Rodeo," *Los Angeles Examiner*, December 26, 1956; another twenty-three horses escaped from the Griffith Park stables: "Pinto Police Cars in Los Feliz Rodeo," *Los Angeles Examiner*, March 28, 1957; see also "Old Dobbin Hates Autos; Leaps on Passing Car; Batters Hood, Driver," *Los Angeles Examiner*, January 12, 1956; "Fleeing Nags Lose Freeway Race to Autos," *Los Angeles Examiner*, July 20, 1958.

29. "Rule Horses Off Streets! That's Plea to City Council," *Los Angeles Examiner*, May 4, 1954.

30. "Girls and Horses," *Los Angeles Times*, July 21, 1968, A24.

31. California Rangers Web site, http://www.californiarangers.org.

32. Blue Shadows Mounted Drill Team Web site, http://www.blueshadows.org.

33. "Youthful 'Horse Set', 6 to 16, Keeps in Shape," *Los Angeles Examiner*, October 18, 1953.

34. Concerns with encouraging patriotism and conformity to American values among youth were paramount during the wartime era. Youth who challenged these norms and values, particularly Mexican American and African American youth, were

often punished for their transgressions, as evidenced by the hysteria surrounding the Sleepy Lagoon murder trial of 1942 and support for the white American servicemen involved in the Zoot Suit Riots of 1943. See Pagán, *Murder at the Sleepy Lagoon.*

35. Bert Heath, "The Pet Show," *Los Angeles Times*, February 23, 1947, F18.

36. Bill Brown, "Horses Riding High Again; Booming Industry Here," *Los Angeles Examiner*, May 16, 1960.

37. Bill Brown, "Man's Best Friend; Good Horse Now Is Hard to Buy," *Los Angeles Examiner*, May 18, 1960.

38. "Riders Plan San Diego, Santa Barbara Trail," *Los Angeles Examiner*, November 14, 1940.

39. "Bridle Trail Group to Meet," *Los Angeles Examiner*, May 12, 1940; "Association Plans Horse Trails on El Camino Real," *Los Angeles Examiner*, November 17, 1940.

40. "San Fernando Mission Ride Plans Complete," *Los Angeles Examiner*, March 20, 1949.

41. "Cholly Angeleno Observes: Valley Horsemen Do," *Los Angeles Examiner*, September 3, 1948; "Sermon Today for Horsemen," *Los Angeles Examiner*, May 6, 1951; "Sermon on Mount for Horsemen," *Los Angeles Examiner*, May 17, 1953; "Valley Horsemen Attend 'Sermon on Mount' Sunday," *Los Angeles Examiner*, May 22, 1954; "80 Worship on Horseback in Glendale," *Los Angeles Examiner*, May 13, 1957.

42. "Powerful Tonic," *Los Angeles Examiner*, October 19, 1941; see also "Desert Vaqueros Near End of Five-Day Journey," *Los Angeles Examiner*, October 26, 1941.

43. "California Horsemen en Route to Palm Springs Meeting," *Los Angeles Examiner*, October 2, 1950; "100 Horsemen to Ride Sunday," *Los Angeles Examiner*, October 20, 1950.

44. Equestrian Trails, Inc. Web site, http://www.etinational.org.

45. "Bridle Trails Project Told," *Los Angeles Examiner*, March 9, 1945; "Horsemen Back Statewide System of Equestrian Trails," *Los Angeles Examiner*, March 10, 1947.

46. "Riding and Hiking Trails Project Wins Backing," *Los Angeles Examiner*, February 2, 1946.

47. "County Backs Trail Plan," *Los Angeles Examiner*, January 9, 1946.

48. "State Riding Trail Backed," *Los Angeles Examiner*, December 12, 1951.

49. "Residents Say Nay to Horse Invasion," *Los Angeles Examiner*, July 27, 1958.

50. *Equestrian: Magazine of the Horse World* 9 (1947): 5.

51. Ibid.

52. Display Ad 74, *Los Angeles Times*, September 15, 1907, II14. Only seven adult males were reported living in the Hansen Heights area as of 1907, and by the 1920 federal census, only about fifty households were counted. Another measure of the area's rural development and sparse population lies in school enrollment numbers: only thirteen students attended the Hansen Heights School when it first opened in 1912. Sarah Lombard, "Verdant Valley Attracts Settlers," *Foothill Record-Ledger*, October 13, 1977.

53. United States Bureau of the Census, *Fourteenth Census of the United States, 1920* [hereafter *1920 Census*], Enumeration District 128, sheet 5B.

54. Ibid., sheet 4B.

55. Marlene Hitt, "Rancho Tujunga Home to Japanese Community," *Foothill Leader*, n.d., accessed in "Shadow Hills" file, Bolton Hall, Tujunga, California.

56. U.S. Bureau of the Census, *1920 Census*, sheet 4B.

57. Paul Tsuneishi, interview by author, Sunland, California, August 14, 2005.

58. Hitt, *After Pearl Harbor*, 58–59; Tsuneishi interview.

59. Pozzo, *Hollywood Comes to Sunland-Tujunga*.

60. See Sugrue, *Origins of the Urban Crisis*, chaps. 7–9.

61. Roderick, "Borders," in *San Fernando Valley*; Ponce, *Hoyt Street*.

62. Roderick, *San Fernando Valley*, 140.

63. Meeker, "San Fernando Valley Profile."

64. Roderick, *San Fernando Valley*, 147.

65. Reuben Borough, "Memo on Pacoima Race Situation, March 22, 1945," box 18, folder labeled "January 1, 1945," Reuben Borough Papers, Charles E. Young Research Library, UCLA.

66. Pacoima Revitalization, Inc., for example, began to recruit industrial employers and commercial stores to locate in Pacoima in the early 1970s. See the Pacoima Revitalization, Inc. collection at the Special Collections and Archives, California State University Northridge.

67. Irv Burleigh and David LePage, "Valley Population Near Million; Growth Slows," *Los Angeles Times*, April 29, 1971, SF 1; "New Councilman Working Hard for Council Workers," *Los Angeles Times*, August 21, 1977, sec. SF, p. B1. Despite the high degree of homeownership, the incomes of first-district residents were relatively low, with a median family income of $13,391 (compared with a citywide average of $15,239) in 1975.

68. Evan Jones [pseud.], interview by author, Shadow Hills, California, August 4, 2005.

69. Los Angeles City Planning Commission, *City Ordinance #122,934*.

70. Robert S. Butts to Everett G. Burkhalter, correspondence of September 18, 1961, Los Angeles City Council File 105850, Los Angeles City Archives and Records.

71. "Horses May Live Closer to Houses," *Los Angeles Times*, May 16, 1962, B8; "'Horse-Raising' Areas Win Tentative Okay," *Los Angeles Times*, July 15, 1962, L32; "Districts for Horses Win Council OK," *Los Angeles Times*, September 30, 1962, 12; Los Angeles City Planning Commission, *City Ordinance #122,934*.

72. "Equestrians to Dedicate Horses Zone," *Los Angeles Times*, March 24, 1963, sec. SF, p. A10.

73. Anonymous to Louis Nowell, n.d.. Los Angeles City Council File #132082, box 2009, Los Angeles City Archives and Records.

74. Anonymous to Louis Nowell, November 24, 1966, Los Angeles City Council File #132082, box 2009, Los Angeles City Archives and Records.

75. "Horse Owners to Fight Rezoning in District," *Los Angeles Times*, April 8, 1965, SF11.

76. "Horse Owners Beat Rezoning," *Los Angeles Times*, April 9, 1965, SF9.

77. "Tract Keyed to Horse Owners Scheduled for Hearing Thursday," *Los Angeles Times*, July 6, 1966, SF8.

78. "Protested Equestrian Subdivision Gets Planners' Unanimous OK," *Los Angeles Times*, August 5, 1966, SF8.

79. "Shadow Hills Zoning Plea Slated Today," *Los Angeles Times*, September 12, 1966, SF8; "Decision Due in Commercial Center Fight," *Los Angeles Times*, October 6, 1966, SF2; "Shadow Hills Development Bid Delayed," *Los Angeles Times*, October 7, 1966, SF9.

80. "Horse Owners Urged to OK New Neighbors," *Los Angeles Times*, October 19, 1966, SF8.

81. "Planners Dismiss Plea for Commercial Center," *Los Angeles Times*, November 4, 1966, SF8.

82. "Council Rebuffs Sunland Foes of Horse Project," *Los Angeles Times*, November 17, 1966, SF1.

83. "Council May Revamp Horsekeeping Zones," *Los Angeles Times*, November 24, 1966, SF2; "Council Committee Asks Study of Better Horse-Keeping Zones," *Los Angeles Times*, December 8, 1966, SF1.

84. Director of Planning to City Planning Commission, *Staff Report*, July 3, 1968, City Plan Case No. 20936, City Council File #135161, box 2056, Los Angeles Archives and Records Department. Since many Shadow Hills lots are very hilly, net square footage refers to the amount of usable flat land on a given property. "City Eases Horse Zone Requirements," *Los Angeles Times*, September 29, 1967, SF8.

85. "Earnings from Small Farm Swell Pension," *Los Angeles Times*, July 10, 1960, SF1.

86. Fanucchi, "Shadow Hills."

87. "Master Plan Hearing Called," *Los Angeles Times*, March 31, 1965, SF9. At a meeting held in August 1965, over two hundred residents were in attendance; see "Master Plan Will Be Late, Residents Told," *Los Angeles Times*, August 20, 1965, SF8.

88. "Sunland-Tujunga Plan Prepared for Adoption," *Los Angeles Times*, October 2, 1968, SF8; Los Angeles City Planning Department, *Sunland-Tujunga-Lake View Terrace-Shadow Hills-East La Tuna Canyon Community Plan*.

89. "Commission OKs Plan for Sunland-Tujunga," *Los Angeles Times*, October 4, 1968, SF8.

90. "Tempers Flare as Bar Loses Police Decision," *Los Angeles Times*, June 24, 1966, SF8; "Plea Set on Trailer Park, Horse Permit," *Los Angeles Times*, August 9, 1966, SF8; "BZA Rejects Variance for Gas Station," *Los Angeles Times*, June 29, 1968, SF9; "Zoning Aide Balks at Foster Home Variance," *Los Angeles Times*, January 23, 1971, SF10; "Homeowners Lose Bid to Stop Sale of Castle," *Los Angeles Times*, October 11, 1973, SF1; "Shadow Hills Homeowners Appeal OK of Nearby Landfill," *Los Angeles Times*, January 10, 1982, sec. V, p. A1; "Homeowners Lose; Plant Gets Zoning," *Los Angeles Times*, February 17, 1967, SF8. In this last case, representatives of the city council told homeowners present at the zoning-change meeting that they were lucky to have such a manufacturing company in

the community, since the company produced high-end optical and electrical equipment rather than more durable, unattractive, and dirty goods.

91. "Animal Lovers Protest Hansen Dam Urban Plan," *Los Angeles Times*, August 2, 1979.

92. "Shadow Hills Horse Owners to Fight Tax," *Los Angeles Times*, August 15, 1972, SF7.

93. "Wilkinson Asks Action on Zoning for Horses," *Los Angeles Times*, October 11, 1972, SF6; "Council Unit Eases Rules for Horses in Residential Zones," *Los Angeles Times*, August 16, 1973, SF1.

94. "Group Calls for Limits on Hillside Tracts," *Los Angeles Times*, January 31, 1989, 9.

95. "Plans Would Limit 'Tacky Homes' Development," *Los Angeles Times*, July 11, 1991.

96. "Hillside Growth Plan Sparks Hot Debate," *Los Angeles Times*, July 11, 1989, 12; "Limits on Hillside Density Get Initial OK," *Los Angeles Times*, July 13, 1990, 3.

97. "Limits on Hillside Density."

98. "Sunland-Tujunga Workshop Scheduled on Community Plan," *Los Angeles Times*, May 1, 1996, 3; "Sunland-Tujunga General Plan Changes O.K.," *Los Angeles Times*, November 19, 1997, 5.

99. Los Angeles City Planning Commission, *San Gabriel/Verdugo Mountains Scenic Preservation Specific Plan*, 2–3.

100. Hines, "Housing, Baseball, and Creeping Socialism"; Cuff, "Chavez Ravine and the End of Public Housing," in *Provisional City*, 270–309. For the representation of ethnic Mexicans and Latinos in various genres of film, including westerns, see Dominguez, de los Santos, and Racho, *Bronze Screen*.

CHAPTER FIVE *Linking Western Heritage and Environmental Justice in the West Valley*

1. Biolchino, "From Rural Village to Metropolitan Suburb," 53–54, 59.

2. Ehrheart, "World's Most Famous Movie Ranch," 29.

3. Martha Willman, "Anywhere U.S.A.: Film Sets Shift to Valley Streets," *Los Angeles Times*, July 12, 1981, V1; Frost, "Reshaping the Destination."

4. Willman, "Anywhere U.S.A."

5. Lawrence Bassoff, "The Last Sunset Hovers over Paramount Ranch," *Los Angeles Times*, October 21, 1979, N3.

6. Huerta, "South Gate"; Macey et al., "Investigation"; Pulido, "Rethinking Environmental Racism"; Rothenberg et. al., "Blood Lead Levels."

7. Pulido, "Rethinking Environmental Racism"; Wolch, Wilson, and Fehrenbauch, "Parks and Park Funding."

8. Pulido, "Rethinking Environmental Racism," 25.

9. Referenced in Pincetl, "Nonprofits and Park Provision," 985.

10. Shaffer, "Scenery as an Asset."

11. Watson, "Open Space and Planning," 26.

12. Charles Bennett and Milton Brievogel, "Planning for the San Fernando Valley," *Western City* (1945): 28–30, quoted in Roderick, *San Fernando Valley*, 124–25.

13. Victor Gruen and Associates, *California State Development Plan Program*, 2.

14. Los Angeles County Regional Planning Commission, *Introducing "Destination Ninety,"* 1

15. Citizens Advisory Committee of the Destination Ninety Forum, *Destination Ninety*, 41–42.

16. Los Angeles City Planning Department, *Open Space Plan*, 14–15.

17. Watson, "Open Space and Planning," 46.

18. Ibid., 51.

19. Preston, "Changing Landscape," 21.

20. Watson, "Open Space and Planning," 77–82.

21. Los Angeles Department of City Planning, *Open Space Plan*, 17.

22. Ehrheart, "World's Most Famous Movie Ranch," 8.

23. For example, Rogers and Evans sponsored a fund-raising drive to preserve and restore the Chatsworth Community Church. Now a historical landmark, the church is considered to be one of the only examples of New England–type architecture left in Southern California. Los Angeles Cultural Heritage Board, *Progress Report*; Chatsworth Community Church Typescript, n.d., box 13, folder 19, p. 2, W. W. Robinson Collection, Charles E. Young Research Library Special Collections and Archives, UCLA.

24. Scott, "High Technology Industrial Development."

25. Biolchino, "From Rural Village to Metropolitan Suburb," 26.

26. Chatsworth Chamber of Commerce, *Chatsworth*, 4.

27. Ibid., 8–9.

28. "Ingram Tract of Simi Valley Filling Up: 22 Lots Are Left," *Moorpark Enterprise*, December 30, 1948, quoted in Biolchino, "From Rural Village to Metropolitan Suburb," 21.

29. "Zoning Stand Is Aired at Simi Meeting," *Moorpark Enterprise*, February 25, 1960, quoted in Biolchino, "From Rural Village to Metropolitan Suburb," 29.

30. "Cavalier Tract Homes Are Half Sold at Simi," *Moorpark Enterprise*, March 24, 1960, quoted in Biolchino, "From Rural Village to Metropolitan Suburb," 30.

31. Al Johns, "Simi Valley Retains Rural Charm in Face of Growth," *Los Angeles Times*, March 5, 1961, 11.

32. Referenced in Biolchino, "From Rural Village to Metropolitan Suburb," 69.

33. Art Seidenbaum, "Simi Valley Seeking an Economic Base," *Los Angeles Times*, April 3, 1977, 14.

34. Biolchino, "From Rural Village to Metropolitan Suburb," 155.

35. Seidenbaum, "Simi Valley Seeking an Economic Base."

36. Historian Lisa McGirr has recorded similar impulses in suburban Orange County, California, where the privatized residential landscape and lack of community identity and communal facilities propelled new suburbanites into conservative activism focused on the defense of property and neighborhood schools. McGirr, *Suburban Warriors*.

37. Lynn O'Shaughnessy, "Simi Valley Mayor Finds Favor with Developers," *Los Angeles Times*, May 3, 1986, sec. V, p. A6.

38. Ken Lubas, "State Aid Sought to Purchase Part of Overland Trail," *Los Angeles Times*, June 3, 1971, SF1.

39. Ibid.

40. "Chatsworth Park OKd," *Los Angeles Times*, May 18, 1958, 30; "Officials Envision Four Park Projects," *Los Angeles Times*, June 5, 1960, SF1; "Chatsworth Park Job for $245,000 OKd," *Los Angeles Times*, January 25, 1962, E2.

41. Santa Susana Mountain Park Association, *Santa Susana*, 8.

42. Ibid., 9.

43. "Planners Order Mountain Park Lands Study," *Los Angeles Times*, January 20, 1971, SF6.

44. Carlton Chase to Janice Hinkston, "Letter regarding Assembly Bill 2470," April 9, 1971, box SSMPA 1, folder 13, Santa Susana Mountain Parks Association Collection, Urban Archives Center, California State University Northridge, hereafter cited as SSMPA Collection.

45. "Park Group to Take Plea on Land to County Board," *Los Angeles Times*, June 9, 1971, SF6.

46. "Supervisors to Study Valley Fund Requests," *Los Angeles Times*, June 22, 1971, SF9.

47. "Park Group to Take Plea."

48. "Mountain Tour Planned Today," *Los Angeles Times*, June 23, 1972, SF7.

49. "Mountain Park Fund Drive to Start Today," *Los Angeles Times*, January 16, 1972, sec. SF, p. B2.

50. Robert Jones to Janice Hinkston, "Letter from Southern California Horsemen's Council," March 11, 1971, box SSMPA 1, folder 13, SSMPA Collection.

51. Walter Frame to Janice Hinkston, "Letter from the Conference of California Historical Societies regarding Santa Susana Mountains," March 28, 1972, box SSMPA 1, folder 15, SSMPA Collection.

52. City of Los Angeles Department of City Planning, "Historic-Cultural Monuments Listing: City Declared Monuments" (December 2008), 4, http://www.preservation.lacity. org/monuments.

53. Ken Lubas, "Overland Trail Option Sought by Park Group," *Los Angeles Times*, October 20, 1971, SF6.

54. "Save the Stagecoach Trail Hike Announcement," January 1972, box SSMPA 1, folder 19, SSMPA Collection.

55. "Hike-in Slated on Stagecoach Trail," *Los Angeles Times*, April 10, 1972, G9; Santa Susana Mountain Parks Association, *Santa Susana*, 4.

56. Laurence Hoge to Janice Hinkston, "Letter from Wells Fargo to Santa Susana Mountain Parks Association," November 29, 1971, box SSMPA 1, folder 14, SSMPA Collection.

57. "Chatsworth to Celebrate 84th Birthday," *Los Angeles Times*, March 5, 1972, sec. SF, p. C4.

58. Robert Cline to Ronald Reagan, "Letter to Governor Reagan regarding Santa Susana Mountain Park Association Fair," February 11, 1972, box SSMPA 1, folder 15, SSMPA Collection.

59. Santa Susana Mountain Parks Association, *Santa Susana*, 4.

60. "Mountain Park Group Sells Book," *Los Angeles Times*, March 22, 1973, SF3.

61. Santa Susana Mountain Parks Association, *Santa Susana*, 4, emphasis in original.

62. Edwin Baker, "Council Asks State to Consider 5 Park Plans," *Los Angeles Times*, March 6, 1974, 26.

63. "Bigger Share of Park Funds Urged for Valley," *Los Angeles Times*, August 11, 1974, sec. SF, p. B7.

64. Ken Lubas, "$12 Million Sought for Parks in Valley," *Los Angeles Times*, April 27, 1975, sec. SF, p. B1.

65. John V. Tunney to Janice Hinkston, "Letter regarding Proposed Parks Bill," August 24, 1972, box SSMPA 1, folder 17, SSMPA Collection.

66. Irv Burleigh, "Disperse U.S. Park Funds, City Warns," *Los Angeles Times*, June 26, 1975, WS1, 7.

67. Ibid., 7.

68. Ibid.

69. Martha Willman, "Last-Ditch Effort Made to Save Mountain Park Land," *Los Angeles Times*, June 9, 1977, SF1.

70. Ken Lubas, "Movers Faster Than Pen in Susana Park Acquisition," *Los Angeles Times*, September 4, 1977, sec. SF, p. B1.

71. Ken Lubas, "Santa Susana Mountains Park Bill Wins Approval," *Los Angeles Times*, August 7, 1977, sec. SF, p. C2.

72. Pincetl, "Nonprofits and Park Provision," 987–88.

73. Wolch, Wilson, and Fehrenbauch, "Parks and Park Funding," 7.

74. Pincetl, "Nonprofits and Park Provision," 981.

75. Martha Willman, "Santa Susana Park Land in Escrow — after 9 Years," *Los Angeles Times*, June 14, 1979, SF1; "San Fernando," *Los Angeles Times*, February 7, 1980, V2.

76. Richard Simon, "Weed Used as Shield in Coach Trail Fight," *Los Angeles Times*, November 16, 1980, sec. V, p. A1.

77. Simon, "Weed Used as Shield," sec. V, p. A5.

78. Fulton, *Reluctant Metropolis*, 178.

79. "Visitor Center at Park to Be Opened Nov. 18th," *Los Angeles Times*, November 8, 1984, sec. V, p. A15.

80. Santa Susana Mountain Parks Association Web site, http://www.ssmpa.com.

81. Ehrheart, "World's Most Famous Movie Ranch," 31.

82. "Corriganville Movie Ranch Will Be Sold," *Los Angeles Times*, October 12, 1963, 17; "$1.6 Million Offered for Corriganville Ranch," *Los Angeles Times*, May 7, 1964, B9; "Film Ranch Sale Stalled by Ex-Wife," *Los Angeles Times*, May 12, 1964, A2; "Broker Says He Bought Film Ranch," *Los Angeles Times*, October 31, 1964, A12; "Deadline Set for Deposit on Corriganville," *Los Angeles Times*, November 18, 1964, 30; "Buyer Will Keep Corriganville Open," *Los Angeles Times*, March 26, 1965, SF8; "Bob Hope Buys Corriganville Movie Ranch," *Los Angeles Times*, April 3, 1965, B9.

83. Michael Levett, "Postscript: Site of Countless Westerns Is Now a Real Ghost Town," *Los Angeles Times*, September 10, 1976, C1; Ken Lubas, "Simi Rodeo to Pay Tribute to Champ," *Los Angeles Times*, September 1, 1977, SF1.

84. "Fire Destroys Last Buildings of Corriganville Film Sets," *Los Angeles Times*, November 1, 1979, A1.

85. "Hopetown Project Gets Tentative Simi OK," *Los Angeles Times*, April 24, 1985, V_A8.

86. Al Martinez, "Two Ladies in Their Middle Years," *Los Angeles Times*, April 11, 1985, V_A7, emphasis added.

87. "State Approval Seen for Park Site Gift," *Los Angeles Times*, February 26, 1961, SF5.

88. Ehrheart, "World's Most Famous Movie Ranch," 8–9.

89. "Remembrance of Westerns Past," *Los Angeles Times*, January 16, 1986, V_C22.

90. Ibid.

91. Doug Smith, "Film Benefit Gives Simi's Cowboy Lore Full Rein," *Los Angeles Times*, July 25, 1985, V_A14.

92. Ehrheart, "World's Most Famous Movie Ranch," 34.

93. David Wharton, "Civilization Stakes a Claim on Crumbling Corriganville," *Los Angeles Times*, January 16, 1986, V_C22.

94. Ibid.

95. Ibid.

96. Thomas Omestead, "Simi Valley Sees Hopetown Land as Possible Park, Site for Museum," *Los Angeles Times*, March 30, 1986, V_A4.

97. Ibid.

98. Ehrheart, "Corriganville Park Master Plan."

99. Santa Monica Mountains Conservancy, "Corriganville Park", http://www.lamountains.com/parks.asp?parkid=99 (accessed April 1, 2008).

100. Pulido, "Multiracial Organizing." For the formation and early activism of the Mothers of East Los Angeles against the proposed state prison, see Pardo, *Mexican American Women Activists*.

101. Pulido, Barraclough, and Cheng, "People's Guide to Los Angeles."

102. Di Chiro, "Nature as Community," 300, emphasis in original.

103. Ibid., 301.

104. Wolch, Wilson, and Fehrenbauch, *Parks and Park Funding*, 15.

105. Tierney, Dahl, and Chavez, *Cultural Diversity*.

106. Wolch, Wilson, and Fehrenbauch, *Parks and Park Funding*.

CHAPTER SIX *Urban Restructuring and the Consolidation of Rural Whiteness*

1. The literature on color blindness is by now extensive and has primarily been developed by sociologists and critical legal scholars. See Bonilla-Silva, *Racism without Racists*; Bonilla-Silva, Lewis, and Embrick, "'I Did Not Get That Job'"; Gallagher, "Color-Blind Privilege." Across national contexts, scholars note that color blindness perpetuates the material, institutional, and structural legacies of white supremacy in new forms. See Ansell, "Casting a Blind Eye."

2. Bobo et al., "Analyzing Inequality in Los Angeles.

3. Ibid.; Bonacich and Appelbaum, *Behind the Label*.

4. Los Angeles Alliance for a New Economy, *Other Los Angeles*, v.

5. Reimers, *Still the Golden Door*.

6. Grant, "Demographic Portrait of Los Angeles."

7. Ibid.; Los Angeles Alliance for a New Economy, *Other Los Angeles*.

8. Center on Urban and Metropolitan Policy, *Los Angeles in Focus*, 58; Los Angeles Alliance for a New Economy, *Other Los Angeles*, vii.

9. Katznelson, *When Affirmative Action Was White*.

10. Frey, "New White Flight."

11. Grant, "Demographic Portrait of Los Angeles."

12. Strait, "Poverty Concentration."

13. Nancy Cleeland, "Rich, Poor Live Poles Apart in L.A. as Middle Class Keeps Shrinking," *Los Angeles Times*, July 23, 2006; Bobo et al., "Analyzing Inequality in Los Angeles," 18.

14. Ethington, Frey, and Myers, "Racial Resegregation."

15. Amanda Covarrubias, "Census Bureau Offers First-Ever Snapshot of San Fernando Valley," *Los Angeles Times*, December 8, 2006.

16. Jim Newton, "In Valley, Pace of Change Is Fast," *Los Angeles Times*, December 20, 2006.

17. Kotkin and Ozuna, *Changing Face*, 3, 4.

18. Ibid., 9.

19. Newton, "In Valley, Pace of Change."

20. United States Bureau of the Census, *Twenty-second Census of the United States*, hereafter cited as U.S. Census 2000. Numbers may total more than 100 percent because of rounding.

21. Ibid.

22. Zweig, "Introduction," 4.

23. Sweezy, *Post-Revolutionary Society*, 79–80.

24. Brace, *Politics of Property*, 7.

25. Harris, "Whiteness as Property," 174.

26. Oliver and Shapiro, *Black Wealth/White Wealth*; Lui et al., *Color of Wealth*.

27. Center on Urban and Metropolitan Policy, *Los Angeles in Focus*, 65.

28. Painter, *Race, Immigrant Status, and Homeownership*.

29. U.S. Census 2000.

30. Fausold and Lillieholm, "Economic Value of Open Space."

31. "Commission OKs Plan for Sunland-Tujunga, *Los Angeles Times*, October 4, 1968, SF8.

32. Donna Reese [pseud.], interview by author, Shadow Hills, California, June 27, 2005.

33. Gary McCullough [pseud.], interview by author, Sunland, California, August 11, 2005.

34. Ibid.

35. Mesch and Schwirian, "Effectiveness of Neighborhood Collective Action"; Benford and Snow, "Framing Processes and Social Movements"; Rose, "Toward a Class-Cultural Theory."

36. U.S. Census 2000.

37. James Huck [pseud.], interview by author, La Crescenta, California, July 7, 2005.

38. Ibid.

39. Richard Eagan [pseud.], interview by author, Shadow Hills, California, August 2, 2005.

40. Evan Jones [pseud.], interview by author, Shadow Hills, California, August 4, 2005.

41. Lisa Burkett [pseud.] and Edward Burkett [pseud.], interview by author, Shadow Hills, California, July 17, 2005.

CHAPTER SEVEN *Beliefs about Landscape, Anxieties about Change*

1. Patricia Wheat [pseud.], interview by author, Shadow Hills, California, March 12, 2003.

2. Wheat interview.

3. Duncan and Duncan, *Landscapes of Privilege*, 8.

4. Linda Ellison [pseud.], interview by author, Shadow Hills, California, 25 July 2005.

5. Eric Franco [pseud.], interview by author, Sunland, California, June 28, 2005.

6. Gary McCullough [pseud.], interview by author, Sunland, California, August 11, 2005.

7. Leslie Forster [pseud.], interview by author, Shadow Hills, California, 9 July 2005.

8. Ellison interview.

9. Ibid.

10. Franco interview.

11. Evan Jones [pseud.], interview by author, Shadow Hills, California, August 4, 2005.

12. Lisa Burkett [pseud.], interview by author, Shadow Hills, California, July 17, 2005.

13. Michael Castalucci [pseud.], interview by author, Sunland, California, July 18, 2005.

14. Ellison interview.

15. Forster interview.

16. James Huck [pseud.], interview by author, La Crescenta, California, July 7, 2005.

17. Franco interview.

18. Donna Reese [pseud.], interview by author, Shadow Hills, California, June 27, 2005.

19. Forster interview.

20. Castalucci interview.

21. Elaine Hillsboro [pseud.], interview by author, Sunland, California, June 23, 2005.

22. Huck interview.

23. Duncan and Duncan, *Landscapes of Privilege*, 8.

24. Meeting of the Shadow Hills Property Owners Association, January 15, 2002.

25. McCullough interview.

26. Meeting of the Shadow Hills Property Owners Association, January 15, 2002.

27. Forster interview.

28. Castalucci interview.

29. Edward Burkett [pseud.], interview by author, Shadow Hills, California, July 17, 2005.

30. Franco interview.

31. Ellison interview.

32. Richard Eagan [pseud.], interview by author, Shadow Hills, California, August 2, 2005.

33. Franco interview.

34. Forster interview.

35. Castalucci interview.

36. McCullough interview.

37. Huck interview.

38. Eagan interview.

39. Franco interview.

40. Ellison interview.

41. Wheat interview.

42. Ibid.

43. Jones interview.

44. Hillsboro interview.

45. Wheat interview.

46. Ellison interview.

47. Huck interview.

48. Forster interview.

49. Eagan interview.

50. McCullough interview.

51. Huck interview.

52. Eagan interview.

53. Ibid.

54. Wheat interview.

CHAPTER EIGHT *"Rural Culture" and the Politics of Multiculturalism*

1. Sonenshein, *City at Stake.*

2. "Northeast Valley Rural Foothills Redistricting Map Committee Summary," March 12, 2002, in author's possession.

3. "Horses and Harleys" flyer, not dated, in author's possession.

4. "L.A. Council Redistricting—Commission Hearing February 11, 2002," flyer in author's possession.

5. E-mail from Nancy Snider to multiple recipients, forwarded to the ETI Corral 20 e-mail Listserv February 15, 2002, copy in author's possession.

6. E-mail from Tim Borquez to undisclosed recipients, forwarded by Brenda McAlpine to the Sunland Tujunga Neighborhood Council Listserv, March 25, 2002, copy in author's possession.

7. Meeting of the Northeast Valley Rural Foothills Redistricting Map Committee, March 12, 2002, Sunland/Tujunga Municipal Building, Tujunga, California.

8. Meeting of the Sunland-Tujunga Neighborhood Council, February 8, 2002, Sunland/Tujunga Municipal Building, Tujunga, California.

9. Ibid.

10. Meeting of the Northeast Valley Rural Foothills Redistricting Map Committee, March 12, 2002.

11. "Demographics for Council District Two," available at http://cd2.lacity.org/cd2_ul.htm (accessed July 21, 2009).

12. This incident was posted as an e-mail to the Listserv of Equestrian Trails, Inc. on June 24, 2002, with the subject line "Rough Ride," copy in author's possession.

13. Ibid.

14. Ibid.

15. Ibid.

16. Ibid.

17. E-mail to ETI Listserv, subject line "Hansen Dam making our presence known ride," dated July 1, 2002, copy in author's possession.

18. Anonymous, *The Hansen Dam Papers*, no. 3, September 10, 2002, p. 6, copy in author's possession.

19. Chavez, *Latino Threat*, 2.

20. E-mail to ETI Listserv, June 20, 2003, copy in author's possession.

21. Herbert, *Policing Space*; Miller, *Search and Destroy*.

22. Tierney, Dahl, and Chavez, *Cultural Diversity*, iv.

23. Kathy McHugh to ETI Listserv, "Real Dirt . . .", April 12, 2002, copy in author's possession.

24. Foothill Trails District Neighborhood Council, Day of the Horse program booklet, October 2003, copy in author's possession.

25. See Leiker's critique of African American participation in the Buffalo Soldiers, particularly with regard to the suppression of indigenous people. Leiker, *Racial Borders*.

26. Deverell, *Whitewashed Adobe*, 59.

27. Foothill Trails District Neighborhood Council E-forum, "Greuel Motions for Citywide Study of L.A. Horsekeeping Regulations," http://www.wildwildwest.org/forum (accessed January 16, 2006), emphasis added.

28. Sterling Andrews, "Greuel's Posse Rides Herd on Equestrian Rights," *Los Angeles Daily News*, October 28, 2002, 4., emphasis added.

29. Joseph Staub, "Hold Your Horses; Valley Has Real Issues," *Los Angeles Daily News*, October 22, 2002.

30. Ibid.

31. E-mail to ETI Listserv, "Today's *Daily News* needs our response! Pls forward," October 23, 2002, copy in author's possession.

32. Richard Eagan [pseud.], interview by author, Shadow Hills, California, August 2, 2005.

33. Gary McCullough [pseud.], interview by author, Sunland, California, August 11, 2005.

34. E-mail to ETI Listserv, "RE: [ETI_C20] Fwd: L.A. Daily News," October 29, 2002, copy in author's possession.

35. Patricia Wheat [pseud.], interview by author, Shadow Hills, California, March 12, 2003.

36. McCullough interview.

37. "Today's *Daily News* needs our response!"

38. Patricia Wheat [pseud.] to JoAnn Yepem, correspondence of October 24, 2002, copy in author's possession.

39. Michael Castalucci [pseud.], interview by author, Sunland, California, July 18, 2005.

40. Eagan interview.

41. Garner, *Whiteness*, 89.

42. Thanks to Don Mitchell for this insight regarding the multiple possible interpretations of these expressions.

43. Eagan interview.

44. McCullough interview.

45. Cassidy, "Social Practice of Racehorse Breeding."

46. Eagan interview.

47. McCullough interview.

48. Eagan interview.

49. Castalucci interview.

50. Elaine Hillsboro [pseud.], interview by author, Sunland, California, June 23, 2005.

51. See Blee, *Inside Organized Racism*.

52. Newitz and Wray, "What Is 'White Trash'?"; see also Hartigan, *Odd Tribes*, especially chap. 1.

53. Castalucci interview.

54. James Huck [pseud.], interview by author, La Crescenta, California, July 7, 2005.

55. Eric Franco [pseud.], interview by author, Sunland, California, June 28, 2005.

56. In Bonilla-Silva's study, respondents claimed that they had "excellent black friends," but when asked about their activities and time spent together, levels of closeness and interdependence were quite low. Alleged "friendships" with blacks were more likely to be acquaintances with coworkers or fellow students than interdependent relationships based on shared interests, worldviews, and commitments. Bonilla-Silva, *Racism without Racists*, 105–11.

57. Linda Ellison [pseud.], interview by author, Shadow Hills, California, 25 July 2005.

58. Huck interview.

59. E-mail to ETI Listserv, "Re: [ETI_C20] Fwd: L.A. Daily News," October 29, 2002, quotation marks in original, copy in author's possession.

60. Huck interview.

61. Wheat interview.

CONCLUSION

1. Steven Holmes, "Leaving the Suburbs for Rural Areas," *New York Times*, October 19, 1997, 34.

2. Scott Baldauf, "More Americans Move off the Beaten Path," *Christian Science Monitor*, August 7, 1996, 1.

3. Pooley and Levy, "Great Escape."

4. Kotkin, "Resurgence of the Rural Life."

5. Frey and Liaw, "Immigrant Concentration."

6. Kotkin, "Resurgence of the Rural Life," 139.

7. Pooley and Levy, "Great Escape."

8. McCarthy and Hague, "Race, Nation, and Nature," 401.

9. Agyeman and Spooner, "Ethnicity and the Rural Environment"; Cloke and Little,

Contested Countryside Cultures; Garland and Chakraborti, "'Race', Space, and Place"; Kimmel and Ferber, "White Men Are This Nation."

10. Agyeman and Spooner, "Ethnicity and the Rural Environment"; Aguiar, Tomic, and Trumper, "Work Hard, Play Hard"; Hjort and Malmberg, "Attraction of the Rural"; Escribano, "Migration to Rural Navarre"; Knowles, "Landscape of Post-imperial Whiteness."

11. Sarah Neal, "Rural Landscapes, Representations and Racism." 144.

12. Knowles, "Landscape of Post-imperial Whiteness," 173.

13. Ibid., 170.

14. Agyeman and Spooner, "Ethnicity and the Rural Environment"; Cloke and Little, *Contested Countryside Cultures*; Garland and Chakraborti, "'Race', Space, and Place"; Kimmel and Ferber, "White Men Are This Nation."

15. Frankenberg, *White Women, Race Matters*; Garner, *Whiteness*.

16. Garland and Chakraborti, "'Race', Space, and Place," 160.

BIBLIOGRAPHY

Abbott, Carl. *The Metropolitan Frontier: Cities in the Modern American West*. Tucson: University of Arizona Press, 1993.

Aguiar, Luis, Patricia Tomic, and Ricardo Trumper. "Work Hard, Play Hard: Selling Kelowna, B.C. as a Year-Round Playground." *Canadian Geographer* 49, no. 2 (2005): 123–39.

Agyeman, Julian, and Rachel Spooner. "Ethnicity and the Rural Environment." In Cloke and Little, *Contested Countryside Cultures*, 197–217.

Almaguer, Tomas. *Racial Fault Lines: The Historical Origins of White Supremacy in California*. Berkeley: University of California Press, 1994.

Amaral, Anthony. *Movie Horses: Their Treatment and Training*. Indianapolis: Bobbs-Merrill, 1967.

Anderson, Kay. "The Idea of Chinatown: The Power of Place and Institutional Practice in the Making of a Racial Category." *Annals of the Association of American Geographers* 77, no. 4 (1987): 580–98.

Ansell, Amy. "Casting a Blind Eye: The Ironic Consequences of Color-Blindness in South Africa and the United States." *Critical Sociology* 32, no. 2–3 (2006): 333–56.

Autry National Center. *Cowboys and Presidents*. Catalog of exhibit of the Autry National Center, Griffith Park, California, April 12 to September 7, 2008. http://www.autrynationalcenter.org/cowboysandpresidents/.

Avila, Eric. *Popular Culture in the Age of White Flight: Fear and Fantasy in Suburban Los Angeles*. Berkeley: University of California, 2004.

———. "Popular Culture in the Age of White Flight: Film Noir, Disneyland, and the Cold War (Sub)Urban Imaginary." *Journal of Urban History* 31, no. 1 (2004): 3–22.

Baker, Alan, and Gideon Biger, eds. *Ideology and Landscape in Historical Perspective: Essays on the Meanings of Some Places in the Past*. New York: Cambridge University Press, 1992.

Barraclough, Laura. "South Central Farmers and Shadow Hills Homeowners: Land Use Policy and Relational Racialization in Los Angeles." *Professional Geographer* 61, no. 2 (2009): 164–86.

Benford, Robert, and David Snow. "Framing Processes and Social Movements: An Overview and Assessment." *Annual Review of Sociology* 26, no. 1 (2000): 611–39.

Biolchino, Louis. "From Rural Village to Metropolitan Suburb: Community Action in Simi Valley, California, in the 1960s." MA thesis, California State University Long Beach, 1980.

Blee, Kathleen. *Inside Organized Racism: Women in the Hate Movement.* Berkeley: University of California Press, 2003.

Blomley, Nicholas. "Law, Property, and the Geography of Violence: The Frontier, the Survey, and the Grid." *Annals of the Association of American Geographers* 93, no. 1 (2003): 121–41.

———. *Unsettling the City: Urban Land and the Politics of Property.* London: Routledge, 2004.

Bobo, Lawrence, Melvin Oliver, James H. Johnson Jr., and Abel Valenzuela Jr. "Analyzing Inequality in Los Angeles." In *Prismatic Metropolis: Inequality in Los Angeles,* edited by Lawrence Bobo, Melvin Oliver, James H. Johnson Jr., and Abel Valenzuela Jr., 3–50. New York: Russell Sage Foundation, 2000.

Bokovoy, Matthew. "Inventing Agriculture in Southern California." *Journal of San Diego History* 45 (1999), http://www.sandiegohistory.org/journal/99spring/agriculture.htm.

Bonacich, Edna, and Richard Appelbaum. *Behind the Label: Inequality in the Los Angeles Apparel Industry.* Berkeley: University of California Press, 2000.

Bonilla-Silva, Eduardo. *Racism without Racists: Color-Blind Racism and the Persistence of Racial Inequality in the United States.* Lanham, Md.: Rowman and Littlefield, 1997.

Bonilla-Silva, Eduardo, Amanda Lewis, and David Embrick. "'I Did Not Get That Job Because of a Black Man . . .': The Story Lines and Testimonies of Color-Blind Racism." *Sociological Forum* 19, no. 4 (2004): 555–81.

Brace, Laura. *The Politics of Property: Labour, Freedom, and Belonging.* Hampshire, England: Palgrave Macmillan, 2004.

Budiansky, Stephen. *The Nature of Horses: Exploring Equine Evolution, Intelligence, and Behavior.* New York: Free Press, 1997.

Camarillo, Albert. *Chicanos in a Changing Society: From Mexican Pueblos to American Barrios in Santa Barbara and Southern California, 1848–1930.* Cambridge, Mass.: Harvard University Press, 1979.

Cassidy, Rebecca. "The Social Practice of Racehorse Breeding." *Society and Animals* 10, no. 2 (2002): 155–72.

Center on Urban and Metropolitan Policy. *Los Angeles in Focus: A Profile from Census 2000.* Washington, D.C.: Brookings Institution, 2003.

Chatsworth Chamber of Commerce. *Chatsworth: A Colorful California Community.* Chatsworth, Calif.: Chatsworth Chamber of Commerce, n.d. Available at the Braun Research Library of the Autry National Center, Griffith Park, Calif.

Chavez, Leo. *The Latino Threat: Constructing Immigrants, Citizens, and the Nation.* Stanford, Calif.: Stanford University Press, 2008.

Citizens Advisory Committee of the Destination Ninety Forum. *Destination Ninety: Policies for Planning; A Citizens' Book of Planning Recommendations for the San Fernando Valley.* Los Angeles: Los Angeles County Regional Planning Commission, 1968.

Cloke, Paul, and Jo Little, eds. *Contested Countryside Cultures*. London: Routledge, 1997.

Conner, Palmer. *The Romance of the Ranchos*. Los Angeles: Title Insurance and Trust Company, 1941.

Corkin, Stanley. "Cowboys and Free Markets: Post–World War II Westerns and U.S. Hegemony." *Cinema Journal* 39, no. 3 (2000): 66–91.

Corriganville Movie Ranch Pictorial Souvenir Book. Los Angeles: Outside Entertainment, 1955.

Cosgrove, Denis. *Social Formation and Symbolic Landscape*. Madison: University of Wisconsin Press, 1984.

Costo, Rupert, and Jeannette Henry Costo, eds. *The Missions of California: A Legacy of Genocide*. San Francisco: Indian Historian Press, 1987.

Crenshaw, Kimberlé. "Color-Blindness, History, and the Law." In *The House That Race Built: Black Americans, U.S. Terrain*, edited by Wahneema H. Lubiano, 280–88. New York: Pantheon Books, 1997.

Cronon, William. *Nature's Metropolis: Chicago and the Great West*. New York: W. W. Norton, 1991.

Cuff, Dana. *The Provisional City: Los Angeles Stories of Architecture and Urbanism*. Cambridge, Mass.: MIT Press, 2000.

Daniels, Roger. *Asian America: Chinese and Japanese in the United States since 1850*. Seattle: University of Washington Press, 1988.

Daniels, Stephen. *Fields of Vision: Landscape Imagery and National Identity in England and the United States*. Cambridge: Polity Press, 1993.

Davis, Mike. *City of Quartz: Excavating the Future in Los Angeles*. New York: Vintage Books, 1990.

Dear, Michael. *From Chicago to L.A.: Making Sense of Urban Theory*. Thousand Oaks: Sage, 2002.

———. *The Postmodern Urban Condition*. Oxford: Blackwell, 2000.

DeFronzo-Haselhoff, Kim. "Motivations for the San Fernando Valley Secession Movement: The Political Dynamics of Secession." *Journal of Urban Affairs* 24, no. 4 (2003): 425–43.

Delaney, David. "The Space That Race Makes." *Professional Geographer* 54, no. 1 (2002): 6–14.

DeLyser, Dydia. *Ramona Memories: Tourism and the Shaping of Southern California*. Minneapolis: University of Minnesota Press, 2005.

DeMarco, Mario. *Horse Bits from the "B" Western Movies and Television*. West Boylston, Mass.: Mario DeMarco, 1990.

Denhardt, Robert. *The Horse of the Americas*. Norman: University of Oklahoma Press, 1947.

De Oliver, Miguel. "Historical Preservation and Identity: San Antonio and the Production of a Consumer Landscape." *Antipode* 28, no. 1 (1997): 1–23.

Deverell, William. *Whitewashed Adobe: The Rise of Los Angeles and the Remaking of Its Mexican Past*. Berkeley: University of California Press, 2004.

Di Chiro, Giovanna. "Nature as Community: The Convergence of Environment and Social Justice." In *Uncommon Ground: Rethinking the Human Place in Nature*, edited by William Cronon, 298–320. New York: W. W. Norton, 1996.

Dominguez, Alberto, Nancy de los Santos, and Susan Racho. *The Bronze Screen: 100 Years of the Latino Image*. Produced and directed by Alberto Dominguez, Nancy de los Santos, and Susan Racho. 120 min. Cinemax Reel Life, 2002. Videodisc.

Duncan, James, and Nancy Duncan. "The Aestheticization of the Politics of Landscape Preservation." *Annals of the Association of American Geographers* 91, no. 2 (2001): 387–409.

———. *Landscapes of Privilege: The Politics of the Aesthetic in an American Suburb*. London: Routledge, 2004.

Ehrheart, William J. "Corriganville Park Master Plan" (excerpted with interpretation). Simi Valley, Calif., 1998. Available at http://faculty.oxy.edu/jerry/corrigan/corrpark.htm.

———. "The World's Most Famous Movie Ranch: The Story of Ray 'Crash' Corrigan and Corriganville." *Ventura County Historical Society Quarterly* 43, no. 1–2 (1999): 1–69.

Escribano, Maria Jesus Rivera. "Migration to Rural Navarre: Questioning the Experience of Counterurbanisation." *Tijdshrift voor Economische en Sociale Geografie* 98, no. 1 (2007): 32–41.

Ethington, Philip, William Frey, and Dowell Myers. "The Racial Resegregation of Los Angeles County, 1940–2000." Available at http://www.rcf.usc.edu/~philipje/CENSUS_MAPS/CENSUS_2.html.

Etulain, Richard, and Glenda Riley, eds. *The Hollywood West: Lives of Film Legends Who Shaped It*. Golden, Colo.: Fulcrum, 2001.

Fausold, Charles, and Robert J. Lilieholm. "The Economic Value of Open Space: A Review and Synthesis." *Environmental Management* 23, no. 3 (1999): 307–20.

Fogelson, Robert. *The Fragmented Metropolis: Los Angeles, 1850–1930*. Berkeley: University of California Press, 1967.

Frankenberg, Ruth. *White Women, Race Matters: The Social Construction of Whiteness*. Minneapolis: University of Minnesota Press, 1993.

Frey, William. "The New White Flight." *American Demographics* (April 1994): 40–48.

Frey, William, and Kao-Lee Liaw. "Immigrant Concentration and Domestic Migrant Dispersal: Is Movement to Nonmetropolitan Areas 'White Flight'?" *Professional Geographer* 50, no. 2 (1998): 215–32.

Frost, Warwick. "Reshaping the Destination to Fit the Film Image: Western Films and Tourism at Lone Pine, California." Monash University Department of Management Working Paper Series, October 2004.

Fulton, William. *The Reluctant Metropolis: The Politics of Urban Growth in Los Angeles*. Baltimore: Johns Hopkins University Press, 1997.

Gallagher, Charles. "Color-Blind Privilege: The Social and Political Functions of Erasing the Color Line in Post Race America." *Race, Gender, and Class* 10, no. 4 (2003): 22–37.

Garcia, Matt. *A World of Its Own: Race, Labor, and Citrus in the Making of Greater Los Angeles, 1900–1970.* Chapel Hill: University of North Carolina Press, 2001.

Garland, Jon, and Neil Chakraborti. "'Race', Space, and Place: Examining Identity and Cultures of Exclusion in Rural England." *Ethnicities* 6, no. 2 (2006): 159–77.

Garner, Steve. *Whiteness: An Introduction.* London: Routledge, 2007.

Gilmore, Ruth Wilson. "Fatal Couplings of Power and Difference: Notes on Racism and Geography." *Professional Geographer* 54, no. 1 (2002): 15–24.

Gonzalez, Gilbert. *Labor and Community: Mexican Citrus Worker Villages in a Southern California County, 1900–1950.* Urbana: University of Illinois Press, 1994.

Grant, David. "A Demographic Portrait of Los Angeles, 1970 to 1990." In *Prismatic Metropolis: Inequality in Los Angeles*, edited by Lawrence Bobo, Melvin Oliver, James H. Johnson Jr., and Abel Valenzuela Jr., 51–80. New York: Russell Sage Foundation, 2000.

Haas, Lisbeth. *Conquests and Historical Identities in California, 1769–1936.* Berkeley: University of California Press, 1995.

Harris, Cheryl. "Whiteness as Property." *Harvard Law Review* 106, no. 8 (1993): 1709–95.

Hartigan, John, Jr. *Odd Tribes: Toward a Cultural Analysis of White People.* Durham, N.C.: Duke University Press, 2005.

Herbert, Steve. *Policing Space: Territoriality and the Los Angeles Police Department.* Minneapolis: University of Minnesota Press, 1997.

Hines, Thomas. "Housing, Baseball, and Creeping Socialism: The Battle of Chavez Ravine, Los Angeles, 1949–1959." *Journal of Urban History* 8, no. 2 (1982): 123–44.

Hintz, Harold Franklin. *Horses in the Movies.* South Brunswick, N.J.: A. S. Barnes, 1979.

Hise, Greg. *Magnetic Los Angeles: Planning the Twentieth Century Metropolis.* Baltimore: Johns Hopkins University Press, 1997.

Hitt, Marlene. *After Pearl Harbor: The War Years in Sunland/Tujunga, California.* Tujunga: Bolton Hall, 2001.

Hjort, Susanne, and Gunnar Malmberg. "The Attraction of the Rural: Characteristics of Rural Migrants in Sweden." *Scottish Geographical Journal* 122, no. 1 (2006): 55–75.

Hoelscher, Steve. "The White-Pillared Past: Landscapes of Memory and Race in the American South." In Schein, *Landscape and Race*, 39–72.

HoSang, Daniel. "Racial Propositions: Genteel Apartheid in Postwar California." PhD diss., University of Southern California, 2006.

Huerta, Álvaro. "South Gate, Calif.: Environmental Racism Defeated in a Blue-Collar Latino Suburb." *Critical Planning* 12 (2005): 93–103.

Hurtado, Albert. *Intimate Frontiers: Sex, Gender, and Culture in Old California.* Albuquerque: University of New Mexico Press, 1999.

Jacobson, Matthew Frye. *Whiteness of a Different Color: European Immigrants and the Alchemy of Race*. Cambridge, Mass.: Harvard University Press, 1998.

Jenkins, Gordon. *San Fernando Valley: Words and Music*. New York, 1941.

Johnson, Walter. *Soul by Soul: Life inside the Antebellum Slave Market*. Cambridge, Mass.: Harvard University Press, 1999.

Jorgensen, Lawrence C. "Chiniginich Is Very Angry." In *San Fernando Valley: Past and Present*, edited by Lawrence Jorgensen, 30–36. Los Angeles: Pacific Rim Research, 1982.

Jurca, Catherine. "Tarzan, Lord of the Suburbs." In *White Diaspora: The Suburb and the Twentieth-Century American Novel*, 20–43. Princeton, N.J.: Princeton University Press, 2001.

Katznelson, Ira. *When Affirmative Action Was White: A New Perspective on Racial Inequality*. New York: W. W. Norton, 2005.

Keffer, Frank. *History of San Fernando Valley*. Glendale, Calif.: Stillman Printing, 1934.

Kim, Claire Jean. "The Racial Triangulation of Asian Americans." *Politics and Society* 27, no. 1 (1999): 105–38.

Kimmel, Michael, and Abby Ferber. "'White Men Are This Nation': Right-Wing Militias and the Restoration of Rural Working-Class Masculinity." *Rural Sociology* 65, no. 4 (2000): 582–604.

Knobloch, Frieda. *The Culture of Wilderness: Agriculture as Colonization in the American West*. Chapel Hill: University of North Carolina Press, 1996.

Knowles, Caroline. "The Landscape of Post-imperial Whiteness in Rural Britain." *Ethnic and Racial Studies* 31, no. 1 (2008): 167–84.

Kobayashi, Audrey, and Linda Peake. "Racism Out of Place: Thoughts on Whiteness and an Anti-racist Geography in the New Millennium." *Annals of the Association of American Geographers* 90, no. 2 (2000): 392–403.

Kotkin, Joel. "Resurgence of the Rural Life." *Forbes*, August 23, 1999, 139.

Kotkin, Joel, and Erika Ozuna. *The Changing Face of the San Fernando Valley*. Sherman Oaks, Calif.: Economic Alliance of the San Fernando Valley, 2002.

Kropp, Phoebe. *California Vieja: Culture and Memory in a Modern American Place*. Berkeley: University of California Press, 2006.

Kruse, Kevin. *White Flight: Atlanta and the Making of Modern Conservatism*. Princeton, N.J.: Princeton University Press, 2005.

La Chappelle, Peter. *Proud to Be an Okie: Cultural Politics, Country Music, and Migration to Southern California*. Berkeley: University of California Press, 2007.

Lankershim Branch Publicity Department. *A Daughter of the Snows: The Story of the Great San Fernando Valley*. Los Angeles: Security Trust and Savings Bank, 1923.

Lassiter, Matt. *The Silent Majority: Suburban Politics in the Sunbelt South*. Princeton, N.J.: Princeton University Press, 2004.

Lawrence, Elizabeth. *Hoofbeats and Society: Studies of Human-Horse Interactions*. Bloomington: Indiana University Press, 1985.

Lee, Erika. *At America's Gates: Chinese Immigration during the Exclusion Era, 1882–1943.* Chapel Hill: University of North Carolina Press, 2003.

Leiker, James. *Racial Borders: Black Soldiers along the Rio Grande.* College Station: Texas A & M University Press, 2002.

Limerick, Patricia. *The Legacy of Conquest: The Unbroken Past of the American West.* London: W. W. Norton, 1987.

Lipsitz, George. *The Possessive Investment in Whiteness: How White People Profit from Identity Politics.* Philadelphia: Temple University Press, 1998.

Lopez, Ian Haney. *White by Law: The Legal Construction of Race.* New York: New York University Press, 1996.

Los Angeles Alliance for a New Economy. *The Other Los Angeles: Executive Summary.* Los Angeles: Los Angeles Alliance for a New Economy, 2000.

Los Angeles City Planning Commission. *Los Angeles City Ordinance #122,934.* Los Angeles, 1962.

———. *San Gabriel/Verdugo Mountains Scenic Preservation Specific Plan (Ordinance 175,736).* Los Angeles, 2003. http://www.cityofla.org/PLN/complan/specplan/pdf/SanGab_Verdugo.pdf.

Los Angeles City Planning Department. *Open Space Plan, An Element of the General Plan of the City of Los Angeles.* Los Angeles, 1973.

———. *Sunland-Tujunga-Lake View Terrace-Shadow Hills-East La Tuna Canyon Community Plan.* Los Angeles, 1991. http://www.ci.la.ca.us/PLN/complan/pdf/sld-cptxt.pdf

Los Angeles County Chamber of Commerce. *Los Angeles County, California: Tujunga Edition.* Los Angeles, 1932.

Los Angeles County Regional Planning Commission. *Introducing "Destination Ninety": A Dynamic Planning Program for the San Fernando Valley Area.* Los Angeles, 1966.

Los Angeles Cultural Heritage Board. *Progress Report, 1962–73.* Los Angeles, 1973.

Los Angeles Valley College Historical Museum Association. *Valley History.* Van Nuys, Calif.: Los Angeles Valley College, 1999.

Lui, Meizhu, Barbara Robles, Betsy Leondar-Wright, Rose Brewer, and Rebecca Adamson, with United for a Fair Economy. *The Color of Wealth: The Story behind the U.S. Racial Wealth Divide.* London: New Press, 2006.

Lukinbeal, Chris. "Cinematic Landscapes." *Journal of Cultural Geography* 23, no. 1 (2005): 3–22.

Macey, Gregg, Xee Her, Ellen Thomas Riebling, and Jonathan Ericson. "An Investigation of Environmental Racism Claims: Testing Environmental Management Approaches with a Geographic Information System." *Environmental Management* 27, no. 6 (2001): 893–907.

Magers, Boyd. *So You Wanna See Cowboy Stuff? The Western Movies TV Tour Guide.* Madison, N.C.: Empire, 2003.

Magliari, Michael. "Free Soil, Unfree Labor: Cave Johnson Couts and the Binding of

Indian Workers in California, 1850–1867." *Pacific Historical Review* 73, no. 3 (2004): 349–89.

Mann, Geoff. "Why Does Country Music Sound White? Race and the Voice of Nostalgia." *Ethnic and Racial Studies* 31, no. 1 (2008): 73–100.

Marx, Leo. *The Machine in the Garden: Technology and the Pastoral Ideal in America.* New York: Oxford University Press, 1964.

Massey, Doreen. "Geographies of Responsibility." *Geografiska Annaler* 86, no. 1 (2004): 5–18.

Massey, Douglas, and Nancy Denton. *American Apartheid: Segregation and the Making of the Underclass.* Cambridge, Mass.: Harvard University Press, 1993.

Mayers, Jackson. *The San Fernando Valley.* Walnut, Calif.: John D. McIntyre, 1976.

McCarthy, James, and Euan Hague. "Race, Nation, and Nature: The Politics of "Celtic" Identification in the American West." *Annals of the Association of American Geographers* 94, no. 2 (2004): 387–408.

McGirr, Lisa. *Suburban Warriors: The Origins of the New American Right.* Princeton, N.J.: Princeton University Press, 2001.

McWilliams, Carey. *Southern California: An Island on the Land.* 2nd ed. Salt Lake City: Peregrine Smith Books, 1973.

Meeker, Marcia. *San Fernando Valley Profile.* Los Angeles: San Fernando Valley Welfare Planning Council, 1964.

Mesch, Gustavo, and Kent Schwirian. "The Effectiveness of Neighborhood Collective Action." *Social Problems* 43, no. 4 (1996): 467–83.

Miller, Jerome. *Search and Destroy: African American Males in the Criminal Justice System.* Cambridge: Cambridge University Press, 1996.

Mitchell, Don. *Cultural Geography: A Critical Introduction.* Malden, Mass.: Blackwell, 2000.

———. *The Lie of the Land: Migrant Workers and the California Landscape.* Minneapolis: University of Minnesota Press, 1996.

———. "Writing the Western: New Western History's Encounter with Landscape." *Ecumene* 5, no. 1 (1998): 7–29.

Montgomery, Charles. "The Trap of Race and Memory: The Language of Spanish Civility on the Upper Rio Grande." *American Quarterly* 52, no. 3 (2000): 478–513.

Montoya, Maria. *Translating Property: The Maxwell Land Grant and the Conflict over Land in the American West, 1840–1900.* Berkeley: University of California Press, 2002.

Morrison, Toni. *Playing in the Dark: Whiteness and the Literary Imagination.* New York: Vintage, 1992.

Nash, Gerald. *The American West in the Twentieth Century: A Short History of an Urban Oasis.* Albuquerque: University of New Mexico Press, 1977.

———. *The American West Transformed: The Impact of the Second World War.* Lincoln: University of Nebraska Press, 1985.

Neal, Sarah. "Rural Landscapes, Representations and Racism: Examining Multicultural Citizenship and Policy-Making in the English Countryside." *Ethnic and Racial Studies* 25, no. 3 (2002): 442–61.

Newitz, Annalee, and Matthew Wray. "What Is 'White Trash'? Stereotypes and Conditions of Poor Whites in the United States." In *Whiteness: A Critical Reader*, edited by Mike Hill, 168–84. New York University Press, 1997.

Nicolaides, Becky. *My Blue Heaven: Life and Politics in the Working-Class Suburbs of Los Angeles, 1920–1965.* Chicago: University of Chicago Press, 2002.

Oliver, Melvin, and Thomas Shapiro. *Black Wealth/White Wealth: A New Perspective on Racial Inequality.* London: Routledge, 1995.

Omi, Michael, and Howard Winant. *Racial Formation in the United States from the 1960s to the 1990s.* 2nd ed. New York: Routledge, 1996.

Pagán, Eduardo Obregón. *Murder at the Sleepy Lagoon: Zoot Suits, Race, and Riots in Wartime L.A.* Chapel Hill: University of North Carolina Press, 2003.

Painter, Gary. *Race, Immigrant Status, and Homeownership.* Los Angeles: University of Southern California Lusk Center for Real Estate, 2000.

Pardo, Mary. *Mexican American Women Activists: Identity and Resistance in Two Los Angeles Communities.* Philadelphia: Temple University Press, 1996.

Pichardo, Nelson. "The Power Elite and Elite-Driven Countermovements: The Associated Farmers of California during the 1930s." *Sociological Forum* 10, no. 1 (1995): 21–49.

Pincetl, Stephanie. "Nonprofits and Park Provision in Los Angeles: An Exploration of the Rise of Governance Approaches to the Provisions of Local Services." *Social Science Quarterly* 84, no. 4 (2003): 979–1001.

Pitt, Leonard. *The Decline of the Californios: A Social History of the Spanish-Speaking Californians, 1846–1890.* Berkeley: University of California Press, 1999.

Ponce, Mary Helen. *Hoyt Street: An Autobiography.* Albuquerque: University of New Mexico Press, 1993.

Pooley, Eric, and Daniel S. Levy. "The Great Escape." *Time,* December 8, 1997, 52–60.

Pozzo, Mary Lou. *Hollywood Comes to Sunland-Tujunga, 1920–1995: A Guide to the Homes of the Stars and Locations of Movies Filmed in the Sunland-Tujunga Area.* Tujunga, Calif.: Sunland-Tujunga Little Landers Historical Society, 1995.

Preston, Richard. *The Changing Landscape of the San Fernando Valley between 1930 and 1964.* Northridge, Calif.: San Fernando Valley State College Center for Urban Studies, 1965.

Professional Rodeo Stock Contractors Association. *100 Years of Rodeo Stock Contracting.* Reno, Nev.: Professional Rodeo Stock Contractors Association, 1997.

Pulido, Laura. "Multiracial Organizing among Environmental Justice Activists in Los Angeles." In *Rethinking Los Angeles*, edited by Michael Dear, H. Eric Schockman, and Greg Hise, 171–89. Newbury Park, Calif.: Sage, 1996.

———. "Rethinking Environmental Racism: White Privilege and Urban Development in Southern California." *Annals of the Association of American Geographers* 90, no. 1 (2000): 12–40.

Pulido, Laura, Laura Barraclough, and Wendy Cheng. "A People's Guide to Los Angeles." Manuscript in progress, available from the authors.

Rand, Yardena. *Wide Open Spaces: Why We Love Westerns*. Manville, R.I.: Maverick Spirit Press, 2005.

Rawls, James. "The California Mission as Symbol and Myth." *California History* 71, no. 3 (1992): 343–60.

Razack, Sherene, ed. *Race, Space, and the Law: Unmapping a White Settler Society*. Toronto: Between the Lines, 2002.

Reimers, David. *Still the Golden Door: The Third World Comes to America*. 2nd ed. New York: Columbia University Press, 1992.

Reps, John. *The Forgotten Frontier: Urban Planning in the American West before 1890*. Columbia: University of Missouri Press, 1981.

Ritter, Tex. *Tex Ritter: Mountain Ballads, Cowboy Songs*. Chicago: M. M. Cole, 1941.

Robinson, William Wilcox. *The Story of San Fernando Valley*. Los Angeles: Title Insurance and Trust Company, 1961.

Roderick, Kevin. *The San Fernando Valley: America's Suburb*. Los Angeles: Los Angeles Times Books, 2001.

Roediger, David. *The Wages of Whiteness: Race and the Making of the American Working Class*. New York: Verso, 1991.

Rose, Fred. "Toward a Class-Cultural Theory of Social Movements: Reinterpreting New Social Movements." *Sociological Forum* 12, no. 3 (1997): 461–94.

Rothel, David. *An Ambush of Ghosts: A Personal Guide to Favorite Western Film Locations*. Madison, N.C.: Empire, 1990.

———. *Those Great Cowboy Sidekicks*. Metuchen, N.J.: Scarecrow Press, 1984.

Rothenberg, Stephen, Freddie Williams Jr., Sandra Delrahim, Fuad Khan, Michael Kraft, Minhui Lu, Mario Manalo, Margarita Sanchez, and Daniel Wooten. "Blood Lead Levels in Children in South Central Los Angeles." *Archives of Environmental Health* 51, no. 5 (1996): 383–88.

Rothman, Hal. *Devil's Bargains: Tourism in the Twentieth-Century American West*. Lawrence: University Press of Kansas, 2000.

Sackman, Douglas. *Orange Empire: California and the Fruits of Eden*. Berkeley: University of California Press, 2005.

Saito, Leland. *The Politics of Exclusion: The Failure of Race-Neutral Policies in Urban America*. Stanford, Calif.: Stanford University Press, 2009.

Samuels, Marwyn. "The Biography of Landscape: Cause and Culpability." In *The Interpretation of Ordinary Landscapes: Geographical Essays*, edited by Donald W. Meinig, 51–87. New York: Oxford University Press, 1979.

San Fernando Valley Chapter of the Daughters of the American Revolution. *The Valley of San Fernando*. No publication information, ca. 1924.

Santa Susana Mountain Park Association. *Santa Susana: Over the Pass . . . Into the Past.* Chatsworth, Calif.: Santa Susana Mountain Park Association, 1973.

Schein, Richard. *Landscape and Race in the United States.* London: Routledge, 2006.

———. "The Place of Landscape: A Conceptual Framework for Interpreting an American Scene." *Annals of the Association of American Geographers* 87, no. 4 (1997): 660–80.

Scott, Allen. "High Technology Industrial Development in the San Fernando Valley and Ventura County: Observations on Economic Growth and the Evolution of Urban Form." In *The City: Los Angeles and Urban Theory at the End of the Twentieth Century,* edited by Edward Soja and Allen Scott, 276–310. Berkeley: University of California Press, 1998.

———. *Technopolis: High-Technology Industry and Regional Development in Southern California.* Berkeley: University of California Press, 1993.

Shaffer, Marguerite. "Scenery as an Asset: Assessing the 1930 Los Angeles Regional Park Plan." *Planning Perspectives* 16, no. 4 (2001): 357–82.

Shaw, Wendy. *Cities of Whiteness.* Malden, Mass.: Blackwell, 2007.

Sherman, Robert. *Quiet on the Set! Motion Picture History at the Iverson Movie Location Ranch.* Chatsworth, Calif.: Sherway, 1984.

Shively, JoEllen. "Cowboys and Indians: Perceptions of Western Films among American Indians and Anglos." *American Sociological Review* 57, no. 6 (1992): 725–34.

Simmon, Scott. *The Invention of the Western Film: A Cultural History of the Genre's First Half-Century.* Cambridge: Cambridge University Press, 2003.

Smith, Henry Nash. *Virgin Land: The American West as Symbol and Myth.* Cambridge, Mass.: Harvard University Press, 1950.

Sonenshein, Raphael. *The City at Stake: Secession, Reform, and the Battle for Los Angeles.* Princeton, N.J.: Princeton University Press, 2004.

A Southern California Paradise, (In the Suburbs of Los Angeles): Being a Historic and Descriptive Account of Pasadena, San Gabriel, Sierra Madre, and La Canada; With Important Reference to Los Angeles and All Southern California. Pasadena, Calif.: R. W. C. Farnsworth, 1883.

Starr, Kevin. *Inventing the Dream: California through the Progressive Era.* New York: Oxford University Press, 1985.

Stong, Phil. *Horses and Americans.* Garden City, N.Y.: Garden City Publishing, 1946.

Strait, John. "Poverty Concentration in the Prismatic Metropolis: The Impact of Compositional and Redistributive Forces within Los Angeles, California, 1990–2000." *Journal of Urban Affairs* 28, no. 1 (2006): 71–94.

Sugrue, Thomas. *The Origins of the Urban Crisis: Race and Inequality in Postwar Detroit.* 2nd ed. Princeton, N.J.: Princeton University Press, 2005.

Sweezy, Paul. *Post-Revolutionary Society.* New York: Monthly Review Press, 1980.

Tierney, Patrick, Rene Dahl, and Deborah Chavez. *Cultural Diversity of Los Angeles*

County Residents Using Undeveloped Natural Areas. Albany, Calif.: United States Department of Agriculture Forest Service Pacific Southwest Research Station, 1998.

Turner, Frederick Jackson. *The Frontier in American History.* New York: Henry Holt, 1920.

United States Bureau of the Census. *Fourteenth Census of the United States.* Washington, D.C., 1920.

———. *Twenty-second Census of the United States.* Washington, D.C., 2000.

Victor Gruen and Associates/Eisner-Stewart and Associates. *California State Development Plan Program, Southern California Region: Reconnaissance and Critique Report.* Los Angeles: The Associates, 1963.

Warner, J. J., Benjamin Hayes, and J. P. Widney. *An Historical Sketch of Los Angeles County, California.* Los Angeles: Louis Lewin, 1876. Reprint, Los Angeles: O. W. Smith, 1936.

Watson, Richard Alan. "Open Space and Planning in the San Fernando Valley." MA thesis, University of California Los Angeles, 1969.

Watts, Jennifer. "Photography in the Land of Sunshine: Charles Fletcher Lummis and the Regional Ideal." *Southern California Quarterly* 87, no. 4 (2005): 339–76.

Weeks, Charles. *One Acre and Independence, or My One Acre Farm.* n.p., 1927.

White, Richard. *It's Your Misfortune and None of My Own: A New History of the American West.* Norman: University of Oklahoma Press, 1991.

Wild, Mark. *Street Meeting: Multiethnic Neighborhoods in Early Twentieth-Century Los Angeles.* Berkeley: University of California Press, 2005.

Williams, Raymond. *The Country and the City.* New York: Oxford University Press, 1973.

Wills, Gary. *Reagan's America: Innocents at Home.* New York: Penguin Books, 2000.

Wilson, Chris. *The Myth of Santa Fe: Creating a Modern Regional Tradition.* Albuquerque: University of New Mexico Press, 1997.

Winant, Howard. "Behind Blue Eyes: Whiteness and Contemporary U.S. Racial Politics." *New Left Review* 225 (1997): 73–89.

———. *The World Is a Ghetto: Race and Democracy since World War Two.* New York: Basic Books, 2002.

Wolch, Jennifer, John P. Wilson, and Jed Fehrenbauch. *Parks and Park Funding in Los Angeles: An Equity Mapping Analysis.* Los Angeles: University of Southern California Sustainable Cities Program, 2002.

Yarbrough, Tinsley. *Those Great B-Western Locations.* Produced and directed by Tinsley Yarbrough. Albuquerque: VideoWest Productions, 1998. 5 videocassettes.

———. "Those Great B-Western Locations." *Western Clippings* 1 (1998): 1–4.

Zweig, Michael. "Introduction: The Challenge of Working Class Studies." In *What's Class Got to Do with It? American Society in the Twenty-first Century*, edited by Michael Zweig, 1–17. Ithaca, N.Y.: Cornell University Press, 2004.

INDEX

Chatsworth (*continued*)
contemporary demographics of, 191,
195, 200; film production in, 98–99,
102–3; history and development of,
155–57; horse-raising in, 129; men-
tioned, 96, 107
Chatsworth Beautiful, 148, 161
Chatsworth Chamber of Commerce, 157,
167
Chatsworth Community Church, 287n23
Chatsworth Park South, 162
Chatsworth Reservoir, 160, 161
Chavez Ravine, 29, 144–45
Chinese, 51, 82–83
Citizens Aware of a Sensible
Environment, 176
citrus industry, 19, 29, 39–40, 65, 78
Cline, Robert, 162, 165, 167, 169
colonias, Mexican, 29, 54–55, 130
colonies, agricultural, 41, 47–48; Little
Landers Colony, 41–46. *See also*
Weeks Poultry Colony
color-blindness: as articulated by white
people, 118, 236, 238, 258, 260–61;
characteristics of, 18–19, 118, 185, 252,
258, 269; emergence of, 18–19, 20,
118, 185; importance of landscape to,
18, 263, 270; role of poor whites in
sustaining myth of, 259; rural culture
as, 19, 231, 248, 253, 258–63
common-interest developments,
213–14
community plans, 153–54. *See also*
Sunland–Tujunga–Shadow Hills–Lake
View Terrace–East La Tuna Canyon
Community Plan
Compton, 108, 124, 126, 155
Concerned Citizens of South Central Los
Angeles, 178, 180
Conference of California Historical
Societies, 164

Congress of Industrial Organizations,
57–58
Connelly, Lex, 96
Cooper, Gary, 95
cooperatives, agricultural, 39
Corrigan, Ray, 99–100, 147, 173, 174; business decisions of, 101, 104, 106–7, 156;
mentioned, 108
Corrigan, Tom, 174
Corriganville Movie Ranch, 85, 99–108,
156, 161; decline of, 147–48; preservation of, 148, 173–78; subdivision of,
173–74
Corriganville Movie Ranch Restoration,
175
Corriganville Park, 149, 177–78, 180
Corriganville Preservation Committee,
175
counterurbanization, 264–70
"country folks," 248, 255–57, 259–60
country-western music, 12
Cranston, Alan, 161–62
critical whiteness studies, 276–77n110
Crosby, Bing, 91
Cusanovich, Lou, 170

Daughters of the American Revolution,
64, 68, 72–83 passim, 166
Dawes General Allotment Act, 10
Day of the Horse Festival, 248–50; mentioned, 232
de Celis, Eugelio, 1, 75
decentralization, 27–29
defense industry, 86–87
deindustrialization, in Los Angeles,
186–87. *See also* economic restructuring, in Los Angeles
DeMille, Cecil B., 95, 156
Depression, Great, 50, 57
Destination Ninety Citizens Advisory
Committee, 152–53, 154

GEOGRAPHIES OF JUSTICE AND SOCIAL TRANSFORMATION

Made in the USA
Middletown, DE
03 June 2021